The Wines of
Chablis

The Wines of Chablis

AUSTEN BISS and OWEN SMITH

First published in Great Britain in 2000 by Writers International Ltd,
PO Box 3229, Bournemouth BH1 1ZS, UK.

A CIP Catalogue record for this book is available from the British Library.
ISBN 0 9538101 0 0

The publishers and the authors will be pleased to receive any information which
will assist them in updating any further editions. Although all reasonable care
has been taken in the preparation of this book, neither the publishers nor the
authors can accept any liability for any consequences arising from the use there-
of, or the information contained herein.

Produced by Deer Park Productions, Tavistock, Devon.
Typeset in Monotype Garamond by PDQ Typesetting, Newcastle-under-Lyme.

Printed and bound in Great Britain by The Baskerville Press Ltd,
6–8 Newton Road, Churchfields, Salisbury, Wiltshire SP2 7QB.

Maps by Eugene Fleury

CONTENTS

List of Photographs

ACKNOWLEDGEMENTS

THE COMPLETION, indeed the start, of this book was due to the encouragement of numerous very kind people both in and out of the wine trade. We must acknowledge the fact that through all its facets, growers, winemakers, merchants, retailers, wine writers and enthusiasts, the wine trade is peopled by some of the kindest people one could meet, and to them all we owe a considerable debt of gratitude.

We would specifically like to thank Clive Coates MW whose help and encouragement were invaluable, for writing the Foreword to the book, giving us the benefit of his considerable experience in Burgundy, and the use of his extensive library.

Special thanks are also due to the following: to Michel and Madame Vignaud at the Hostellerie des Clos for looking after us so well on our many visits; to Lorraine Carrigan of Domaine Laroche for historical notes; to Jean-Paul Durup for providing so many details of wine production statistics and much more; to Jean-Bernard Marchive of Domaine des Malandes for information on Le Syndicat; to Ann Smith for the poem; to Alex Biss M.PHIL.CANTAB, Austen's son, for geological information; to Haywards Chartered Surveyors for the use of their computer equipment; to both Sue Hooper and Anita Nyman for secretarial assistance; to the late Robert Mapley and to Howard Ripley for our introduction to fine Burgundy and the Wednesday Wine Club and to all past and present members of that illustrious group.

However, this book would not have been possible without the generosity, enthusiasm and friendship shown to us by the growers of Chablis. To them all, many many thanks.

FOREWORD

Austen Biss and Owen Smith are neither wine professionals nor journalists. They are *amateurs du vin* – lovers of wine – and the wines that most transfigure their imagination and taste buds are the bone-dry, steely but nevertheless rich-finishing wines of Chablis. Over the past years the two of them have sampled countless wines of this individual and, as they point out, unfairly neglected wine region, and made repeated visits to the area.

In the summer of 1998 they approached me with the first draft of this book. Had I any suggestions? Would I write a Foreword? I said I would be honoured to do so, and furthermore that I would be delighted to help them fine-tune what was already, I felt, a splendid achievement.

The result – and I claim no credit whatsoever, for the work is all theirs – is the most comprehensive guide to this region ever accomplished. The place, its history and its wines are splendidly delineated. The *domaines*, their proprietors and their individual wines come alive in the pages which follow.

This is the definitive guide to Chablis: an area neglected by wine writers for fifteen years. It well deserves a place on your bookshelf.

Clive Coates MW
January 2000

INTRODUCTION

THIS BOOK does not set out to bore the reader with facts and figures in which the average wine consumer has not the slightest interest. It may indeed achieve this end result, but such is not the intention. A few necessary supporting statistics have been included but these can easily be skipped without much loss of continuity.

The writers have spent the past twenty years or so visiting the Yonne and Chablis, tasting, expectorating in approval or not as the case may be, consuming and enjoying some of the finest wines to emanate from France. The vast majority have been above the average standard of produce we have come to expect from some other wine regions of the world. The Chablisiens can be proud of their ancient tradition and achievements.

The purpose of this book is to sort out just where the consistently reliable sources are to be found, and to call into question the plethora of wine writers who too often ignore or denigrate this fascinating region and its wines.

We have tried to be as precise as possible, giving details, as are reasonably obtainable, of the geography and history of the region, the origin and history of the leading domaines, and an assessment of their wines. We have adopted a star rating for the domaines visited where we consider that this is warranted, and many others are shown as deemed worthy of note. This shows that in our opinion the Chablis growers indeed have reason to be proud of their métier.

We also call into question the unadventurous face of much of the general commercial wine trade in the extremely limited range of Chablis which can be found in the larger supermarkets. In order to widen consumer choice to include fine or finer wine – which need not cost an arm and a leg – as well as the indifferent quality stocked by the mass market, it is necessary for experienced buyers and tasters to get out there in the field and show some enterprise in their commercial choice for the shelves. As it is, the Chablis lover must look to the reputable merchant for those quality bottles.

We do not attempt to sort out the wines which are so-called 'value for money'. Who are we to presume judgement on the reader's bank balance? Value is very subjective, it is for the reader to make that decision when she or he knows something about the wine and its price. Indeed, wine assessment itself is very subjective, but if we didn't stick our necks out sometimes there would be no point in this book anyway.

We present to you our recommendations for the domaines and their wines, and where to buy them, with reasoned judgement and just a little favouritism.

To Sue and Ann

A wine that confesses and obsesses
A perfume so sublime
Not from the gods this nectar comes
But soil that's aged in time.

Coloured like some ancient jewel
So pure a joy to see
Did Bacchus have this future dream
A wine qui s'appelle Chablis?

Wander through this little town
And sip the wine of great renown
Then let its pleasure fill your soul
'Til Saint Martin's bell shall cease to toll.

PART ONE

①

CHABLIS –
THE GOLDEN GATE OF BURGUNDY, AND
THE DÉPARTEMENT DE YONNE

. . . .

AS YOU DRIVE south-east out of Calais on the A26 towards the massive interior of France, before any viticultural geographical features are noticed, you will be greeted with a number of place names famous for historical events and battles of the Middle Ages and the two world wars – Champ de Drap d'Or, Vimy Ridge, Cambrai, etc. At a steady 80 mph or so, after a couple of hours, looming up on the right-hand side, the Montagne de Reims announces that we are in Champagne country. It is almost as though we are being warned of Champagne's not insignificant past association with the area to come. Skirting Reims, the countryside breathes a sigh of regret flattening out to a degree but remaining fertile and vital. Another hour, clearing the mists of the Marne, leaving the motorway network outside Troyes, the soil darkens, the meadows become more verdant and the scenery gains in beauty by leaps and bounds – rolling hills, Charolais cattle and picturesque villages. There are two routes to Chablis from Troyes, but the eastern road through Tonnerre is far preferable as it affords a lovely view of the Grand Cru vineyards before crossing the River Serein into the town of Chablis itself. Alternatively, Chablis can be reached via the autoroute of renown – the A6 some 110 miles from Paris via Auxerre, or from Dijon travelling north on a return from the Côte d'Or.

Chablis is a small but delightful little town of 2,300 inhabitants whose lifeblood is wine: it is known as the Golden Gate of Burgundy, a term probably originating from the sale in 1215 of gold from the altar of Saint-Martin de Tours to raise the necessary sum for the purchase of a prime site belonging to Guy de Montréal, after which the monks referred to the wine as 'bottled gold'.

The visitor will find a number of fascinating historical attractions including La Collégiale Saint-Martin, originally dating from 1160, a church built as a smaller replica of the Cathedral of Sens; the fifteenth-century Obédiencerie, the cellar of which received the remains of Saint-Martin c. 877, and which now houses an old wooden wine press from the twelfth century, not unfortunately on public view; the 'Synagogue', situated in the

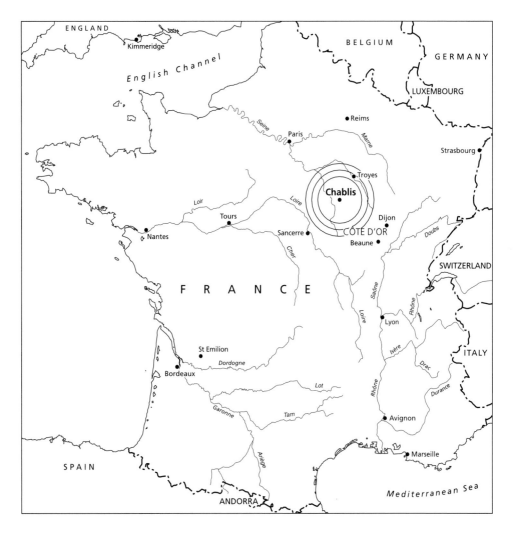

France – Location

Rue des Juifs, a building with a Renaissance facade believed to be the old Synagogue of a one-time community, and in need of considerable work of restoration; the two towers of the Porte Noël built in 1778 replacing the original fifteenth-century fortifications; L'Hospice, probably dating back to the twelfth century and containing a fourteenth-century chapel dedicated to John the Baptist; Le Petit Pontigny, of which more later; Le Prieuré Sainte-Cosme – Joan of Arc slept here one night in February 1429; and the twelfth-century Eglise Saint-Pierre. The Tourist Office will supply full information on these and other places of interest. Not least is the serenity and beauty of a small French town, walks by the river and through the vineyards followed at the end of the day by food and wine second to none.

The history of Chablis is very ancient, the vignoble older even than the twelfth-century Abbey of Citeaux near Dijon, but the development of the vineyards owes much to the monks of Citeaux. The oldest *cave* in Chablis still existing to this day, the cellars of Petit Pontigny, were constructed by these monks in the twelfth century, the same period which saw their formation of the famed Clos Vougeot in the Côte de Nuits.

Seven hundred years later, in the nineteenth century, the wines of Chablis were exported to numerous countries, principally England, Holland, Belgium and Germany, the United States and Russia. Tolstoy in *Anna Karenina* describes Russian society of the period as appreciative of all things French, and mainly two wines, Champagne and Chablis.

Undoubtedly the great reputation of the wine in all the nineteenth century wine consuming countries of the world has been the cause of many abusive uses of the name on any number of mediocre dry white wines, not least in the United States where the word 'Chablis' is often used to refer to any dry white. The large Gallo organisation at one time produced a wine in California labelled 'Gallo Mountain White Chablis'. The Bureau Interprofessionnel des Vins de Bourgogne (BIVB) estimates that a probable 3 to 4 million hectolitres of dry white wine produced in North America, including Canada, 500,000 hectolitres in Australia and 200,000 in South America are sold under the name of Chablis. This practice is unacceptable to the Chablisien and a problem which must be addressed.

The name 'Chablis' is sacrosanct to those entitled to it, and should be recognised as such by international law. The Champenois have the volume and financial clout to assure their heritage against abuse. The Chablisien do not. **Chablis only comes from Chablis, as Champagne only comes from Champagne. THERE ARE NO EXCEPTIONS.**

Walking around the town, it is possible to reach most producers on foot, at least those in the town itself or nearby Milly. But a car is advisable as many growers will gladly sell their produce at the cellar door, and the outlying districts such as Beines, Maligny and Chichée are just that little too far even for the most athletic. There are not many restaurants, but what are there are sufficient and of good quality. The Hostellerie Des Clos is a delight and affords a welcome sanctuary for the weary imbiber – the Fruits de Mer as part of the Menu Gourmande is to die for, as is the cheese board. The wine list is a reference book on Chablis, but is not totally parochial – try the Simon Bize Savigny Vergelesses 95 with the cheese. Monsieur and Madame Vignaud who have owned the hotel for many years are welcoming hosts, known for their restaurant, where Michel Vignaud excels, and also for the very comfortable rooms on the floors above where the weary traveller suitably fed and wined can rest until the morrow. For this and other hotels and restaurants in the area, see Chapter 19.

Not too far away is the town of Auxerre, famous for many historical escapades – also for its football team and its supporters who number amongst them Jean-Paul Durup, featured prominently later in this book.

Chablis is a story of wine, in fact it is the story of two wines, quite different from each other, yet both paradoxically the epitome of the style of wine associated with the name, when well made that is! It is the story of oak and no oak. As will be seen, it is also the story of two soils, Kimmeridgian and Portlandian, and of two opposing camps set in their beliefs on soil type and use of oak. This sounds as though there is a continual cold war at the heart of Chablis but, as explained later, both factions have now adopted a benign tolerance of each other and go their merry ways alone, and both produce fine wines. Do not be led to believe that the oak camp will give wines prominently tasting of wood, new or old. In capable hands, nothing is further from the truth. The wines of René et Vincent Dauvissat and Jean-Marie Raveneau, advocates of wood, are sublime in the extreme.

So how did all this begin?

②

The History of Chablis

. . . .

IF THE HISTORY of France could be condensed to just one town, then Chablis, through its good and bad times, could be that town. As far back as can be recalled, that is with the benefit of historical hindsight, it would seem that people have loved to live in this little corner of Burgundy, and the life of the village has in effect closely mirrored the events of French history.

One finds traces of a village dating back to the Neolithic period, in the remains of a fortified farm of an early Gallic settlement. But the real beginning for Chablis starts with the Roman occupation and the construction of a villa in the valley of Vaucharmes. The Romans seldom moved or settled without vines, and in AD 276 the Emperor Probus reversed Domitian's edict of AD 92 which had forbidden the further planting of vines in Gaul to encourage grain production. Gradually viticulture came to the area in the third century AD and the first wines of the Chablisien were born.

The first mention of Chablis was in the year 510 AD when Sigismond, first Christian king of the Burgundy lands, established a little monastery dedicated to Saint Loup. Slowly, the village grew and at the beginning of the ninth century the Emperor Charlemagne erected a church dedicated to Sainte Marie. About twenty years later, Chablis received unexpected support. To avoid the Vikings backing up to the River Loire, the monks of Tours carrying with them the remains of Saint Martin sought refuge close to the Abbey of Auxerre. In 865 Charles the Bald gave them the monastery of Saint Loup and the town,[1] and from that moment the wines of Chablis were assured, for at that period of history, the friar was the vine. It was as much a necessity to them as the prestige and hospitality of their Abbey.

The first concern of the monks was the sale of the produce, and Chablis was central enough for that purpose, being near Auxerre, and hardly any great distance from Paris.

Tours retained ties with Chablis for over 900 years, and under the auspices of the Abbot construction was commenced in 1138 on the Collégiale

---

1. Bernard Ginestet, in his indispensable volume on Chablis in the series The Vineyards of France, gives an informed and delightful interpretation of this gift – the *Cella nomine Capleiam* – a cellar of Chablis wine, later supported by the construction of a little chapel consecrated to Saint Loup.

Church of Saint Martin, still today the parish church of Chablis.

At about this time – the precise date is unclear – the Abbey of Pontigny, founded by the monks of Citeaux in 1114 and situated about 15 kilometres north of Chablis, needed to expand its vineyard holding, and entered into an agreement in which the Abbey of Tours guaranteed them the right to farm 36 *arpents* (about 22 hectares) of vineyard in Chablis plus use of a building known to this day as Le Petit Pontigny, in return for an annual rent of ten muids of wine, equivalent to some 10 barrels in today's terms, payable to the monks of Tours. A very early example of *métayage*? The early years were difficult, Chablis suffering at the expense of the renown of the wines of nearby Auxerre, not exactly helped commercially by the wine merchants and brokers who praised the Auxerre wines at the expense of Bordeaux, Beaune and Chablis.

Yet over the years, the reputation of Chablis grew, gradually supplanting that of Auxerre. It came at the right time, and in the course of centuries the distribution lines were established, strengthened by the markets of Champagne. The wine found its way to England via Rouen, to the north, and Flanders via Compiègne. In 1455 the ledgers of 'Compagnies Françaises' reveal the transfer of 67 barriques of Chablis wine agreed by a merchant of Maubeuge. The name of Chablis was on the map, its renown assured.

The beginning of the fifteenth century saw the construction of the city walls and ramparts with 29 towers and 3 gates, necessary fortifications during the times of the Hundred Years War. In 1477, Chablis became part of the Duchy of Burgundy, from that date associating the wines with those of the Côte d'Or rather than Champagne. Chablis was now growing in importance, and in 1478 Pierre Lerouge established in the town the fifth printing press in France. Fifty years later the town counted 4,000 inhabitants – a high point of Chablis' development – at this time there were more than 700 vineyard owners having grown from 450 recorded two hundred years earlier. But in February 1568 the ravages of another war took their toll, as the town was burned, looted and devastated by the Huguenots. It took another two hundred years or so before prosperity returned to the same level, helped no doubt by the wine's many appearances on the dining table of the kings of France.

The most formidable opponents were yet to come. Severe frosts and miserable winters mixed irregularly with abundant vintages were obviously quite commonplace, but the events of the last two hundred years were not. The French Revolution brought to a sudden end the association of the town with the Church, as the vineyards and property of the Abbeys were auctioned off. The populace were not the main beneficiaries, as the principal plots were acquired by wealthy merchants and property owners. But development continued, and the fame of Chablis continued to spread far and wide.

It would be obvious to think that the coming of the railways in the mid-nineteenth century would have been a welcome development. In one way it was – the improved communications and ease of travel all over France. Up to then, the waterways had been the mainstay of transport, the wines of Chablis and the Yonne travelling by road the short distance to Auxerre, and thence by boat or barge down the River Yonne to the Seine, the tables of Paris, northern France, Flanders and the Netherlands. Exporting to England and beyond was easy. But the railways had another effect, not so welcome. It enabled the distribution lines to be opened up for the hitherto relatively unknown cheap wines of the Midi. Chablis now had severe competition, not least from mass-produced wines of the Yonne from high-yielding grape varieties, and all was not well as cheap light wines flooded into Paris to take their place on the café tables. Dr Guyot in *Etude des Vignobles de France* (1868) refers to 38,000 hectares of vines in the département providing the income for 38,000 families or 152,000 people, just under half the total population of 372,589.

In 1870 the Franco-Prussian war was a financial drain on the community, as the Prussians raised capital by ransoming the town as a reprisal for the death of one of their minor officers.

Then at the end of the nineteenth century, after an epidemic of oidium or powdery mildew had been successfully seen off, a most insidious little aphid made its devastating début in the vineyards of France. Phylloxera had arrived from the United States via a greenhouse in Hammersmith, in a bunch of vine cuttings, a parasite feeding off vine roots and destroying its host. It was slow to take hold, but by the turn of the century, the Chablisien vignoble had been decimated. Never had Chablis known such a difficult period, virtually everything being destroyed. After numerous attempts to find the solution, including the application of chemicals and even flooding the vineyards, a nationwide remedy was eventually discovered which involved the grafting of vines on to Phylloxera-resistant American root stock. The epidemic was thus mastered but not for another sixty years or so were fortunes to be turned round. The Great War had another effect, depriving the area of its workers and horses, to such an extent that only women, the old and children were left to work the land. The coming of peace did not bring with it a return to full labour – the lure of better paid employment in the cities and the bright lights of the capital aided the decline of rural life.

The Chablis growers are used to the vagrances of the weather and, as we shall see, frost is a serious problem in these vineyards, much more so before effective methods of control were employed. They were not, however, prepared for the next insidious little aphid, Hitler. The town and area suffered terribly from the bombardment during the Second World War: a stray bomb rearranged the town centre. By the end of the war the vineyards had shrunk to a mere 400 hectares.

Now things began to happen as the Chablisiens dusted themselves off yet again. Over the next two decades, two important events gave renewed confidence to the growers: the introduction of the tractor and mechanisation, and effective frost control methods, both discussed in later chapters.

As a symbol of renewed confidence and determination, 1949 saw the creation of the Fête des Vins, a festival which has been repeated every year since. This was followed in 1952 by the founding of The Order of the Piliers Chablisiens – the Pillars of Chablis – a brotherhood whose purpose is the promotion of the wines of the region, the encouragement of high quality and the pursuit of pleasure and happiness, the wines of Chablis being an undoubted aid to that purpose. Les Piliers was the idea of one Maitre Sotty, the former *notaire* of Chablis, who took inspiration from pillars in the crypt of Mont St Michel and decided that Chablis and its wines needed similar architectural support of a strong foundation, especially during a difficult post-war era of deprivation and severe winters. The organisation of the brotherhood is likewise architecturally based, not in Masonic terms, but bearing such titles for the officers as The Architrave, Pedestals, Corniche (cornice) and Chapiteau (capitals). The members are divided into Stylobates, Fûts (shafts) and Frises (friezes). It works, it works well and the whole is conducted with good humour. The annual November festival is when new members deserving of the honour are *intronisé* (initiated) at Le Petit Pontigny, sometimes at other times of the year in various locations. The events are a source of friendship, companionship and a lot of fun, the cause of not a few morning-after hangovers – but never any regrets.

③

WHAT IS CHABLIS?

. . . .

THIS MAY SEEM a silly question at this stage, but the answer is far from silly, and we should consider just what it is that the producer of fine Chablis is trying to achieve. Here we use the word 'producer' as opposed to 'grower' deliberately, as will be seen there are many instances of *négociants* producing wine of fine quality to put alongside the growers' wines, not unfortunately a common occurrence in other areas of France.

To take the most obvious comparables, the wines of Bordeaux and the Côte d'Or of Burgundy are easier to define in terms of overall style. Fine Claret combines the winemaker's art of growing and blending Cabernet Sauvignon, Merlot and Bouchet to produce a recognisable house style – everyone knows what is required in a fine Cabernet and if achieved will recognise it as a work of art according to taste. No less a fine red Burgundy, but considerably more difficult to achieve, due to the capricious nature of the Pinot Noir grape – but when everything gels, not least the skill of the winemaker, the red nectar of the gods will show what elegance and finesse can be found in a glass. Imagine raising a Riedel glass of mature Dujac Bonnes Mares to the nose – you don't have to taste, just be wafted away to the Elysian Fields on the breath of perfumed air.

So, why this deviation into dreams, dubious feelings perhaps not universally appreciated? Because the appreciation of fine Chablis is even more subjective and indeed elusive than any other wine in France. Even the experts get it wrong – let us quote Charles Albert d'Arnoux in his *Dissertation sur la situation de Bourgogne* of 1728:

> The good gourmets taste by the nose before they put the wine in their mouths: and all the other vineyards of Bourgogne like Chablis and Auxerre have not a single quality of the true wines of Burgundy though they may be fairly made and produced.

Charles Tovey in 1877 – 'Chablis is very fine, firm and dry: it is in perfection at five to six years old, but it is liable to get cloudy when much longer in bottle' – where did he get his bottles from? But Tovey goes on to talk about the unjust reputation of Chablis which it does not deserve, and it's probably Pouilly Fuissé anyway. Therein lies the problem.

Frank Schoonmaker and Tom Marvel wrote of Chablis in 1934:

> Like the great Burgundies of the Côte d'Or, this wine is magnificent when genuine, but rarely genuine. It is necessary to distrust not only any bottle marked simply 'Chablis', but any bottle that does not bear on its label the same triple specification that authentic Côte d'Or wines bear: the name and address of the shipper, the year, the name of a definite vineyard.

Schoonmaker then rails against Muscadet Nantais, 'a pale self-effacing little wine', being blended and sold as 'Export Chablis'.

Like many works of art, over the years Chablis has suffered as a result of its own popularity. Bastardised and copied – mostly badly – for decades, the full worth of the genuine article is not yet fully appreciated for what it is, at least not in modern terms. Chablis is from the Chardonnay grape alone. It is above all a food wine, a perfect partner for oysters and other shell fish, white fish dishes, *fruits de mer* and light white meats. It is a wine of distinction and individuality like no other. Light green-tinged gold, bright and clear, it possesses neither the muscle power nor gout of fine Meursault or Puligny, but all their finesse and elegance, not their vegetal – in the nicest sense, that is – character or oak base, but their Chardonnay fruit nuances, not their toasty oaky noses but their gentle perfumes and fragrances. It is a wine of crisp freshness when young, often with mouth-puckering acidity, developing subtle nutty 'oaky' type overtones, and mouth-filling fruit long on the aftertaste, and to cap it all that flinty miner-ally character keeping alive the famous *typicité* to the end of its life. Chablis can be and frequently is drunk when young, often too young, but its true nature comes alive after a few years in the bottle – as a rough rule of thumb at least five years for a Premier Cru and ten years for a Grand Cru. But as we have already mentioned and shall see again, a fine village wine can be a joy for many years.

Chablis has been the subject of many ancient and modern quotes, hardly surprising when one considers the historical importance of the wine and area; the Yonne was, after all, at one time the largest wine-producing area in France.

Here are just a few well-known and not so well-known quotes:

> The wines of Chablis.....have body and finesse, and a charming per-fume, their whiteness and clarity are remarkable. But they are distin-guished above all by their hygienic and digestive qualities, and by the gentle stimulation full of lucidity that they give to the brain.
>
> Dr Jules Guyot

How delectable these wines can be ... the light wines of the 2èmes and 3èmes Crus adapt themselves as the most delightful thirst-quenchers at tennis parties or picnics.

Charles Walter Berry

Chablis, agreeable in itself, makes everything you eat with it taste better.

Stephen Gwynn

I do not think I shall ever tire of Chablis: it defies description.

Rosemary George

The scent and flavour that develop are the quintessence of an elusive character you can miss if you only ever drink Chablis young. I can only define it as combining the fragrances of apples and hay with a taste of boiled sweets and an underlying mineral note that seems to have been mined from the bowels of the earth.

Hugh Johnson

Bernard Ginestet playfully takes Hugh Johnson to task over the boiled sweets, stating that he has never tasted nor has any intention of tasting such bonbons. Perhaps this is the same reaction to the 'sweaty saddles' when nosing a glass of Australian Shiraz — the writers thankfully have never smelled a recently vacated saddle nor have any intention of so doing.

Alexis Lichine, having never eaten a piece of flint, eschews this comparison:

> ... a great Chablis cru of a good vintage which has been vinified correctly presents a strange combination of austere vigour and hardness as well as the elegant fruit imparted by the Chardonnay and the pebbly soil lying over limestone.

④

The Appellation Laws
and their Development

. . . .

IT WOULD BE USEFUL at this stage to take a look at the development of the appellation laws from the very beginnings of attempts at self-control by the Chablis producers themselves. To some degree this can be self-defeating and rather boring for the reader. After all, the purpose of this book is to aid the pleasure and enjoyment of wine to the enthusiast, but a précis of the important events leading to the established status quo could be considered informative for the understanding of past and present attitudes.

As we have seen, Chablis was a name used back in the nineteenth century to describe any dry white wine emanating from the Yonne region, irrespective of the grape variety and location of production. Cyrus Redding in 1833 refers to the best class of white wine of the Yonne being produced from the *pineau blanc* alone. Whether this refers to the Pinot Blanc as we know it today or to the Chardonnay is unclear. What is clear is his reference to character: very white, dry, diuretic, flinty; and a quality order: first, Val Mur; second, Vaux-desir; third, Grenouille: fourth, Blanchot; fifth, Mont-de-Milieu. This differed from André Jullien's earlier unofficial classification in *Topographie de Tous Les Vignobles Connus* (1822) which divided the white wines into three classes:-

Première classe
Tonnerre Côtes de Vaumorillon and des Grisées, 'which give wines full of
   body, finesse and especially *spiritueux:* they approach the quality of the
   finest Meursault.'
Chablis-'highly regarded wines, occupying the second division immediately after the best Meursault *cuvées* ... the most sought after being (i).
   Le Clos (ii), Valmur and Grenouilles as they don't keep as long as Le
   Clos, (iii) Vaudésir, Bouguereau and Mont de Milieu ... All of these
   need to be kept two years in *tonneau* and one year in bottle. By the third
   edition of 1832, Jullien suggests bottling in the second year!

Deuxième classe
La Côte Delchet (Côte de Lechet) at Milly, Fourchaume at Maligny, a part
   of the Côte de Troëne at Poinchy, Vaucompin at Chiché, Blanchot at Fiey,

and Fontenay.

Tonnerre Charloupe, Bridaines, Boutoirs and Maison Rouge.

Chablis Chapelot, Vauvilien, a part of Bouguereau and Preuse, Vaulovent, Vossegros and the lower part of Le Clos.

Champs and Saint-Bris — various *lieu dits*.

Troisième classe
Vivier, Beru and Fley. Roffey, Serrigny, Tissey, Vezannes, Bernouil, Dié, Tanlay. Milly, Maligny, Poinchy, Villy, Chiché, Ligny-le-Châtel, Poily, Chemilly, Courgy, 'and several others also giving *des vins d'ordinaire et des vins communs.*'

By the third edition, Blanchot had been elevated to first class, but so also had Préaux and Pitoy in Tonnerre, Côte des Olivotes in Dannemoine, and Vins Mousseaux of Tonnerre, Dannemoine and Epineuil. Montmains is a new entry at number two with Vivier, Beru and Fley joining that class in an upgrade. The third class had now been amalgamated with a fourth, and Bennes (Beines) makes a late entry at number four in the edition of 1866.

A much more simplistic approach but no less sincere was penned at about the same time as Jullien's first thoughts by A. L. Henderson in *The History of Ancient and Modern Wines* (1824). Henderson's ideas created just two classes of white wine in Burgundy:

First class — the best *crus* of Mont Rachet.
Second class — the best *climats* of Meursault: Vaumorillon and Les Grisées at Tonnerre; Valmur, Grenouilles, Vaudésir, Bouguereau and Mont de Milieu in Chablis; Pouilly and Fuissé in Macon.

Thus, unofficial attempts had been made at classification, with Jullien's considered opinions held in high esteem, not before time and much needed, but the journey ahead was long and fraught with difficulties.

Things came to a head in 1898 at the height of the Phylloxera epidemic when a *négociant* from Chablis bought a large quantity of Spanish wine which appears to have been resold as Chablis. There was serious need to establish a system of control, to clearly define the permitted area of production to prevent fraud and protect the name of Chablis. The first tentative steps were taken at the turn of the century with the formation of a union of growers, 'Union des Propriétaires-Vignerons de Chablis' whose purpose was to guarantee the authenticity of the wines, and 1908 saw the introduction of the 'Certificat d'origine de Chablis' — a wax seal would be affixed to each barrel bearing the stamp of the union, which of course did not carry with it any legal standing. Some 140 growers were members of this union.

In 1919 appeared the first law on the appellation origins based on quantitative control. The Grand Crus were broadly mapped out by the growers, and the first suggestion that only Chardonnay should be the permitted grape variety was mooted, and only wines from certain communes – Chablis itself, Fontenay-Près-Chablis, Fyé, Milly, Poinchy, Chichée, Fleys, Courgis, La Chapelle-Vaupelteigne, and Beine should be given the Chablis Village Appellation. The rest were to be given the umbrella protection, if that is the word, of Petit Chablis.

(For reference and completeness, the 19 communes outside of Chablis are: Poilly, Chemilly, Préhy, Chichée, Béru, Viviers, Courgis, Fleys, Milly, Fyé, Rameau, Beine, Poinchy, Fontenay, La Chapelle Vaupelteigne, Lignorelles, Villy, Maligny, Ligny-le-Châtel.)

However, the growers' submissions were largely ignored and the Chablis Appellation was awarded by the Commission set up for the purpose to all wines made from Chardonnay almost throughout the entire region of the Yonne.

The Burgundy Commission considered an appeal by the growers in 1920, and correspondingly proposed a revision into three appellations:

1. Grands Vins de Chablis, i.e. the Grand Crus
2. Chablis Village Supérieur for all Beaunois wines (Chardonnay) of Chablis, the above-mentioned communes plus Ligny-le-Châtel, Lignorelles, Maligny, Villy, Beine, Viviers and Chemilly-sur-Serein
3. Chablis Village for all other white wines of these communes, but this Appellation was never subsequently applied.

Various lawsuits followed as the growers fought with extreme difficulty to enforce the new definitions but, in 1921, the Union itself extended Chablis Village appellation to any Chardonnay wine from the Canton of Chablis plus further communes in Ligny-le-Châtel and Tonnerre. This followed a judgement in late 1920 which named 'Kimmeridgian' soil as the soil for the genuine article, thus excluding wines from Lignorelles and Villy from being sold as Chablis without mention of Village or Village Supérieur. Thus our little Dorset village was now firmly established on the Chablis wine map.

There followed years of wrangling, more law suits, representations and pronouncements during which the terms Chablis Village and Petit Chablis were abandoned, and new arguments evolved naming not only Kimmeridgian soil and the Chardonnay grape as a basis, but also local methods of production. At last the term Petit Chablis was officially used to refer to any Chardonnay wine from non-Kimmeridgian soil, but it was not to last.

In 1929 the Tribunal d'Auxerre ratified an agreement made between the growers and the Yonne Syndicat de Commerce stating that only wine from the communes of Chablis and from Chardonnay could be classified as Chablis Appellation. Everything else was called 'Bourgogne des Environs de Chablis' and both Appellations of Chablis Village and Petit Chablis would be extinguished. No mention is made of Kimmeridgian soil, and one could be forgiven for thinking that progress was not a word in common usage. (Stephen Gwynn writing in 1934 sets out this situation, which was known at that time in England, despite a London Club offering a wine called Chablis-Meursault on its list, the label indicating clearly that it could be neither.)

January 1938 changed all that. The new Inspector General for Agriculture, Georges Chappaz, was responsible for drawing up the laws of Appellation d'Origine Controllé, and a decree was issued by CNAO, in effect combining the 1929 ruling of the Tribunal d'Auxerre and the earlier agreement on soils. Thus the Chablis Appellation would be restricted to Chardonnay wines from the twenty communes grown on Kimmeridgian soil only.

This was fine as far as it went, but to establish for certain just which vineyards comply, or more exactly do not comply as regards soil composition, proved almost impossible at the time. Geologists didn't agree, soil experts didn't agree, and especially vignerons didn't agree what was and what was not Kimmeridgian, there was no clear division, no clear start or finish, but the CNAO were unconvinced and insisted that there was a distinct difference, although failing to define it themselves. And what about those areas where Chardonnay was grown on sites most definitely composed of the 'other' soil, Portlandian – Lignorelles, Villy and Maligny? In another about-turn, the INAO (as CNAO had now become) in 1943 re-created Petit Chablis for this purpose (much to the disgust of William Fèvre) but without precisely delimiting the area. So the Kimmerigdian War was firmly declared.

Appeal followed appeal but it was not until 1956 that a new commission was set up by INAO to investigate the possibility and which recommended the extension of the Chablis Appellation by 500 hectares, but this extended area was broadly restricted to sites of Kimmeridgian soil. There was a general feeling of satisfaction with this decision, and together with the introduction of effective methods of frost control during the 1960s, things were looking up and trade substantially improved.

January 1967 saw the classification and delimitation of the Premier Crus, discussed in greater detail later. (Forty years earlier, it was already very clear as to the principal growths of Chablis, as listed by P. Morton Shand in *A Book of French Wines* (1928), dividing the growths into first and second class. He was understandably very accurate with the first or Grand Crus, and fairly accurate with the second or Premier Crus. His third class lumped everything else together, including the wines of Chichée and Milly-Lechet.) But all was not well in the ranks, particularly the growers of Maligny who were aggrieved at the effect on the Chablis Appellation and discontent continued. As we will see, two distinct groups polarised representing the opposing sides of the expansionist argument, the nays led by William Fèvre and the ayes by Jean Durup, who rightly claimed that the orientation and microclimates of a site were as important as soil composition in establishing its status. This was especially so of the Premier Crus and it was a claim to which the authorities could hardly turn a deaf ear. But the appellation laws are not just concerned with the delimitation of the areas, they also control yields through the INAO declaring annually a *'rendement de base'* taking all factors of the vintage into consideration, after due consultation with the local experts, and adding 20 per cent to that figure. Control also extends to alcohol content of the four levels plus the amount of chaptalisation allowed.

In 1976 and confirmed two years later, INAO recommended an extension of 148 hectares to the Premier Crus, 860 hectares to the Chablis Appellation, which established an overall area of some 1,500 hectares as Petit Chablis. The new approved areas of AOC, not necessarily in production, were as follows:

Chablis Grand Cru	112 hectares
Chablis Premier Cru	742 hectares
Chablis Village	4,420 hectares
Petit Chablis	1,562 hectares.

The list of Premier Crus was finally published in 1986 and is given complete in the discussion on the areas of production in the following chapter.

The growers are no longer at open war, but opinions are still firmly divided and held on the respective merits of expansion, consolidation, Kimmeridgian and Portlandian. This is referred to in more detail in Chapter 11.

In 1994, there were 6,800 hectares of AOC, 3,600 in production.

Bernard Ginestet in his book *Chablis – Guide to the Vineyards of France* states that his attempt to sum up the appellation situation is somewhat simplified, yet the above is probably an oversimplification of a very involved and complex issue. We commend to all readers Monsieur Ginestet's masterly essay on the subject.

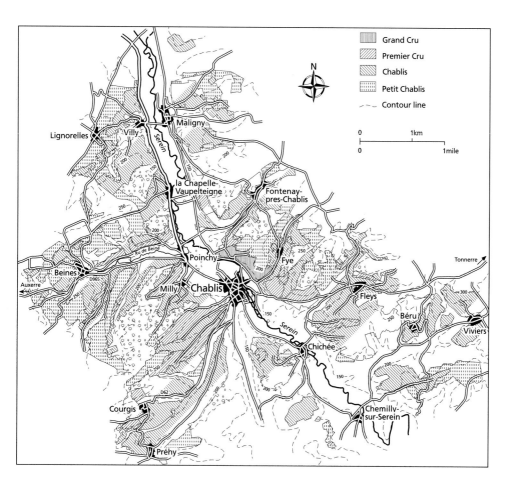

General Appellation Map

⑤

Areas of Production

. . . .

WINE IS PRODUCED in Chablis by some 300 growers, at four quality levels, all Appellation Controllé, all from the Chardonnay grape alone. One third of all the production is bottled and sold separately, the other two thirds are marketed through the *négociants* and the co-operative La Chablisienne. The four Appellations in ascending order are Petit Chablis, Chablis Village, Premier Cru and Grand Cru.

Petit Chablis

Average yield is 54.4 hectolitres per hectare (average 1987–1996 based on INAO figures).

At the most basic level, Petit Chablis comes from the flatlands at the base of the Côtes and surrounding areas – approximately 475 hectares, most of it Portlandian soil. Many do not consider this worthy of the name Chablis, but this is a sweeping judgement and does not allow for the produce of a fine winemaker, e.g. Jean Collet whose Petit Chablis is excellent quality, fresh, crisp and fruity, even with some depth, and for early enjoyable drinking.

With INAO's acceptance and agreement to the expansion of the Chablis Appellation, the initial effect was the upgrading of much Petit Chablis land, particularly at Maligny, with the resultant decreased area in the lower appellation. Recent figures show a reversal of this trend, as more plantings come into production. The area is, however, still small in relation to the much larger area of village Chablis.

The minimum level of natural alcohol under the Petit Chablis Appellation regulations is 9.5 per cent.

Chablis Village

Approximately 2,678 hectares (1996 figure) from specific areas in 19 communes with varied exposure from north-east to south-west. Average yield is 57 hectolitres per hectare (average 1987-1996 based on INAO figures).

Village Chablis is produced from the lower slopes or foothills, so to speak, and well-sited flatter ground abundant in the area. The soil is mostly Kimmeridgian clay-limestone which in good hands produces wine typical of the area, flinty pale green, minerally with ripe fruit and mouth-puckering acidity. In the best hands, Village Chablis can age well, although made for relatively early drinking. An example of Jean Durup's Chablis Village Vieilles Vignes 1983 from 90-year-old vines, tasted in 1997 was a revelation, nutty, biscuity, developed like a fine delicate Meursault, wonderful. This is what can happen to un-oaked Chablis, atypical, but that is the joy of it. Unfortunately, this particular vineyard was destroyed by 30 degrees of frost in 1985.

The minimum level of natural alcohol under the Chablis Appellation regulations is 10 per cent.

Chablis Premier Cru

The Premier Cru vineyards, 747 hectares in 1996, the mainstay of the district upon which the high reputation is broadly based, are mostly sited on the low hills with south-eastern to south-western exposure on Kimmeridgian soil, and on both banks of the river. The 10-year average yield from 1987 to 1996 based on verified returns was 58.9 hectolitres per hectare.

There are 40 named Premier Cru vineyards, but generally only 17 names are used as being the principal crus of which the others form part. This is a recent increase from only 11 names. The following list of the 40 Premier Crus gives the commune in which they are sited and the main cru of which they form part:

Premier Cru	Commune – right bank of Serein	Principal Cru
Berdiot	Fyé	Berdiot
Chapelot	Fyé	Montée de Tonnerre
Côte de Bréchin	Fyé	Montée de Tonnerre
Côte de Fontenay	Fontenay	Fourchaume
Côte de Prés Girots	Fleys	Les Fournaux
Côte de Vaubarousse	Fyé	Côte de Vaubarousse
Fourchaume	La Chapelle Vaupelteigne	Fourchaume
L'Homme Mort	Maligny	Fourchaume
Les Fourneaux	Fleys	Les Fourneaux
Mont de Milieu	Fleys	Mont de Milieu
Montée de Tonnerre	Fyé	Montée de Tonnerre
Morein	Fleys	Les Fourneaux
Pied d'Aloup	Fyé	Montée de Tonnerre
Vaucoupin	Chichée	Vaucoupin
Vaulorent	Poinchy	Fourchaume
Vaupoulent	La Chapelle Vaupelteigne	Fourchaume

Premier Cru	Commune – left bank of Serein	Principal Cru
Beauroy	Poinchy	Beauroy
Beugnons	Chablis	Vaillons
Butteaux	Chablis	Montmains
Chatains	Chablis	Vaillons
Chaume de Talvat	Courgis	Chaume de Talvat
Côte de Léchet	Milly	Côte de Léchet
Côte de Cuissy	Courgis	Les Beauregards
Côte de Jouan	Courgis	Côte de Jouan
Côte de Savant	Beine	Beauroy
Forêts	Chablis	Montmains
Les Beauregards	Courgis	Les Beauregards
Les Epinottes	Chablis	Les Beauregards
Les Lys	Chablis	Vaillons
Mélinot	Chablis	Vaillons
Montmains	Chablis	Montmains
Roncières	Chablis	Vaillons
Sécher	Chablis	Vaillons
Troesmes	Beine	Beauroy
Vau de Vey	Beine	Vau de Vey
Vaillons	Chablis	Vaillons
Vaugiraut	Chichée	Vosgros
Vosgros	Chichée	Vosgros
Vau Ligneau	Beine	Vau Ligneau
Vaux Ragons	Beine	Vau de Vey

If a wine is wholly from a vineyard, under Appellation laws it can be labelled either with the name of the Premier Cru as such, or with the name of the vineyard, e.g. Chablis Premier Cru – Fourchaume, or Chablis Premier Cru L'Homme Mort, but not both. There is an increasing tendency nowadays for the vineyard to be specified, and who can blame a grower like Jean Durup for doing just that, when his wines are superb examples of *typicité*.

The minimum natural alcohol level for the Appellation Chablis Premier Cru is 10.5 per cent.

One would be forgiven for thinking that the 17 are the best known and most popular Premier Crus of the 40. Well, no! In reality, and in France reality is often separate and distinct from French law, the list can be reformed as follows:

Les Fourneaux
*Mont de Milieu
*Montée de Tonnerre

The Grand Crus

CHABLIS

La Moutonne
Vaudésir
Preuses
Bougros
Grenouilles
Valmur
Les Clos
Blanchot

Serein

Chemin de Chablis à Flogny
Chemin dit de la ferme couverte
Chemin dit de la preuse
Chemin départemental de Joigny
Chemin dit des V.audésirs
Chemin dit des V.audésirs
Chemin dit de Valmur
à Avallon Chemin
Chemin dit des V.audésirs
Fontaine de...
Chemin rural dit du Travers des Clos
de sentier
le sentier des Clos
le grand sentier
Chemin de Chablis à Vézannes
Voie-meurtrière
Rue de Fie
Rue de Fie
Chemin de Chablis à Fie
Chemin de Chablis à Collan
annexe de Chablis

Bonny-sur-Loire
Neufchâteau

N

0   1km
0   1mile

Vaulorent
*Fourchaume
*Beauroy
*Vau Ligneau
*Vau de Vey
*Côte de Léchet
 Les Lys
*Vaillons
 Beugnons
 Butteaux
 Forêts
*Montmains
*Vosgros
 Vaucoupin

This list follows the geographic order in anti-clockwise sequence around the town of Chablis. We have shown with an asterisk (*) the ten best known of all the Premier Crus and we have endeavoured to give their various characteristics in the later chapter.

In addition to the above, many growers and *négociants* are using with greater frequency the names of Chapelot (Montée de Tonnerre), Côte de Fontenay (Fourchaume), l'Homme Mort (Fourchaume), Vaugiraut (Vosgros), Châtains and Sécher (both Vaillons).

French spelling of these names can be a bit perverse; for example, you are likely to see Forêts, Forêt, Les Forêts, even Forest. There should, however, be no doubt to which vineyard the bottle is referring. We shall endeavour to use the spelling which appears on the grower's label.

In the words of BIVB – French wine law is complex, reality is more complex.

Chablis Grand Cru

There are seven Grand Crus, totalling 106 hectares (1996 figures) and all occupying a crown-shaped area on the right bank of the Serein, in the hills to the north-east and within sight of the town, and that is exactly what the vineyards are, the crown of the district, producing wines of depth, concentration, finesse and elegance, supreme examples of what Chablis is capable of. The exposure is southern to south-western.

Average yield is 53.9 hectolitres per hectare (10 year average 1987-1996 based on INAO figures).

Grand Crus – areas in production (hectares)
Blanchot	12.71
Bougros	12.63
Grenouilles	9.38
Les Clos	26.05

Preuses	11.44	includes La Moutonne
Vaudésir	14.71	see Long-Depaquit
Valmur	13.20	
Total	100.12	

The minimum natural alcohol level under Chablis Grand Cru regulations is 11 per cent.

The basic yield figures are interesting from the point of view of consistency between the Appellations. Admittedly the Grand Cru figure is lower, but not substantially so. These yields are also affected by the increase in vineyard area over the years particularly in Petit Chablis and Chablis as new plantings come on line. The figures below show the most dramatic increases between 1987 and 1996 of vineyard area in production:

Petit Chablis	1987 –	160 ha	1996 –	475 ha
Chablis Village	1987 –	1432 ha	1996 –	2678 ha
Premier Cru	1987 –	593 ha	1996 –	747 ha
Grand Cru	1987 –	94 ha	1996 –	100 ha

Average yield in hectolitres per hectare

Year	Gr. Cru	1er Cru	Chablis	P. Chab.
1987	53.8	58.8	58.1	60.5
1988	53.9	59.9	59.5	58.5
1989	54.2	56.3	55.2	49.7
1990	53.9	60.0	58.5	56.8
1991	53.4	57.6	47.9	37.1
1992	53.7	59.3	59.6	59.0
1993	57.3	65.2	66.7	69.7
1994	43.3	51.6	53.4	50.0
1995	54.1	60.1	59.9	59.1
1996	49.2	56.6	57.9	58.5
Average	52.68	58.54	57.67	55.89

These figures are distorted by new plantings and additional areas coming into production during the ten-year period, especially the Premier Crus, but they give a guide to the consistency of the four appellations. Note Petit Chablis in 1991 and the Grand Crus in 1994 hit by spring frost, and the generally abundant harvest of 1993 resulting in some rain-diluted fruit and corresponding diminished quality.

⑥

ORIENTATION OF THE CRUS

. . . .

A VINEYARD'S ABILITY to produce quality fruit depends on a number of characteristics, some tangible, some intangible – the concept of *terroir*. Not least of those essentials is its orientation to the sun, wind, rain and other climatic conditions, the slope in relation to surrounding or adjoining vineyards, its drainage and innumerable factors making up its very individual microclimates. Like fingerprints, no two vineyards have exactly the same form: unlike fingerprints, each vineyard has different sections where those very microclimates differ.

The Grand Crus clearly have the best orientation and slopes being sited on the right bank of the Serein. All have south-east, south or south-west facing slopes which are very steep and well drained. The Valley of Vaudésir runs through the middle of the Grand Crus in which there are some northwest facing slopes classified as Chablis Appellation and are not included in the Grand Cru classification.

Blanchot facing south-east nearest to Fyé is the smallest. **Les Clos** facing almost due south with a lovely wooded top is the most prominent and the largest cru, followed in a northerly direction by **Valmur** which faces mainly south west. **Grenouilles**, identified by its château, so named as its slopes run down to the river and reportedly were frequented by frogs, is the lowest of the Grand Crus in terms of height, and possibly produces the most delicate of the wines as a result.

Vaudésir and **Les Preuses**, both south facing, have excellent orientation and very steep well-drained slopes, the steepest areas being where the **La Moutonne** monopole is situated, somewhat reminiscent of the Valley of the Kings at Luxor and almost as hot at the height of summer, trapping the sun's rays in its embrace. This leaves **Bougros**, well exposed at the northern end, slopes facing south/south-west possibly with the least attractive orientation.

The best Premier Crus on the right bank are **Mont de Milieu** which faces due south and has a lovely location with good slopes under a wooded hilltop. This Premier Cru is separated from **Montée de Tonnerre** by a dip forming a valley giving limited sunny aspects and the area is thus designated as generic Chablis. Montée de Tonnerre ('Thunder Climb') is so named as it was the hill to be crossed on the journey from Chablis to Tonnerre in bygone days, no easy matter. This is all south-facing with well-drained steep slopes. The *lieu-dit* within this cru, named **Chapelot,** as described later, is deemed to be of Grand Cru quality, but change of status is unlikely.

Fourchaume, by far the largest and best known of the right-bank Premier Crus, is extensive, stretching from the road to Fontenay as far as the approach to the village of Maligny. The slopes are well drained with wooded hilltops and have south-east, south and south-west facing elevations. **L'Homme Mort,** which forms part of Fourchaume, is located at the northern end towards Maligny and is a special favourite of the writers particularly in the hands of Domaine Jean Durup who own a large parcel. Jean-Paul Durup told us that the name is attributed to the number of condemned miscreants buried there after being hanged near his Château de Maligny just up the road, before he took over, that is.

On the left bank we would list the better known as **Montmains,** a large area extending between Chablis and Courgis with rounded slopes facing south and south-east. A section of Montmains named variously **Les Forêts, La Forêt,** even **Forest** at the southern end is particularly well favoured. The other large Premier Cru **Vaillons** includes a number of other names, **Les Lys** and **Sécher** to name but two, this area lying between two valleys and having slopes with varying steepness and orientation.

Côte de Léchet, however, is the Premier Cru most noticeable from the road leading from Chablis to Beines (or Beine, depending upon your mood), and these marvellous south-facing slopes dominate the area around Milly. The reason for the outstanding wines it produces is there to see and appreciate. It can hardly be coincidental that some of its leading exponents are located in the village below.

This brings us very neatly to the question of the value of upgrading certain Chablis vineyards to Premier Cru status. The tasting notes in Part Two support our view that some of these areas clearly do not justify this status, either on the grounds of soil and elevation or in some cases due to recent plantings where land has been brought into production to gain recognition before time has shown whether this is justified or not. This comment applies to some of the lesser known Premier Crus on both banks of the Serein and to such now well-known names as Vau Ligneau, Vau de Vey, Beauregards and Vaugirot. The findings, however, also include many of the new crus towards the villages of Beines, Courgis and Chichée which are located on the far outposts of the Chablis appellation, and indeed it has to be said, of Kimmeridgian soil.

⑦

THE CHARACTER AND CHARACTERISTICS OF THE WINES AND THE VINEYARDS

. . . .

THE *TYPICITÉ* OF CHABLIS in general is defined by pale greenish straw colour, not too yellow as this can denote age or oxidation (obviously colour can and does change with age), flowery nose, steely flinty fruit on the palate, crisp acidity and a fresh aftertaste. As far as it goes, this is fine, but to the experienced palate each and every vineyard and wine has its individual taste, and should be recognisable in blind tastings.

A joke – and for those who have heard it, forgive us and bear with it for a few seconds, but not all the readers of this book will be experienced tasters – Harry Waugh of international wine fame was once asked if he had ever mistaken a Claret for a Burgundy. As quick as a flash came the brilliant reply 'Not since lunchtime.'

Blind tasting can be a mug's game, fun for amateurs, serious for the professionals, as it is the only way to judge a wine free from unwanted external influences. To state that a wine has certain characteristics may be subjective, even if agreed by others at a blind tasting. But if certain characteristics are aimed for by the winemaker, this is objective. When the two meet successfully, this is magic.

Set out below are the characteristics of the wines from the best known vineyards. It is a suggested guide to what to look for in the glass of wine in front of you – it is not infallible.

Chablis Village

Greeny straw or lemon, flowers, green apples, crisp acidity, flinty mineral character, easy drinking but ageing well if a balanced vintage from a good grower.

Premier Crus

Fourchaume

Very floral nose, feminine wine with an elegant and fresh palate, overall flinty and mineral with a touch of peach, develops nuts and biscuits with age. Fourchaume in the hands of a good grower is often referred to as being of Grand Cru status; however, from an indifferent producer it can sometimes be dull and disappointing. **L'Homme Mort** is a *lieu-dit* within Fourchaume at its northern end which displays an attractive earthy flavour with an added dimension.

Best growers: Billaud-Simon, Boudin, Durup, Grossot, Louis Michel, Gerard Tremblay, Vrignaud.

Côte de Léchet
Flowery nose, perhaps English roses, minerally, flinty, develops butter, plums, crème brûlée, gives wines of lovely elegance, never brutal or harsh. One of our very favourites on the left bank.

Best growers: Daniel Dampt, Daniel-Etienne Defaix, Laurent Tribut.

Montée de Tonnerre
More powerful masculine wine, typical minerally Chablis flavours, fresh fruit, flinty, develops nuts and honey. **Chapelot**, a *lieu-dit* within Montée de Tonnerre, has claims for it to be upgraded to a Grand Cru, principally by Domaine Raveneau, and judging by examples we have tasted, we can see why. If any Chablis can be described as succulent and voluptuous, in Raveneau's hands this is it.

Best growers: Billaud-Simon, J.-P. Droin, Duplessis, Durup, Louis Michel, Raveneau, Philippe Testut.

Mont de Milieu
Fragrant nose of spring flowers, steely acidity with fresh fruit flavours, lighter in style which develops quickly, drink relatively young.

Best growers: Billaud-Simon, Louis Moreau, Pinson.

Montmain
Fresh, crisp, light and perfumed wine with steely acidity, more masculine than Vaillons, generally not of the greatest elegance and the least characterful of the Premier Crus. **Forêt**, **Forêts** or **Forest** is a *lieu-dit* within Montmain, which in the hands of the best growers is outstanding.

Best growers: Adine, René et Vincent Dauvissat, Louis Michel, Pinson, Raveneau, Philippe Testut, Laurent Tribut, Vocoret.

Vaillons
Spicy fruit, flinty, develops honey butter and almonds, sometimes truffles, soft feminine character particularly in **Sécher**, a *lieu-dit* within the Vaillons Cru. Can be succulent and voluptuous.

Best growers: Billaud-Simon, Daniel Dampt, René et Vincent Dauvissat, Daniel-Etienne Defaix, Drouhin, Laroche, Long Depaquit, Louis Michel, Raveneau.

Grand Crus

Blanchot

A wine of elegance and finesse, intensely perfumed, spring flowers with lovely fruit. Not quite the power and structure of the other Grand Crus but usually delightful.

Best growers: Billaud-Simon, Daniel-Etienne Defaix, Laroche, Long Depaquit, Raveneau, Vocoret.

Bougros or Bouguerots

The least known of the big seven, up-front wines of power and generosity without the finesse and elegance of the others. Can be disappointing.
Best grower: Laroche.

Les Clos

Nicknamed by the writers 'Big Daddy', the epitome of Grand Cru Chablis, powerful yet gentle, great depth but great charm, very mineral-complex fruit flavours, warm, takes the longest to mature and should keep for ages.

Best growers: René et Vincent Dauvissat, J.-P. Droin, Drouhin, Laroche, Long Depaquit, Louis Michel, Pinson, Raveneau.

Grenouilles

Very perfumed when young, fresh mineral taste, fat, round and elegant. Superb wine from the best growers, but location of parcels is important as this is the lowest cru on the slopes. Perhaps the lightest of the Grand Crus but ages well.

Best growers: J.-P. Droin, Louis Michel, Philippe Testut.

La Moutonne

Although not listed as a Grand Cru in its own name, **La Moutonne** – a *monopole* owned by Long Depaquit – is mainly within Vaudésir with a small section of Les Preuses, and in our view combines the best qualities of both. Soft, elegance and finesse, usually a wine of sheer delight.

Best growers: Although solely owned by Long Depaquit, older vintages can be found from Drouhin.

Les Preuses

Most forward of the Grand Crus and approachable relatively early, round and intensely fruity, full flavoured perhaps less subtle than the others.

Best growers: Billaud-Simon, Jean et Sebastien Dauvissat, René et Vincent Dauvissat, Drouhin, Long Depaquit.

Valmur

Floral perfumed, generally rich and full bodied showing generous fruit and capable of long ageing.

Best growers: J.-P. Droin, Raveneau, Gerard Tremblay, Vocoret.

Vaudésir

Floral bouquet, concentrated spicy fruit which develops nuts and oaky characteristics. Can be drunk young, but ages gracefully and beautifully. Is this the best Grand Cru? Possibly!

Best growers: Billaud-Simon, J.-P. Droin, Drouhin, Long Depaquit, Louis Michel.

(8)

The Climate and Frost Control

. . . .

4 DEGREES EAST, 48 DEGREES NORTH – with the exception of Champagne and Alsace, Chablis must be the most northerly vineyard in the world of major importance. There are, of course, others in Canada, Belgium, England and Mosel in Germany, but for a vignoble of significance, both historically and commercially, 48 degrees north is a distinct disadvantage. Cyrus Redding writing in 1833 gives 51 degrees or half a degree north of Coblentz (Koblenz) as the limit 'south of which wine is made that will repay the grower from fruit reared in the open air'. The inland district of the Yonne not directly affected by the vagrances of the sea can claim hottish summers and very cold winters. Only Champagne is colder at both ends of the scale.

The warmth and beneficial effects of sunshine are at a premium in such northerly climes; enough of it is essential to photosynthesis, the process whereby the chlorophyll in the leaves of a plant acting as a catalyst converts carbon dioxide to sugar and oxygen during daylight, reversing this at night and giving out carbon dioxide but to a lesser extent – hence the worldwide problem caused by deforestation; however, this is another subject.

The vine is an **autotrophic organism**, i.e. self-nourishing, which obtains its photosynthetic energy source of water and carbon dioxide from the physical environment. The reaction which occurs can be summarised by the following simplified formula:

$$\text{water} + \text{carbon dioxide} \xrightarrow{\text{sunlight}} \text{oxygen} + \text{glucose} + \text{water}$$

More specifically:

$$12H_2O + 6CO_2 \xrightarrow{\text{sunlight}} 6O_2 + C_6H_{12}O_6 + 6H_2O$$

where $C_6H_{12}O_6$ = glucose. This is the fundamental basis of vine activity.

April to the end of the vintage in October is the critical period, and Chablis survives on an average of just under 1,300 hours of sunshine during this time, as opposed to over 1,400 in the Côte d'Or and only 1,200 in Champagne.

Rainfall, the other main constituent of a balanced climate, is fairly well spread throughout the year, but obviously a dry warm period leading up to the vintage concentrates the sugar levels in the fruit and ensures that the grapes are not swollen with diluting water. Rain is not the main problem in Chablis, it is frost.

Frost and Frost Control

Spring frost is a real hazard in the Chablis region and over the years has been responsible for much devastation. Many *vignerons* have suffered losses of substantial proportions – the 1945, 1951 and 1953 vintages were all but wiped out, in 1957 it was wiped out. The danger period is 15 to 31 May, but a careful watch is necessary from the end of March. The Grand Crus can be the worst hit, but Jack Frost knows no social boundaries and takes his toll of all the appellations. The crucial elements here are the May buds which when attacked by frost below −5°C are totally destroyed, the plant being incapable of rebudding at this stage of the growing season.

Frost was a greater problem a few years back when there were large areas of uncultivated land in the middle of the Premier Crus and particularly the Grand Crus. Greater density of planting and fewer uncultivated patches reduces the risk of frost. With the wider acceptance of weedkillers there are fewer weeds, thus less humidity and less frost. Also there is less need for hoeing and disturbing the ground, again less humidity and less frost.

However, the greatest strides towards improved conditions and more reliable yields came with the introduction of effective measures of frost control during the 1960s. One of the two accepted methods was discovered more or less by accident, or so legend has it – a *vigneron* walking home one morning in the early hours, somewhat worse for wear from a night on the tiles, needed to answer the call of nature, and having no tree behind which to disappear, and too drunk anyway to find one, chose to relieve himself by artificially watering one of his vines. In the morning, it was apparent that frost had destroyed the entire vineyard, all except one solitary vine on which the buds had been preserved under a yellow layer of ice. The aspersion method of frost control had been discovered by a Chablisien imbibing Chablis – how appropriate!

The theory behind the aspersion method is that buds can be protected, by ice at zero degrees Celsius, from lethal frost which can fall way down to -20°C, as happened in 1985. The theory works in practice but there is a downside. Many growers have now installed underground piping serving sprinkler systems (supplied from the River Serein or an artificial lake situated outside Beines) throughout their vineyards and the system is effective provided that the spraying commences immediately the temperature drops to zero, the early hours of the morning being the danger period, and continues uninterrupted during the whole time that the temperature remains below zero. Any interruption caused by a failing supply of water, blocked pipes, etc. is fatal, as the effect is worse than if spraying had not taken place at all, probably due to the natural resistance of the vine and bud being lowered. The spray can also be affected by high winds, causing interference with one's neighbour's vines. The likelihood of the need for spraying, indeed also for the operation of the other main control method, heating the vineyard, is usually fairly accurately forecast every day on a recorded telephone message by the local *Station Météorologique*. The principal argument against aspersion is the increased risk of further frost due to increased humidity. What seems to be forgotten is the simple fact that ice exists at zero degrees and all temperatures below, so the snug coating for the precious buds can be a killer in itself.

The other main method of control is by heating the vineyards. This is accomplished by the installation, generally in mid-April, of oil or paraffin burners stationed at strategic intervals between rows of vines, but many growers have now installed heating systems which are supplied with fuel automatically. Just as, if not more, effective than aspersion, the only drawback is the cost of the fuel and labour for lighting and maintenance. The cost of aspersion is minimal for maintenance, but expensive for installation. It is not unusual to see both methods in use in the same vineyard, and the sight of hundreds of *chaufferettes* or burners glowing in the cold dark night is reminiscent of a scene from Dr Who and the Daleks.

Experiments on two further systems of protection have been recently commenced. The first, which was introduced in 1995 ('la Bâche de Protection'), involves covering the vines for a two-month period until about the end of May with plastic sheeting, holes at various intervals allowing the penetration of the sun's rays and the free flow of atmospheric gases. This creates an artificial greenhouse effect and thus prevents the formation of frost and ice – at least, that's the theory, and the experiments have proved a success according to Veronique Drouhin. It is a very expensive method of frost protection, as the sheeting has to be replaced every three years or so and may therefore not become universally accepted. The newest method, in a very early experimental stage, has two practitioners and another two growers considering its merits – this involves the laying of electrical heating elements to warm the area around the vines. It is a costly method, and in its infant stages.

All methods work but, at the time of writing, the *chaufferette* is the most widely used aid. Protection has been a major element in the battle to improve yields beyond the short odds risk, resulting in renewed confidence and the upsurge of Chablis in recent years.

9

VITICULTURE

. . . .

As we shall see later, the substance of the Chablis soil is rich in lime-based oyster fossils. Because of this very nature, the Yonne vines must be grafted onto lime-resistant root stocks. Many trials have taken place in recent years, learning from past mistakes, such as errors in the Côte d'Or with a clone known as 41B, and successes with SO4. With the arrival of virtual virus-free clonal root stocks, almost all replanting in the Chablis region is clonal, lime-resistant, high sugar content, early ripening Chardonnay – known as the Beaunois locally, which in any case is a prolific vine.

The local soil is richer than the Côte d'Or, and over-production can be and is a problem. Pruning is done according to the double-Guyot system, two fruit-bearing canes generally trained downhill after the risk of spring frost has abated, and close to the soil for warmth. This also keeps the green vegetation in check, encouraging production of the fruit. The quality grower will ensure that there are no more than six to eight buds for fruit production, and rub out any excess. Green pruning, or the removal of too much foliage in the summer, allows the sun's rays to reach that part of the plant not otherwise exposed and to create greater movement of air around the bunches to avoid the setting in of rot. This is done by those viticulteurs who believe in the practice – not all do.

During the growing season, the vine is or should be given various treatments, spraying with Bordeaux mixture (copper sulphate) to combat oidium and mildew, insecticide for red spider, and other anti-rot chemicals, but there is a very strong movement today towards organic and biological farming avoiding the use of herbicides, fertilisers and chemicals. The excessive use of potassium fertilisers certainly causes lower acidity levels. Anne-Claude Leflaive of Domaine Leflaive in the Côte d'Or states that her soils have improved immeasurably since using biodynamic methods and the reputation of the Domaine has returned to the No.1 position among white Burgundy growers in the Côte d'Or. It will be interesting to see who follows in Chablis, although cost is a material factor, as stressed by Christian Adine in Courgis.

Most important is the yield, which should be controlled to as low a level as possible within the parameters of the quality being sought by the grower. A specific plot of land has an exact amount of goodness to yield up, likewise the vine on which it grows. If the vine is encouraged to produce the best grapes possible by careful and prudent husbandry of the plant and soil, then that grower will have the best, most concentrated sweet fruit with the right level of acidity, from which to make his wine.

It is plainly apparent that many Chablis growers farm for as much as they can get, in terms of both production and financial returns. If that is the stated aim, we are not knocking it – everyone has to make a living the best way they can and according to their ability. However, this approach does not produce the best wines, the most concentrated, the most intense, the most characterful, and those who adopt its methods, we are sure, will be the first to agree, in private. Certainly this is more prevalent *pro rata* in the Côte d'Or, but unfortunately Chablis has too high a proportion. With particular reference to the top crus, this practice is as reprehensible as elsewhere in Burgundy. We have concentrated our efforts in bringing you, the reader, to the tasting table of those growers who are more interested in the quality of their wines than a quick buck – a slow buck is just as valuable, and ultimately returns greater satisfaction from a finer reputation, e.g. Vincent Dauvissat, Raveneau, Jean-Paul Droin, Laurent Tribut, to name but a few with low yields.

The table at the end of Chapter 5 shows the variance in rendements achieved over the four appellations, yet points to the relative values of the Grand Crus and down the scale. The top producers will attempt and achieve low yields as a matter of routine by rubbing out surplus buds, stringent pruning and foliage control. Six to eight buds per fruit-bearing cane is quite sufficient – any more would sap the strength of the vine, concentration of the fruit, acidity and sugar levels. Jean-Marie Raveneau and Vincent Dauvissat are reluctant to give precise details of their rendements, but like Leroy and Romanée Conti in Vosne, they are very severe in the control of yields, sometimes as low as 28 hectolitres per hectare, but always well below average levels. Domaine Servin is very open about its yields: the 96 Chablis was a mere 37.7 hl/ha and the Montée de Tonnerre 46.6 hl/ha. But the practice here does not seem consistent – the 94 Vaillons, not being severely frost damaged, was harvested at 58 hl/ha. The yields show in the tasting notes.

Louis Moreau of the Domaine de Biéville vineyard keeps well below average, determined that his Chablis will not develop the same mass-produced reputation of the namesake *négociant* house. Bernard Marchive of Domaine des Malandes is a grower who is very conscious of the benefits of good husbandry, and it shows in the wines.

We feel that commercialisation is uppermost in the philosophy of many well-known domaines whose wines are widely available, the control of yields not being as tight as one would hope for, allowing *rendements* to rise above acceptable levels equating to quality production. These wines too often lack that needed degree of concentration and depth as revealed in the tasting notes attached to the domaine profiles in Part 2.

Mechanisation

A vigneron's life is not an easy one — there must be easier ways of making a living. A century ago there was hardship on the land, all work was manual, back-breaking and exhausting, a twenty-four-hour day minimum and still ends hardly met. The fragmented vineyards, as in Burgundy, still meant that a grower was expected to work a minuscule domaine of 2 or 3 hectares on average, tending the vines which could be on steep slopes, harvesting and vinifying the wines often involving taking the grapes to the travelling press used by numerous other vignerons, and selling the resulting wine through the Beaune or Chablis *négociants*. This was rarely enough to keep the family fed and warm through the long hard winters, and many growers supplemented their wine production by keeping livestock — pigs, cows, chickens — and horses to do the donkey work in the vineyards. They would also grow cereals, make hay, and even cultivate cherry trees. It is interesting to note that the Groupement d'Étude Technique Vinicole et Arboricole de Yonne, an organisation of growers founded in 1957 for the protection of the vineyards from frost damage, is concerned not only with viticultural and vinicultural matters but also with those cherry trees.

Any method of lightening the load would therefore be attractive and when Robert Vocoret first introduced a tractor into his vineyards in 1951 it seemed logical that this new mechanical horse would be quickly taken up by the overworked and underpaid *vigneron*. But tractors are expensive items of machinery, in any case they were new and had to be viewed with suspicion. By the end of the decade it had caught on, and with growing confidence in the market, spurred by the introduction of the methods of frost control and improving yields, the growers found that viticulture provided a better return than before and as a result turned more and more to the vine as a sole provider of their livelihood.

With the introduction of the tractor, the vineyards became smaller overnight, they were better controlled and tended, and time was created for better efficiency. Now was the time to look further afield, to expand, but even more was to come which would lighten the load of the still hard-pressed vigneron — the mechanical harvester.

These monsters were introduced into Chablis at the right time. It is fascinating to watch them at work, even more so when staring at them after their work is done, and realising that they are capable of such a delicate and sublime operation as the harvesting of the grape. Their *raison d'être* is not just the obvious labour-saving exercise (one harvester can do the work of several pickers), it is also cost cutting, saving the expense of paying, feeding and housing the pickers for the length of the harvest. Many tests have been carried out and several types of machine have been tried. The principal objection to mechanical harvesting is the tendency for a substantial part of the crop to arrive at the press with unwhole or damaged grapes which can result in some oxidation; however, in most cases the advantages of the machines outweigh the disadvantages: quicker harvesting gets the crop to the presses sooner with less chance of exposure; if it rains in the middle of the harvest it can be stopped, avoiding excess water on the skins; surplus labour can be put more economically to other tasks in the chain. Petrol and maintenance cost less than board and lodging for dozens of workers. Roger Séguinot, a doyen among growers, changed to mechanical harvesting in the late 1980s, carrying out many comparative tastings with wines made from a section of the vineyard still manually harvested at that time and is convinced by the results then and now that there is no difference in the taste of the wines from the two methods. Not all producers have changed over completely, some not at all, and not all who have changed are utterly convinced of the advantages. Indeed, much of the Grand Cru area is too steep, and is consequently still picked by hand. Perhaps not such a bad thing!

In the main, the growers talk about their method of harvesting with a matter-of-fact attitude '… that's my method, next subject!' But the subject obviously occupies their minds far more than they are letting on. Unrepentant and immovable hand harvesters include Vincent Dauvissat and Joseph Drouhin. Raveneau hand picks, but is far from convinced by the sole practice. It would be easy to claim that Grand Cru owners eschew machines, but that is not true either – Domaine Servin uses a mixture of hand and machine harvesting for their Grand Crus, machines obviously on the not-so-steep sections – and it must be remembered that Servin was one of the first to experiment with machine harvesting back in 1982. Another reason for maintaining a firm hold on the manual practice could of course be a financial one – these machines are expensive. Alice and Olivier de Moor in Courgis harvest their Chablis Village land manually, but it is only 3 hectares and it is a very young estate.

Jean and Sebastien Dauvissat began mechanical harvesting in 1987 since when the results have been encouraging, with impressive improvements in quality. This is not to imply that the improvements are due only to this changeover – we just mention this as a possible contributing factor. Maybe the rapid picking and bringing of the fruit to the presses suits their style more, and maybe the ability to stop the harvesting during heavy rain limits the amount of water on the skins significantly, thus aiding concentration of fruit. Bernard Defaix changed to machines – he has no Grand Crus – and finds it preferable because he can avoid rain dilution during picking. If only the results showed this! Jean-Paul Droin, on the other hand, uses mechanised harvesting for the lower appellations only – his results are undoubted, as are those of Long Depaquit where Gerard Vullien only allows part of the basic Chablis appellation to be mechanically harvested. Jean Durup machine harvests from necessity (he does, after all, farm over 170 hectares), and his quality level is also very high. Jean-Claude Martin of Domaine Beauregards in Courgis has no Grand Crus, but insists that quality begins in the vineyards and his 3.5 hectares of Premier Crus and 8.5 hectares of Chablis are harvested entirely by hand – no chances are taken here – with excellent results.

Putting together the growers' comments and results, it would be possible to arrive at a general consensus on whether mechanical harvesting produces inferior wines or not, but this exercise would be futile. What is important is that the introduction of mechanical harvesters in Chablis has had a dynamic effect on production, the commerce of the area and the confidence of the growers. There are those who resolutely adhere to the old ways and produce very good wines, such as Jean-Claude Martin, magnificent wines in the hands of Dauvissat, Raveneau, Long Depaquit and J-P. Droin. There are those who have made all or mostly all the change and, coupled with careful and resourceful husbandry and a watchful eye on quality, have continued to produce fine wines – Vocoret, Durup, Jean Dauvissat. And there are those who have changed through necessity or desire and who need to look more closely at other operations within their domaines in order to complement the new system with more thorough methods of yield and fermentation control – those domaines will be commented on in Part Two.

Mechanisation was introduced into the region over a number of years during the 1970s and 1980s. It is not complete but it is here, and here to stay. To be totally effective it must be considered only part of the renaissance of Chablis. It is not the cure for all ills – if it is considered as such, the only improvements will be in the grower's bank balance not his reputation.

Vinification, *Élevage* and the Use of Oak

. . . .

THE METHOD OF vinification and *élevage* differs distinctly from producer to producer. As is the nature of the production of Chablis and its disputes, particularly the use of oak or some oak or no oak, vinification procedures will be noted where appropriate in the domaine profiles. There is no single way, and fine wine can be made in vastly differing methods. Some wine-makers gently crush the grapes in pneumatic presses, others use a hydraulic press. Some allow settlement of the must by natural *débourbage*, others use a centrifuge. Some sulphur a lot, some a little. Some use natural yeasts, some do not. Dried yeast cultures are often used as it is believed this brings about more regular fermentation, giving cleaner more dependable wines. Lactic bacteria are sometimes introduced to bring on the malolactic fermentation more quickly, the action of converting apple-tasting malic acid to lactic acid. Most important is the method of temperature control of the fermenta-tion vats and the chosen temperature. Obviously control is easier with stainless steel and can be accomplished without changing the prevailing temperature of the cellars, which is frequently done if oak *foudres* are used; then there is the question of the time taken for ageing, whether to *batonnage* or not, fine or filter or both, whether to cool the wine to precipi-tate the tartrates if wood has not been used, and then to bottle early or late – so many methods and so many variations. The quality winemaker will have few hard and fast rules, except those imposed by the chosen equipment and installations, and will judge the nature of each vintage and each cuvée on its characteristics at the time.

Where the domaine has provided such information, as was generally the case, this is included in the profile.

Before or during the course of fermentation, the winemaker may decide on chaptalisation which is the process of adding sugar to the fermenting must to increase the potential alcohol content of the wine. In Chablis this is a usual practice as the natural sugar content in the fruit is frequently insuffi-cient due to the cooler northern climes. Chaptalising (named after chaptal, a Frenchman who thought of the idea) is often frowned upon by producers in other French regions whilst emptying the sugar bags themselves, unless of course sunshine is not rationed as in the South West and Provence. Antipodean producers pour scorn upon the very idea, but perhaps they should consider their favoured geographical aspect before casting stones. The practice is sanctioned in Burgundy and particularly Chablis under the provisions of the Appellation regulations which stipulate a minimum level of natural sugar in the fruit before additions are allowed, and a maximum amount of added sugar in order to attain a specified alcohol percentage. As an example, 13.5 per cent is the maximum alcohol level allowed for a Grand Cru; to attain this, sugar may be added if the natural content in the must falls below 170 grammes per litre.

In Burgundy the regulations specify that adding sugar should be done at the beginning of fermentation and not in stages, obviously a rule made by bureaucrats not winemakers, as judging the amount required is a delicate task and is much more effective in smaller amounts as fermentation proceeds than a great big dollop at the start which can well upset temperature control. No one asks whether this particular regulation is vigorously observed or not. Chaptalisation can be a much abused practice by the unscrupulous, but is also a much maligned and misunderstood practice often derided by the misinformed.

As in the case of all Burgundy, the quality of the wine depends almost entirely on the quality of the grower/winemaker. A winemaker dedicated to quality by low yields, hygienic and controlled production, minimal interference with the *élevage*, one who puts his experience and knowledge to the service of the soil, vine, grape, wine, bottle and customer, without a constant glance over the shoulder at the profits, is one who will make the most of the materials to hand. We will harp no further, enough has already been said and written on the subject by such luminaries as Clive Coates, Remington Norman, Anthony Hanson, Robert Parker *et al*.

The Use of Oak

The use of oak, new or old, in fermentation or *élevage*, is a controversy which has beset the winemakers and *éleveurs* of Bordeaux and Burgundy for many years, none more so than Chablis. Whereas for most areas and wines the arguments and differences concern the amounts, whether new or old, and for how long if at all, oak has sharply divided Chablis into two opposing camps.

Let us just consider first what oak has to do with wine anyway – why oak, how the use of it began and where it is leading.

Wine is as old as the hills. Well, maybe not quite, but its existence certainly pre-dates ancient history, although it was possibly not the first alcoholic beverage to be discovered. That honour falls to mead – our caveman forebears probably delighted in the after-effects of drinking the watered down honey which had been forgotten and left in a disused corner of the cave, naturally fermenting away unnoticed. The honey bee was far more universal and prevalent in those days than the vine, and the chance discovery of a bowl of fermented squashed grapes was a long way off.

However, in terms of history, the progress of wine paralleled the evolution and development of civilised society. It was already part of the staple diet of the Ancient Egyptians even before the building of the Great Pyramid and the construction of the Temple of Karnak at Luxor. Forty years after the Exodus *circa* 1400 BC Moses at great cost for doubting the word of God sent scouts into the Promised Land to report back on what they could expect to find in a land flowing with milk and honey. They returned laden with bunches of grapes so large that it took two men with the aid of wooden poles to carry them. In later years wine was to become an integral part of the ritual in King Solomon's Temple mirrored even now in synagogue and church services. The importance of wine to the consumer and to religion continued into the Greek and Roman eras: it had become a valuable commodity for trade, and the more that could be moved, the greater the profit. But stone jars and amphorae for storage and transportation were large, heavy and unwieldy.

The making and selling of wine was fast becoming a commercial reality. The problem of containing and storage for long or short periods was solved by the fashioning of wood into staves and then into barrels, the metal containing hoops made in the same way as the rims of chariot wheels. Wood was a conveniently available commodity, easily transformed and replenished, and easily transported. The precise date, indeed the precise century, that saw the introduction of the barrel is uncertain, but it clearly goes back to Biblical days – according to Herodotus, wine was transported to Babylon in barrels made of palm wood.

Oak became preferred to other woods because of its abundance, durability and strength. It was a very adaptable material, but two important effects of its use were noticed: first, an acceptable flavour of vanilla was imparted to the wine, the newer the oak the stronger the flavour; and second, somehow the structure of the wine seemed to be supported. We know now that the wine gets some of its tannins from the wood, which under the right conditions aids the balance and hence the ageing process. In our sophisticated understanding of the processes which occur in winemaking today, the use and effect of oak has been commandeered and commercialised to satisfy the thirst of oak enthusiasts worldwide – especially those in the New World and the UK. There is a noticeable tendency for oak flavour to be the dominant factor in the production, judging, selling and drinking of a wine, be it Claret, Burgundy, Californian, Antipodean, Cabernet, Pinot Noir, Syrah (Shiraz), Chardonnay, or even Sauvignon Blanc, perhaps losing sight of the purpose of wood which is to add support to the wine's structure. The flavour of it, however pleasant it may be, should integrate not dominate. The oak camp is internationally strong and exerts a major influence on Burgundian winemakers, some of whom have been known to produce two cuvées of the same wine, one for America and the other for Europe. But the British should not gloat – too often nowadays an unsuitable wine is treated and labelled as 'oak aged' just to attract the unsuspecting supermarket shopper. Oak sells.

This is all very well for Bordeaux and the Côte d'Or – oak is an integral part of the make-up of their wines – but Chablis is a different matter altogether. The very nature of the region's Chardonnay means that it does not require any dominant characteristic to smother the delicate flavours, and that is the basis of the controversy which still rages today. There are those who oppose its use *per se*, insisting that it goes against the spirit, style and character of the wine, swamping the perfumed flowery mineral flavours for which fine Chablis is known, preferring to vinify and age their wine in stainless steel or cement, glass-lined vats. But there is the opposite camp which holds totally to the reverse view, claiming that with oak the wine is better structured and better endowed for ageing, whilst retaining its freshness and fragrance. Some of these producers may have a point, but their arguments are far from convincing and tasting fine old oak-free Chablis from the cellars of Louis Michel and Jean Durup, for example, weights the balance firmly in favour of the no-oak camp as their wines are capable of ageing brilliantly, developing honeyed, nutty, even those 'oaky' characteristics themselves. But then there is the exception to the rule as usual, in the form of Raveneau's supreme wines, all aged in old *pièces*, Jean Collet's Vaillons mostly fermented and aged *en foudres* and Robert Vocoret's range of Premier and Grand Crus all fermented and aged *en foudres*. Often as not, the decision whether to use oak is governed by practicalities, such as the difficulty of cleaning and maintenance of hygiene, and also the expense of renewing the barrels or vats when deemed necessary. *Élevage* in oak for a time during the winter months assists in crystallising out the tartrates before bottling, and this may also be a consideration. A happy medium is struck by some, and when oak is used by a quality producer, it is usually discreet and seldom swamps the delicate flavours of traditional Chablis.

Jean-Marie Raveneau and Vincent Dauvissat, two of the supreme producers, are committed oak users, never new but well-aged barrels averaging out at six to eight years old. Their art is unquestioned, their Chablis a wine of great beauty never lacking *typicité*. It is noticeable that vignerons will readily tell why they don't use oak, but seldom give positive reasons for so doing – if that's the way it has been done for generations and the results are unquestionably fine, then that is the right method!

Jean-Paul Droin is an oak producer *par excellence*, mixing the age of his barrels from new to ten years old *pièces* for his Premier and Grand Crus, but is at pains to point out that each cuvée and each vintage is different and must be judged on its merits and its ability to accept the oak, which should never dominate or overwhelm the delicate aromas and flavours. As for the provenance of the wood, each forest having its own individual characteristics, Droin favours a mixture of five oaks including wood from Nevers, Allier and Vosges, three of the most widely used forests in France, claiming that the diversity adds complexity to the wine, and few would argue with this. Interestingly for a French producer, Jean-Paul often uses American and

Russian oak, but whatever the source, it is the staves of the barrel which are mixed by his tonnelier, not usually the barrels themselves, adding with a wink that American and Russian staves are never placed adjacent to each other lest their tannins and flavours argue too much.

Michel Laroche is a firm believer in the benefit of oak ageing of all his Grand Crus, the Fourchaumes and Vaillons in 228-litre Allier barrels, but uses nothing newer than four years old, sometimes mixing the provenance of the oak to aid complexity.

Louis Pinson is another oak producer with an undoubted ability to hide and integrate its flavours within the Chablis character. The ageing here is in Allier oak barrels between two and six years old, never new. Laurent Tribut is another fine domaine using oak ageing discreetly and turning out lovely wines.

There is, of course, the continuing practice of vinification in large oak *foudres*, maybe not quite as controversial as *élevage*, but nevertheless scorned by the majority as unhygienic and uncontrollable. Most winemakers have moved to temperature-controlled stainless steel, or glass or enamel-lined fermentation vats, but a few have persisted in the old tradition maybe just for selected cuvées. Jean and Sebastien Dauvissat ferment their Vieilles Vignes and Les Preuses *en fut*, and are specific in their choice of Troncais oak as suiting their style of wine. Vincent Dauvissat part ferments in barrel, Pascal Bouchard vinifies his Grands Crus in one- to four-year-old Allier oak, and Jean Collet varies his use of barrels and casks to complete the fermentation of the Valmur and some Premier Crus according to the character of the vintage.

Joseph Drouhin firmly believes in fermenting Grands Crus Vaudésirs and Les Clos in 100 per cent oak, 15 per cent of it new. Raoul Gautherin reserves his large old *foudres* of 6,300 litres for part of his Vaillons. All of these producers who believe in some fermentation in wood do so from the conviction that this adds to complexity, and in most cases they are right, but the use of this method has to be well thought out and discreet. As a general rule, the Grand Cru cuvées can stand up to the treatment more than most Premier Crus, although Vaillons appears often to benefit from some oak because of its hardy nature, but not the village appellations.

Some winemakers, we do not know why, seem to be encouraged to give the oak treatment – whether for fermentation or *élevage* – to the wines of Côte de Léchet. In our view this is one Premier Cru which should emphatically *not* be oaked in any way. The delightful character of this most gentle of the top crus is positively overwhelmed by such treatment, although Laurent Tribut who is aware of the nature of the cru manages to integrate the flavours well. The wines of Daniel Dampt are the epitome of elegance here, as are often Daniel Defaix's wines.

The opposition in the oak wars was lead by Louis Michel and Jean Durup. Louis Michel said that the only useful purpose of oak is for decoration, whilst the mere mention of the word to Jean-Paul Durup elicits a wry smile. The word itself is anathema to both men. Yet to taste fine old Chablis from these great producers is to cause wonderment at the way the wines age, developing those same oaky biscuity aromas reminiscent of a fine Côte d'Or whilst retaining that essential Chablis character.

In reply to our question about his attitude to oak, Christian Adine waves an expressive hand skywards with the remark, 'The only wood here is in the roof' – a typical reaction confirming the firmly held opinions of all the no-oakers!

All these growers make very fine wine, and where wood is used, it is used with thought and consideration for the end product, as an aid to wine-making and not as the primary objective to appeal to mass oak-thirsty markets. If only that was always the case! On a recent visit to Peter Hall's worthy Breaky Bottom estate, deep in the Sussex Downs (possibly the best source of English wine), when asked whether he oaked the wines or not and how much, the rather surprising answer was oak chips. Peter proceeded to extol the virtues – mainly cost – of dropping little bits of wood into the maturing liquid, and insisted that the practice is widespread, in California, Bordeaux and Burgundy, even Chablis. Politely, we made no comment. Perhaps this process of adulteration is indeed widespread, but definitely *not* by the reputable winemakers with whom we are concerned. We can honestly state that we have not encountered this in Chablis – yet! All the oak producers we have visited have their barrels proudly on display. Oak chip use would be obvious in tasting, and would destroy their reputation.

But what of the producers who obstinately stick to their established oak practice without question or adaptation? Walking round William Fèvre's impressive establishment and also La Chablisienne, it is impossible to miss the show of new barrels, in Fèvre's case imported from the Côte d'Or. Regrettably, in the past these wines too often tasted of it, masking the special Chablis flavours. These two are not alone in the practice, as will become evident, but we can report that Henriot-Bouchard, the new owners of William Fèvre's otherwise magnificent heritage, have taken a long, hard look at those barrels and changes have already been made.

It is essential to bear in mind that Chablis is renowned for fresh dry crisp white wines of finesse and elegance, packed with flinty minerally fruit. To quote Michael Broadbent (*The Great Vintage Wine Book II*, Mitchell Beazley 1991) in reference to the Chablis 1986 vintage: 'I do note the increasing use of oak. For me, Chablis should be dry, clean as a whistle, crossing the palate rapier-like, with a crisp acidic finish. Increasing the oak increases the flavour: buttery, oaky Chablis might well be speciously attractive, but is it classic Chablis?'

The two camps in *La Guerre de Chêne* are poles apart, but seem to adopt a benign acceptance of the other's existence. Not so in the continuing battle of the expansionists, a subject we shall come to very soon.

EXPANDING THE BOUNDARIES
OF CHABLIS

. . . .

HERE WE HAVE two sides of an argument that apparently will never agree to the exact outer limits of the Chablis Appellation. The leader in this battle is Jean Durup, president of La Fédération des Viticulteurs Chablisiens, who understandably is working to persuade the authorities to expand the permitted area of vineyard, claiming back those vineyards devastated by spring frosts, the ravages of two world wars and the Phylloxera epidemic of a hundred years ago. It should, of course, be remembered that the pre-Phylloxera area covered by Auxerre, Chablis and the Yonne was the largest in France, in its heyday approximately 40,000 hectares, supplying Paris with its everyday drinking wines. At the commencement of its appellation before the Second World War Chablis had dwindled to a mere 400 hectares. By 1994, this had recovered to 3,600 hectares in production, and the total area covered by the Yonne to 4,935 hectares (figures furnished by M. Durup, June 1995). It should be stressed that these are the areas actually in production and not just with AOC as shown in the table in Chapter 15.

Jean Durup's opposite number in this conflagration was another major vineyard owner of Chablis, namely William Fèvre of Domaine Maladière, until recently the president of Le Syndicat de Défence de l'Appellation de Chablis, who claims, not without some justification, that an increase in vineyard area is synonymous with lowering standards, especially as this relates more to Chablis Village and Petit Chablis. He wished to maintain the present areas and boundaries, and concentrate improvements within, firmly believing that Kimmeridgian soil and Kimmeridgian only is the basis for quality Chablis, not Portlandian soil as is the case with Petit Chablis and some Chablis Village, and certainly not 'Jurassic' located outside the recognised area. The Syndicat at present comprises some one hundred growers representing 1,100 hectares, about a quarter of the vignoble: William Fèvre recently handed over the reins of the group to Jean Bernard Marchive of Domaine des Malandes who continues the work with the same enthusiasm.

Thus the lines are drawn and battle commences, a battle which Monsieur Durup is not about to lose. As the history of past skirmishes are given in Chapter 15, let us just comment on the most significant recent movements.

Kimmeridgian soil is the fundamental basis of the arguments, and when the Chablis Appellation was extended by 500 hectares following INAO's decision to set up a special commission to consider this in 1956, the expanded area was largely restricted to those of Kimmeridgian origin. In 1967, INAO recommended approval to a new classification and delimitation of the Premier Crus, not universally popular especially with the growers of Maligny, and thus Jean Durup, who felt that the Chablis Appellation in his locality was being ignored. Years of wrangling, protests, appeals and petitions followed, accompanied by bad feeling between the two opposing factions, culminating in the 1976 recommendation of INAO to an extension to the Premier Crus of 148 hectares, and a resounding 860 hectares to the Chablis Appellation. Some 1,500 hectares of Petit Chablis were finally established in total. These extensions were confirmed two years later, but not put in official print until 1986.

The effect of all these additions was to change the overall picture of Chablis as was known at the time, as recent as that time was! Suddenly, new Premier Crus with unpronounceable names were created, bottles appearing in the shops almost immediately. Generic Chablis was abundant, with production shooting skyward in the 1980s, and a new perception of Chablis as a wine was created regrettably countered by the increase of misuse of the name by producers in other countries.

Not all of the changes within the Chablis area, however, were for the good. Unfortunately, not all producers are of the quality of Jean Durup whose generic Chablis is a fine wine, and he makes pretty good Petit Chablis too. Much too much basic Chablis is just that, very basic, the result of over-cropping and slap-dash wine making, in our view the biggest culprits being the *négociants* who seem to think that Chablis is just another everyday white wine. It isn't, it's special. This is proved by Louis Moreau of Domaine de Bièville who from a 65-hectare single parcel at Viviers produces a Village Chablis of Premier Cru quality by restricting yields and giving it as much tender loving care as his superb Fourneaux. Les Fourneaux is a result of the changes, a newly designated and good Premier Cru in its own right, formerly part of Mont de Milieu, and Moreau makes a point of using the new name to distinguish his wine from the larger more famous section, but he is at liberty to choose either name if desired. And here is the crux of the matter, whether or not all of the new Premier Cru creations deserve the label. The authorities have, of course, restricted the new 'A' level sites to those on Kimmeridgian soil, but as discussed in the next two chapters, it is not just the soil which produces the wine, it is 'terroir'. Let us leave this emotive subject until then. To be frank, the writers have not yet been convinced of the value of some of the new crus. Possibly in a hundred years or so the 'terroir' will have caught up to enable the right quality fruit to be grown for quality wine; until then, in our view, certainly at present, some of these *climats* are just too young, with poor orientation and location. We cite as examples Côte de Cuissy and Côte de Jouan at Courgis; Côte de

Savant, Troesmes and Vaux Ragons at Beine; Côte de Bréchin and Berdiot at
Fyé; Morein and Côte de Prés Girots at Fleys.

The slightly more favoured sites of Vau de Vey and Vau Ligneau also at
Beine can be disappointing, but these crus are improving, particularly in
the capable hands of Jean Durup, Alain Geoffroy and Louis Moreau.

It must be said that the extension of some of these disappointing Premier Crus has regrettably devalued the reputation of Chablis, whereas the
extension of the Village Chablis land has had some compensating effect and
under proper control has to be encouraged.

Geology and Soils

What are these soils, and what connection is there with the remote little
Dorset village of Kimmeridge?

To answer this, we must go back to the Jurassic period, 195 million years
ago, to a time when the land that is now France was at a similar latitude to
present-day Nicaragua and Cambodia. Dinosaurs were roaming the Earth,
whilst birds were making their first appearance. Mammals, however, were
no match for the dinosaurs and remained at a sensibly discreet size, no
larger than a rodent, and at a discreet distance for health reasons.

At that time, Chablis was located at the bottom of the sea, being
swamped by small lime-rich (calcium) oysters and other organisms dying
in untold numbers, with sediment being swept in from the surrounding
rivers. Humans, of course, hadn't evolved yet, but life in the sea was abundant, teeming with tropical fish, seafood and microscopic life. By the time
the sea had receded at the end of the Jurassic era, about 59 million years
later, a thick layer of calcium carbonate ('lime' or, in petrified form, 'limestone') made up of the skeletons and shells of trillions of tiny sea animals,
formed the bedrock of the area.

During the course of this 59 million years, the balance did change a
little. After a quarter of the way into the Jurassic, the supercontinent of
Pangaea – all the continents as merged into one mass – had split into
two: Laurasia, essentially the northern continents minus India, and Gond-
wanaland, the remainder. Laurasia started to make its way north towards
the mid-latitudes, and by the end of the Jurassic, France lay at a similar
latitude to present-day Morocco. Europe's great journey northwards
brought about the sort of climatic and environmental changes that one
might expect and these changes are imprinted upon the sediments laid
throughout this period.

Around the seas there still existed land exposed to the vagaries of weath-
ering and erosion that broke down the rock into boulders, smaller rocks,
gravel, sands and silts and, importantly here, clays – so-called secondary
minerals produced by chemical reaction. The smaller and lighter the parti-
cle, the further it was transported by river towards the sea. Clays, being
particularly small, microscopic in fact, were carried beyond the estuaries
and coastal areas, and settled in the calmer and deeper waters beyond.

As a result, not even the limestones are composed of pure calcium carbonate but include clay as well as sand and silt-sized minerals in varying proportions. The proportion of lime to clay is related to the rate at which sedimentation occurred from the two different sources: (i) calcium, secreting marine life living within the sea, i.e. calcium skeletons and shells, and (ii) mineral input from surrounding rivers and coastal erosion. Generally, when the sea was shallow and tropical it produced a purer lime sediment, but as the sea deepened and the environment became relatively colder, the proportion of clay increased leading to a clayey limestone and finally a marl (lime/clay mix).[2] We can see this in the area of the Yonne – if one walks due east from Chablis towards Viviers, one would walk over the three types of bedrock, in effect tracing the 59-million-year voyage of France and Europe from tropical to Mediterranean latitudes.

But how do the limestones and marls found in the Yonne differ from those found elsewhere? The simple answer is not a coral, a cocolith or a crustacean this time, but a type of mollusc. Encouraged by warm waters and depths not much greater than 30 metres, Exogyra Virgula, a tiny type of oyster, steals the show, and it is this in abundance which identifies and distinguishes the Chablis soil from others. Although it would be difficult to prove scientifically, we owe our thanks to this creature for its undoubted contribution to the sublime taste of Chablis. It is cruelly ironic that we choose to devour this gem chased by the blood of its descendants.

What has all this to do with Kimmeridge? These sediments which extend from France across to England, along with those laid before and after, were disturbed from the horizontal by the clash of continents and alpine-mountain-building phase that began 35 million years ago and still continues today, the net effect of which was to create a basin – its base raised above sea-level and the boundaries folded into hills.

As we have seen, not all limestones are the same, but most have characteristics specific to that strata. In the Chablis area, the limestone is called Portland limestone because it shares many of its characteristics with that found in Dorset's Isle of Portland. More importantly, the marl in the Chablis area is referred to as Kimmeridgian marl because it has the same characteristics as a marl that is found in the Kimmeridge area of Dorset just 12 kilometres or so east of Portland, both rich in those precious calcium-based minerals and oyster fossils. This is not surprising, since the south coast of England and the rolling hills of the Yonne are respectively the north-west and the south-east boundaries of the Paris basin created in the period of mountain building. At these two points the marl and limestone strata, which are buried elsewhere under later sediments, outcrop and form

2. This is, of course, a simplification. There were many other smaller scale variations that resulted in a greater variety of sediments. For example, in some areas there was a high presence of microscopic marine organisms such as *Foraminifera*, single cell amoeba-like creatures, that in relatively pure form produce a type of limestone referred to as chalk but here were only in sufficient numbers to produce a chalky-limestone.

the surface geology. Walking along the sea shore at Kimmeridge, the abundance of oyster fossils is visible to the naked eye, as when sifting through a handful of Grand or Premier Cru soil. Why, you may ask, are the soils and rocks not referred to by the names of French towns or villages? Seemingly British scientists got there first!

All this geology would be academic if it didn't have a significant effect on the wine. But it does, and this is illustrated by a simple comparison of the vineyard sites with the geology. As can be seen in the cover plates, there is a clear connection between Grand Cru, Premier Cru and most Chablis Village *climats* and soils overlying Kimmeridgian marl ('Kimmeridgian soils'). Petit Chablis is largely confined to soils that are overlying Portlandian limestone ('Portlandian soils') where, because of the lack of clay, the soils are thinner and lack the right structure and mineral content. Further inspection of the diagram reveals the added importance of topography. It is no accident that the sunny and well-drained south- and south-west facing slopes capping the town of Chablis are where the Grand Crus originate.

Thus, Kimmeridgian soil, light, very porous and draining well, gives to its wines that very mineral character of which it is comprised, the roots of the vine reaching deep under the surface layer towards the mineral-rich bedrock for its nourishment. The clay particles are chemically charged and as a result cling on to essential cations, e.g. calcium, potassium and sodium, releasing them opportunely for the vine. Clays are also useful because they retain water, in this case just the right amount to maintain good drainage. Sand, because the particles are relatively large, allows air to circulate through the soil, facilitating better drainage. Finally, lime as a natural fertiliser contains essential calcium and prevents excessive soil acidity. Kimmeridgian is an almost perfect soil for vines, but certainly regarded as infertile for other purposes. It is important to remember that generally speaking the vine is planted in 'poor' soil to encourage the roots to penetrate deeper to gain stability and search for essential foods. Strength springs from adversity. A visit to some of the deepest cellars in Saint Emilion is an eye-opener, when one sees the roots appearing through the cellar walls and ceilings.

Portlandian soil is perhaps not so very different from Kimmeridgian except, as we have seen, in its proportions; even the local experts fail to agree where one ends and the other begins. There is no firm demarcation line. But, as Rosemary George explains, the CNAO, now the INAO,[3] back in 1938 refused to acknowledge any similarity between the two soils. With hindsight it is easy to understand their obstinacy. After all, one could hardly expect wines from Portlandian soil to approach Premier Cru quality – indeed there are no examples of Petit Chablis and very few of Portlandian

3. The Comité de National d'Appellations d'Origine (CNAO), formed in the 1930s for the purpose of defining Appellation Controlé, became the Institut National des Appellations d'Origine (INAO) in the early 1940s.

based Chablis Village wines in this category. One can also understand the William Fèvre philosophy *'Le Kimmeridgien est sacré!'*

However, it is a fact that both soils are complete in their chemical composition for growing grapes, and Portlandian soil can and often does produce very good wines.

The Concept of *Terroir*

Having considered the geological aspect and the question of soils, perhaps we should spend just a little time on the emotive subject of *terroir*, the precise definition of which is somewhat elusive. Clive Coates in *Côte d'Or* (1997), the bible of great Burgundy (our comment) and Anthony Hanson in *Burgundy* (Faber & Faber, second edition 1995), both give extensive discourse and scholarly discussions on this issue. These books are a 'must read' for all Burgundy enthusiasts and wine buffs everywhere and we can do no better than précis this information and summarise the principal points.

One of the glories of wine is its ability to vary in character and style according to the desire of the winemaker, but a good winemaker will always subject this desire to the character and style naturally dictated by the grape and land on which it is produced. For example, Jacques Seysses of Domaine Dujac in Morey Saint-Denis will always ensure that his Bonnes Mares reflects the finesse and elegance associated with the vineyard together with his inimitable style of fragrant Pinot Noir, a wine which is or should be instantly recognisable as Bonnes Mares. This reflected character obtained from the *terroir* cannot be repeated anywhere else: copies and imitations can be tried but the success rate would be nil.

As with soils and oak, the very concept of *terroir* is emotive, but this time it is not a purely Chablisien subject but more particularly Burgundian in general. Of course, Bordeaux has its *terroirs* but we are only considering Burgundy in this context.

Here is a very generalised definition of the term *terroir*:

> A plot of land or site, with its own individual fingerprint, made up of geological features, soil composition and structure, mineral content, exposure to general weather conditions, micro-climates, rainfall and drainage, sunshine, degree and variation in orientation, slope, all of which may vary in content and make-up throughout the site, and which has been so used for the growing of the vine through generations resulting in the land being composed of its natural constituents for that purpose.

Even this definition just scratches the surface of a very complex subject.

Bill Jekel of Jekel Vineyards (one of the nicest, most knowledgeable men in the wine world) in *Decanter Magazine* (August 1982) disputes the value of the soil's mineral content to the quality level of fine wine, a reasoned argument claiming that it is the soil's structure which is important, not the composition, ending with the claim that if he chooses to put manure on his vegetable garden, he does not expect manure-tasting vegetables. Very true, but that is something of a red herring, for manure is used to revitalise the nitrogen cycle and has little to do with mineral content. As a positive example, mineral lime-rich soil adds a character, a Chablis character, to Chardonnay, which would not be present if those Chablis grapes were grown in the Côte d'Or. *Nous répétons 'Le Kimmeridgien est sacré!'* One of us had inconclusive correspondence on this subject with Mr Jekyl in 1982 following the article. Here we have a living example of *terroir*, and a New World attitude to it!

But *terroir* as a concept is a reality and should not be dismissed out of hand, as it is by some populist British writers and broadcasters who appear to be echoing the protests of Antipodean producers, as relative newcomers to viticulture, unable in their wildest dreams to claim *terroir* of such a nature. Using our example again, Louis Michel could no more produce Grand Cru quality Chablis from the Hunter Valley than Jacques Seysses could produce his Bonnes Mares from vines planted in Barossa.

To conclude, let us quote Anthony Hanson:

> A future line of soil research is to quantify the proportion of soil of vegetal, rather than mother-rock, origins in Burgundy's vineyards. Old root cells from buried decayed vines may make up 70 per cent of some soils, so recent scannings by Claude Bourguignon suggest. So six centuries of monoculture – or more – could prove to be the real creators of these soils.
>
> If these observations can be verified Burgundians could relax. It will be centuries before the best New World *terroirs* catch up, and by then Burgundian *terroirs* will be somewhere else.

Recent Chablis Vintages

. . . .

1998 – patchy but generally good

The night of 14 May brought devastation to many vineyards, Grand Crus particularly and some of Vaillons, from a hail storm that was as selective as it was ferocious. Apart from that, as far as the climate is concerned, this was a fairly typical year for Chablis.

Budding occurred at the beginning of April and was followed by a sunny May. Frost was minimal this spring and the good weather conditions encouraged healthy growth and the flowering in June. Then problems occurred with a cold and grey July followed by a scorching August when temperatures in some vineyards touched 40°C. This resulted in a lot of burnt grapes and delayed the full development until the middle of the month.

In September, there were two weeks of rain, mainly at night and the *ban de vendange* was declared on the 25th. Many domaines started picking immediately, some preferring to hang on for a few days, e.g. Michel Laroche waited until 1 October for that extra degree of ripeness, reporting natural alcohol levels at 11 per cent comparable to the 1995 vintage and with acidity similar to 1997.

Some good wines have been produced here, especially by those who avoided the dilution of the late rains. Much of the Grand Cru production was lost due to the hail and we trust that prices will not be too drastically affected.

1997 – very good indeed

Due to a generally warm March, by the end of the month the vines were already three weeks ahead of the average, but this was followed by an extremely cold April when temperatures fell below zero for 15 consecutive nights. Frost control was brought into operation for most of this period and losses were contained to a minimum as a result of dry conditions and a lowest recorded temperature of –5.5°C . Development now returned to almost normal progression and 75 per cent of the vines flowered under good conditions by 15 June. Then the cold returned in the second half of June together with rain and continued until 10 July when summer was felt at last. The late flowering vines suffered during the cold and rain leading to *coulure* and *millerandage*.

July alternated between sun and rain, while August was very hot and dry. Then on 1 September the rains came with a vengeance, 50mm of it and very welcome it was too after such a heat wave. The remainder of September was dry, sunny and nicely hot, natural sugar levels were high and the vintage began on the 22nd. Many picked late during continuing good weather, particularly the Premier and Grand Crus at the end of the month.

With a satisfactory harvest, very good aromatic wines are the order of the day, much in the style of the 92s, but perhaps without the same keeping potential.

1996 – very fine

In Chablis, the flowering developed on two fronts. The Grand and Premier Cru vineyards in general reached the floraison early at the end of May in cold weather, affected by *coulure* and *millerandage*, with small bunches and small grapes both imparting quality at the expense of quantity. The Village Chablis and Petit Chablis in later developing areas flowered about the middle of June in much better conditions, forming normal plump fruit.

Throughout the Chablisien, the yields were about average as the weather had been predominantly dry during the year and the grapes had never been fat. At the final stage of maturation in September, all the necessary elements (sugar, acidity, fruit etc.) concentrated together, with the aid of a drying north wind and fresh temperatures. The vintage began early on 23 September. The fruit was sweet and concentrated, beautifully balanced with acidity.

The wines reflect that marvellous concentration, rich, fresh, crisp and aromatic. They have the potential for long ageing, especially the top levels; but do not ignore the village wines, there are some really lovely wines here. This is a vintage to put alongside the fabulous 89, 90, 92 and 95.

1995 – fine

The Chablis vintage began on 28 September, a date later than normal for precocious years, as 1994. But late vintages do not necessarily signify lack of quality or *typicité*. Whilst the abundance of sunshine in the early ripening years precipitate earlier maturity of the fruit, and give wines of generosity, richness and alcohol, they are often less well balanced. Cold and rain at the flowering explains the date of the vintage in 1995. Floraison occurred around 23 June.

At vintage time, the vines were in perfect condition, fine foliage and rot-free grapes, in spite of the September rains, 82mm between 1 and 20 of the month, but the drying rays of the sun followed and the vintage continued in near-perfect conditions. A thunderstorm on the night of 4 October temporarily disturbed the work and caused localised hail damage.

Porte Noël, Chablis – The Gateway to Burgundy

This is a vintage of well above average quality, but of a distinct character. The wines are forward and approachable relatively early, but are keepers. They are aromatic, very fruity and well balanced, with good acidity but not the crispness or freshness of the yet to come 1996. The Grand and Premier Crus will age very well and develop honeyed luscious and voluptuous flavours. Leave the Grand Crus for at least eight years, the Premier Crus five years.

1994 – good

The year boded well with an early budding at the beginning of April, but a heavy frost during the night of the 14/15 caused widespread damage. Flowering occurred in good weather around 20 June. The vines were thankful for July and August which were very sunny and warm, followed by rain at the beginning of September. The *ban de vendanges* was 24 September, and the vintage continued in fine conditions. But Jack Frost had done some bad work this year.

Fine wines were made in 1994 although in reduced quantity. Good growers produced rich and balanced wines of quality, many to compare with the best years of Chablis.

1993 – fair/good

A mild spring favoured an early budding which was not frustrated by frost. Continuing good weather conditions allowed an early, rapid and uniform flowering, early sign of a good vintage. A humid July and a particularly sunny August led to a harmonious development of the fruit. At the beginning of September the grape sugar content was almost the equal of the 92s at the same period, with superior acidity and an almost perfect condition. The harvest thus began on 21 September, and then the rains came, dashing hopes of a great vintage.

Some good wines were made in 1993, lively, fresh, aromatic, with Chablis *typicité*, mainly by those producers who were able to minimise the effect of the rain, but it was a difficult year for real quality; choosing well is imperative.

1992 – very fine

For once, the Chablisien benefited from excellent climatic conditions not unfortunately mirrored in other French regions. Thanks to a winter and spring particularly mild and dry, the budding started on 20 April. Continuing good weather allowed an exceptionally early and rapid flowering during the first week of June. Some rain at the beginning of July was welcome. The *véraison* naturally followed early due to a hot August, and the vintage commenced on 21 September in the best of conditions, as in 1990. Fresh nights before the vintage hindered the development of any botrytis, so the grapes were in fine fettle, with excellent sugars and acidity.

The resultant wines of 1992 are comparable with the best of Chablis vintages, beautifully balanced and harmonious, rich, elegant, structured with fine ageing potential. Well-chosen village wines are very good, Premier and Grand Crus very fine.

1991 – good

This year the damage caused by the spring frosts was minimalised by the effective methods of frost control employed by many vignerons. The flowering was a little late, but continued in good conditions. This was followed by two months of dry hot sunshine which helped a rapid maturity and the *ban des vendanges* was fixed for 5 October. The harvest proceeded well and was completed by about the 15th. The sugar content of the fruit was not quite at 1990 levels, but still well above average, particularly on the Crus. The acidity was comparable to 1990 and made for balanced wines of *typicité*. 1991 is a good year for well-chosen Premier and Grand Cru wines.

1990 – exceptional

A particularly warm and sunny summer gave hopes for a great vintage. Rain on 30 and 31 August came at the right time, and September nocturnal temperatures helped to preserve the needed acidity to balance the excellent sugar content. The vintage was early and proceeded in excellent conditions.

1990 Chablis is a very fine vintage, the wines are intensely fruity and opulent with a clean non-aggressive attack, lively and fresh. These wines age beautifully and harmoniously.

1989 – very good indeed

The climatic conditions for the Chablis area were exceptionally favourable, allowing an advance on all the growing stages, but one night of severe frost considerably damaged the predictions of a fine harvest on some slopes. Fortunately, a long warm period limited the effects of the cold and by the end of August the vines had benefited from as much sunshine as is usually had by 30 September. The vintage was finished in the Chablisien by the date it usually starts.

The 89s are rich, fat and fruity, full bodied and structured with great generosity. It is a vintage where the wines can be appreciated young but the best wines will develop beautifully.

Earlier notable vintages

1988 – As a generalisation, high yields resulted in a lack of concentration. Some producers rose above this, e.g. Joseph Drouhin, Jean Durup, Louis Michel.

1986 – A late harvest here produced some fair wines despite questionable concentration. Choose carefully.

Chablis – View from the Grand Crus

Chablis – Winter view from the Serein

River Serein – Tranquility

Village of Milly and Côte de Lechet

1985 – Freezing conditions in January and severe frost made life difficult, many areas suffered severe loss of vines. Reasonable summer weather saved what remained and some really beautiful wines were made by the careful producer.

1983 – Rich fruity wines high in alcohol, the best wines had charm and personality and kept well.

1981 – Severe frost damage resulted in a vastly reduced crop but a warm summer compensated for what was left and a few lovely wines resulted.

1978 – Together with 1971 the vintage of the 1970s produced some wonderful wines, fabulous ripe fruit and crisp acidities. Find them if you can!

⑬

OTHER WINES OF THE YONNE

. . . .

WHEREAS this book deals with the wines of Chablis, some producers are concerned also with the wines of the region in a wider sense. A few words on this for the sake of completeness. We are in no way denigrating these wines as they can be very acceptable everyday drinking wines and good value, but this is a book on Chablis. However...

Jullien in 1822 noted the division of the Yonne into five *arrondissements* — Auxerre, Avallon, Joigny, Sens and Tonnerre, the first and last named particularly celebrated for quality of produce, 36,000 hectares producing 900,000 hectolitres, 250,000 of which were consumed by the local populace, with the surplus exported to Paris, the north of France and other thirsty countries. As noted earlier, the Yonne was the largest wine-producing area in France before Phylloxera, supplying the café tables and private houses of Paris and beyond with cheap readily available plonk at reasonable prices. The present day legacy is somewhat small in comparison, and comprises principally four sources well known today, namely Saint-Bris-le-Vineux, Chitry, Irancy and Coulanges-la-Vineuse.

The history of the area is closely linked with that of Chablis, vines existing in the valley of the Yonne around Auxerre at the end of the seventh century. Auxerre wines were the favourites of kings and princes and enjoyed a fine reputation in the French and English courts for centuries. Oidium, Phylloxera and CNCF changed all that.

Spreading out the Michelin road map No. 65, one observes the west-to-east spread of the three northerly wine regions, Auxerre to the west, Chablis at the epicentre and Tonnerre to the east. Epicentre is not a word idly chosen, for Chablis does indeed govern the area as far as the market is concerned, with market movements reflected in the outer areas as prices rise or fall in the centre. 'When Chablis catches cold, Auxerre sneezes.' One could hardly expect otherwise, given the relative importance of Chablis. But the 'other' areas have been going through something of a renaissance in the past twenty years or so, and it is not too difficult to find their wines in the shops in France and the UK, especially the Auxerrois.

The villages of the Auxerrois include Bleigny-le-Carreau, Champvallon, Mige, Quenne, Senan, Vaux, Volgre and Venoy, as well as the four most famous mentioned above. The Tonnerrois wines comprise Tonnerre itself and Epineuil, with further *vignobles* located on the Côte Saint-Jacques above

Early Spring buds

Spring rape – Looking towards Montmain

Old Chablis – Shutters

Old Chablis – Rue des Juifs

Joigny to the north of Auxerre, Vézelay to the south, and the Châtillonnais to the east of Tonnerre.

The following is a summary of those areas:

Auxerrois

La Grande Côte d'Auxerre

In the nineteenth century, vines covered almost 140 hectares outside Auxerre, and the wines produced were a popular market commodity. We have seen what happened to the district as a result of the advent of the railways and resulting competition from the cheap wines of the Midi, the devastation of the vineyards caused by Phylloxera, the Great War, rural depopulation and the Second World War. Today only a mere 3 hectares remain, the Clos de la Chainette, producing white and rosé wine in contrast to the past fame of Auxerre red wines. André Jullien in *Topographie de Tous les Vignobles Connus* (1822) gives his own classification of the wines of the region placing La Chainette and a suitably named vineyard La Migraine (which by accounts produced strong wine high in alcohol) in the first category of reds alongside the wines of Dannemoine and Tonnerre. Cyrus Redding in 1833 refers to the reds of the Auxerrois from the black *pineau* grape alone of 'good colour, and agreeable bouquet, with strength and alcohol, and yet does not injure the head or stomach.' Of the white wine, Roger Dion in 1959 relates the following description attributed to a thirteenth-century monk Frère Salimbene – 'a white wine, sometimes golden, that has aroma and body, a generous and exquisite flavour, that fills the heart with a merry confidence.' P. Morton Shand in 1928 continues the quote: 'So strong are the wines of Auxerre that the outsides of the jars which contain them weep with sweating.' Wow!

La Chainette is now owned by the Psychiatric Hospital, and its situation in these days of urban expansion places it in the middle of the hospital complex in Avenue des Clairions and Auxerre itself, sheltered and warmed by the radiated heat from the surrounding buildings. Thank heaven, it is a protected vineyard and safe from the greedy hands of property developers – we hope! The wines produced by traditional vinification methods are Appellation Bourgogne and reportedly pleasant, unsophisticated, easy drinking, popular but hard to find.

Saint-Bris-le-Vineux

One of the four main communes of the Auxerrois with vineyards dating back to the twelfth century. The village seems to have borne the brunt of military attacks during the middle ages resulting in fortifications which survived until well into the last century. The savagery of the attacks must have been of the utmost severity, as there still exists a vast maze of cramped cellars beneath the town where the local populace would seek shelter from the marauding troops. Their use today is of a more peaceful nature.

High-yielding and inferior grape varieties abounded in the area, gradually replaced by Pinot, Chardonnay, Aligoté, Sacy, Gamay, César and surprisingly Sauvignon Blanc – perhaps imported from Sancerre with whom there is a trading history. Although other wines received Appellation status, Sauvignon Blanc as a foreigner did not, and from 1974 was sold only with the designation of Vin Délimité de Qualité Supérieure (VDQS) but it would seem not for long. Its popularity is on the increase. due no doubt to the public thirst for dry crisp fruity wines and the reluctance to pay Sancerre, Pouilly Fumé or Bordeaux prices. The total area of Sauvignon Blanc has remained fairly constant in recent years, but from the 1995 vintage the wine carries Appellation status and with it official recognition, and Sauvignon de Saint-Bris of good quality is now readily available in both France and the UK.

Saint-Bris-le-Vineux's fame rests on this very interesting white wine, certainly good value for what it is, crisp clean gooseberry fresh, typical Sauvignon when well made. Keep a look out for Domaines Jean-Marc Brocard, William Fèvre, Ghislaine Goissot, Bersan, Félix, Patrice Fort and Verret et Fils.

Aligoté is another white grape produced at Saint-Bris, making a sharply acidic, blandly fruity wine, but it's fine in Kir, in fact try the Kir locally, delicious! Kir originated in Dijon, being the name of the then mayor of the town who found that he could sell vast quantities of his blackcurrant juice by adding it to the unwanted Aligoté wine of the Côte d'Or.

Chardonnay locally in Saint-Bris produces a generic Bourgogne Blanc and also sometimes finds its way into the *cépage* for Crémant de Bourgogne which used to be produced in Saint-Bris from an inferior white grape, the Sacy, thankfully now almost entirely replaced by Pinot Noir, Sauvignon, Aligoté and Chardonnay, with a little Gamay for the rosé. In 1971 a cooperative, the Société d'Intérêt Collectif Agricole du Vignoble Auxerrois (SICAVA) was formed for this purpose, following the collapse of the German market, the wine having previously been sold for the mass production of the insipid Henkel Trocken. The Crémant now emanating from the co-op has a reputation as a fresh zippy wine of good value – maybe the wine is indeed fresh and lively, but it doesn't hold a candle to the excellent quality Blanc de Blancs Crémant de Bourgogne from the Cave de Lugny in the Maconnais.

Irancy

Pinot Noir and César are the red wine grapes of this village situated in the centre of vineyards. Bourgogne Irancy is just another amongst the plethora of general Bourgogne Rouges, mostly Pinot Noir, but some growers add a little César supposedly to beef up the body of an otherwise rather undistinguished red. Anthony Hanson has more than a kind word to say about César, a grape probably brought to the area by the Romans. César produces long bunches of grapes, loosely hung, so being less susceptible to rot, is high in potential alcohol and low yielding, and it is ideal as a *vin de médecine*

Frost control – Chaufferettes

Frost control – La bâche de protection

Les Piliers Chablisiens – Cellars of Le Petit Pontigny

Au Vrai Chablis

if it is to be used as such, i.e. for beefing up, darkening and colouring otherwise pale Pinots. Some producers have in the past made cuvées of pure César, Michel Esclavy and Luc Sorin. Simonnet-Febvre still does; drink it locally if you must as an experience, but this is not a wine to take seriously.

As in all Burgundian matters, the quality of the producer governs the quality of the wine. Bourgogne Irancy is a light, pleasant everyday drinking red wine. In the best hands the wine has depth and some ageing potential. Leading producers include Bersan, Bienvenu, Cantin, Colinot, Delaloge, Félix, Patrice Fort, Simonnet-Febvre, Sorin and Verret.

Chitry-le-Fort
Situated between Chablis and Auxerre, the village of Chitry historically sat astride the border between the provinces of Champagne and Bourgogne. Prior to 1929 and especially in the nineteenth century the wines were sold as Chablis, but as we have already seen all that changed with the introduction of Appellation laws. Nowadays, it is a centre for white wine production, mainly Bourgogne Blanc from Chardonnay and Bourgogne Aligoté; some Gamay is grown for Bourgogne Grand Ordinaire, a most appropriate name. The Bourgogne Blanc is worth seeking out when visiting the area – a nice crisp refreshing wine on a hot summer day – try the local bars and cafés, and Domaine Joel Griffe.

Coulanges-la-Vineuse
The principal wine here is red from Pinot Noir, and not to be sniffed at, except in a glass whilst seated contentedly at a local establishment contemplating the culinary achievements of Monsieur Le Patron or Madame La Patronne.

The history of the ancient town is fascinating, and relates the story of the devastation of the town and its church by fire in 1676. Because of a lack of water to quell the flames Mme de Villefranche had thirty barrels of wine broken open and the wine thrown on the flames to stop the disaster. A bad restoration of the church commenced immediately, but it really remained in ruins until 1732 when work started in earnest. In 1742 the reconstruction was completed, the funds for which came entirely from a tax levied on the wines. Hence 'la Vineuse'?

The wine is going through something of a revival with more and wider plantings of Pinot Noir, but is still a very minor part of the greater Burgundy scene. The wine in dedicated hands is capable of ageing well, reportedly with fine vintages such as 1969, 1976 and 1978. We look forward to tasting more recent vintages. For the curious, try the wines of Raymond Dupuis, Jean-Pierre Maltoff and Pierre Vigreux.

Joigny
About 27 kilometres north-west of Auxerre lies the town of Joigny through which flows the once-upon-a-time lifeline Yonne river wending its way

down to Sens and joining the Seine at Montereau-Fault-Yonne. At Joigny, there still exists one small vineyard outside the town to the north, the Côte Saint-Jacques, all that remains of a once proud vignoble of some 700 hectares. Thankfully there is a revival of interest in the area, and high-yielding and minor grape varieties which used to help fill Parisian restaurants before the advent of the railway system and the ravages of Phylloxera are being replaced with Chardonnay, Pinot Gris and Pinot Noir.

Jacques Vignot is the pioneer in the revival, with his son Alain from Paroy-sur-Tholon and nephew Serge Lepage from Champlay, villages on the left bank of the River Yonne. The future could be interesting. Look out also for the co-operative run by Michel Lorain who turn out Bourgogne Blanc from some 15 hectares of replanted vines. Most if not all the wines produced are for the home market – at present.

Vézelay

Not strictly speaking part of the Auxerrois, this small town 50 kilometres directly south of Auxerre and 13 kilometres west of Avallon, separated from the Côte d'Or by the hills of the Morvan, is still within the département of the Yonne and a historic part of Burgundy. Surrounded by pine forests and woodland, the beautiful hilltop town of Vézelay is situated on the River Cure, a tributary of the Yonne which it joins at Vermenton 28 kilometres to the north. Like its vinous cousins, the area traces its history back a long time, very long, for it is believed that the Romans brought the vine here two thousand years ago. The town was founded by Girart de Roussillon, a Count of Burgundy, when he established a Benedictine monastery and founded the Abbey of Vézelay consecrated by Pope John Vlll in 878. This Abbey, the Basilica of St Mary Magdalene, at one time housed the relics of Mary Magdalene and was a great place of pilgrimage. It was at Vézelay that St Bernard preached the Second Crusade in 1146, and Richard the Lionheart met Philippe-Auguste of France before their departure on the Third Crusade. The Huguenots and the French Revolution brought the Abbey to a low point in its history and virtual dereliction until renovation and restoration works under Viollet-le-Duc in the middle of the nineteenth century rebuilt the church to its former state of glory.

The town itself is beautiful and captivating. Walking up through the narrow winding streets of the old town to the Basilica can ease the most troubled of souls. Climb the 200 steps to the platform at the top of the Basilica tower for a spectacular view over the Cure valley and the Morvan.

As for the vignoble, by the middle of the nineteenth century, the whole of the much larger area of the Avallonaise boasted some 4,000 hectares, now long gone. Once again, a vast vignoble was decimated by the common adversaries.

The current revival was spearheaded by a local grower Bernard Basseport, and later by a well-known Chablis name, none other than Bernard Raveneau, Jean-Marie's brother who in 1990, following family disagree-

Hostellerie des Clos – Courtyard and garden

Hostellerie – Exterior

ments and departure from the family domaine, joined La Vézelienne the local co-operative and brought his own brand of expertise to the venture producing wines for sale at non-Raveneau prices, Bourgogne Chardonnay and Pinot Noir. Bernard has recently rejoined the family domaine. A small amount of Melon de Bourgogne, otherwise known as Muscadet – another story – is also cultivated.

Apart from the co-operative, *viticulteurs* of the area include Bernard Basseport, Domaine Guyard and Domaine Villiers.

Tonnerois

Moving eastward, we come to Tonnerre, just 16 kilometres from Chablis and a different vignoble, that of the Tonnerrois, which includes the village of Epineuil, and served by the Armançon, yet another tributary of the Yonne. Also with a thousand years of history, the wines flourished in royal France and England transported like so many others by barge down to the River Seine and Paris. Jullien's classification favoured both the red and white wines of Tonnerre. Following the devastation of the vineyards, rural depopulation and the Second World War, the revival in interest in the area was led and inspired by André Durand, one-time Mayor of Epineuil. Realising the potential of the now fallow land, and starting from a low point of a mere 12 hectares of surviving vineyards, he encouraged interest from outsiders from Champagne, Châteauneuf-du-Pape and Paris to re-plant the land which was still within the Bourgogne Appellation. One of the leading growers in this revival is Jean-Claude Michaut, a viticulteur with considerable Chablis experience but producing red and rosé wine in addition to his Bourgogne Blanc, Chablis Vaucoupin and Village.

To date there are a total of some 210 hectares planted in the district and in production, and that is some notable revival. The main grapes for the area are Pinot Noir and Chardonnay.

Mention must also be made of the co-operative Caveau des Fontenelles and Emmanuel Dampt in Collan, also a good producer of Chablis.

Two further *vignobles* are:

Bernouil

Just a few kilometres to the north-west of Tonnerre is the little village of Bernouil, where due to its predominantly sandy soil, pre-Phylloxera vines still grow producing Bourgogne Blanc.

Châtillonais

This ancient vignoble is situated some 50 kilometres to the east of Tonnerre and just 10 kilometres from the Aube vineyards of Champagne, still under the umbrella protection of the Yonne Département. Centred on Châtillon-sur-Seine, the vineyards were decimated in the same way as the other areas of the Yonne. Nowadays there are a number of growers in the surrounding villages cultivating Pinot Noir, Chardonnay, Pinot Blanc and

Gamay for red, white and rosé Bourgogne, Crémant de Bourgogne and Passetoutgrains. Producers include the co-operative at Belan-sur-Ource and Gilbert et Régine Brigand at Massigny.

Staying and Eating Out
in Chablis and Surrounding Area

. . . .

We have mentioned before that the Chablis area does not abound in eating establishments, but bearing in mind that all of the villages are relatively small, what is there is sufficient and of good to excellent quality. Here are some suggestions:

Hostellerie des Clos

Rue Rathier	Tel: 03 86 42 10 63
Chablis	Fax: 03 86 42 17 11

The best hotel and restaurant in town, owned and run by the Chef Michel Vignaud and his charming wife. The attractive restaurant is reached through a small comfortable lounge opening up into a lovely and tasteful dining area with glazed alcoves overlooking the garden at the rear. Refurbishment in 1999 has added a further lounge area with a lovely roaring open fire in winter.

It is no surprise that Michel has a Michelin star. The à-la-carte menu is extensive, the Oeufs-en-Meurette is authentic, the red mullet is a dream, and the Menu Gourmande FF375 is a feast of the best Burgundian cuisine. There are also two lower-priced menus FF275 and FF185 of very good value. The wine list is a book itself on the wines of Chablis – it includes 200 different growers' wines in bottles, 35 in magnum and 40 in half bottles as well as a good selection of other Burgundies and Clarets.

The first-floor bedrooms have all been refurbished to a very high standard with well-equipped ensuite bathrooms and TV.

A good buffet breakfast is provided in a lovely morning room which looks out on to the enclosed lawn and garden to the front of the hotel. Car parking is available at the rear or on the forecourt.

We have stayed here on many occasions and are always welcomed and extremely well looked after. Fresh flowers and a friendly atmosphere pervade. Booking ahead is essential – this hotel is renowned.

Hotel de L'Etoile
Rue des Moulins
Chablis   Tel: 03 86 42 10 50

The oldest hotel in Chablis, close to the central square and often used in the past by visiting people in the wine trade.

However, in 1998 we found the hotel to be in need of extensive improvement, the bedrooms are ill equipped, some without ensuite bathrooms or even WCs, and this is not acceptable in our spoiled molly-coddled millennium days; maybe thirty years ago, but not now! Many of the rooms are shabbily furnished and decorated.

The restaurant has very limited local menus, perfectly edible, but the wine list is not good enough for a hotel in a wine town. Things have changed regrettably since Stephen Gwynne was writing in 1934 about the late Monsieur Briand always having a meal here on his way to and from Geneva, the days when Club des Cent awarded a diploma to the hotel.

The owners Roger and Michèle Prévost are welcoming and helpful and we only hope that the hotel is upgraded very soon. Limited car parking is available through the archway at the side.

Hotel Ibis
Route d'Auxerre   Tel: 03 86 42 49 20
Chablis   Fax: 03 86 42 80 04

A modern commercial hotel in the Ibis chain of 450 hotels, situated on the fringe of town opposite the large Moreau wine complex, providing functional rooms and a small simple restaurant. Originally known as Les Lys, the hotel has now been upgraded to provide good clean accommodation with en-suite facilities and TV.

We made a brief visit in February 1999 in order to be able to report here. A good buffet breakfast is served at a very moderate cost and a budget menu is available for evening meals. Ample car parking is provided.

Friendly staff provide for a very convivial stay but this is essentially a bed and breakfast hotel for short visits with no frills.

La Syracuse Restaurant
19 Rue de Maréchal de Lattre de Tassigny
Chablis   Tel: 03 86 42 19 45

Located in the main street opposite the town square and reached through a small courtyard with tables for summer use. The restaurant is at first-floor level with an attractive vaulted ceiling at the front.

There is an excellent choice of menus with no-nonsense French cuisine providing a very satisfying and inexpensive lunch or evening venue, clearly well supported by the local Chablisien. The wine list has a good range of Chablis in both bottles and half bottles. Well worth a visit.

Restaurant Vieux Moulin
Rue des Moulins
Chablis   Tel: 03 86 42 47 30

As the name suggests, this restaurant has been built over an old water-mill above the Serein. Entrance is from the Rue des Moulins only a short distance from the main square, giving access to restaurants at ground and first-floor levels.

The first-floor restaurant has an attractive beamed ceiling, and the windows overlook the river. The atmosphere is relaxed and friendly, the Patronne always willing to explain the delights of the local speciality Andouilette, not a dish for everyone and guidance is essential.

The restaurant is always very busy at lunchtime even out of season, always a good sign. A varied and very reasonable menu is available, together with a good but limited wine list. We liked it very much. Park in the main square – if space is available.

Au Vrai Chablis
6 Place du Général de Gaulle
Chablis   Tel: 03 86 42 11 43

A quaint café/restaurant in the main square directly opposite Jean-Marc Brocard's shop and impossible to miss. Wonderful lunchtime venue with a local atmosphere, but get there early to be sure of a table.

There is always an attractively priced menu of the day, well cooked and reasonably substantial, a good thing if you are wine-tasting again after lunch. The wine list may be fairly limited but it is good with Chablis and local Auxerrois wines.

This is clearly another meeting place for the locals which always creates a good ambience.

Hôtel Le Relais Saint-Vincent
Ligny-le-Châtel   Tel: 03 86 47 53 38
Nr. Chablis   Fax: 03 86 47 54 16

A small hotel in the centre of this village about 7 miles north of Chablis. The building at the front is attractively presented with reception and restaurant areas providing local menus at attractive prices. Local vignerons recommend the restaurant but we have not sampled it yet for ourselves.

A small number of bedrooms are located in the main building and in the annexe at the rear. Car parking is limited.

There is also another restaurant nearby in Ligny-le-Châtel known as the **Auberge du Bief**.

Restaurant Barnabet
14 Quai République
Auxerre   Tel: 03 86 51 68 88 Fax: 03 86 52 96 85

No visit to Chablis is complete without a detour to the lovely old town of Auxerre with its magnificent cathedral and the colourful quais along the River Yonne giving at night almost a Mediterranean aura.

Set right on the riverside almost beneath the cathedral itself is the splendid Restaurant Barnabet. The approach is through a delightful courtyard and garden giving way to a very elegant restaurant at the rear. This most sought after establishment in Auxerre well merits its high recognition in *Guide Michelin* and its rosette. The Chef is always in attendance to speak to his guests.

A wide selection of à la carte dishes are available and a Menu Gourmande with accompanying wines is extremely good value at FF450. The wine list is very comprehensive and most of the recognised Chablis producers are represented. Prices are quite sensible for a restaurant of this standing.

Easy car parking is available on the banks of the Yonne. A highly recommended destination for a delightful and relaxing evening's diversion following a hard day's tasting! The cuisine is exceptional and the table settings give a very delightful and relaxed feel to an evening's dining experience.

Auberge La Beursaudière
Nitry 89310   Tel: 03 86 33 62 51 Fax: 03 86 33 65 21

A Michelin restaurant some 10 miles south of Chablis in the centre of the village of Nitry. Reached by the Route d'Avallon south out of Chablis, this is a delightful evening jaunt across rolling open farm land. We arrived in the dark and in torrential rain but the lights of this quaint rustic auberge were clear to see and most welcome.

This is a restaurant on two floors with exposed timber beams and tiled floors enjoying a reputation amongst vignerons wishing for a quiet night out of town. The same comment applied to two rather weary wine writers and one wife who had been weather beaten walking around the shops, what there is of them anyway.

The menu was a tour-de-force and complicated to unravel. The food was varied in price, menus ranging from FF95 to FF180 with an à la carte menu to match. Good Burgundian no-nonsense cuisine with an expansive wine list of Chablis and other French wine regions – yes, even Bordeaux.

A well-recommended restaurant, and shortly to have some rooms added for overnight stay.

Restaurant Le Saint-Bris
13 Rue de l'Eglise
Saint-Bris-le-Vineux   Tel: 03 86 53 84 56

Situated in the centre of the delightful small town of Saint-Bris-le-Vineux, immediately opposite La Poste, this restaurant under the direction of owner/chef M. Pouillot is a wonderful venue for lunch. The timbered walls and ceiling, tiled floor and roaring log fire in the winter are most welcoming.

The menu described as Cuisine Artisan is extensive, with a strong bias towards fish dishes and cooked in any number of ways. Monsieur Pouillot is in constant touch with the front room to check on his customers' satisfaction with a friendly smile, appreciative of any plaudits which may come his way.

The wine list is simple but contains as one would expect the Sauvignon de Saint-Bris, and Auxerre red and white wines of the area plus a limited Chablis selection.

This restaurant is well worth a visit.

Restaurant La Charmaille
4 Route de Boiloup
Chevannes   Tel: 03 86 41 24 80
Nr. Auxerre   Fax: 03 86 41 34 80

A Michelin-starred restaurant run by the Famille Siri situated in the quiet village of Chevannes some 8 km south-west of Auxerre off the road to Nevers. The restaurant can be difficult to find: it is located behind the church overlooking open farmland towards Vallan. An attractive gravelled entrance leads to the rustic range of buildings arranged round a courtyard. Ornamental facades and doorways give an incongruous Tudor appearance and the illusion continues when entering the stone and timbered restaurant which radiates a relaxing ambiance for a great gastronomic experience.

The menus are changed daily and are reasonably priced. The presentation of dishes here is different from other starred restaurants in the area and the journey is well worth a visit 'out of town'.

Wines recommended from the locality include a Chardonnay from Vézelay and a Bourgogne Rouge from the nearby village of Coulanges les Vineuses, both provided as part of a mid-priced menu, from which we both chose the Rognons de Veau. Delicious!

This restaurant is a must!

PART TWO

SECTION A
THE DOMAINE PROFILES

Introduction
to the Domaine Profiles

. . . .

Marketing

Today, Chablis is a much easier commodity to buy than not so many years ago. Every off-licence worth its salt has at least one source to offer, though that may not be a very enterprising choice. Supermarkets and chains offer less than a reasonable choice, but the best supplies are obtainable from your reputable wine merchant or specialist store. We hope the information given will assist in your search.

Right up to the days before the Second World War, the market was substantially controlled by the commissionaires or brokers, who acted between the growers and *négociants*. The sale and purchase of wine was by the *feuillette* – the Chablis barrel of 132 litres – very little by the bottle to private clients. Very gradually over the years, the proportion of commercial and private clients increased. In the early 1960s, three quarters of the total Chablis production passed through the hands of the main *négoce* of Beaune and Bordeaux. One fifth was sold to Chablis *négociants*, which left a mere splash of wine for *vente directe*. Today, the trend has swung much further towards direct sales by the growers, as more and more domaines show their independence.

The dramatic change is demonstrated in today's figures which show that about 50 per cent of growers sell all or some of their produce in bottle. This indicates the continuing improvements in vineyard holdings, advancement in viticultural and vinification techniques, and the growing confidence of the domaines.

Chablis has often been criticised as being overproduced from inferior growers and marketed at prices which compare unfavourably with wines from the Nantais, Gascony and areas of the Dordogne. Inappropriate comparisons are also made with the Chardonnays of California, New Zealand and Australia by certain wine writers and publicists. In other words, in many quarters Chablis has had a bad press, price-wise as well as otherwise. The following quotations highlight the point that we are making:

> Most Chablis, no matter the quality, is overpriced for the wine one gets in the bottle.
>
> Robert Parker on Burgundy

Genuine Chablis is never cheap because there is little of it.
André Simon in 1920

Chablis has always been known for allowing prices to soar when there is little wine to sell of whatever quality, and for selling its wine too quickly and too cheaply when there is a prolific vintage.
Serena Sutcliffe, *The Wines of Burgundy*

As long as prices are not at the top of a cycle, Chablis is a must if only for its wonderful partnership with seafood generally and oysters in particular.
Jasper Morris, *The White Wines of Burgundy*

All around £11 a bottle. Chablis Premiers and Grand Crus are not the most accessible Chardonnays available. However, they are not produced on a large scale. You should expect to pay around £13 a bottle for a similar style California Chardonnay produced in higher quantities.
Decanter Magazine August 1997.

The first and the last quotations speak volumes for the attitude of some wine writers when comparing Chablis with wines from the New World.

We have attempted in this book to separate the wheat from the chaff, the good Chablis from the not-so-good Chablis, and where those bottles can be found.

Prices, needless to say, are as always governed by supply and demand, and in good years such as 1982, 1985, 1989, 1990, 1992, 1995 and 1996, prices from the best domaines will reflect the quality of the wine produced, whether it is straight Village Chablis, one of the better Premier Crus or a Grand Cru. In lesser years such as 1984, 1987, 1991, 1993 and 1994 bargains can be found and some 1984 Grand Crus are drinking well now if they can still be found at auction sales. But always be aware of the quality of the producer.

Regular fine wine sales are held in London by both Christies and Sothebys at which cases of white Burgundy often appear and Chablis from both recent and older vintages can be found. Provincial sales are also held in towns such as Salisbury, Honiton and Abergavenny, to name but a few; and, of course, well-publicised auctions are becoming a regular feature in major cities of the United States.

It should be remembered that approximately one third of all production is through the Chablisienne Co-operative, much of which is sold to *négociants* in Beaune and elsewhere and then finds its way on to supermarket shelves as well as the more specialised wine merchants. We have, however, concentrated on where the individual growers' wines can be located and the schedules are limited to our own experience and are in no way comprehensive

Who is and is not included

In the early 1980s, Rosemary George in her treatise on Chablis examined the difficulties in compiling a complete list of growers: the vineyards sometimes being apparently cultivated in the names of several different family members of one domaine; the multitude of lists available in the *Mairie*, one for each commune; and the non-definitive nature of the *syndicats*. Therefore, the *déclaration des rendements* which may be inspected at the town hall cannot be relied upon for this purpose. Monsieur Tucki at La Chablisienne also reported the same problem and it is clear that a definitive list of individual domaines is impossible.

We have compiled the domaines pictured here from our own perspective, all having been visited and with notes on all wines tasted, together with notes from a substantial amount of tastings both in France and the UK over the years. We like to believe that all the leading and most prominent growers and *négociants* have been included. If not, we apologise.

It is our intention to update this section at some future date if our readers wish to see further reviews.

The choice of which domaines should be profiled in this book was probably the most difficult decision we had to make. We have endeavoured to include domaines large and small, famous and the less well known. We have even found some that have been keeping themselves to themselves but with gentle coaxing have been persuaded to reveal their secrets. If we have omitted anyone we should not have omitted, we can only say sorry and if they make themselves known to us, we will visit them next time around.

As neither of the writers is infallible, we cannot guarantee that our selection is totally comprehensive, but we have covered almost half of the growers producing all or some of their wine in bottle. Growers selling all their grapes or must to the co-operative or the *négoce* are omitted as the wine is not available for purchase.

Our periodic update will include any new estate which we have been able to visit, as well as any revision in the ABOS Classification, our key to quality – see below – and the addition of recent vintages and tasting notes.

The tasting notes

The tasting notes are given in plain English. We do not liken smells and tastes to slithers of bitter grapefruit pip, Scandinavian lingonberries, women's eel-skin purses, or the revving up of an outboard motor on a boat and a slick of paint, all of which have been used in journalistic vinous descriptions – this approach has now ceased to be amusing.

The tasting notes are our opinion of the wines tasted and how they appeared on the day. We would stress again that they are our opinions, some people may disagree with the verdict and they are just as right or wrong as we may be: we can only give a guide to the best of the ability of our noses and palates, but having tasted well over a thousand Chablis in the past two years, we trust that the guide is comparative and helpful.

We would draw attention to the dates given with the reviews of Premier and Grand Cru wines. These are an estimation for **optimum drinking** – they are not hard and fast, wines may be drunk with pleasure before, and they will probably in most cases last well after. No dates have been given for Chablis and Petit Chablis as these are basically early-drinking wines.

Marking the wines

There are various methods of marking or evaluating wines. One system used extensively in the United States is the 100-point system. Marking wines out of 100 is all very well but requires a degree of accuracy and subjectivity beyond reason. We believe that this method is declining in popularity, and wholeheartedly applaud this decline for a number of reasons, not least being the impossibility of being able to judge to such a fine degree whether to give a mark of, say, 86 to one wine and 87 to another. Where is the cut-off point and what criteria are used to fine-tune to a degree which is obviously totally subjective and unreliable? A marking of 85 or 87.5 is more realistic, and it follows mathematically that this can be brought down to the 20-point system without any loss of judgement ability, i.e. 17 or 18 out of 20 is 85 or 90 and 17.5 is 87.5.

The numerical marking of new wines is even more risky: in our case the 1998 Chablis was incomplete, and the 1997s or any wines still in *cuve* or barrel are too much in their infancy to mark so meticulously.

As far as Burgundy is concerned, as we all know, the quality of a wine relates almost entirely to the quality of the grower and winemaker, and the star system of rating here is as valid as the evaluation of the resultant wines, where a more finely honed description can be employed. The power of the English language is far more telling than numbers – the simple word 'fine' speaks volumes more than '90' under the 100 point method or even 18 under the 20-point method.

Therefore we have used the star system for rating the domaines, and good old fashioned English for the wines.

∾

Note:

A word about the names, addresses, telephone and facsimile numbers, e-mail and internet addresses. We believe that these were all correct at the time of going to press but give no guarantee of the continuance of such. This is of especial note for the UK stockists – at the moment, the French and Americans do not appear to have contracted 'Brit communications disease', the annoying habit of continually changing head office telephone numbers at a whim under the pretext of better customer service, which it never is! To make matters worse, the recent change by BT in national prefix numbers is horrific!

All information regarding stockists, which include importers and retailers, has been supplied to us by the agents, distributors or retailers themselves. Readers are advised to telephone or fax their enquiries prior to making any journey or shopping expedition.

Due to the size and scope of the US retail system, we have obviously been unable to list comprehensively the shops and suppliers of the wines. We hope that the limited number of names given will enable our American readers to obtain the bottles they desire. Regretfully we were also unable to find the telephone numbers of a few US suppliers but addresses are given where known.

~

The ABOS classification of Chablis

Like the Côte d'Or, there is no official classification of the domaines of Chablis. So, to be controversial, and as a generally helpful guide for the consumer, we are going to stick our necks out and categorise the leading domaines into starred groups – three stars, two stars, one star and other domaines worthy of note. The stars reflect the capability of the domaine to consistently produce fine wine as judged by results over several years through good, bad and indifferent vintages. Remember that it is the domaines which are being starred, not the wines. Particular wines from some growers and *négociants* may justify a higher rating and this should be covered by the profiles and tasting notes that follow.

New estates and recent improvements are separately noted and inwardly digested. This list therefore will be regularly updated to take account of any improvements and changes. It is subjective and not authoritative.

★★★ – outstanding
Domaine Billaud Simon
Domaine René et Vincent Dauvissat
Domaine Jean-Paul Droin
Domaine Louis Michel et Fils
Domaine Raveneau

★★ – excellent
Domaine Joseph Drouhin
Domaine Gérard Duplessis
Domaine Jean Durup et Fils
Domaine Long-Depaquit
Domaine des Malandes
Domaine Louis Moreau

★ – very good
Domaine de Chantemerle – Boudin Père et Fils
Domaine Jean Collet
Domaine Daniel Dampt
Domaine Daniel-Etienne Defaix
Domaine Laroche
Domaine Sylvain Mosnier
Domaine Louis Pinson
Domaine Servin
Domaine Gérard Tremblay
Domaine Laurent Tribut
Domaine Vauroux
Domaine Vocoret

Other domaines worthy of note
Domaine Joëlle et Michel Barat
Domaine Pascal Bouchard
Domaine Jean-Marc Brocard
Domaine du Chardonnay
Domaine de la Concièrgerie
Domaine du Château de Fleys
Domaine Jean et Sébastien Dauvissat
Domaine Alain Geoffroy
Domaine Jean-Pierre Grossot
Domaine Thierry Hamelin
Domaine des Marronniers
Domaine de la Meulière
Domaine Alice et Olivier de Moor
Domaine Gilbert Picq et ses Fils
Domaine Denis Pommier
Domaine Denis Race
Domaine Philippe Testut
Domaine Vrignaud

The Co-operative La Chablisienne and the **négociants** have not been classified in the list above as they are not domaines and their wines are not
necessarily the same or from the same source each year. However, these
firms have a reputation to uphold and many of them consistently produce
very good wines. We would unhesitatingly recommend:

La Chablisienne
Maison Chanson Père et Fils
Maison Louis Jadot
Maison Verget

Errata

Page 4 line 8. The reference to Chapter 19 should refer to Chapter 14.

Page 44 lines 15 and 33. The references to Chapter 15 should refer to Chapter 4.

We apologise for these typographical errors

DOMAINE HERVÉ AZO

2 Rue de Champlain
Milly   Tel: 03 86 42 43 56
89800 Chablis   Fax: 03 86 42 49 98

15.5 hectares

Production:
Premier Crus   Beauroy   1.00 ha
                        Côte de Léchet   1.50 ha
                        Vau de Vey   8.40 ha

Chablis Village and Petit Chablis

Hervé Azo runs an interesting domaine, but he is rather difficult to find – not the two premises, but the one he is in at any particular moment. No matter, for Monsieur Azo is a fine wine maker and is worth seeking out.

A Groucho Marx lookalike with a dry sense of humour and a twinkle in his eye, Hervé will gladly talk about his wines with infectious enthusiasm, nineteen to the dozen. He lives in the heart of the village of Milly just a kilometre or two north of Chablis, but the workings of the domaine are divided between the village property and an ultra-modern factory unit located at the rear of the only supermarket in Chablis town, near the Ibis Hotel.

The holdings comprise three Premier Cru sites including a sizeable chunk of Vau de Vey of more than 8 hectares, as well as Chablis Village and Petit Chablis. Most of the vines were planted between 1982 and 1988 and are harvested by machine, except for the steep slopes of the Premier Crus which still require manual picking.

Vinification is in a mixture of stainless steel and enamelled *cuves* with no wood to be seen anywhere: Hervé shakes his head so vigorously at such a suggestion that his Groucho moustache is in danger of falling off. And here is the main individualistic idea of the domaine – the vinification is carried through without temperature control – 'purely natural' Hervé insists. Idiosyncratic certainly, but it works for him. The wines are fined with bentonite and kieselguhr-filtered before bottling in the spring following the vintage, continuing until September as necessary.

The total annual production is divided two thirds for the lucky *négoce* and one third representing some 30/35,000 bottles for the home market and export to the UK, USA and Germany.

At the risk of repeating ourselves, we like the guy, we like the wines.

Tasting notes
Petit Chablis 98 – lots of fruit here and well balanced. Should be a good Petit Chablis.

Petit Chablis 97 – good nose, like the above lots of nice fruit and well balanced acidity. This is good.

Vau de Vey 97 – fragrant nose, lovely minerally fruit and acidity with some length, fine balance and finish. Very good. (2001–2003)

Côte de Léchet 97 – closed nose, rather sour appley fruit, perhaps lacks a bit of crispness. Fair/good. (2000–2003)

Petit Chablis 96 – lots of crisp green appley fruit and acidity. Good Petit Chablis.

Vau de Vey 96 – quiet fragrant nose just a little closed, wine of *typicité*, steely appley fruit rather hidden but good concentration. Needs time. Good. (2002–2004)

Côte de Léchet 96 – honeyed fruits on nose, good fruit extraction with a dry mineral finish, well-balanced acidity, not exactly typical of the *climat*. Good. (2001–2004)

Vau de Vey 95 – tight nose, fruit and acidity is there but more closed than the 96, well-balanced wine. Still needs time. Good. (2001–2003)

Côte de Léchet 95 – butter biscuits, honey and nuts, lovely elegant fruit if not too long, well balanced. This is a delicious wine. Very good. (2000–2003)

Wines are available from the **CELLAR DOOR** and from stockists in:

UK
Hall Batson & Co., Norwich, Norfolk. Tel: 01603 415115 Fax: 01603 484096

USA
Beaune Imports, Berkeley, California. Tel: 510 841 9815

DOMAINE JOËLLE et MICHEL BARAT

6 Rue de Léchet
Milly   Tel: 03 86 42 40 07
89800 Chablis   Fax: 03 86 42 47 88

16 hectares

Production:

Premier Crus	Côte de Léchet	3.0ha
	Mont de Milieu	1.0ha
	Fourneaux	2.0ha
	Vaillon	3.0ha
Chablis Village		

Located in the centre of Milly on a steep road leading down to the Côte de Léchet, the domaine, partially hidden by a high brick wall, comprises an impressive detached house and office facing on to a paved courtyard. The magnificent old vaulted cellars date back to 1725.

Joëlle and Michel Barat, in their very youthful early fifties, both come from a long line of *vigneron* families, six generations, soon to be followed by son Ludovic working with Michel in the vineyards, and daughter Angèle on the administration and commercial side with Joëlle – a true family estate. Michel is a very personable, amiable and highly intelligent man, initially cautious with his two visiting wine writers but very soon relaxed and laughing. He is devoted to his métier and modestly very proud of his family's achievements. When we asked which of his wines pleased him the most, he smilingly replied that the Vaillons was Papa's favourite, but pressed further he expressed a love of the Côte de Léchet. We are not surprised, the Côte de Léchet is a lovely wine as our notes below indicate.

Harvesting here is all mechanical, and traditional vinification methods are applied with fermentation in temperature-controlled stainless steel vats. No wood is used at Domaine Barat. Bottling is carried out in May to preserve freshness, and if possible the wines are not sold until the following September. 70 per cent of the total production of around 80,000 bottles per annum is exported.

This is a domaine worthy of note, a very good source of delicious Chablis.

Tasting notes
The following wines were tasted at the domaine in October 1998 and February 1999, the 98s in London in August 1999 by courtesy of Adam Bancroft Associates:

Chablis 98 – pale colour, shy nose which needs encouragement to peek through, fruit is there and well balanced, a slight appley finish. Should be good but needs a little more time.

Vaillons 98 – mineral nose, good concentration of fruit, Granny Smith apples, crisp but a very dry finish. Still a very good wine. (2002-2005)

Côte de Léchet 98 – perfumed nose, terrific concentration of ripe appley fruit, again with a bone dry finish. Good. (2002–2004)

Fourneaux 98 – gentle fruity nose, minerally, lovely ripe appley fruit, crisp acidity, good length and depth. Very good. (2002–2005)

Chablis 97 – clean flowery nose, good fruit, fine length, lovely wine.

Vaillons 97 – little on nose, sweet fruit with some depth and lovely aftertaste. Very good. (2000–2002)

Côte de Léchet 97 – more closed than the Vaillons, rather discreet now, well balanced wine, should develop well into an elegant wine. (2001–2004)

Fourneaux 97 – flinty and floral, very round elegant wine with length and depth, delicious. What a lovely Premier Cru this is! Very good. (2001–2004)

Mont de Milieu 97 – very dry aromatic wine, acacia and peaches, fine concentrated fruit with depth. Lovely wine. Very good. (2001–2004)

Côte de Léchet 96 – wine of *typicité*, closed but encouragement reveals elegant ripe fruit, balance and length. Lovely wine for the future. Very good indeed. (2002–2005)

Mont de Milieu 95 – mineral nose as expected but fruit a bit flabby, a little short on the finish. Still good though. (2000–2002)

Côte de Léchet 95 – a lovely developed nose and palate, great fruit with a delicious aftertaste. Very good wine. (2000–2002)

Côte de Léchet 87 – tasted blind, was this a test of age? A lovely wine of intensity, fine fruit, *sous-bois*, mushrooms and violets, great complexity. Still young with just a little ageing. Really lovely for the vintage. Fine. (2000–2002)

Wines available from the **CELLAR DOOR** and stockists in:

UK
Adam Bancroft Associates, London SW8. Tel: 020 7793 1902 Fax: 020 7793 1897

USA
Burgundy Wine Co. Ltd, New York. Tel: 212 691 9092 Fax: 212 691 9244
Calvert Woodley, Washington DC. Tel: 202 966 4400. Fax: 202 537 5086
Vinifrance Imports Inc., 1608 S. Arlington Ridge Road, Arlington VA 22202.

DOMAINE BEAUREGARDS

Jean-Claude Martin
5 Rue de Chante Merle
Courgis   Tel: 03 86 41 40 33
89800 Chablis   Fax: 03 86 41 47 10

13 hectares

Production

Chablis Premier Crus	Montmains	1.00 ha
	Beauregards	2.30 ha
	Les Forêts	0.25 ha

Chablis Village

Domaine Jean Claude Martin is a small estate created in 1981 by the young husband and wife team of Jean Claude and Jacqueline Martin. Tradition and quality are the bywords for their produce, and this is declared from the outset by the attractive and tasteful nature of the wine labels. The *cuverie* and *chai* is incorporated on the ground floor of the large but not unattractive family property built in one of the valleys overlooked by Premier Cru Beauregards. Visitors are received in the modern, well-fitted-out tasting room usually by the charming Jacqueline Martin proudly producing the bottles out of nowhere whilst keeping her questioners firmly in their place with an air of 'I'll tell you what you need to know'. She even produced a bottle of Forêts for tasting, probably from the family's private stock.

The bulk of the estate is 8.5 hectares of Chablis Appellation, with a sizeable 2.3 hectare chunk of Premier Cru Beauregards. A single hectare of Montmains and a minuscule quarter of Forêts make up the remainder. In all, the Martins aim for a *rendement* of 50 hl/ha, as naturally organic as possible. The pruning as usual is the Guyot Double system, and the harvest is entirely manual.

The harvest is received at the *chai* and treated on three levels, proceeding to the pressing and then *débourbage* by gravity. The fermentation is in stainless steel and enamelled *cuves* temperature-controlled at 18-20°C, followed by *élevage* in *cuve*. Bentonite fining and a light filtration precede bottling under inert gas. Oak is not a word to be used at Domaine Martin.

On average, the domaine produces about 120,000 bottles annually, half of which is exported to the UK, 10 per cent each to Belgium and Germany, and the remainder for the home market.

Seek out these bottles, the Martins make very good wines.

Tasting notes
The following wines were tasted at the domaine in May 1998 and February 1999:

Chablis 98 – good fruity wine, nice acidity, crisp.

Chablis 97 – shows good fruit and acidity, fresh and crisp.

Montmains 97 – lovely fruity nose, concentrated fruit and balance, perhaps lacks a bit of length, but still should become a very good wine. (2001–2004)

Beauregards 97 – more earthy minerally flavour, but lacks a little bit of depth and concentration, but could evolve well. Good. (2000–2003)

Forêts 97 – this is also a bit thin, the fruit is there and acidity, and with some length. Could be good given time. (2001–2004)

Beauregards 96–forward flinty nose, full of fruit, minerally, apricots, good balance, very good wine. (2000–2004)

Montmains 96 – minerally appley fruit, reasonable acidity, a bit blousy, dry finish. Nevertheless good wine. (2001–2004)

Wines available from the **CELLAR DOOR** and stockists in:

UK
Bordeaux Direct, Reading, Berks. Tel: 0118 948 1718

DOMAINE BEGUE-MATHIOT

Les Epinottes   Tel: 03 86 42 16 65
89800 Chablis   Fax: 03 86 42 81 54

11 hectares

Production:
Premier Crus   Fourchaume   0.30 ha
                      Vaillons   1.50 ha
                      Vaucoupin   0.45 ha
                      Vosgros   0.15 ha
Chablis Village

This is a fascinating little domaine run by husband and wife team Joel Begue and Maryse Mathiot, a thirty-something couple with an apparent in-built distrust of wine writers – who can blame them?

The domaine can be found behind the town of Chablis on the lower slopes of Premier Cru Vaillons in the location known as Les Epinottes. Sticking out like a sore thumb, the buildings comprise an attractive family house set apart from a barn-cum-factory-like *cuverie* and *chai*. On entering, one is immediately struck by the untidy, apparently disorganised and slapdash operation, where lots of love is lavished on the customers, as it should be. When eventually attention is turned to the nosey journalist, to coin a phrase, getting information is like getting blood from a stone. To complete this profile, we had to telephone three times on our return to London in order to establish further facts.

This small 11-hectare estate includes in its holdings four areas of Premier Cru sites, three of them tiny by any standard, but a fair-sized 1.5 ha chunk of Vaillons on which the domaine rests. Over 8 hectares of Chablis Village completes the portfolio.

All the grapes are harvested mechanically and vinified in stainless steel and enamelled vats packed tightly into the adjoining cuverie. *Elevage* is *en cuve*. The wines are fined with bentonite and given a kieselguhr filtration before bottling in July or August.

Of the total production 90 per cent is destined for the négoce whilst 5,000 bottles are earmarked for the home market.

We are not certain why the Begue-Mathiots were so unwilling to show more than one wine, i.e the one being bought by the customers present. Judging by the quality of this wine, the Vaillons 97, they had no reason to fear. It was delicious. As for being uncommunicative, perhaps we called at an inconvenient moment. We shall call again, it's fun here!

Tasting note
Vaillons 97 – quite a forward wine, fresh fruity nose, minerally fruit on palate, delicious crisp acidity, well balanced, clean finish, lovely after-taste. Very good. (2001–2004)

Wines are available from the **CELLAR DOOR.**

DOMAINE BERSAN

20 Rue de l'Eglise	Tel: 03 86 53 33 73
89530 Saint-Bris-le-Vineux	Fax: 03 86 53 38 45

40 hectares includes 4.5 hectares of Chablis Appellation

Production:

Premier Crus	Montmains	0.50 ha
	Beauroy	minimal
Chablis Village		

Sited at the rear of the eleventh-century church in the picturesque hill town of Saint-Bris-le-Vineux, stands Domaine Bersan, built over cellars originally constructed by the Knights Templar during the Crusades. The buildings, gathered around a cobble-stone courtyard, mostly date from the last century with some modern attachments and additions, but the cellars – restored to use by Bersan Père 30 years ago – remain intact, on two levels, very cold, very extensive, and to us the most fascinating in Burgundy. On our tour, Owen, having left his coat in the car, voiced through chattering teeth his fear of getting lost in the maze of tunnels and caves through which Monsieur Bersan threaded his way so nonchalantly. 'Oh, no problem,' shrugged our host, 'I was practically born down here.'

This fine domaine is run by two brothers, Jean-Louis Bersan and our guide Jean-Francois, two very charming and informative vignerons. The mainstay of the estate is naturally Sauvignon de Saint-Bris which together with Bourgogne Aligoté, Côtes d'Auxerre and Irancy account for some 90 per cent of the production. Chablis is represented by two *cuvées*, basic Chablis with the vineyards located near the village of Préhy, and Premier Cru Montmains of which Bersan has half a hectare.

The harvest is gathered by machine and the grapes receive a slow pneumatic pressing. Vinification is traditional, temperature controlled in stainless steel *cuves* at 20° to 23°C and no wood, despite the array of hundreds of barrels in the cellars, some of which seem to have been lying in the same haphazard positions as if the Knights had dropped them in their hurry to take the fight to Saladin – at least some of them appear that old!

The wines are bottled in April or May following the vintage, and after satisfying the home market, many find their way to the UK. These wines are good and well worth seeking out. The Sauvignon de Saint-Bris is the best we have come across: the 97 and 98 are delicious fruity crisp wines with gooseberry overtones and mouth-puckering acidity – the 97 is the summer house wine at Chez Biss.

Tasting notes
The following wines were tasted at the domaine in February 1999:

Chablis 98 – nice Chablis nose, delicious fruity wine, well-balanced acidity. Good food wine.

Chablis 97 – intense fruity nose, lots of concentrated fruit here with some length, light on the acidity, but a lovely easy drinking basic Chablis. Very impressive.

Montmains 97 – closed nose but mineral character comes through, fair concentration of fruit with reasonable acidity and a mineral dry finish. Good. (2001–2003)

Chablis 96 – this is a lovely wine, minerally honeyed fruit on nose, delicious depth of fruit well balanced with nice crisp acidity, dry long finish. Very good.

Montmains 96 – flowery mineral nose, quite forward, dry minerally steely flinty fruit, long, balanced and delicious. A real Montmains of typicity. Very good. (2002–2004)

Wines are available at the **CELLAR DOOR** and stockists in:

UK
Gallery Wines, N.Ireland. Tel: 028 70833891. Gomshall, Surrey Tel: 01483 203795

Oddbins branches . Tel: 020 8944 4400 Fax: 020 8944 4411 (Sauvignon de Saint-Bris)

H. G. White & Co., Eastbourne, Sussex. Tel: 01323 720161 Fax: 01323 649362

The Wine Shop, Heeley, Sheffield .Tel: 01142 553301 Fax: 01142 551010

DOMAINE BESSIN

Jean-Claude Bessin
Rue des Cours
La Chapelle Vaupelteigne   Tel: 03 86 42 46 77
89800 Chablis   Fax: 03 86 42 85 30

12 hectares

Production:

Grand Cru	Valmur	2.00 ha
Premier Crus	Montmains	3.00 ha
	Fourchaume	2.00 ha
Chablis Village		

Situated in the rustic village of La Chapelle Vaupelteigne, the domaine is well tucked away out of sight under the church, literally under the church for the cellars are buried within the church walls, complemented by the lovely old buildings and modern *cuverie* and *chai* making up this most original of domaine locations.

The domaine was created in 1878 and is now run by Jean-Claude Bessin, an upright friendly man with an easy manner who admits to being a foreigner (he was born in Normandy). His father-in-law sold grapes to Regnard until 1993, since when he has bottled the wines himself with the help of a travelling bottler, usually in September.

The harvesting is manual for the Grand Cru Valmur, Fourchaume and some of the Montmains, the rest by machine. Vinification is divided between stainless steel and enamelled *cuves*. In all this is a very tidy operation.

The total production is 45,000 bottles a year, and export markets include Germany, Holland, Japan as well as the UK and USA. This is a domaine producing good Chablis. The 98s are a knockout.

Tasting notes
The following wines were tasted at the domaine in February 1999, the 98s later in the year in London by courtesy of Morris & Verdin:

Chablis 98 – why can't all Chablis Village wines taste like this? Lovely minerally and nutty nose, bags of fruit, good concentration, crisp acidity, all there. Very good.

Montmains 98 – closed nose, lots of minerals and steel on palate, very good concentrated fruit with intensity, gentle acidity, good length. Very good. (2002–2005)

Fourchaume 98 – very minerally nose, appley and citrus fruit, good concentration and length, slightly bitter aftertaste but should integrate to give a very good wine. Needs time. Very good. (2003–2006)

Chablis 97 – good aroma, lovely fruit if perhaps a little sharp. Good basic Chablis.

Montmains 97 – mineral nose, fruit is there but little else, rather lacks definition, surprising as the vines are partly in Forêts. Good only. (2001–2004)

Fourchaume 97 – floral aromas, fruit slightly bitter on attack, needs more time to settle. Good. (2001–2004)

Valmur 97 – nose totally closed as would be expected, tight fruit but all there, great concentration and depth. Should be very good. (2002–2007)

Chablis 96 – good nose, lovely steely fruit and acidity. Good Village Chablis.

Montmains 96 – lovely nose, minerally, more depth of fruit than the 97, beautifully balanced. Very good. (2002–2006)

Fourchaume 96 – very closed, good concentration of fruit with good length but needs a bit more zip! Good. (2002–2006)

Wines are available from the **CELLAR DOOR** and stockists in:

UK
Morris & Verdin, London SE1. Tel: 020 7357 8866 Fax: 020 7357 8877.

USA
Kysela Père et Fils, Chestnut Grove Road, Winchester VA, 22603.

DOMAINE BILLAUD-SIMON ★★★

1 Quai de Reugny
BP46-89800 Chablis

Tel: 03 86 42 10 33
Fax: 03 86 42 48 77

20 hectares

Production:

Grand Crus	Les Clos	0.44 ha
	Blanchots	0.18 ha
	Vaudésirs	0.71 ha
	Les Preuses	0.40 ha
Premiers Crus	Montée de Tonnerre	2.80 ha
	Mont de Milieu	2.30 ha
	Vaillons	3.50 ha
	Fourchaume	0.25 ha

also various Vieilles Vignes cuvées at these levels

Chablis Village – Cuvée Tête d'Or and Petit Chablis.

This domaine was originally established on a site known as 'Domaine de la Maison Blanche' in 1815 by Charles-Louis Noël Billaud, indeed the original name is still proudly carried by the estate on its literature. The domaine buildings face the River Serein in a delightfully peaceful location yet within easy walking distance of the centre of the town; the new large *cuverie* and cellars are somewhat reminiscent of a military academy and out of character with the fine old houses fronting Quay de Reugny, but are tactfully set back at the rear of the parade ground, leaving the family home to greet approaching visitors from the Quay.

It was not until the end of the Second World War, however, that the estate took off in a big way under the direction of Jean Billaud *fils* and his father-in-law Jules Simon. Jean Billaud's sons André and Bernard continued this family tradition. With the next generation, the domaine moved into the modern technological era, André's son Samuel overseeing the conversion from wood to stainless steel temperature-controlled fermentation vats and wood presses to pneumatic presses. There has not been a complete break with the old ways, for some oak casks have been retained, but the operation is now streamlined, hygienically and technically without losing sight of the traditions of generations past.

Bernard and Samuel now run the operation together from an office at the rear of the house, combining the expertise and flair of two generations

Billaud-Simon, like any estate, has its own particular methods – frost protection from 350-400 burners per hectare, harvesting manually for the Grand Crus and Vieilles Vignes, mechanically for the remainder, natural low temperature *débourbage*, temperature control through all vinification processes with fermentation maintained between 16°C and 21°C. *Elevage* is in oak casks – 60 per cent new – for the special cuvées produced from *vieilles vignes* over 40 years old. There is no refrigeration for precipitation of tartrates. The wines are given a light fining with isinglass or kieselguhr filtration prior to bottling.

This is clearly a well-run operation; we like the style of wines produced by this fine domaine which has now in our estimation moved into the top rank. Billaud Simon regard Les Clos as the masterpiece among their Grand Crus, but their Vaudésir, Preuses and Premier Cru Montée de Tonnerre are all outstanding.

The wines are readily available in the UK and USA as well as being exported generally to Western Europe and Japan.

A three-star estate now well established and one to be recommended. We shall visit again and again.

Tasting notes
The following wines were tasted at the domaine in May 1998 where stated, and February 1999. The 98s were tasted in London in January 2000:

Chablis Tête d'Or 98 – mineral nose, very concentrated fruit, apples and pears, with lovely balance and depth but needs time to come together. Should be very good.

Mont de Milieu 98 – lovely minerally nose and palate, good concentration of flinty appley fruit and good length. Very good. (2002–2006)

Montée de Tonnerre 98 – lovely Chablis nose and delicious appley minerally fruit, good concentration and depth, crisp acidity, very long. Needs time to develop. Very good. (2002–2006)

Chablis 97 – quiet nose, fruit hidden, a bit short. Fair.

Vaillons 97 – little nose yet, citrus fruit, minerally, crisp acidity, dry finish. Good wine. (2002–2005)

Mont de Milieu 97 – gentle nose, good fruit and acidity but lacks a little concentration, dry minerally finish. Good. (2002–2005)

Fourchaume 97 – fragrant and flowery, lovely supple elegant fruit with a hint of *sous-bois* and mushrooms, fine concentration, balance and depth, great length. Very good. (2002–2005)

Montée de Tonnerre 97 – fruity nose, Cox's apples and apricots, well balanced acidity, good concentration and fair length. Very good. (2002–2005)

Mont de Milieu Vieilles Vignes 97 – 40 per cent wood – a little oak on nose but not too obtrusive, lovely concentrated ripe fruit, peaches and mangos, fine balance, lovely wine. Very good/fine. (2002–2007)

Vaudésir 97 – steely fruit on nose but well hidden on palate. Is there enough concentration or depth for the long term? Probably yes, but judgement reserved. Should be good/very good. (2003–2007)

Les Preuses 97 – quinces and friesia on nose, gorgeous fruit, figs and nuts, well-balanced acidity and length, very elegant. Very good/fine. (2003–2007)

Les Clos 97 – closed, immense concentrated fruit, balance, great length. Should be a wine of supreme elegance. Fine. (2004–2009)

Blanchots Vieilles Vignes 97 – 100 per cent wood – gently oaky nose, supple wine, voluptuous fruit, fine balance, delicious acidity, great length and depth. Very good indeed. (2004–2009)

Chablis 96 –closed nose, bags of fruit, apricots, good balance, long, nice aftertaste. Very good. (May 98)

Vaillons 96 – well-developed nose, bags of fruit, minerally and flinty, good depth, acidity and length. Very good. (2001–2006)

Montée de Tonnerre 96 – closed nose but lovely mineral fruit, more intense and concentrated, finely balanced acidity, dry finish, good length. Very good/fine. (2002–2006)

Mont de Milieu 96–greenish tinged, closed nose, good concentrated fruit and acidity, long and lovely. Very good. (2000–2004) (May 98)

Mont de Milieu Vieilles Vignes 96 – 50-year-old vines, 50 per cent inox, 50 per cent oak: 10 per cent new the rest up to 5 years old. Good intensity of fruit, fine depth and concentration on nose and palate, lovely wine. Very good. (2002–2006) (May 98)

Vaudésir 96 – all in inox. bottled December 97. Delicate perfumed nose, fabulous fruit with tremendous length, very long. Fine. (2005-2010) (May 98)

Les Clos 96 – closed up as expected, gentle elegant fruit of great concentration, fine depth and very long. Very good/fine. (2004–2009)

Blanchots Vieilles Vignes 96 – 100 per cent wood 2-4 years old. Oaky nose apparent here but a wine of immense concentration needing time to evolve and integrate the oak. Should be very good. (2004–2009)

Mont de Milieu 95 –not much on nose, but full-bodied wine, some fruit, good balance of acidity, fairly good length, but needs more personality. Good. Drink now. (November 97 in London)

Blanchots Vieilles Vignes 94 –100 per cent in barrel. Lovely bright lemon yellow, brilliantly clear, nuts and biscuits and a little toasted oak, honeyed, intense, big and powerful yet delicious, very long indeed. Very fine wine. (Drink now–2004) (May 98)

Preuses 92 – no oak. Plenty there for the future, lovely wine of depth and concentration, develops an oaky character, honeyed fruit, well balanced. Lovely wine. Very good. Drink now. (May 98)

Wines available from stockists in:

UK

Adam Bancroft Associates, London SW8. Tel: 020 7793 1902 Fax: 020 7793 1897

Bentalls of Kingston, Surrey. Tel: 020 8546 1001 Fax: 020 8549 6163

Berry Bros. & Rudd, London SW1. Tel: 020 7396 9669 Fax: 020 7396 9611 and Basingstoke, Hants. Tel: 01256 323566 Fax: 01256 340106

Ian G. Howe, Newark, Notts. Tel: 01636 704366 Fax: 01636 610502

Longford Wines, Sussex. Tel: 01273 480761 Fax: 01273 480861 e-mail: longwines@aol.com

Montrachet, London SE1. Tel: 020 7928 1990 Fax: 020 7928 3415

Freddy Price, London W5. Tel: 020 8997 7889 Fax: 020 8991 5178 e-mail: freddywine@aol.com

Selfridges, London W1. Tel: 020 7318 3730 Fax: 020 7491 1880

Charles Taylor Wines, London SE1. Tel: 020 7928 8151 Fax: 020 7928 3415 e-mail: charles.taylor.wines@dial.pipex.com

Wine Trading Co., N. Yorks. Tel: 01423 872425

The Wine Society, Stevenage, Herts. Tel: 01438 741177

Noël Young Wines, Cambridge. Tel: 01223 844744 Fax: 01223 844736

USA

Garnet Wines & Liquors, New York, 10021. Tel: 212 772 3211 Fax: 212 517 4029

Hi-Time Wine Cellars, Costa Mesa, California 92627. Tel: 949 650 8463 Fax: 949 631 6863

Langdon Shiverick Inc., 2220 Superior Avenue, Cleveland, Ohio.

DOMAINE DE BOIS D'YVER

Georges Pico-Race
Grande Rue Nicolas Droin
Courgis
89800 Chablis

Tel: 03 86 41 46 38
Fax: 03 86 41 46 39

20 hectares

Production:

Grand Cru Blanchots	small area
Premier Cru Montmain	5 ha
Chablis Village	

The domaine of Georges Pico-Race, whose wife is a distant cousin of Denis Race in Chablis, is located literally at the lower end of the village of Courgis, overlooking a valley of vineyard slopes, a very pleasant outlook if you don't look away. Unfortunately in the other direction the view is less attractive as the domaine's buildings are a large modern industrial complex set on a site more resembling a motor repair garage than a winery. But outward appearances can de deceptive, for within those walls lurks an impressive *cuverie* and *chai* constructed in 1990, and housing an ultra-modern operation producing some 130,000 bottles per annum.

The Pico-Race family have 20 hectares of vines, 5 of which are Premier Cru Montmains. Relatively speaking, this is a young domaine now in its second generation. Georges's father-in-law originally owned a small parcel of land in Chablis to which much was subsequently added to bring the domaine to the size it is today. Following the conventional period of study at Oenology College in Beaune, Georges Pico proceeded to build the domaine's reputation and achievements. His business partner is the charming and elegant Eleana Puentes from Colombia who accompanied us on an extensive tour of the *cuverie*. The soft veneer, however, conceals a very tough cookie underneath – business wise that is! One of the domaine's largest and most important customers is none other than Harrods – the basic Chablis is their house Chablis and at £10.95 a bottle not exactly the bargain of the century, but then it is Harrods! Nobody argues with such a client, although Eleana does have misgivings that such a large regular order from one source has its own commercial dangers. They are clearly very proud of their illustrious client and intent on providing their Chablis, and the best quality possible, for years to come.

The vinification here is largely traditional in temperature-controlled stainless-steel and enamelled *cuves*, each operation under the personal supervision of Georges himself; when we were there he was perched precariously at the top of a very high ladder leaning against one of the tall *cuves* and directing the necessary moves for cooling the over-heating fermentation vessel of the recently harvested 1998 vintage.

A little Blanchots is vinified in wood *barriques*, but this is made from grapes bought in for the purpose. We are not sure where this is sold and none was available for tasting.

In the comfortable showroom-cum-tasting room after the tour, Georges makes his appearance taking over from Eleana who retorts tongue-incheek that having done the hard bit, the tour, Georges takes the easier and tastier part sitting down.

The tasting that followed was somewhat of an anti-climax, the 97s only, Georges exclaiming that all the 95s and 96s have thankfully been sold. All? Nothing left at all? Hmmm! Never mind, the elusive bottles turned up in London, thanks to Enotria Winecellars. Maybe there was a reluctance to show us these wines? Judging by the tasting notes below, any misgivings on Georges's part were totally unnecessary. This is a domaine to watch for in the future.

The wines are marketed in the UK and throughout Europe, Japan and the USA.

Tasting notes

The following wines were tasted in Courgis and London in October 1998:

Chablis 97 – very pale, dumb nose, fair fruit if a little sharp but nothing jumps out of the glass, clean finish though. Fair wine.

Montmain 97 – pale wine with a closed nose as expected, good fruit with some concentration and length, once again clean finish. Tasted again in March 99 – nose opening out but otherwise same note. Good. (2000–2003)

Chablis 96 – perfumed nutty nose, bags of concentrated fruit, almonds, peaches and Granny Smith apples in the nicest sense, a big mouthful of flavour, good depth, balance and length. Is this really only a village wine? Very good indeed. If Harrods have any left, go for it!

Montmain 96 – gentle mineral nose of *typicité*, steely, excellent ripe flinty fruit, green appley and crisp mouth-puckering acidity, very dry, good concentration, balance and depth. Typical Montmain. Needs a little more time. Very good. (2000–2003)

Montmain 95 – quiet nose but with encouragement revealing a floral character, really lovely ripe honeyed fruit, quite forward, good concentration, elegant, long delicious aftertaste. Lacks a little acidity and will not last too long. But very good nevertheless. Drink now.

Wines available from the **CELLAR DOOR** and stockists in:

UK

Enotria Winecellars, London NW10 (trade only). Tel: 020 8961 4411 Fax: 020 8961 8773

Hall Batson & Co., Norwich, Norfolk. Tel: 01603 415115 Fax: 01603 484096

Harrods, London SW1. Tel: 020 7730 1234

Whittaker Wines Ltd, London SW14. Tel: 020 8878 2302 Fax: 020 8876 5580

Wine Importers, Edinburgh. Tel: 0131 556 3601

Wine Trading Co., Harrogate, N. Yorks. Tel: 01423 872425

USA

Touton Selection, NY.

DOMAINE PASCAL BOUCHARD

Parc des Lys   Tel: 03 86 42 18 64
89800 Chablis   Fax: 03 86 42 48 11

32 hectares

Production:

Grand Crus	Les Clos	1.70 ha
	Vaudésir	1.60 ha
	Blanchot	0.75 ha
Premier Crus	Fourchaume	8.00 ha
	Mont de Milieu	5.00 ha
	Montmain	3.50 ha
	Beauroy	4.50 ha
	1er Cru	5.00ha

Chablis Village and Petit Chablis

Pascal Bouchard married into the Tremblay family, and with his wife Joëlle – sister of Lyne Marchive of Domaine des Malandes and cousin to Gerard Tremblay, runs the family estate which now extends to more than 32 hectares. It was in 1979 that they took over André Tremblay's fine family domaine thus securing the continuation and succession through generations of vignerons.

The *cuverie* and *chai* are now based in a very modern but attractive building built in 1995 just off the road to Beines, combining traditional methods with modern technology. Pascal has been encouraged by his domaine's commercial success, and has expanded the business in the *négociant* direction, now vinifying the production of about 160 hectares including his own holding. In addition to the Chablis Appellations, the domaine produces a wide range of Yonne Burgundies.

The emphasis in the vineyards is low yields. The grapes are given a pneumatic pressing, and 10 to 12 hours quiet contemplation in stainless steel *cuves* for *débourbage*. Fermentation in inox is temperature controlled between 18° and 20°C using selected yeasts. The Grand Crus, however, are vinified in *fûts de chêne*, Allier oak of 1 to 4 years of age. After the malolactic fermentation, and ageing 6 months in 3- to 4-year-old wood for the Grand Crus, the wines are fined with bentonite or isinglass, given a *passage de froid* for precipitation of tartrate crystals and a kieselguhr filtration. A second light membrane filtration directly precedes bottling.

As can be seen below, the wines can be good, indeed very good and worth seeking out, which should not be too difficult as 65 per cent of the production is destined for export. A domaine worthy of note.

The domaine also has an excellent shop in the Rue Porte Noël in the centre of the village, right behind the Porte Noël itself.

Tasting notes
The following wines were tasted at the domaine in May 1998 and February 1999, the 98s in London in August 1999:

Chablis 98 – nose of *typicité*, good citrus fruit flavours with balanced acidity, reasonable concentration but finishes a little bitter. Fair.

Fourchaume 98 – fruity nose, citrus fruit flavours with good intensity but a little short. Should improve. Fairly good. (2001–2004)

Petit Chablis 97 – little on nose but lemon fruit flavours and fair acidity. Not too crisp but a good Petit Chablis.

Chablis 97 – Whoof! What a big fruity nose, lots of concentrated fruit, good balance of acidity and a clean finish. Very good wine.

Chablis Vieilles Vignes 97 Grand Réserve du Domaine – from 25- to 45-year-old vines. 30 per cent matured in old barrels for two months. Impressive name and treatment, but the results are rather bland. We preferred the above in every way.

Montmains 97 Grand Réserve du Domaine – 50 per cent old barrels for two months – gentle restrained nose but the minerals and apricot fruit are there, wine reflects the *climat*, well balanced, dry crisp apple finish. This is good. (2002–2004)

Fourchaume 97 Grand Réserve du Domaine – same vinification as above – floral nose comes out with lots of encouragement and warming of glass, good fruit extraction, fair acidity, minerally dry finish. Good. (2001–2004)

Fourchaume 97 Standard cuvée – this lacks some class and style, fruit is a bit bland by comparison with the above, but has a mineral characteristic and gentle acidity. Fair length. Fair/good. (2001–2003)

Vaudésir 97 – 100 per cent old oak barrels for four months. Lovely biscuity nose, bags of ripe fruit here, steel and minerals, long on the finish, good grip, fruit still rather overtaken by oak but a good wine. (2002–2007)

Chablis 96 – lovely discreet nutty nose, good steely fruit and acidity, long. Good.

Fourchaume 96 –closed nose, concentrated minerally fruit, depth and length, a lot there, lovely wine. Good. (2000–2002)

Vaudésir 96 – hazelnuts and Petit Beurre biscuits on nose, big voluptuous wine still rather too oaky but bursting with fruit, fine acidity and length. Very good. (2002–2006)

Blanchots 96 – elegant fruity nose, lots of fruit here, wine of depth and length, lovely clean finish. Needs time to gain more character. Very good but not great. (2002–2006)

Les Clos 95 – reluctant but lovely nose with encouragement, perfumed fruit, a wine of depth and concentration, great length. Very good. (2002–2006)

Wines available from the **CELLAR DOOR** and stockists in:

UK
Albion Wine Shippers, London WC1. Tel: 020 7242 0873
Bablake Wines, Coventry. Tel: 024 7622 8272
Bordeaux Direct, Theale, Berks. Tel: 0118 903 0903 Fax: 0118 903 0130
   e-mail: orders@bordeaux-direct.co.uk
Byron Vintners, Notts. Tel: 01159 704682
European Wine Growers, Nr. Lancaster. Tel: 01524 701723
Hayward Bros., London SE1. Tel: 020 7237 0576
Ian G. Howe, Newark, Notts. Tel: 01636 704366 Fax: 01636 610502
William Morrisons Stores, N. England. Tel: 01924 412303
H. Needham & Sons, Kent. Tel: 01732 740422
O'Neill Fine Wines, Liverpool. Tel: 0151 924 5767
Terry Platt Wines, N. Wales. Tel: 01492 592971
Waterloo Wine Co., London SE1. Tel: 020 7403 7967
Wine World of Cornwall. Tel: 01637 851372

USA
Hi-Time Wine Cellars, Costa Mesa, California 92627. Tel: 949 650 8463 Fax:
   949 631 6863
Opici, 25 De Boer Drive, Glen Rock, New Jersey 07452. Tel: 201 689 1200
   Fax: 201 251 8081

DOMAINE JEAN-MARC BROCARD

Domaine Sainte-Claire
Préhy   Tel: 03 86 41 49 00
89800 Chablis   Fax: 03 86 41 49 09
                                           http://www.aja.tm.fr/brocard

80 hectares

Production:
Own estate
Chablis Premier Cru   Montmains
                           Côte de Jouan
                           Beauregard
                           Vaucoupin
                           Total 1er Cru area   4 ha
Chablis village   55 ha
Petit Chablis   5 ha

Négociant wines:
Grand Crus   Les Clos, Bougros, Vaudésir and Valmur
Premier Crus   Beauregard, Montmains, Vaucoupin,
                           Montée de Tonnerre, Beauroy, Fourchaume

Chablis Vieilles Vignes from vines over 55 years old
Chablis Village and Petit Chablis

Jean-Marc Brocard came to the Chablis region as recently as 1972, having married a *vigneronne* from the village of Saint-Bris-le-Vineux in the Yonne. His first Chablis vintage was the following year, but for now he continued with the overall production of the wines of the Yonne. Between 1980 and 1982 Brocard moved the business to the village of Préhy, centred on the fine fifteenth-century church of Sainte-Claire, built a large modern cellar in 1989 and gave more prominence to the production of the wine of the local appellation.

M. Brocard began his viticultural life with a solitary hectare from his father-in-law Emile Petit, building over a comparatively short span to an impressive 80 hectares plus the successful *négociant* arm. Curiously enough, it was another Petit of no relation, Louis, an experienced *vigneron* guru who is Jean-Marc's guide and inspiration to this day, having made his own Chablis for many previous years using some wood ageing. Stainless steel is now the order of the day, with wood relegated to the 'other wines'. Jean-Marc says that Chablis must retain its steely flinty fresh *typicité*, in the modern tradition.

Visiting Jean-Marc's domaine in Préhy is always a pleasure. Driving up to the ultra-modern complex, you are likely to catch a glimpse of a bundle of black fluff darting across the front of your car, and coming to a halt, two paws and a wet nose appear at the driver's window. At the other end a violently oscillating tail informs you that you have arrived Chez Brocard. The very commercialised *chai* is laid out principally to accommodate customers who in the season visit in droves. It may well also be considered a shrine to Auxerre FC, whose team portraits are plastered all over. His regular attendance at matches with his friends Alain Geoffroy and Jean-Paul Durup may well be called 'blind faith'.

An important factor to M. Brocard is the need to preserve at all costs the characteristics of each vineyard and wine, and the *élevage* and bottling is adapted accordingly. A new cellar built in 1992 with up-to-the minute technology is continually updated, with pneumatic presses, temperature-controlled stainless steel vats, *élevage* on fine lees, fined, filtered and bottled. Mechanical harvesting is adopted throughout the domaine.

This is a source of good easy-drinking Chablis, nothing too pretentious, perhaps lacking that final degree of concentration and personality. They are excellent bottles to consume with seafood and that after all is what wine is about. Don't let popularity put you off, there are some very good wines to be found here, especially the Vieilles Vignes – to be put away for a few years, if you have the patience. This is a domaine worthy of note.

In addition to his holdings of Chablis Appellations, M. Brocard also produces Bourgogne Rouge and Blanc, Irancy, Aligoté, Passetoutgrains, and Sauvignon de Saint-Bris. His Sauvignon de Saint-Bris is outstanding and is proved to age well as evidenced by the tasting note below.

Tasting notes

The following wines were tasted at the London International Wine Trade Fair, May 1999:

Chablis Vieilles Vignes 98 – ripe sweet fruit on nose, good concentration but not very crisp, low on acidity, fairly good length.

Vaucoupin 98 – very mineral nose, good concentration and fair acidity, appley fruit, lovely aftertaste. Good. (2001–2003)

Beauregards 98 – quiet nose, lots of fruit, not a lot of character. Prefer the Vaucoupin. Fairly good. (2001–2003)

Montmains 98 – not a lot of concentration, earthy, finishes short. Fair only. (2001–2003)

Fourchaume 98 – more intensity and a bit more concentration, but a little sour. Fair. (2001–2003)

Montée de Tonnerre 98 – picked late – mineral nose, more concentration, riper fruit, good length, dry and crisp. Good. (2001–2004)

Côte de Jouan 98 – some intensity and acidity, unripe Granny Smiths. May improve. Fairly good. (2001–2003)

Les Clos 98 – some concentration, but not enough for a Grand Cru and short. Judgement deferred.

Bougros 98 – minerally, could be a Premier Cru, not enough concentration or staying power although some length and better aftertaste. Fairly good. (2003–2007)

The following wines were shown at the BIVB/SOPEXA tasting in London, January 1999 and at the domaine in February 1999:

Petit Chablis 97 – little on nose and palate. Not the best of Petit Chablis.

Chablis 97 – minerally on nose and palate, no great concentration but some length. Fair.

Chablis Vieilles Vignes 97 – more concentration here, and more length, good balance. This is a good typical Chablis.

Côte de Jouan 97 – gentle nose, appley fruit, not the greatest concentration (vines only 12 years old) but balanced and crisp. A good Côte de Jouan. (2001–2004)

Beauregards 97 – good typical nose, fair fruit on the palate, green apples, but lacks concentration, fades away. Fair/good. (2001–2004)

Vaucoupin 97 – once again a good typical minerally nose, lots of fruit, concentration, intensity and length. This really is good. Vaucoupin produced some interesting wines in 97, provided of course they are made well. Good. (2001–2004)

Montmains 97 – steely mineral nose but poor concentration on the palate, fades away. This suggests a too high *rendement*. Still, some crisp fruit if rather astringent, may get better in a year or so. (2001–2004)

Fourchaume 97 – a typical mineral nose and flinty palate, fair fruit but not over concentrated. Still, a good wine. (2000–2003)

Bougros 97 – the fragrance wafted out of the glass across the table, lovely concentrated fruit here, but lo and behold falls a bit short again! There is some potential but doubts exist whether this will ever be a great wine. What a pity!

Les Clos 97 – totally closed nose as expected, good concentrated fruit, nice acidity, this wine does have length and fine potential for the future. Will not be an enormous wine, but elegant. Very good. (2002–2007)

The following wines were tasted at the domaine in May 1998:

Petit Chablis 96–very light and ineffective wine. Disappointing.

Chablis Village – various bottlings as named:-

Chablis 96 Chichée – closed and acidic, but fruit is there if a bit bitter on finish. Disappointing.

Chablis 96 Boissonneuse – no nose and bland fruit. Disappointing.

Chablis 96 Malante – 25-year-old vines, most perfumed of the three, balanced fruit and acidity, clean and crisp, long, fair to good.

Chablis Malante Vieilles Vignes 96 – 55-year-old vines, very low yield hence more concentration, deeper coloured, sweet fruit, perhaps not so much acidity therefore less crisp. Fair.

Côte de Jouan 96 – nose of *typicité*, Granny Smiths, good fruit but perhaps a bit sour. Tasted again at London Wine Fair May 98. Not really Premier Cru quality. Disappointing.

Beauregards 96 – fruity appley nose, Cox's, better fruit and length than above and better wine. Tasted again at the London Wine Fair May 98. Fair to good. Drink now.

Vaucoupin 96 – closed nose, crisp and fresh, good fruit and length but a little sour, more flinty and minerally, could develop given a year or two but drink now.

Montmains 96 – completely closed but with encouragement aroma develops in glass, however fruit is still a bit bland and sour. Tasted again at London Wine Fair May 98. Fair to good. This had improved a year later – pale lemon colour, minerally nose with a hint of peaches, good fruit and acidity but not a lot of depth and an element of unripe Granny Smiths. Good length though and some intensity. Can't see great riches for the future but may still improve a bit further. Good. (2000–2003) (July 1999)

Bougros 96 – quiet nose but good fruit on palate, rather short and bland again, Vaucoupin better. (*Négoce* wine). Tasted again at London Wine Fair May 98. Fair. (2002–2005)

Further wines tasted in London and elsewhere in 1998:

Chablis Vieilles Vignes 96 – bright yellow straw, lots of fruit and lots of sulphur too, probably very good but not fair to judge at this stage after bottling. Re-tasted a year later – this has *typicité*, mineral and flinty fruit, but for a 96 VV lacks concentration and it falls short again. Not very impressive.

Les Clos 96 (négoce wine) – deep colour for a young Grand Cru, lovely nose, good viscosity, concentrated succulent fruit, good depth, long delicious finish, will now close up. Very good. (2003–2007)

Côte de Jouan, Cuvé St. Celine 95 – (under the label of Paul Brocard) pale colour, green tinged, lovely fruity nose, good typicité, goodish length, well balanced with fine crisp acidity, a little oak as a base but unobtrusive, gained character in glass. (January 98)

Beauregards 95 – sweet fruit, almost too sweet, good wine but won't set the world alight. Drink now.

Beauregards 95 (under the label of Domaine St. Julien) light straw gold with green tinge, fragrant nose, sweet fruit, good *typicité*, fresh, crisp, very long, fine potential. (January 98)

Chablis 94 – lemon with a green tinge, slight perfume on nose but it needed to be worked, on palate good flinty Chablis character, with depth and concentration, good fruit and acidity, and fair length. Good. Drink now. (December 97)

Montmains 92 – nose of *typicité* but nicely mature, biscuits and apricots, well developed and balanced, clean finish, fair length, powerful wine. Good. Drink now.

Montmains 90 – perfumed intensity on nose, biscuity, more finesse, a bit dry on finish but this has aged well. Good. Drink now.

Sauvignon de St. Bris 89 – lovely mature honey nutty nose, expansive mouthful of flavour, not exactly gooseberries, but very delicious and long. It's amazing how this has stood up. Was mistaken by a well-known MW for Côte d'Or Chardonnay, and a good one. (July 98)

Wines available from the **CELLAR DOOR** and stockists in:

UK
Adnams, Suffolk. Tel: 01502 727222 Fax: 01502 727273
Julian Baker Fine Wines, Essex. Tel: 01206 262358
Balls Brothers, London E2. Tel: 020 7739 1642 Fax: 020 7729 0258

Berkmann's Wine Cellars, London N7. Tel: 020 7609 4711 Fax: 020 7607 0018

Matthew Clark (Grants of St. James's), Bristol. Tel: 01275 891400 Fax: 01275 836726

Justerini & Brooks, London SW1. Tel: 020 7493 8721 Fax: 020 7499 4653 and Edinburgh. Tel: 0131 226 4202 Fax: 0131 225 2351

Longford Wines, Sussex. Tel: 01273 480761 Fax: 01273 480861 e-mail: longwines@aol.com

Le Nez Rouge, London N7. Tel: 020 7609 4711

Oddbins, branches and fine wine shops nationwide. Tel: 020 8944 4400 Fax: 020 8944 4411

Charles Taylor Wines, London SE1. Tel: 020 7928 8151 Fax: 020 7928 3415

Waitrose Direct and supermarket branches in Southern England. Tel: 0800 188881 Fax: 0800 188888

The Wine Society, Stevenage, Herts. Tel: 01438 741177

Noël Young Wines, Cambridge. Tel: 01223 844744 Fax: 01223 844736

Young & Co., London SW18. Tel: 020 8875 7000 Fax: 020 8875 7009

USA

Garnet Wines & Liquors, New York, 10021. Tel: 212 772 3211 Fax: 212 517 4029

Hi-Time Wine Cellars, Costa Mesa, California 92627. Tel: 949 650 8463 Fax: 949 631 6863

Martine's Wines Inc. 1201a Andersen Drive, San Rafael, California 94901.

DOMAINE CHRISTOPHE CAMU

50 Grande Rue
Maligny   Tel: 03 86 47 57 89
89800 Chablis   Fax: 03 86 47 57 98

7 hectares

Production:

Grand Cru	Les Clos	0.07 ha
Premier Crus	Côte de Léchet	0.60 ha
	Beauroy	0.25 ha

Chablis Village, Vieilles Vignes and Petit Chablis

Christophe Camu runs this modest family domaine from his headquarters in Maligny. Four generations precede him, so he has a good foundation on which to build. Two small parcels of Premier Crus Côte de Léchet and Beauroy are complemented by a minuscule area of Grand Cru Les Clos, the bulk of the estate being made up of over 6 hectares of Chablis, including some very old vines in excess of 50 years of age, and Petit Chablis.

The harvest is mostly gathered mechanically and fermentation is in temperature-controlled enamelled *cuves* for most of the Chablis, but a part is vinified and *élevé en fût de chêne* of 2 to 4 years of age. The Premier Crus and Les Clos are also raised in oak. Fining is with bentonite and a kieselguhr filtration precedes bottling in March or April.

The production totals approximately 25,000 bottles per annum with just a very little for the *négoce*. Export markets include the USA, Spain and Japan. UK importers are keenly being sought.

As the tasting notes indicate, there are some good wines to be found here, but taste in the shop first.

Tasting notes
The following wines were tasted in Chablis February 1999, the 98s later in the year in London:

Chablis 98 – flinty mineral nose, good fruit here, crisp green apples, good balance, length and lovely aftertaste. Good.

Beauroy 98 – lovely perfumed nose, citrus fruit flavours but very dry with a slightly bitter finish. Should improve though. Fairly good wine. (2001–2004)

Petit Chablis 97 – good fruit and fair acidity. Good for what it is.

Chablis Vieilles Vignes 97 – little on nose but good fruit and balance, with some concentration. Nice clean finish and aftertaste. Very good.

Chablis 96 – fruity nose but a bit marked by oak. Fair depth and balance. Not bad.

Côte de Léchet 96 – closed on nose but lovely concentration of almost sweet fruit, nicely minerally, well balanced, good length, even some elegance. Very good. (2001–2004)

Wines are available from the well-fitted tasting room and shop at **1 Rue Rampon Lechin** in Chablis. Tel: 03 86 42 44 01

DOMAINE de CHANTEMERLE ★

C.Boudin Père et Fils
27 Rue du Serein
La Chapelle Vaupelteigne   Tel: 03 86 42 18 95
89800 Chablis   Fax: 03 86 42 81 60

15 hectares

Production:
Premier Crus   Fourchaume   5.0 ha
                          L'Homme Mort   0.2 ha
Chablis Village and Petit Chablis

Run by Adhémar and Francis Boudin, this is a domaine with a fine reputation. Adhémar is a typical old-style *vigneron* with a suspicious smile well able to recount the history of the domaine and indeed the history of Chablis itself. He is everybody's romantic vision of a typical French *vigneron*. Father is now joined by son Francis who we suspect runs the operation on a day-to-day basis and well able to counter the ways of the father with the new methods of today. Even a fax machine has been installed.

Situated in the centre of La Chapelle Vaupelteigne, a very rustic village along the Serein just a short drive from Chablis, the domaine's buildings occupy a corner site with entrance to the *cuverie* from the main road and with the family house at the rear of a lovely unmade cul-de-sac. The whole scene could have been lifted right out of *Clochemerle*.

Elusive to contact, at the third attempt father and son received us heartily and were clearly very enthusiastic about the production of the domaine. The *vendage* is completely manual, enamelled *cuves* are used, vinification is traditional, *passage au froid*, bentonite fining, plate filtration and wines not bottled until May following the vintage.

The Boudins were the first to bottle L'Homme Mort, as distinct from Fourchaume. The story of L'Homme Mort as told by Adhémar differs totally from that of Jean Durup and we imagine is more based on folklore. Adhémar's version refers to a battle taking place across the Serein between the forces of the Compte de Champagne and the Compte de Bourgogne which resulted in a bloody massacre in the area of the vineyard. Quite who won the battle became rather difficult to understand in his excited retelling of the events. Which version to believe is up to the listener – 'you pays your money, you takes your Homme Mort' – but as an aside, just look at the river Serein at this point. Any proficient athlete could long jump across with ease; if not, it is hardly deep enough to cause any natural barrier to an invading army. Nevertheless, it is clear that the Boudin L'Homme Mort is a superb wine, as indeed is its rival produced by Jean Durup. The *terroir* is clearly very special, whatever the history.

Most of the wines from this fascinating estate reflect the personality of their maker, elusive and full of character. This is a star domaine.

Tasting notes

The following wines were tasted at the domaine in October 1998 and on a return visit in February 1999 except where noted:

Chablis 97 – restrained nose, good fruit but lacking a little character, good length and aftertaste. A good basic Chablis.

Fourchaume 97 – floral nose of violets, lots of fruit, some length, gentle wine and elegant. Good. (2001–2004)

L'Homme Mort 97 – more minerally than Fourchaume with tremendous concentration of fruit and great intensity, fine depth and balance. A superb wine, very fine and one to keep. (2002–2007)

Chablis 96 –pale green tinged, gentle fruity nose with encouragement, full flavoured on palate, green apples and hay, a lot there to develop. Fine concentrated fruit, weighty, good depth with plenty of character, excellent balance, very long. This is a very good Chablis indeed. (January 98 in London and October 98 at domaine)

L'Homme Mort 96 – a lovely fragrant nose just fading a bit in glass, super minerally fruit, well balanced and long. Needs time. Very good. (2002–2006)

L'Homme Mort 95 – lovely nose, beautiful balance of fruit and acidity, earthy, fine length and depth, a lovely wine. Very good. (2000–2005) (May 98 in London)

Fourchaume 95 – green tinged, floral nose still closed but opening out in glass, gentle elegant wine with good length and lovely aftertaste. Very good. (2000–2005) Tasted in October 98 and February 99 both times as good.

Chablis 94 – What a lovely Village wine, green/yellow tinged, character of new mown hay, great fruit and intensity, good depth, very long. Fine.

Chablis 92 – How well these wines keep! Lovely perfumed nose, fruit and acidity still there in abundance, intense yet elegant. Very good.

Wines are available from the **CELLAR DOOR** and stockists in:

UK

Ian G. Howe, Newark, Notts. Tel: 01636 704366 Fax: 01636 610502
Lea & Sandeman, London branches. Tel: 020 7376 4767 Fax: 020 7351 0275
Majestic Wine Warehouses, branches nationwide. Tel: 01923 816999
Wine Trading Co., Harrogate, N. Yorks. Tel: 01423 872425 Fax: 01423 873435

USA

Branded Liquors Inc., Norwood MA.
Burgundy Wine Co. Ltd., New York. Tel: 212 691 9092 Fax: 212 691 9244
Dionysos Imports Inc., Lorton VA.

Garnet Wines & Liquors, New York, 10021. Tel: 212 772 3211
   Fax: 212 517 4029

North Berkeley Imports, Richmond, CA.
Vintner Select, Cincinnati Ohio.
Willett Distributing Inc., Alexandria, KY.

DOMAINE du CHARDONNAY

Moulin du Patis	Tel: 03 86 42 48 03
89800 Chablis	Fax: 03 86 42 16 49

32 hectares

Production:

Premier Crus	Montmains	3.80 ha
	Montée de Tonnerre	2.12 ha
	Mont de Milieu	0.60 ha
	Vaillons	1.00 ha
	Vaugiraut	1.30 ha

Chablis Village and Petit Chablis

Located at the northern end of Quai Voltaire, the approach to this domaine is through a park driveway running alongside the River Serein, and marked by its name prominently displayed on an old water mill set over the river. This belies the size of the domaine which on entering the barn-type building adjoining the family cottage, leads unerringly from one area to another, and one building to another. Massive construction and development is continuing so as to eventually relieve the rather cramped conditions of the various departments.

The winemaker Etienne Boileau, a charming and accommodating man, secretary of Le Syndicat de Défence de l'Appellation de Chablis under the presidency of Jean-Bernard Marchive, created the domaine in 1987 and initially used the facilities of William Fèvre for vinification and bottling. However since 1993, and with two *associés*, Christian Simon and William Nahan now involved providing extra capital, the domaine is now self-sufficient and clearly expanding rapidly.

Within this conglomeration lurks an impressive operation. Temperature-controlled stainless steel and enamelled vats for vinification with oak *pièces* used for 25 per cent of the Montée de Tonnerre and Mont de Milieu. Most of the Premier Cru vines are 40-60 years old except for Vaugirot and this shows through in the wines.

Production has now reached 180,000 bottles per annum leaving just a little for the *négoce*, and exports go to the UK and Western Europe, Japan and the USA. This domaine is on the up and up and Monsieur Boileau has shown his métier. Certainly a domaine worthy of note, soon to reach star status.

Tasting notes

The following wines were tasted at the domaine in October 1998, the 95s and 98s in London:

Chablis 98 – mineral and gently perfumed nose, citrus fruit flavours, fruit and acidity well balanced, some intensity and good length. Very good.

Montmains 98 – gentle fruity nose but the fruit bursts through on the palate, apricots and peaches, well balanced and concentrated. Very good. (2001–2004)

Montée de Tonnerre 98 – surprisingly more mineral than the Montmains, restrained nose, not as much individuality as the above but good fruit and acidity, well balanced with a clean finish. Good. (2001–2004)

Petit Chablis 97 – terrific perfumed mineral nose, bags of fruit, very dry. Try it with *moules*. A lovely Petit Chablis.

Chablis 97 – lovely floral nose and depth of fruit, beautiful balance with lovely finish. Very good.

Vaugirot 97 – very steely dry elegant wine, full of fruit, all up front. Very good. (2000–2002)

Montmains 97 – closed nose, good mineral flavours, crisp apples, well balanced. A very good wine. (2001–2004)

Montée de Tonnerre 97 – 25 per cent oak. Closed nose, oak noticeable but not overpowering and should integrate well with lots of lovely fruit. Well balanced. Very good. (2002–2007)

Mont de Milieu 97 – lovely mineral nose and flavours here, oak already well integrated. Good balance and length, dry finish. Fine wine. (2002–2007)

Chablis 96 – floral nose, fruit well advanced as *batoné* with lees during *élevage*. Good wine but drink now.

Vaugirot 96 – flowery but steely elegant wine, well balanced, some length, good wine. We like M. Boileau's Vaugirot. (2000–2003)

Vaillons 96 – rather strange nose, perhaps fruit drops, fruity wine, peaches. Needs time. Should be good. (2001–2006)

Montmains 96 – lovely yellow gold colour, closed nose, lots of good ripe fruit, minerally and flinty, nice acidity, needs time. Very good wine. (2000–2004)

Mont de Milieu 96 – lovely nose of *typicité*, fruit in abundance, minerally dry finish, good balance, concentration and length. Elegant lovely wine. From 50-year-old vines, this is Mont de Milieu at its best. Very fine. (2001–2006)

Chablis 95 – brilliant pale gold, some maturity on nose, good *typicité*, lots of lovely fruit, a little nutty, almost sweet, delicious now, reasonable length, well balanced, very good for vintage. (March 98)

Chablis Vaillons 95 – pale lemon, closed nose, succulent fruit, good *typicité*, long, well balanced, elegant wine, very good, still needs time – March 98. A bottle drunk in October 98 showed that the nose had opened out, but revealed a slight lack of depth. Good wine though and drinking well now.

Wines available from the **CELLAR DOOR** and stockists in:

UK

Wine Treasury Ltd, London SW8. Tel: 020 7793 9999 Fax: 020 7793 8080
Champagne & Château, London SW4. Tel: 020 7498 4488 Fax: 020 7498 4499

USA

Hi-Time Wine Cellars, Costa Mesa, California 92627. Tel: 949 650 8463 Fax: 949 631 6863

CHATEAU DE CHEMILLY

c/o Domaine Laroche
L'Obédiencerie
22 Rue Louis Bro
89800 Chablis

Tel: 03 86 42 89 09
Fax: 03 86 42 89 29
e-mail: lorraine.carrigan@domainelaroche.fr
http://www.vinternet.fr/DomaineLaroche

33.73 hectares

Production:

Premier Cru Vosgros	1.27 ha
Chablis Village	29.30 ha
Petit Chablis	3.16 ha

In 1996, Domaine Laroche acquired a one-third holding in Château de Chemilly, a property which at the time of writing is at some future date to undergo extensive renovation. It is located 7 kilometres from Chablis in the village of Chemilly sur Serein within the picturesque valley of the River Serein. During the fifteenth century the village was in the ownership of the Budé family, but the château itself owes its more recent reconstruction to the Count of Villeneuve who was the owner from 1824 to 1902.

The vines have an average age of 22 years and, as at Domaine Laroche, organic methods are employed. Vinification is in stainless-steel tanks temperature-controlled at the low level of 14° to 16°C. *Elevage* takes place in the vat. After the malolactic fermentation has been completed, the wines are transferred to Domaine Laroche HQ for bottling. The whole process is carried through by the Michel Laroche team under the watchful eye and experienced palate of their trained oenologist and quality control manager Florence Gras.

The first vintage here was the 1997 reported below. We trust that the new enterprise goes from strength to strength.

Tasting notes
The following wines were sent to us for tasting in London in March 1999:

Petit Chablis 97 – brilliantly clear, the wine just sparkles in the light, sour appley nose, rather heavy for a Petit Chablis, grapefruit and citrus flavours, but a little short on acidity. We must confess, however, that the wine grows on you. This is good and drinking well.

Chablis 97 – this is disappointing after the wine above. No nose, the fruit is there but it lacks a little acidity and is a bit short. Rather dull and bland.

Vosgros 97 – lovely wine! Minerally fruity nose but a little reticent at this stage. Good intensity, citrus fruits and brioche, well balanced and with good length. This is a real mouthful, refreshing and crisp, feminine in character, drinking well now but will keep for some time. Delicious. Very good. (2002–2005)

At the time of writing, these wines are not available in the UK or USA, but can be bought at Domaine Laroche's **CELLAR DOOR,** i.e. the shop in Chablis town. We are informed that, by the time of publication, some exports to the UK will have taken place.

DOMAINE DANIEL COLBOIS

8 Promenade du Tertre	Tel: 03 86 41 42 86
89530 Chitry	Fax: 03 86 41 45 80

30 hectares, 20 hectares of which is Chablis, the remainder Bourgogne

Production:

Premier Crus   Montmain
                 Côte de Jouan   } 7.5 ha Premier Crus in total
                 Côte de Cuissy

Chablis Village and Petit Chablis

12 kilometres to the south-west of Chablis lies the old fortress town of Chitry-le-Fort, where historically the centre of the main street marked the border between the provinces of Champagne and Bourgogne. Nowadays this is a delightful village with a fortified church nestling in the valley, and reached by a picturesque road from Chablis crossing the A3 Autoroute through a short tunnel.

Domaine Daniel Colbois is situated in the centre of the village, impressive period-timbered buildings tastefully modernised, comprising the office, reception and tasting rooms, the *cuverie* and *chai* surrounding a small courtyard which must have reverberated to the atmospheric sound of horses' hooves not so very long ago.

Daniel's parents and grandparents were *vignerons*, but the domaine was created by Daniel in 1974 starting with just 3 hectares of vines. He hopes that his two teenage sons will eventually follow into the family business.

Most of the vinification here is done in enamelled and stainless steel *cuves*, although some new wood is used for a special cuvée made from 40-year-old vines.

Apart from Chablis Appellations, the domaine also produces a Bourgogne Chitry from Chardonnay, a Bourgogne Aligoté and a Bourgogne Chitry Rouge solely from Pinot Noir grapes. Premier Cru Chablis accounts for the produce of about 7.5 ha, of which Côte de Jouan is the largest area.

The total production averages 260,000 bottles per annum and the markets are spread wide, with 78 per cent exported to the UK, Denmark, Sweden, Germany and the USA. The domaine gives the impression of a very clean commercial enterprise, but unfortunately for us they seem to 'miss the boat' as the tasting notes below clearly indicate. But there are some good wines to be found here.

Tasting notes

The following wines were tasted at the domaine in October 1998 except where stated, the 98s in London August 1999:

Petit Chablis 98 – boiled sweets on nose, good fruit on palate, crisp acidity. Good Petit Chablis.

Chablis 98 – just bottled. Lots of fruit here and fair balance but needs a bit of time to recover from bottling shock. Should be good. (London, May 1999)

Côte de Cuissy 98 – quiet nose but nice fruit and balance, good length, crisp finish. Good. (2001–2003)

Côte de Jouan 98 – very pale colour, dumb nose, some fruit but rather insipid and not up to Premier Cru standard. Not our favourite cru, but Colbois did better with his 97. Fair only. (2001–2003)

Montmain 98 – what a difference! Lovely fragrant nose, good concentrated fruit, good length and depth. Nice finish with a lovely aftertaste. Shows what a competent winemaker can do with the right raw materials! Very good. (2002–2004)

Chablis 97 Val de Mercy – little nose despite the aromatic nature of the vintage, appley flavour but rather sour. Tasted again in London, May 1999, when it had developed to show good fruit base, gentle acidity, good length. Good Chablis.

Côte de Jouan 97 – appley flavour with a bitter aftertaste, not enough fruit extract. Disappointing.

Côte de Cuissy 97 – this is a much better wine with good fruit and better balance of acidity. Good wine for current drinking. (2000–2003)

Premier Cru Prestige Cuvée 96 – mainly from Butteaux vines. Good intensity on nose with lots of concentrated fruit, soft and nutty, very good length. Very good wine: we wish they were all like this! (2000–2003) (London, May 1999)

Montmain 96 – lovely nose, fair fruit extract here but still no length for a Premier Cru.

Petit Chablis 95 – shown first. Quiet nose, appley flavour with slightly bitter aftertaste.

Chablis 95 – lovely nose, flinty fruity and biscuity, big mouthful of flavour, straw and green apples, scrumpy fruit, reasonable acidity for the vintage, good intensity and length. A bottle was drunk with freshly cut home-grown English garden asparagus – none better – delicious! Unfortunately, two hours later, the remainder of the bottle showed a hint of oxidation, betraying a lack of balancing acidity. (June 98)

Montmain 95 – fine nose with some intensity, green apples and newly mown grass, lots of ripe fruit, fair acidity, plenty of character, some length. But like the above wine, there is an underlying weakness in structure, and it cannot all be blamed on the vintage. (June 98)

Montmain 94 – impression of unripe grapes, very sour with unpleasant after-taste. What went wrong here, and why was it shown?

Montmain 93 Cuvée Alexis – new wood very prominent which after 5 years has not integrated although typical Montmain mineral flavour there in the back of the throat. Good wine if you like obvious wood in your Chablis. Drink soon.

Wines available from stockists in:

UK
Anglo-International Wine Shippers, Esher, Surrey. Tel: 01372 469841
Fax: 01372 469816
Village Wines, Bexley, Kent. Tel: 01322 558772
Oxford Wine, Oxford and London. Tel: 01865 820789
The Vineyard, London W14. Tel: 020 7371 6553

DOMAINE JEAN COLLET ET FILS ★

15 Avenue de la Liberté   Tel: 03 86 42 11 93
89800 Chablis   Fax: 03 86 42 47 43

34 hectares

Production:

Grand Cru	Valmur	0.51 ha
Premier Crus	Vaillons	9.60 ha
	Montmains	5.67 ha
	Montée de Tonnerre	2.29 ha
	Mont de Milieu	0.32 ha

Chablis Village and Petit Chablis.

There have been three generations of Collets in Chablis, the first – Marius – married Agnes Pinot whose own ancestors, all *vignerons* in their time, can be traced back two hundred years. Jean Collet, who succeeded Marius in 1952, at that time sold most of his grapes to *négociants*; by 1959 he had begun to bottle and export the wine himself to the USA.

Domaine Jean Collet et Fils was formed in 1979 when Gilles, the third generation son, entered the family business. From small premises in the centre of town, success and expansion led to larger state-of-the-art premises just off the road to Auxerre where traditional methods are combined with new technology. Father Jean died in 1996 and the estate is now capably run by Jimmy Edwards lookalike Gilles, who has a handle-bar moustache and sense of humour to match. Gilles is an extremely busy and elusive man, and it was only on our third visit that we managed to tie him down, but the wait was worth it for he is most erudite in his explanations and descriptions of the processes he employs and, strangely for such a successful *vigneron*, he is full of praise for some of his rivals' wines. All said, he is a delightful and very knowledgeable person.

The Petit Chablis 1996, the best we have ever tasted, and Chablis Village wines together with Premier Cru Montmains are vinified in stainless steel with the Grand Cru Valmur and Premier Crus Montée de Tonnerre and Mont de Milieu all in barrels of one to six years of age. The Valmur is never allowed to stay in contact with the oak for longer than twelve months. Idiosyncratically, the Vaillons is fermented and *élevé* in large wooden *foudres* or Burgundian barrels two to three years old. Another very individual practice is to fine the wines with bentonite during the *passage au froid* – the precipitation of the tartrate crystals.

The wines are given both a kieselguhr filtration and, just prior to bottling, a very light plate or polishing filtration. The timing of the bottling is necessarily varied, March for the Petit Chablis, April or May for the Chablis, June or July for the Montmains and Vaillons, whilst the Mont de Milieu and Valmur have to wait until September or October, unless Gilles considers that an earlier *mise* in July might be better to preserve freshness. The entire programme here is carefully planned with that freshness in mind.

As reported elsewhere in this book, we are not supporters of the use of oak for the vinification and *élevage* of Chablis, except by producers who ensure that its effect is well integrated and to the service of the wine. In our view, oak is acceptable only if the end result reflects the *terroir* of the vineyard. And this is the crux of the matter. Gilles Collet feels that the use of wood serves well those cuvées for which it is used, regrettably we do not always agree. Some readers like oaky wines, and those who do will undoubtedly enjoy such wines and need not hesitate to buy. We have to be more circumspect and report accordingly.

In spite of this general criticism which we fully realise may not be echoed by all Chablis lovers and is certainly not confined solely to Domaine Collet, we very much like this domaine which produces fine wines from year to year with perhaps the occasional blip, readily acknowledged. The Premier Crus are expected to keep from 3 to 6 years, while with proper cellaring of fine vintages 10 to 15 years is expected, especially for Grand Cru Valmur.

This is a star domaine to visit time and again to see how their wines develop with differing *élevage*, as will be seen from the tasting notes below.

Tasting notes
The following wines were tasted in London in September 1999:

Chablis 98 – mineral nose, very very dry fruit, minerals and steel, but lovely fruit indeed, apples and pears, mouth-puckering acidity, good length. Very good.

Montmains 98 – dumb nose but apricots eventually come through, very dry and steely, mineral flavoured fruit and lots of it, good depth, crisp finish. Very good. (2002–2006)

Vaillons 98 – brilliant colour greenish tinged, perfumed nose, lovely concentrated fruit, slight oak background, long lovely finish. Needs time. Very good. (2002–2006)

The following wines were mostly tasted at the domaine in February 1999, but also on our visits in October 1997 and October 1998:

Petit Chablis 97 – little on nose, some fruit and acidity. Fair only. This had improved no end after another 6 months in bottle by February 99

Chablis 97 – nice fruit here, Cox's apples, reasonable balance, Good.

Vaillons 97 – good nose but oak too prominent all round. Good fruit and balance but much too marked by the oak. We found this the same in Octoer 98 and February 99. Fair to Good. (2001–2004)

Mont de Milieu 97 – acacia flowery nose, minerally and flinty, a wine of *typicité*, reflects the *climat*, but aftertaste not quite clean. Good. (2001–2004)

Montmains 97 – closed nose but lovely fruit and acidity here, steely and minerally, good balance and finish. Will get even better. Very good wine. (2000–2004)

Montée de Tonnerre 97 – some oak here but well integrated, minerally, crisp green apples, complex wine, long dry finish, even elegance. Very good. (2001–2004)

Valmur 97 – gently oaky nose, perfumed fruit, fat, lots of concentration here, wine of depth and complexity, long way to go. Very good indeed. (2003–2007)

Petit Chablis 96 – this wine was a real revelation, quite unlike the Petit Chablis often found in supermarkets and larger wine stores in England and France. Real Chablis with good acidity and fruit. Well worth buying either to gently sip as an aperitif or to accompany Coquilles St. Jacques. Retasted many times and still delicious. Very good. (October 97 to January 99)

Chablis 96 – not a patch on the Petit Chablis, no nose, sour appley fruit but crisp. Fair wine. (October 98). This had improved when retasted in London in January 99 with better fruit and aftertaste, but too cumbersome for a standard Chablis. No better than good.

Vaillons 96 – lovely nose, lots of appley fruit and oak should integrate with it. Well balanced wine – malo blocked here. Fair length. Very good. (2002–2006)

Montée de Tonnerre 96 – oak also marks the fruit here, but the fruit extract is good, good balance, a slightly bitter dry finish. Should improve. Good. (2002–2006)

Valmur 96 – oak marks the wine once again but the fruit can take it, good concentration and depth, nicely fat and rich, exotic spices, balanced and long. Very good. (2003–2007)

Montmains 95 – little showing on the nose, rather vegetal in flavour and dull. Fair only. (October 97)

Vaillons 95 – fermented and *élevé* in 3-year-old oak *foudres*. At this stage, the oak is masking the fruit, but this wine has potential, and will benefit from a few more years in bottle. Good to very good. (2000–2002). (October 97)

Valmur 95 – honey, biscuits, grapefruit and a mêlée of citrus flavours, delicious acidity, great balance. Very good. (2001–2005)

Montmains 94 – an entirely different wine to the 95. Showing good fruit with some length, flinty, Chablis *typicité*. (October 97) Retasted many times since, a delicious wine, nose of new mown hay and honey, lovely fruit and acidity, long, lovely mineral aftertaste. Very good. (2000–2002)

Valmur 94 – golden coloured, honeyed fruit and fair acidity but it's on its way out. Disappointing, Fair. Drink up.

Valmur 93 – still some fruit here but little acidity and fading fast. Drink up.

Montmains 92 – expected to be fine and it is. A truly lovely wine of concentration and depth, rich intense fruit, good acidity length and balance. Fine. (2000–2004)

Valmur 92 – another fine example, nuts and honey, hugely concentrated, complex and rich, powerful, very long. Fine. (2001–2004)

Valmur 91 – surprisingly good, with a lovely mature nose of toast, nuts and honey, still some depth of fruit, truffles and *sous-bois*, fair acidity and by no means suffers after the last two wines. Very good. (2000–2003)

Wines available from the **CELLAR DOOR** and stockists in:

UK

Heath Street Wine Co., London NW3. Tel: 020 7435 6845 Fax: 020 7431 9301

Ian G. Howe, Newark, Notts. Tel: 01636 704366 Fax: 01636 610502

Laytons, London NW1 and branches. Tel: 020 7388 4567 Fax: 020 7383 7419 e-mail: sales@laytons.co.uk http://www.laytons.co.uk

Le Picoleur, London W2. Tel: 020 7402 6920 Fax: 020 7402 5066

La Reserve, London SW3. Tel: 020 7589 2020 Fax: 020 7581 0250

Le Sac à Vin, London SW6. Tel: 020 7381 6930 Fax: 020 7385 5513

USA

Robert Chadderdon Selections, Rockerfeller Plaza, New York, NY 10112. Tel: 212 757 8185 Fax: 212 262 7039

Garnet Wines & Liquors, New York, 10021. Tel: 212 772 3211 Fax: 212 517 4029

DOMAINE DU COLOMBIER

Guy Mothe et ses Fils
42 Grande Rue
Fontenay-près-Chablis
89800 Chablis

Tel: 03 86 42 15 04
Fax: 03 86 42 49 67

35 hectares

Production:

Grand Cru	Bougros	1.20 ha
Premier Crus	Fourchaume	2.00ha
	Vaucoupin	1.00ha

Chablis Village and Petit Chablis

The attractive village of Fontenay nestles in the valley between Fourchaume and Montée de Tonnerre just a stone's throw off the road to Maligny. This is rural France at its best: signs direct the visitor to the various domaines. This domaine can be found in the centre of the village, within a rather out-of-character and dominating modern industrial complex surrounding a large distribution yard which includes the family home.

The domaine is now run by young M. Mothe, the fourth generation of family vignerons, who appears to spend as much time on his telephone as in the cellars or vineyards, somewhat lacking in personal communication skills, brusque but nevertheless outwardly friendly. He produces 200,000/ 250,000 bottles a year from his 35 hectares including 1.2 ha of Bougros.

Vinification is in enamelled vats and stainless steel, with *élevage en cuve* for 6 to 12 months. No wood here.

The production is for home consumption and export to UK, Europe and the USA. We gain the impression of a fairly large commercial concern making wines in bulk for supermarkets but with some quality buyers, e.g. Field's Wine Merchants and Goedhuis & Co. in the UK.

Tasting notes

The following wines were tasted at the domaine in May 1998 and February 1999, the 98s in London August 1999:

Chablis 98 – mineral and flinty, fruit is there but not a lot of concentration or depth. Finishes dry.

Vaucoupin 98 – gentle nose, lovely fruit, well balanced with reasonable length. Good wine. (2001–2004)

Fourchaume 98 – similar nose, fruit is there but doesn't show a lot of concentration, finishes a bit short and slightly bitter but should improve with a little time. Fair at present. Needs a retaste. (2001–2004)

Chablis 97 – the four cuvées which make up the assemblage have produced as expected a forward fruity wine, minerally and well balanced, with good length. This is a good basic Chablis.

Vaucoupin 97 – violet creams obvious and flowery, quite concentrated, good light wine. (2000–2004)

Fourchaume 97 – great minerally fruit, acidity and intensity. Should be good. (2001–2004)

Bougros 97 – from 40/50-year-old wines and tastes like it, great intensity of fruit, very good wine (this was the note when tasted in vat). A year or so later some doubts creep in, the concentration of fruit was just not there. Judgement deferred.

Chablis 96 – little on nose but good appley fruit, mineral *typicité*, crisp acidity. Very good.

Fourchaume 96 – this is a big wine, lovely perfumed and fragrant nose, like a box of violet creams, full long delicious wine of depth and concentration, bags of fruit and beautifully balanced, well forward but should have a good long life. The fruit is amazing, a wonderful wine. Very good. (2000–2004) (March 98 in London)

Wines currently available from stockists in:

UK
Asda supermarkets. Tel: 0113 243 5435
Continental & Overseas Wines, Timperley, Cheshire. Tel: 0161 976 3696
Field's Wine Merchants, London SW3. Tel: 020 7589 5753
Goedhuis & Co., London SW8. Tel: 020 7793 7900 or e-mail:
  goodhuis@btinternet.com

USA
Geerings & Wade, Canton, Massachusetts 02021. Tel: 617 821 4152
Jaydor Corp, Millburn, New Jersey.
USA Wine West, 2512 9th Street, Suite 6, Berkeley, California 94710.
Windstock Importers, 1 Lexington Avenue, White Plains, NY 10601.

DOMAINE DE LA CONCIÈRGERIE

Christian Adine
2 Allée du Château
Courgis   Tel: 03 86 41 40 28
89800 Chablis   Fax: 03 86 41 45 75

17.5 hectares

Production:

Premier Crus	Butteaux	1.10 ha
	Montmain	3.60 ha
	Côte de Cuissy	0.90 ha
Chablis Village		

Christian Adine was born in 1949 in the same family house in which he still lives, a house which was the old caretaker's lodge of the eighteenth-century chateau which gives its name to the domaine. His father Maurice was a *vigneron*, now retired, as were his maternal and paternal grandfathers and great grandfathers, truly a family tradition.

The Adine family name can be found on the civil registers at the beginning of the seventeenth century, and it is thought that they were already cultivating the vine at this time. Of Christian's three daughters, Nicole the eldest is destined to take over the domaine. In 1993 the estate was formed into a company EARL Christian Adine with two responsible managers, Nicole and Christian. A shrewd business man, Christian is a friendly man, slightly quizzical, who probably doesn't suffer fools gladly.

The estate has grown rapidly, from a mere 3.77 hectares in 1982 to a healthy 17.5 hectares in 1998, with fine holdings in three Premier Crus, Butteaux, Montmain and Côte de Cuissy totalling more than 5 hectares and over 11 hectares of Village Chablis. Christian points out that the viticulture is normal: he tried organic methods for the three vintages 1992 to 1994, but found it not to be very commercial, adding FF18 per bottle. He comments 'so why bother when only one importer was interested, the expense was not justified.' A sound commercial decision, but we would like to have tasted the results!

Christian describes his Côte de Cuissy as lively and generous for drinking within 5 years, the Montmain as a good keeper developing finesse and elegance, and the Butteaux as racey and round with a delicate bouquet. Different wines for different tastes, but we liked the Montmain in particular.

A new chai and vinification plant was constructed in 1989 only a short distance away, fitted out with a Vaslin mechanical press, and temperature-controlled stainless steel and enamelled *cuves* — fermentation is generally held at about 20°. There is no wood here, except in the new roof. Precipitation of the tartrates is by refrigeration and a membrane filtration precedes bottling (April to July depending on the cuvée and conditions) by a travelling bottler.

The resulting wines are of high quality, with good *typicité*, and sold 25 per cent in bulk to the *négoce*, 15 per cent in bottle to the domestic market, and the remainder exported to Asia and Europe.

A well-organised estate, a good source and well worth seeking out. This is a domaine worthy of note which we would expect soon to reach star status.

Tasting notes
The following wines were tasted at the domaine in May 1998 and February 1999 except where stated:

Montmain 98 — already nutty and biscuity, delicious wine, lots of concentrated fruit, good acidity and length. Very good. (2002–2005) (London, August 99)

Chablis 97 — one month in bottle, rather austere fresh fruity wine with a clean finish. Good.

Côte de Cuissy 97 — rather bland wine of little depth but pleasant enough. Should this be a Premier Cru? Disappointing.

Montmain 97 — mineral bouquet, typical Chablis, flinty fruit, good acidity. Good. (2000–2003)

Butteaux 97 — bright yellow colour, gentle fruit, burst of exotic flavours, delicious. Very good. (2001–2004)

Chablis 96 — pale yellow/greenish tinged, good youthful nose, good fruit and acidity with some depth, long. Lovely village wine, delicious. Very good. (April 98 in London and May 98 at the domaine)

Montmain 96 — bright yellow, little on nose, just a tiny amount of sulphur from the recent bottling, soon disappeared, bags of concentrated fruit bursting out, Granny Smith apples, good depth and length, fine balancing acidity, delicious wine, really lovely. Fine (2000–2004) (April 98 in London and May 98 at the domaine)

Wines available from the **CELLAR DOOR** and stockists in:

UK

Laytons, London NW1 and branches. Tel: 020 7388 4567 Fax: 020 7383 7419 e-mail: sales@laytons.co.uk http://www.laytons.co.uk

USA

Vigneron Imports, Oakland, California. Tel: 510 530 1616 Fax: 510 530 2325

DOMAINE DE LA COUR DU ROY

Mignard

40 Rue Auxerroise   Tel: 03 86 42 12 27
89800 Chablis   Fax: 03 86 42 49 32

6.6 hectares

Production:

Chablis Grand Cru	Bougros	0.50 ha
Chablis Premier Crus	Vaillons	2.50 ha
	Montée de Tonnerre	0.38 ha
	Les Lys	0.25 ha
Chablis Cour du Roy 'Cuvée du Domaine' and Village		

This is a small family domaine run by Christian Mignard a sprightly 60ish years young, with a history going back three generations. Christian and his wife Lucette effectively control the everyday running of an estate boasting some very fine crus of which they are justly proud. A period of ill health made this work difficult, and they have the worry of succession as at present this lovely couple do not have any family members willing to take over. On our return visit, we were delighted to see Christian in better form, darting hither and thither and enjoying the tour of the domaine himself. Their small house down a narrow lane just off the Rue Auxerroise in the Rue du Foulon is immediately opposite the *cuverie*, and despite all his troubles he is very welcoming and accommodating.

The winemaking process is fairly traditional – temperature-controlled vinification in enamel-lined *cuves*, *élevage* for 8 to 10 months with a light filtration prior to bottling. However, Christian is at pains to point out that chaptalisation is kept to an absolute minimum, usually less than 2 grammes per litre, which is indicative of ripe, healthy, late-picked fruit.

Depending on the vintage, the Grand and Premier Crus have good ageing potential. Although the general results are rather patchy, there can be some good wines here. Taste first if you can.

The domaine sells most of its wine to the French restaurant establishment, but also exports to Belgium, Holland, Germany, Spain, Switzerland and a little to the UK.

Tasting notes

These wines were tasted at the domaine in May 1998 and February 1999, except as stated:

Chablis 97 – very pale lemon colour, the fruit is there but rather bitter, lacks a little acidity. Fair only.

Montée de Tonnerre 97 – very pale colour again, closed on nose, some fruit but no great concentration or depth. Difficult to believe this is Premier Cru quality. (2000–2003)

Chablis Cuvée Cour du Roy 96 – this is really rather good, pleasant fruity nose, some intensity, fat wine, quite voluptuous fruit, apricots and honey, well balanced, nice aftertaste. Very good. (March 99)

Bougros 96 – closed nose and also on palate, does not appear too concentrated. Difficult to see what's there for the future. Judgement deferred.

Vaillons 95 – good fruit, some acidity, good for the vintage and easy drinking. Drink now.

Les Lys 95 – dumb nose, good fruit and balance, tails off a bit but a lovely aftertaste, also good for the vintage and a good food wine. Drink now.

Bougros 94 – still closed up, fruit and acidity there, somewhat strange aftertaste, but could blossom out. (2000–2004)

Wines are available from the **CELLAR DOOR.**

DOMAINE JEAN-CLAUDE COURTAULT

Domicile:
4 Rue du Moulin
Maligny
89800 Chablis
Tel: 03 86 47 44 76

Cuverie & Chai:
1 Route de Montfort
Lignorelles
89800 Chablis

14 hectares

Production:
Chablis Village and Petit Chablis

Monsieur et Madame Courtault run this small estate from their home, a lovely corner house close to the Château de Maligny and the River Serein, in a picture-postcard setting, but the *cuverie* and *chai* are situated in the village of Lignorelles a couple of miles up the road to which the visitor is directed. The working hub of the domaine is located at the top of a hill above the village in well fitted functional buildings newly erected in 1995.

The approaching guests are greeted by the Courtault's black Labrador who then proceeds to indicate the side door for access to his master. Jean-Claude, President of the Syndicat de la Yonne, is an amiable talkative man who planted up the estate in 1984, in principally Beines, Lignorelles and Villy, producing his first vintage in 1989. Examples of yields are an average of 60 hl/ha in 1997 and 45 hl/ha in 1994 despite the frost.

Vinification here is fairly traditional – pneumatic pressing of the grapes, temperature-controlled fermentation in stainless steel and enamel *cuves*, *passage au froid*, bentonite fining and a kieselguhr filtration with bottling July to September. Jean-Claude admits to a 30 per cent blocking of the malolactic fermentation in 1997.

However, what is disturbing is the experimentation with oak barrels, 15 of them, of French and American provenance. One must remember that this is a Chablis and Petit Chablis estate only, and with the one exception of Alice et Olivier de Moor in Courgis, oak involvement is a risky practice. The lower appellations do not need and generally cannot support oak. Even without the influence of wood, we cannot at present wholly enthuse about these wines. A pity, for the expertise and enthusiasm are here.

Of the total production, 40 per cent is sold to the *négoce*, while the remainder is for home consumption and export to the UK, Belgium, Holland, Austria and Japan.

Tasting notes

The following wines were tasted at the domaine in October 1998, except as stated:

Chablis 98 – some fruit but not very intense on nose, mineral characteristics but no great concentration and a little sulphur. Fair only. (August 99, London)

Petit Chablis 97 – atypical perfumed Petit Chablis, good fruit, well made but no more.

Chablis 97 – rose petals on nose but sour apples on palate. Not a good wine.

Chablis 96 – better nose, more minerally, more fruit, good balance but rather ordinary.

Petit Chablis 95 – little on nose but good fruit on palate, a little petillante but very drinkable, a good Petit Chablis. (May 98, London)

Chablis 95 – little on the nose, sulphur on the palate. Disappointing.

Chablis 92 – golden colour, honeyed nose, had good intensity of fruit but short finish and now past its peak.

Wines available from the **CELLAR DOOR** and stockists in:

UK
Mayfair Cellars Ltd, London EC4. Tel: 020 7329 8899 Fax: 020 7329 8880

DOMAINE DANIEL DAMPT ★

17 Rue de Champlain		Tel: 03 86 42 43 27
Milly 89800 Chablis		Fax: 03 86 42 46 41

25 hectares

Production:

Chablis Premier Crus	Beauroy	0.50 ha
	Côte de Léchet	4.30 ha
	Fourchaume	0.50 ha
	Vaillons	4.70 ha
Chablis Village		

Occupying a modern single-storey building (plus basement cellar) the domaine is located on the edge of Milly surrounded by vineyards and with a lovely view of Chablis itself and the Grand Crus behind. This is an up-to-date operation rapidly gaining in reputation and knocking on the door of two-star status.

Run by a husband and wife team, this domaine has an impeccable pedigree, as the charming Madame Dampt is none other than the daughter of Jean Defaix, a long-established and well-respected producer and head of the Defaix dynasty of Milly. Daniel Dampt has been in charge here since 1986.

The history of the domaine goes back to the beginning of the nineteenth century when some *vignerons* from the Dampt and Defaix families earned their living from agriculture, viticulture and *élevage*, often all three together. By the dawn of the twentieth century, it was apparent that Phylloxera had totally destroyed the vineyards of the region. Cultivation of the vine was abandoned, and the growers turned mainly to agriculture. With the arrival of the Great War, much of the land became fallow and unexploited. Then over a period of some 50 years, the Chablis Vignobles, little by little, were reclaimed: Jean Defaix, whose parents had a small piece of land, was one who chose to re-establish viticulture.

Purchasing some fallow land, he put it back into condition, and replanted. This was an uphill struggle even though latterly facilitated by mechanisation, but hard work was a very important investment at this time and was eventually repaid.

Daniel and his wife came on to the scene in the 1980s to continue the enterprise. They replanted about 10 hectares of vineyard and constructed the buildings which now head an estate of some 25 hectares of vines, with basic Chablis Appellation – their Chablis is anything but basic – and Premier Crus Vaillons, Beauroy, Fourchaume and particularly Côte de Léchet whose splendid slopes can be seen from the *chai*, and receives the ultimate expression of Chablis *typicité*, finesse and elegance in their capable hands. Daniel gives Côte de Léchet as his preferred Premier Cru – he says this always allows him some bottles to keep and drink later, much later. We agree that they do age beautifully.

Vinification, solely in stainless steel, is personally supervised by Daniel who believes that Chablis should not be vinified in wood as its individual taste of *terroir* is sufficient in itself without the addition of oak.

The Dampt family enterprise should continue to prosper as their two sons Vincent and Sebastien wish to follow in their parent's footsteps; the elder Vincent is at the Lycée Viticole de Beaune and the younger son will follow him very soon.

Domaine Dampt adheres to family traditions, aided by modern know-how and common sense. The style of the wines is for rich fruity flowery authentic Chablis, *vins de garde*, and invariably this is achieved by attention to detail in the vineyard and *cuverie*, low yields, careful selection, and more than just an eye to quality production, with personal supervision throughout all the processes.

Undoubtedly a star domaine, this is one of the great Chablis estates. Delightful people, delightful wines!

Tasting notes
The following wines were tasted at the domaine in October 1997 and February 1999 (the 97s) plus others as stated. The 98s were tasted in London:

Chablis 98 – gentle nose but lovely fruit here, good concentration and some length. Good Chablis.

Vaillons 98 – gentle nose again, fruity palate, lovely concentration and depth with a very dry mineral finish. Very good. (2002–2005)

Beauroy 98 – discreet nose, lovely fruit with mouth-puckering acidity and good length. Very good. (2002–2005)

Côte de Léchet 98 – quiet nose, absolutely delicious exotic fruit flavours, steely, long, clean and elegant. This wine sings. Daniel at his best. Fine. (2002–2006)

Chablis 97 – nice floral nose and palate, dry and minerally, long and stylish basic Chablis. Very Good.

Vaillons 97 – closed nose, good concentrated minerally fruit and acidity, steely but not a lot of length. Good only. (2001–2004)

Beauroy 97 – quiet nose, lots of lovely fruit here, a bigger wine, good balance, length and depth, clean finish. Very good. (2002–2005)

Côte de Léchet 97 – what a lovely Premier Cru, and how well Daniel expresses it! Gentle nose as yet, lovely mineral fruit with splendid balance, crisp and very long. Fine. (2002–2007)

Fourchaume 97 – gentle floral nose, ripe fruit, round wine with good concentration, good acidity, long. Very good. (2002–2007)

Chablis 96 – good steely acidity and fruit, fine balance, a lovely wine. (October 97/November 97/April 98)

Beauroy 96 – wine of depth and concentration, lovely fruit, very stylish (October 97) – closed up since tasting at the domaine, but still shows to be a wine of depth and concentration, really lovely fruit and a very stylish wine. This is for the long term. Exquisite. Fine. (2001–2006) (April 98)

Côte de Léchet 96 – closed nose as to be expected, lighter in style than the Beauroy, flinty, hidden depth of fruit and acidity, nice clean finish, well balanced, very good wine and will get better. Very good. (2001–2005) (October 97/November 97/October 98))

Vaillons 96 – closed nose, minerally flinty wine, good fruit, rich concentration but very dry. Long. Needs 2/3 years at least. Very good. (2002–2006) (Feb 99)

Fourchaume 96 – closed again, round fat wine with lots of ripe fruit, well balanced, terrific length. Lovely wine. Fine. (2002–2006) (February 99)

Vaillons 95 – youthful appearance, but some maturity already, old viney, raisiny in the nicest sense. Needs time. Should be very good. (2001–2004) (October 97)

Côte de Léchet 95 – classic Chablis, steely, flinty mineral character with lovely fruit, voluptuous, wine of depth and concentration. Absolutely delicious. Fine. (October 97) Retasted on many occasions – virtually same note as when tasted at the domaine, a really lovely wine, one of the best for the vintage, classic Chablis, steely, flinty, minerally, lovely fruit, voluptuous, classy, intensity, depth and concentration. Absolutely delicious now. The Côte de Léchet really is a wonderful Premier Cru. (2000–2003) (Bedford Fine Wine Club tasting March 98 and London May 98 at CSWS)

Chablis 94 – lovely biscuity nose, big mouthful of fruit with some length, terrific acidity for the vintage – a lovely wine! Very good. Drink now. (May 98)

Vaillons 92 – this is what a Premier Cru Chablis should taste like after five years, full flavoured, buttery, nuts and toast, developing oaky characteristics without the vanilla pods. Lovely wine. Very fine. (Drink now to 2002) (October 97)

Wines are available from stockists in:

UK
Daniel Dampt label –
Bacchus 'Les Vignobles de France', – London SW12. Tel: 020 8675 9007
Ballantynes, S. Glamorgan. Tel: 01446 774840 Fax: 01446 775253
Haynes Hanson & Clark, London SW1. Tel: 020 7259 0102 Fax: 020 7259 0103 and Stow-on-the-Wold, Glos. Tel: 01451 870808 Fax: 01451 870508
Playford Ros Ltd, Thirsk, Yorks. Tel: 01845 526777 Fax: 01845 526888
Waters of Coventry, Coventry, Warks. Tel: 01926 888889 Fax: 01926 887416

The Vine Trail. Hotwells, Bristol. Tel: 0117 921 1770 Fax: 0117 921 1772
Jean Defaix label –
Georges Barbier of London, London SE12. Tel: 020 8852 5801 Fax: 020 8463 0398

USA
T. Edward Wines, 66 West Broadway, New York, NY 10007.
Michael Skurnik Wines Inc., 575 Undermill Boulevard, Syossett, New York 11791. Tel: 516 677 9300

DOMAINE EMMANUEL DAMPT

3 Rue de Tonnerre   Tel: 03 86 54 49 52
89700 Collan   Fax: 03 86 54 49 89

15 hectares

Production:
Chablis Village

The pretty village of Collan is best reached from Chablis through Fleys on the Tonnerre Road and then up through a winding undulating road passing woodland and open farmland before descending down into Collan.

The domaine fronts the main road quite prominently, and the whole scene could very well be lifted out of a brochure advertising summer walking holidays in the Tyrol, wooded, hilly and deserted. The stone-built house has a delightful tasting cellar below, but the *cuverie* and *chai* are located elsewhere at the top of the village.

Emmanuel Dampt, a cousin of Daniel Dampt in Milly, followed his father Bernard into the business in 1989. Whereas previously the wine had been sold to the *négoce*, he now sells some 50,000 bottles annually, to the home market and exports to the UK through Direct Wine – we found it advertised by the Sunday Times Wine Club. Other markets include Belgium, Denmark and Germany.

A personable young *vigneron*, whose ambition is to make his way in this world, Emmanuel is very definite about his methods whilst maintaining a pleasant air of modesty mixed with pride at his achievements. He carries out his vinification in stainless steel although some polyester *cuves* are used for the alcoholic fermentation using both indigenous and added yeasts.

The age of the vines vary between 15 and 30 years the oldest vinified separately, and the various cuvées are blended to produce his best available wine. Being situated in the Tonnerrois Vignoble, he also produces a Bourgogne Tonnerre for which he has won many medals.

When we arrived at the domaine, he was awaiting a party to visit for a group tasting, so he is obviously very commercially minded as well as a good winemaker.

Tasting notes
The following wines were tasted at the domaine in February 1999:

Chablis 97 – nose rather hidden, as is the fruit, it is there but needs a bit of time to show, should improve. Fair/good.

Chablis 97 cuvée Prestige – wine from vines in Fyé close to Fourchaume. Rather tight but good fruit and acidity, dry finish. Much preferred to the basic Chablis. Good wine.

Chablis 96 – lovely perfumed nose, quite different to the 97, pear-drop flavours, more austere but will be lovely when it comes through. Very good.

Chablis 95 – a little honey on the nose, lovely balanced wine and drinking well. Good plus.

Chablis 94 – honey and hazelnuts, very good fruit which has held up well for the vintage. Good wine.

Wines are available at the **CELLAR DOOR** and in the **UK** through: Domaine Direct, London WC1. Tel: 020 7837 1142

DOMAINE JEAN et SÉBASTIEN DAUVISSAT

3 Rue de Chichée   Tel: 03 86 42 14 62
89800 Chablis   Fax: 03 86 42 45 54

9 hectares

Production:

Chablis Grand Cru	Les Preuses	0.75 ha
Chablis Premier Crus	Vaillons	3.33 ha
	Séchet	0.44 ha
	Montmains	1.22 ha
	1er Cru cuvée	1.37 ha
Chablis Village		

Domaine Jean Dauvissat was established in 1899 and is centred on the seventeenth-century family house and cellars in the Rue Chichée. The cellars were enlarged and improved in 1987-88 and father and son welcome visitors for impromptu tasting and purchasing of their fine bottles.

The estate now extends to more than 9 hectares, with an average vine age of between 15 and 35 years, except for the Vaillons Vieilles Vignes Cuvée which is from vines planted in 1932. The largest holding is in Vaillons, over 4 hectares, the mainstay of the domaine. The other wines which make up the portfolio are fine examples of their origin and have been frequently mentioned in dispatches, especially since 1990. Cuvée Saint-Pierre is a Premier Cru cuvée. A short blip in the mid-1980s was soon overcome – Sébastien mentions that mechanical harvesting began in 1987 with very good results. Modernisation has taken place – electric press, pumps, fermentation in stainless steel; however, *en fut* for the Vieilles Vignes and Grand Cru. The oak used is Tronçais. Dauvissat still believes that filtration advances the wine too much and risks stripping the fruit of its freshness, so it is only used if absolutely necessary after fining with bentonite.

Sébastien emphasises that it is necessary to try to take the best of progress, respecting the Appellation, and not to take the easy way out. A refreshing attitude.

The domaine has not always enjoyed a good press, perhaps suffering under the weight of its illustrious namesake's reputation. All this is changing, and the name of Jean et Sébastien Dauvissat is a Chablisien name to reckon with. A domaine worthy of note.

Markets for the wines include the UK, Germany, Belgium, Switzerland, Japan and USA.

Tasting notes
The following wines were tasted at the domaine in February 1999:

Chablis 97 – good fruit, balance and acidity, a good basic Chablis.

Vaillons 97 – closed, Cox's apples, good balance, dry mineral finish. Good wine. (2002–2005)

Séchet 97 – quite closed, and the fruit is rather reticent, this needs time to show its paces. Balanced with some length. Good. (2002–2004)

Montmains 97 – closed, very minerally, lacks some concentration, dry finish. Fair. (2002–2004)

Vaillons Vieilles Vignes 97 – closed on nose but concentrated fatter fruit here, appley but a little bitter, steely minerals, fairly good length as the fruit takes over. Good. (2002–2005)

Preuses 97 – gentle perfumed flowers, this is a bigger wine, concentrated fruit, long and balanced. Good/very good. (2003–2007)

The following wines were tasted at the domaine in May 1998:

Montmains 96 – floral and minerally nose with some oak, good fruit of depth and concentration, good length, fresh and clean finish, good wine. (Now–2004)

Vaillons Vieilles Vignes 96 – 40 per cent vinified in wood and it tells on nose, not yet integrated. Fruit and acidity, clean finish and fine aftertaste, Vieilles Vignes concentration and intensity. Will it integrate? Only time will tell! Should be good. (2000–2005)

Preuses 96 – perfumed wine, oak already integrated, masses of fruit, will be an elegant and lovely wine. Very good. (2002–2006)

Chablis 95 – musty nose, bitter taste, some fruit and acidity but not to our liking.

Vaillons 95 – dumb nose, good fruit and length, good concentration and intensity, clean finish. Fair. Drink now.

Montmains 95 – how a Premier Cru should be when young, pale straw with developing flowery fragrant nose, big long full and fruity, plenty of underlying depth, fine balance. Fine. Retasted in London August 98 – a delicious wine. (Now–2004)

Wines available from the **CELLAR DOOR** and stockists in:

UK

John Armit Wines, London W11. Tel: 020 7727 6846

Enotria Winecellars, London NW10 (trade only). Tel: 020 8961 4411
   Fax: 020 8961 8773

Nicolas, branches nationwide. Tel: 020 7436 9338

USA

Calvert Woodley, Washington DC. Tel: 202 966 4400 Fax: 202 537 5086

Hi-Time Wine Cellars, Costa Mesa, California 92627. Tel: 949 650 8463 Fax: 949 631 6863

Neal Rosenthal, Select Vineyards, PO Box 658, Route 83, Shekomeko, New York 12567.

DOMAINE RENÉ et VINCENT DAUVISSAT ★★★

8 Rue Emile-Zola	Tel: 03 86 42 11 58
89800 Chablis	Fax: 03 86 42 85 32

11 hectares

Production:

Chablis Grand Crus	Les Preuses	1.0 ha
	Les Clos	1.7 ha
Chablis Premier Crus	Forest	4.5 ha
	Séchet	0.8 ha
	Vaillons	1.4 ha
Chablis Village and Petit Chablis		

The name of Dauvissat is a very old Chablisien name, dating back probably to the sixteenth century. The Dauvissat family had always been in wine, at least they had always worked the vine – Vincent Dauvissat muses that his great-great grandfather had been a *tonnelier*. The domaine was created by his grandfather Robert, who as a *vigneron* wished to produce and market his own wines and, beginning with the 1931 vintage, he managed to place his bottles with the Paris restaurant establishment.

Since then, father René has developed the vineyard holdings, and still holds to the same philosophy: love of a fine craft, faith in the vineyards and the *terroir*; respect of the vine, the vintage, and the end product is paramount. Vincent, who joined his father in 1976, has this same approach.

The family home and *cuverie* in Rue Emile-Zola is well hidden from public gaze and hard to locate, only an old barrel-end bearing the name of Dauvissat in fading letters gives any clue to what treasures may be found beyond – this may be augmented in February by a bunch of coloured balloons announcing a birthday party for Vincent's young daughter.

The vaulted cellars with its array of old barrels are very similar to Raveneau's, just a stone throw away, perhaps announcing that they both contain supreme examples of the winemaker's art.

This superb domaine now cultivates some 11 hectares in total, divided between the four appellations, Grand Crus Preuses and Les Clos, Premier Crus Forest (part of Montmains), Séchet (part of Vaillons) and Vaillons itself. Chablis Village accounts for a little over a hectare, and there is a small amount of Petit Chablis to complete the holding. The annual production is generally about 70,000 bottles depending on the vintage. Vincent will not be drawn on which he considers to be his best *climat*, merely that each has its own character and *typicité*. We rate his Les Clos as an outstanding Grand Cru; of his Premier Crus, Forest is not only the largest holding but clearly his best as the tasting notes clearly indicate.

The average age of the vines remains a constant 39 years. This stems mainly from a *sélection massale* and grafting with *greffes précoces:* clonal selection is now down to just 10 per cent *portes greffes* – 161.49 with a little SO4 and 41B. Fruit of the finest maturity is the aim, and the harvest is hand picked. We are told that the rendements during good years is 50 hectolitres per hectare for the Grand Crus and 60 for the Premier crus, but inevitably this varies from year to year due to climatic conditions. We find it hard to understand how these high yields produce wines of such tremendous quality – maybe Vincent's comments on his rendements were a little tongue-in-cheek!

Vinification is the simplest possible. Pneumatic pressing of whole bunches, fermentation – part in enamelled steel vats, part in barrel. Following *assemblage, élevage* is from 6 months to a year in 6- to 8-year-old wood – average age – to encourage the tartrates to crystallise during the cold months.

The results are spectacular, and the fine restaurants of Paris are still a major outlet. Ravishing wines! If at all possible, these wines get better and better with each year and Vincent Dauvissat's reputation as a high flyer with Domaine Raveneau is more than ever fully justified. A three-star domaine plus.

(The production is also sold under the name of Dauvissat-Camus. Laurent Tribut is a brother-in-law of Vincent Dauvissat and some bottles may bear his name.)

Tasting notes
The following wines were tasted at the domaine in February 1999 in bottle, and also earlier in cask in May 1998:

Petit Chablis 97 – oh! the fruit of this Petit Chablis, and wonderful intensity. A model example. Brilliant.

Chablis 97 – lovely aromatic nose, fruit and acidity, good length, drinking well now. After bottling, the nose closed up and a little oak was apparent but this will go. Very good.

Séchet 97 – gentle floral nose, quite tight but lovely luscious concentrated fruit, well balanced, wine of finesse and elegance. Very good/fine. (2003-2010)

Vaillons 97 – minerally and floral *typicité*, dry steely flinty fruit, fat, long dry crisp finish, delicious acidity, this had certainly opened out from when tasted in barrel. Fine. (2003–2008)

La Forest 97 – more closed on nose, elegant soft fruit, immense concentration and depth, a big wine for the future, lovely fruit and balance, complex, long, delicious. Fine. (2003–2008)

Les Preuses 97 – intense nose of complexity, flowers, mushrooms and sousbois, so much there, long and complex, lovely balance, but starting its hibernation – let it sleep. Very fine. (2004–2010)

Les Clos 97 – already asleep but spices on nose, once again all there, rich intense concentration yet refined, great depth, wonderful length and elegance. Very fine. (2005–2012)

The following wines were also tasted at the domaine in May 98 except where stated:

Petit Chablis 96 – lovely biscuity nose, great *typicité* and intensity.

Chablis 96 – fruity nose, like someone else's Premier Cru, lovely fruit, quite forward, terrific length for a village wine. Very good.

Séchet 96 – toasted oak and hyacinths, what a lovely wine! Minerally fruity and long, very long. Fine. (2002–2006)

Vaillons 96 – more closed on nose, intense fruit and good acidity, not quite up to the Séchet standard, but very good. (2002–2006)

La Forest 96 – wonderful complexity and intensity, gentle oak on nose, biscuity, full of fruit and balanced, long, another fine example. 6 years. Very fine. Star wine! (2004–2010)

Les Preuses 96 – no oak, more ordinary on palate, needs time, perhaps a sleeping giant. Tremendous aftertaste. Fine. (2004–2008)

Les Clos 96 – apricots on nose, a little more open than the Preuses, fabulous fruit, this will last and last. Don't touch until 2006. Very fine. Star wine! (2006–2015)

Les Preuses 90 – wonderful toasty nose, so intense it hurts to hold it in the mouth, so much fruit here, spice and a mélange of flowers, so complex and so much wine. Believe it or not, it still needs a little time. Truly wonderful. Star wine! (2002–2010) (February 99)

Les Preuses 86 – lemon/straw colour, lovely honeyed nose, wonderful mouthful and fine texture but not too long on the aftertaste. A very good wine. Drink now.

Further wines tasted in London in April 98 at Michael Schuster's tasting of the Chablis 96 vintage:

La Forest 96 – lovely gentle nose, but – wow! A big and luscious wine, wood showing but not overpowering, honeyed character, fabulous concentration and depth, bags of fruit, complex, beautifully in balance and very very long. Will last 'for ever' and it's only a Premier Cru. Star wine! (2004–2010)

Les Clos 96 – again, this a big wine but laced with finesse and elegance, concentrated fruit, nuts and more than a hint of oak, great depth and real style, lovely balance, long, very long. (2006–2015) Star wine!

Les Preuses 96 – bright yellow/green, restrained nose, the fruit is there well hidden nicely concentrated, long and fine overall, but not as fine as Les Clos. (2004–2008)

Vaillons 95 – a wine of elegance and finesse, closed but encouraged to reveal bags of fruit underneath, fine balance and length. (2000–2004) Very good. (Bedford Fine Wine Club tasting March 98)

Wines are not sold direct, but are available from stockists in:

UK
Domaine Direct, London WC1. Tel: 020 7837 1142
Ian G. Howe, Newark, Notts.. Tel: 01636 704366 Fax: 01636 610502
Justerini & Brooks, London SW1. Tel: 020 7493 8721 Fax: 020 7499 4653
    and Edinburgh. Tel: 0131 226 4202 Fax: 0131 225 2351
Lea & Sandeman, London branches. Tel: 020 7376 4767
Tanners, Shrewsbury, Salop.. Tel: 01743 234500

USA
Burgundy Wine Co. Ltd., New York. Tel: 212 691 9092 Fax: 212 691 9244
Calvert Woodley, Washington DC. Tel: 202 966 4400 Fax: 202 537 5086
Garnet Wines & Liquors, New York, 10021. Tel: 212 772 3211 Fax: 212 517 4029
Robert Haas, Vineyard Brands, Birmingham, Alabama. Tel: 205 980 8802 or web site: http://www.vineyardbrands.com

Hi-Time Wine Cellars, Costa Mesa, California 92627. Tel: 949 650 8463
Fax: 949 631 6863

DOMAINE BERNARD DEFAIX et FILS

17 Rue du Château Milly   Tel: 03 86 42 40 75
89800 Chablis   Fax: 03 86 42 40 28

25 hectares

Production:

Chablis Premier Crus	Côte de Léchet VV	1.5 ha
	Côte de Léchet	7.5 ha
	Vaillons	2.0 ha
	Chablis Village VV	1.0 ha
	Chablis Village	11.0 ha
	Petit Chablis	2.0 ha

Bernard Defaix's domaine is located in the village of Milly just to the west of the centre of town and enjoys a lovely view of the Côte de Léchet both from the garden and the *chai*.

Bernard is the fourth generation of a renowned family of *vignerons*, starting his own estate in 1959 with two hectares of vines. To date, the domaine has grown to over 25 hectares, of which 9ha are Premier Cru Côte de Léchet – Defaix is the largest single owner in this *climat*, and part of his holding here was planted in 1955. There are 12ha of Chablis Village land including 1 hectare of *Vieilles Vignes* more than 40 years old.

In 1994 Bernard's two sons Sylvain and Didier, having completed their studies in viticulture and oenology, joined their father as partners adding the knowledge of modern technology to experience, and giving him the comfort of knowing that the future of the estate will be in capable hands, so much so that Bernard is now *en retraite*. The family never lose sight of the ultimate need for the production of fine quality wine, as Didier Defaix says 'Le vin est évidemment très important mais les hommes qui le font le sont tout autant.' (The wine is obviously very important, just as much the men who make it.)

Defaix stresses that the first step to successful vinification is taken in the vineyard to produce the ripest healthiest fruit. Admirable sentiments, we assume this also refers to control of yields! (*Rendements* vary from 35hl/ha for the Côte de Léchet Vieilles Vignes to 60hl/ha for the Petit Chablis). Harvesting is done mechanically, and this is found preferable to picking by hand, one reason being that the harvest can be stopped when it is raining. The grapes are given a gentle pressing pneumatically so that the must produced requires less *débourbage*.

Both fermentations take place in stainless steel, left on its lees, racked and fined with bentonite or isinglass. *Elevage* is from 3 to 8 months according to the nature of the cuvée and vintage, followed by a light plate filtration and bottling.

There is a cuvée of Côte de Léchet Vieilles Vignes Reserve which is partly vinified in oak barrels where it stays for 8 months with regular *batonnage*. The wine is then racked and returned to barrels for another 4 to 6 months before tasting and *assemblage* with the same cuvée in inox. The idea of this method is to produce a more powerful example of Côte de Léchet, but retaining *typicité* with elegance. We have our doubts about such treatment of a lighter delicate Premier Cru!

Above all others, Didier rates the Côte de Léchet Réserve Vieilles Vignes as his best wine. He claims that this shows off its elegance and the power of the *terroir* reinforced by the complexity given by *élevage en futs*. We part company with him so far as Côte de Léchet is concerned and our tastings indicate to us that this *climat* does not benefit from oak, indeed we preferred his un-oaked wine.

In our consideration of this domaine, although there is undoubted potential and expertise here, we prefer to say that the jury is still out. We do not wish to be negative, but regret that the wines do not please us at the moment. Something is needed here to restore the reputation of an otherwise fine estate. Cutting down on the sulphur and the use of oak would be a good starter. Perhaps the corner has been turned with the 1998 vintage.

70 per cent of the production is exported, mainly to Europe.

Tasting notes

The following wines were mostly tasted at the domaine in May 1998 and February 1999, with the 98s tasted in London in August 1999:

Chablis 98 – mineral nose with fruity background, lovely citrus flavours, good acidity, intense and long. Very good Chablis.

Vaillons 98 – only two weeks in bottle, so recovering from shock. Sulphur on nose, sulphur on taste, where is the fruit? Rather bland and sour. Judgement deferred. We prefer the village Chablis. Fair. (2001–2003)

Côte de Léchet 98 – four weeks in bottle. No nose to speak of but more fruit on palate, juicy green apples, some concentration, good acidity. Fairly good. (2001–2003)

Petit Chablis 97 – little on nose, fruit rather slight and too much sulphur.

Chablis 97 – again little on nose but better concentration of fruit with acidity and some length. Good basic Chablis.

Vaillons 97 – minerally sulphurous nose, fruit rather masked by this. Doubt whether it will get much better. Fair only. (2001–2004)

Côte de Léchet 97 – better depth of fruit here but not much, some length but little personality, a bit of sulphur but fairly good. (2001–2004)

Chablis Vieilles Vignes 97 – 30 per cent wood. Nil on nose, fair amount of fruit but with little character, sulphur again with woody overtones. Not for us.

Côte de Léchet Vieilles Vignes 97 – from 50-year-old vines. The wood treatment was completely masking the fruit. Why do this to Côte de Léchet? Judgement deferred.

Petit Chablis 96 – very acidic, no obvious fruit, just bottled so maybe recovering.

Chablis 96 – somewhat austere but good typical nose, good fruit but low on acidity, poor aftertaste. Disappointing.

Chablis Vieilles Vignes 96 – December 97 bottling, 15 per cent *en fût*, acidic sour apple flavour not improved by wood. Disappointing.

Vaillons 96 – floral nose, more concentrated fruit and acidity, good intensity but where is the length? Disappointing.

Côte de Léchet 96 – getting better, floral nose, more fruit, more depth, some length, nice wine – 0 per cent wood as it should have! Good. Drink now.

Côte de Léchet Vieilles Vignes 96 – no precipitation and no filtration. Some biscuits on nose but quite closed, tastes of oak and shouldn't – 30 per cent. Bottled February 98. Disappointing.

Chablis 95 – no oak. Still totally closed nose, good acidity and fruit, some length, good wine.

Côte de Léchet Vieilles Vignes 95 – not as interesting as the 96, a bit dull on nose and palate, rather ordinary and bland, oak problem again!

Côte de Léchet 94 – surprisingly youthful pale lemon/greenish tinge, good Chablis nose to begin with which disappeared after a minute or so. Fullish wine of *typicité*, good sour-apple fruit and crisp acidity, but not a lot of individuality, weighty finish, good length. Fair. Drink now.

Wines available from the **CELLAR DOOR** and stockists in:

UK

Bibendum, London NW1. Tel: 020 7916 7706 Fax: 020 7916 7705
   http://www.bibendum-wine.co.uk
Dartmouth Vintners, Devon. Tel: 01803 832602
Gelston Castle, Castle Douglas, Scotland. Tel: 01556 502164
Harrison Vintners, London EC1. Tel: 020 7236 7716 Fax: 020 7332 0343
Richards Walford, Stamford, Lincs. Tel: 01780 460451 Fax: 01780 460276
Peter Watts Wines, Essex. Tel: 01376 561130 Fax: 01376 562925
   e-mail: pwwines@aol.com

USA

Robert Kacher Selections, 28000 V. Street, NE Washington DC, 20018.

DOMAINE DANIEL-ETIENNE DEFAIX ★

Aux Celliers du Vieux Château
23 Rue de Champlain
Milly
89800 Chablis

Tel: 03 86 42 42 05
Fax: 03 86 42 48 56
http://perso.wanadoo.fr/chablis.defaix.chateau

25 hectares

Production:

Grand Cru	Blanchot	0.20 ha
Premier Crus	Côte de Léchet	4.00 ha
	Vaillon	4.00 ha
	Les Lys	4.00 ha

Chablis Village and Petit Chablis

This is one of the most ancient domaines in Chablis, with a history stretching back eight centuries. Château de Faix in the Avallonais was originally planted with vines in the sixteenth century, but modern history begins with Etienne-Paul Du Jer De La Croix De Faix who, after a long fallow period, restarted the family tradition in the eighteenth century continuing to the present day where it flourishes under the inspired direction of Daniel Defaix. Daniel, proud family man, is also an astute business man with an amazing flair for very individual winemaking, which he accomplishes with precision and hands-on control whilst remaining calm and detached with a sparkling wit and sense of humour.

In 1990, work of restoration began on the old château at Milly where the first wines of Chablis were vinified by the monks from Pontigny one thousand years ago. The *terroir* is still used today. The *cuverie* is located in a modern building in the village of Milly and the domaine also boasts a well-stocked shop at 14 Rue Auxerroise in the centre of Chablis.

The area of this fine domaine is some 25 hectares, mostly of Kimmeridgian soil, limestone-clay rich in oyster fossils. The aspect is for the most part south-east. The average age of the vines is 38 years, which are planted 6,700 per hectare. Harvesting is of the ripest and healthiest grapes, with a severe *trie* to eliminate any unripe or rotten berries. A gentle pressing leads to *débourbage* for 18 hours, and up to 21 days alcoholic fermentation in stainless steel using indigenous yeasts, at a low temperature (18°C). Following the malolactic fermentation, the wine is *batonnée* every month for 18 months. Filtering and fining are used very rarely, as Daniel Defaix says 'we don't want to take out the things we have spent so long putting in.'

The Chablis Village Vieilles Vignes from 45-year-old vines, is kept for 2 years in bottle, and the Premier Crus between 4 and 6 years before release. The ultimate aim is for wines of structure, richness and aroma, wines which age well and give pleasure. They may not be wines of Chablis *typicité per se*, but they are good and very often very very good indeed.

Tasting Chez-Defaix is a real hoot! This took place in the large modern tasting-room-cum-sales area on the first occasion, but on our return visit we were firmly ensconced in Daniel's office crammed round his desk perched precariously on tiny wooden stools and the bottles kept on coming and coming. These things are sent to try us! A star domaine.

Tasting notes
The notes dated February 1999 were taken from a tasting at the domaine, the May 98 notes were taken in Chablis and the February 97 notes at the Selfridges tasting given by Daniel Defaix. The October 97 notes are from a tasting at the domaine. The others are from various tastings in London and Chablis:

Chablis Vieilles Vignes 97 – from 4-5 to 75-year-old vines, this is a very special cuvée – Cuvée Millennium. Exceptional nose, exceptional fruit, very rich and concentrated, wine of depth and length, an almost semi-sweet aftertaste. This is a really lovely wine. (2002–2007) (February 99)

Chablis Vieilles Vignes 96 – lovely wine, fine fruit and acidity, great potential. (May 98) Tasted again July 98 – lovely Chablis nose, concentrated with some length, apricots and honey, well-balanced acidity. Very good village Chablis. Delicious. Tasted again in February 99 and just as lovely. (2002–2007)

Chablis Vieilles Vignes 95 – lemon/gold colour, flowery lively nose, well balanced fruit and acidity, develops citrus flavours in glass, grapefruit and nuts, fair length, not exactly flinty but delicious. Very good. (October 97/March 98)

Les Lys 95 – Cuvée Paul Etienne, Daniel's 3-year-old son. Flowery fruit, dry, perhaps lacks just a trifle concentration, good acidity though. Very good. (2001–2004)

Vaillon 95 – gently mineral perfumed nose, good fruit, dry finish, this is a wine of *typicité*. Very good. (2001–2004) (February 99)

Côte de Léchet 95 – this is still closed on the nose but the elegant concentrated fruit is there, well-balanced acidity, good length and finish. Fine. (2001–2004) (February 99)

Chablis 94 – lots of fruit but a bit short, fair Chablis style, short on acidity, not exciting. Fair. (November 97)

Chablis Vieilles Vignes 94 – bright pale yellow, super nose, real Chablis flavour and steely character, good fruit, tails off in the glass. Good. (February 97)

Vaillon 94 – good minerally flinty fruit here, nuts and apricots, good concentration and depth, lovely length, fine finish. Very good. (Now to 2002) (February 99)

Les Lys 93 – lovely floral nose, delicious fruit and good length. A very good 93. Optimum now. (May 98)

Côte de Léchet 93 – minerally nose, great fruit but perhaps the acidity is a bit lacking. Will not get any better. Fair wine. Drink up. (May 98)

Côte de Léchet 92 – light gold, flinty but flowery nose, mineral, ample, generous, buttery fruity wine of depth, good balance and length. Will keep well. We both loved this wine very much. Fine wine. (Drink now to 2004) (February 97/October 97)

Vaillon 92 – light gold, gives much on the nose, some maturity, smooth, buttery, good fruit and length. Not typical Chablis but a good wine. Should age well. Not a patch on the Côte de Léchet though. Drink now. (October 97) This showed better in May 98 at the BIVB tasting. Lovely wine!

Les Lys 92 – pale lemon colour, toasty nutty nose which follows through to palate, full bodied and full flavoured, slight austerity, perhaps not typical but a very good big mouthful, powerful and long, fine aftertaste, well-balanced wine, now fully mature. Very good. (Now to 2002) (December 97)

Chablis Vieilles Vignes 91 – nuts, honey, toast, mature Chablis nose, mushrooms, delicious fruit, lovely length. Fine. Drinking now. (February 99)

Côte de Léchet 91 – pale yellow, more open nose than the 90, good fruit, delicious and very drinkable, good acidity, some elegance, long. (February 97) but in November 97 light lemon gold, mature nose and palate, full, good weight, minerally but a bit vegetal, lacks some concentration but this is the vintage. Improved substantially in glass. Good. Drink soon.

Vaillon 91 – pale yellow, not giving much on the nose but on the palate a delicious wine with good length, very good for the vintage. Drink now. (February 97)

Côte de Léchet 90 – this is a lovely wine, youthful and vigorous, with depth and concentration, well balanced, and a good long life 10-15 years. Should be better even than the 89, not so open or soft, but the austerity is more Chablis-like. Very good. (Drink now to 2005) (Several notes, last tasted September 98)

Vaillon 90 – bright pale straw, prominent fruity nose, quite forward, depth and concentration, delicious fruit, a lovely wine. Very good. Drink now. (February 97)

Côte de Léchet 89 – youthful colour but mature nose, nutty and biscuity, buttery, long and lingering mouthful, utterly delicious now. Very good. (December 96)

Les Lys 89 – holding up beautifully, Chablis *typicité*, fine steely mineral fruit and depth, still youthful. Very good. (Drink now to 2002) (November 97)

Côte de Léchet 88 – yellow greenish tinged, lovely mature nose, taste of apricots and honey, tremendous depth, gets even better in the glass. This proves Defaix wines can keep well. Fine. (Drink now to 2002) (August

98/February 99)

Les Lys 84 – fine old Chablis, honey nuts and biscuits, lovely fruit, good weight, fine balance, good length. Very good. Drink soon. (November 97)

Chablis Très Vieilles Vignes 83 – deep yellow, rather stale vegetal nose. This has not held up, a no-no. (February 97)

Vaillon 81 – deep yellow, sweet vegetal nose, too old, also a no-no. (February 97)

The wines may be found in the shops sometimes labelled Defaix-Raveneau. They are the same wines as the regular label.

Wines available from the **CELLAR DOOR** and stockists in:

UK
Balls Brothers, London E2. Tel: 020 7739 1642 Fax: 020 7729 0258
Gardner's Folly (UK Agent), Minchinhampton, Glos. Tel: 01453 731509 Fax: 01453 731134
Goedhuis & Co., London SW8. Tel: 020 7793 7900 or e-mail: goodhuis@btinternet.com
Haverlock Wines, Bedford. Tel: 01234 272766
Holland Park Wine Co., London W11. Tel: 020 7221 9614
Ian G. Howe, Newark, Notts. Tel: 01636 704366 Fax: 01636 610502
Lay & Wheeler, Colchester, Essex. Tel: 01206 764446 Fax: 01206 560002 http://www.layandwheeler.co.uk
Robersons, London W14. Tel: 020 7371 2121
Satchells, Burnham Market, Norfolk. Tel: 01328 738272
Selfridges, London W1. Tel: 020 7318 3730 Fax: 020 7491 1880
T & W Wines Ltd., Thetford, Norfolk. Tel: 01842 765646 Fax: 01842 766407 e-mail: contact@tw-wines.co.uk
Tanners, Shrewsbury, Salop. Tel: 01743 234500 Fax: 01743 344401
Thresher Group, branches nationwide including Bottoms Up and Wine Rack. Tel: 01707 328244 Fax: 01707 385000
The Wine Society, Stevenage, Herts. Tel: 01438 741177 Fax: 01438 761167 e-mail: winesociety@dial.pipex.com
Noël Young Wines, Cambridge. Tel: 01223 844744 Fax: 01223 844736

USA
Calvert Woodley, Washington DC. Tel: 202 966 4400 Fax: 202 537 5086
Garnet Wines & Liquors, New York, 10021. Tel: 212 772 3211 Fax: 212 517 4029
Neal Rosenthal, Select vineyards, PO Box 658, Route 83, Shekomeko, New York 12567.

DOMAINE JEAN-PAUL DROIN ★★★

8 Boulevard de Ferrières   Tel: 03 86 42 16 78
89800 Chablis   Fax: 03 86 42 42 09

20 hectares

Production:

Grand Crus	Vaudésir	1.03 ha
	Les Clos	0.99 ha
	Valmur	1.02 ha
	Blanchot	0.16 ha
	Grenouilles	0.48 ha
Premier Crus	Vaillons	4.82 ha
	Montée de Tonnerre	1.75 ha
	Montmains	0.90 ha
	Vosgros	0.58 ha
	Fourchaume	0.38 ha
	Côte de Léchet	0.10 ha
	Vaucoupin	0.14 ha

Chablis Village and Petit Chablis.

This domaine has an impressive entrance from the top end of the Boulevard de Ferrières close to the war memorial. The family live in a large period house facing the road and the cellars are reached through an archway leading on to a secluded and well manicured garden.

To say that Jean-Paul Droin is a charming man is an understatement. A welcoming and entertaining host, Jean-Paul displays all the virtues of an astute and successful businessman with none of the usual arrogance and I-know-better attitude often associated with the breed. Coming from an ancient Chablis family, vignerons from 1640 and 12 generations of them, he admits that he learned his trade on the hoof, and learned it very well it would seem, as this domaine is one of the finest stars in the Chablis firmament. Droin junior, Benoit, the thirteenth generation and his sister are poised to join the family business and continue the fine tradition, but Jean-Paul's eldest son is 'in computers'. Well, someone has to be!

The vineyards here are machine harvested. The Petit Chablis and Chablis are vinified in stainless steel, the Premier and Grand Crus largely in *pièces*, from new up to 10-year-old oak, but each year is different in content and make-up, e.g. Montée de Tonnerre sees more oak than the Fourchaume but the Grand Crus are all fermented *en barrique*. The provenance of the wood used is different from the usual Allier barrels in common usage by the Chablis oak camp, Jean-Paul preferring a mixture of five different forests often making up a single barrel as well as individual barrels. This makes for additional complexity. American and Russian oak is also sometimes used, although he stresses not side by side!!

In February or March the wines are racked into old barrels or *cuves*. Interestingly, the Grand Crus are *batonnée* twice per month. More interestingly, and not a common practice, after the Grand Crus have been racked, some of the Premier Crus are racked onto the Grand Cru lees, usually the Côte de Léchet and Vaucoupins onto Les Clos. The 97 Vaillons was in fact racked onto the Montmains lees. *Elevage* obviously varies with the cuvée, from 6 months for the basic Chablis to 10 or 11 months for the big boys!

Somehow Droin usually manages to avoid any overwhelming taste of oak, integrating the flavours well without too much hiding the *typicité*. Jean-Paul rates his Montée de Tonnerre his best Premier Cru and somehow we feel this is also given special attention. As our tasting notes testify, this wine stands out against the others although it does need time for the oak to fully integrate.

The Valmur and Les Clos are the outstanding Grand Crus in the stable, and Jean-Paul is particularly proud of his Les Clos. This is a lovely wine which would seem sometimes to be more forward than the Montée de Tonnerre but will clearly keep for a long while.

This is a three-star domaine, and a wonderful one to follow.

The markets for the wines are world-wide, almost all of Europe, the Far East, and the USA.

Tasting notes

The following wines were tasted at the domaine in May 1998 and February 1999 except as stated. The 98s were tasted in London by courtesy of Richards Walford:

Chablis 98 – pale green tinged, flinty nose, lovely concentrated fruit in abundance, perfect balance, terrific length, all that a Chablis Village should be and more. Very good.

Montmains 98 – lovely perfumed fruit, great concentration and depth, showing a touch of oak which will be absorbed. Very good. (2003–2007)

Vaillons 98 – fragrant nose, delicious ripe steely fruit, intense and concentrated, very long and lovely aftertaste. Fine. (2003–2007)

Vaudésir 98 – closing up, so intense, so concentrated, such depth, such rich elegant fruit. This is an immense and complex wine, slightly oaky now but will integrate. Wonderful wine. Will be fine. (2004–2010)

Les Clos 98 – totally closed, a big big wine, rich powerful and intense concentration, great complexity, wonderful length and depth. Again the oak will integrate. Very fine. Star wine. (2004–2010)

Fourchaume 97 – perfumed mineral fruit galore, biscuity, rich, very long and lovely. Very good/fine. (2002–2005)

Montmains 97 – typical steely nose, excellent fruit extraction, oak integrated since tasting in barrel, soft acidity, lovely length. Good/very good. (2002–2005)

Montée de Tonnerre 97 – honey and nuts already, beautiful fruit and balanced acidity, a very elegant wine. Very good indeed. (2002–2006)

Blanchots 97 – closed nose (J-P. D. says 'discreet'), oak now integrated, lovely citrus flavours, wine of depth, length, well balanced and supremely elegant. Very good /fine. (2003–2009)

Valmur 97 – tremendous nose, oak also now well integrated, big concentrated wine of intensity, depth and elegance, gorgeous fruit, supple and lovely, a Wow of a wine. Fine. (2003–2010)

Les Clos 97 – what an improvement since tasting in barrel. Now a toasty buttery wine with hidden depth and elegance, just a hint of oak on the palate. Lovely fruit, limes, peaches and a mêlée of fruits, very complex, very rich, steel and mineral elements, amazing balance and length. Very fine. (2003–2010)

Vaudésir 97 – élevée in 1-year-old Russian oak from the borders of the Black Sea. Immense fruit, fairly closed in comparison to the other Grand Crus, holding it all back! Should be very good indeed. (2003–2009).

Grenouilles 97 – élevée in 3-year-old French oak from five forests. The oak is not too prominent here, quite a forward wine, smokey and toasty, spices, fine concentrated fruit, balanced and long. Sells this wine to La Gavroche and Tante Claire. Very good. (2003–2010)

Montée de Tonnerre 96 – forward wine, not so closed, good concentration of fruit, good acidity but not really long and a dry aftertaste. Here the wood masks the quality at the moment, but should be a good wine. (2002–2006)

Valmur 96 – Whoof! Oak and perfume, big and powerful, immense fruit but needs ages for development and integration (J-P. D. thinks this is too marked by the oak). Nicely long, should be delicious! Fine. (2005-2010)

Montée de Tonnerre 95 – Truffles on nose, well-balanced fruit with slight oaky flavour, fair depth and length. Lovely wine. Very good. (2000–2004) (June 98/January 99)

Valmur 95 – the oak is well integrated here, lots of lovely fruit, fair acidity for the vintage, good length. Very good. (2003–2007)

Les Clos 95 – just as an oaked 'big Daddy' would be, lovely perfumed nose, beautiful fruit, the oak is already integrating, lovely wine for earlier drinking . Fine. (2002–2007)

Valmur 94 – Cinderella year! Honey, flowers and nuts, and a hint of marmalade, almost sweet long delicious fruit. And this is in a bottle! Fine. (2000 –2005)

Vaudésir 94 – like the Valmur but a bit more restrained, elegant fruity, limes and violets, lovely flavours. Both are delightful. Fine. (2000–2005)

Grenouilles 90 – 15 per cent demi-sec, a truly lovely aperitif wine, honeyed fruit, long and delicious, very special. Very good. Drink now.

Vaudésir 85 – light golden, mature nose of nuts and honey, good weight,

plenty of lovely fruit, fair length. Very good. Drink soon. (November 97)
Les Clos 85 bottled by Labouré Roi – good nose, fully mature wine holding up
well, but not a lot of flavour. Fair. Drink soon. (April 98)

Wines available from the **CELLAR DOOR** and stockists in:

UK
Berry Bros. & Rudd, London SW1. Tel: 020 7396 9669 Fax: 020 7396 9611
and Basingstoke, Hants. Tel: 01256 323566 Fax: 01256 340106
Bibendum, London NW1. Tel: 020 7916 7706 Fax: 020 7916 7705
e-mail: sales@bibendum-wine.co.uk http://www.bibendum-wine.co.uk
Domaine Direct, London WC1. Tel: 020 7837 1142
Goedhuis & Co., London SW8. Tel: 020 7793 7900
e-mail: goodhuis@btinternet.com
Harrods, Knightsbridge. Tel: 020 7730 1234
Ian G. Howe, Newark, Notts. Tel: 01636 704366
Raeburn, Edinburgh. Tel: 0131 332 5166
Richards Walford, Stamford, Lincs. Tel: 01780 460451 Fax: 01780 460276

USA
Block Distribution, San Antonio, Texas 78208. Tel: 210 224 7531
Direct Import Wines, 2700 River Road, Suite 303, Des Plaines, Illinois
60018.
European Cellars, Suite 801, 236 W. 27th Street, New York City 10001.
Tel: 212 924 4949
Grape Expectations, 1091 Essex Avenue, Richmond, California 94801
Hi-Time Wine Cellars, Costa Mesa, California 92627. Tel: 949 650 8463
Fax: 949 631 6863
Roanoke Valley Wine, Dalleville, Virginia 24083. Tel: 540 992 3285
Santé Wine Distributors, 112 South Duke Street, Durham NC 27701.
Tel: 919 688 6774
The Henry Wine Groupe, 531 Getty Court, Bénicia, California 94510.
Tel: 707 745 8500
USA Wine, 285 West Broadway, New York. Tel: 212 941 7133
Western Importers, 5270 Fox Street, Denver, Colorado 80217.

DOMAINE JOSEPH DROUHIN ★★

Moulin de Vaudon	7 Rue d'Enfer
Chichée	21200 Beaune
89800 Chablis	
	Tel: 03 80 24 68 88
	Fax: 03 80 24 84 25
45 hectares	

Production:

Chablis Grand Crus	Les Clos	1.03 ha
	Vaudésir	1.41 ha
	Preuses	0.23 ha
	Bougros	0.33 ha
	(produced under a Grand Cru label)	
Chablis Premier Crus	Vaillons	2.11 ha
	Montmains	1.80 ha
	Séchers	1.50 ha

Montée de Tonnerre, Mont de Milieu and Morein blended as Premier Cru
The total Premier Cru area is   7.16 ha
Chablis Village and Chablis Domaine de Vaudon

Drouhin owes its place in this section to the fact that the *négociant* house owns about 45 hectares of Chablis vineyards, including some prime Grand Cru sites, operating from the Moulin de Vaudon in Chichée, a lovely old house and watermill. Historically, Domaine Drouhin originated in Beaune when in 1918 the famous Clos des Mouches was acquired by Maurice Drouhin, son of the founder Joseph Drouhin, although the trading rights of the house were purchased nearly 40 years earlier in 1880. Proudly following the family line, Robert Drouhin assumed control in 1957 continuing the expansion of the domaine in the Côte d'Or and enhancing its reputation worldwide. The vineyards in Chablis were brought into the estate in 1968.

Robert's children Frédéric, Philippe, Véronique and Laurent are now fully involved with the running of the company: Philippe manages the estates of the Côte d'Or and Chablis, while Véronique, a trained oenologist, supervises the Oregon winery purchased in 1988, where she spends some months each year whilst retaining a close involvement in the French vineyards.

The story of the house connection with Chablis goes back to Robert's first visit there, when like us all he fell in love with the place. Since it was possible to control frost and cultivate steep slopes with tractors, it became clear that what was fine for him in the Côte d'Or could be successfully duplicated in Chablis. After painstaking research studying old maps, talking to long-experienced *vignerons* and tasting old bottles from abandoned *terroirs*, Robert Drouhin was able to locate the best parcels, especially those located in the valley of Vauvillen. Vaudon comes from the slopes between Montée de Tonnerre and Mont de Milieu on the right bank of the Serein, and gives its name to one of the house cuvés.

The domaine now has some 3 hectares of Grand Cru and 7 hectares of Premier Cru vineyards under cultivation. Yields are carefully controlled and at the *vendage* the grapes are hand-picked and pressed at the domaine's *chai* in Chablis. The juice is then transferred to the company cellars in Beaune, some of the oldest and most immaculately preserved cellars in the Côte d'Or, where fermentation of the village cuvé takes place in stainless-steel tanks and the wine is bottled after 7 or 8 months. 100 per cent oak is used for the Vaudésir and Les Clos, 15 per cent of it new, and perhaps just a smidgen for the Vaillons. Chablis Vaudon receives 50 per cent old oak. These proportions may vary with the vintage.

Rendements vary from year to year, but always below the maximum permitted levels. In 1994 it was as low as 33 hl/ha, in 1995 58hl/ha, in 1996 41 hl/ha and in 1997 43 hl/ha.

Véronique, who kindly escorted us to the vineyards on our first visit and was no less engaging when we visited Drouhin HQ in Beaune, regards her Vaudésir or Les Clos as being their best wine for a *Grand Répas* and the Domaine de Vaudon for oysters. At lunch we drank a 1988 La Moutonne from the cellars of the Hostellerie, a rare treat, for which a tasting note is given below. Drouhin are certainly in the top league of Chablis producers even though they are better known for their Côte d'Or wines.

Tasting notes
The following wines were tasted in London in September 1999:

Chablis 98 – lovely colour, little on nose but good fruit base, Cox's apples and peaches. Lovely basic Chablis.

Domaine de Vaudon Chablis 98 – good colour, quiet nose, good depth and concentration, not so much up front but lovely length and finish, dry and steely. Very good.

Vaillons 98 – good concentration here but yet little on nose, lovely fruit and length. Needs time. Should be very good. (2002–2005)

The following wines were tasted in the Drouhin Cellars in Beaune in February 1999:

Chablis Domaine de Vaudon 97 – fragrant nose, lovely fruit, apricots, fair length. Good wine.

Montmains 97 – lovely wine with good acidity, some oak there on the palate but should integrate well. Good. (2002–2005)

Séchers 97 – fruity nose, good well-balanced citrus fruits, more depth and longer than the Montmains. Very good. (2002–2005)

Vaudésir 97 – delicate floral nose, some oak there but well integrated already and balanced. Very similar to the 86. Very good. (2003–2007)

Les Clos 97 – from 60-year-old vines – nose hidden, good depth of fruit with good length, perhaps too oaky at this stage but should be very good in time. (2003–2007)

Les Clos 95 – darker colour, rather strange flavour, perhaps not enough acidity to balance the fruit and oak. Rather disappointing for Les Clos. Good only. (2002–2007)

The following wines were tasted in the Drouhin vineyards in May 1998:

Chablis 97 – lovely nose and really fruity Chablis, this is our style! Very good.

Vaillons 97 – bursting with fruit and fine acidity, very typical, fine wine. (2002–2006)

Chablis Domaine de Vaudon 96 – delicious fruit and acidity, a lovely Chablis. Tasted whilst looking at the vineyard – a wonderful experience. Very good. Retasted at MW 96 Burgundy Tasting in March 1999 and just as good.

Vaillons 96 – 10 per cent oak, all a bit closed but lovely fruit and beautiful balance. Very good, maybe fine. (2002–2006)

Vaudésir 96 – very oaky nose masking the fruit but should integrate. Not a wine of *typicité* but delicious and long. Should be fine. (2004–2008)

Les Clos 96 – similar state to Vaudésir and should ultimately be a bigger wine. Delicious, shows well. Should be fine. (2005–2010)

La Moutonne 88 – made when Drouhin had a 15 per cent interest in the vineyard: deep yellow colour, lovely biscuity nose, tremendous fruit, apricots, succulent, delicious, beautifully balanced, very long. Star wine! (Drunk with lunch following the tasting May 98.)

Wines available from stockists in:

UK

Ballantynes, S. Glamorgan. Tel: 01446 774840 Fax: 01446 775253

Mentzendorff & Co (UK Agents), London SE1. Tel: 020 7415 3200 Fax: 020 7415 3222

James Nicholson, County Down. Tel: 028 44830091

Stones of Belgravia, London SW1. Tel: 020 7235 1612

Wine Importers, Edinburgh. Tel: 0131 556 3601

USA

Dreyfus Ashby & Co., New York 10165. Tel: 212 818 0770 Fax: 212 953 2366
http://www.dreyfusashby.com

Garnet Wines & Liquors, New York, 10021. Tel: 212 772 3211 Fax: 212 517 4029

Hi-Time Wine Cellars, Costa Mesa, California 92627. Tel: 949 650 8463
  Fax: 949 631 6863
Sherry-Lehmann Inc., New York. Tel: 212 838 7500 Fax: 212 838 9285

DOMAINE GÉRARD DUPLESSIS ★★

5 Quai de Reugny	Tel: 03 86 42 10 35
89800 Chablis	Fax: 03 86 42 11 11

7 hectares

Production:

Chablis Grand Cru	Les Clos	0.36 ha
Chablis Premier Crus	Vaillons	1.30 ha
	Montmain	2.90 ha
	Fourchaume	0.44 ha
	Montée de Tonnerre	1.20 ha
Chablis Village		

Driving along the Quai de Reugny early one morning after a splendid breakfast at the *hostellerie* round the corner, we perceived an upright bearded man standing outside his gate contemplating the river and ready to welcome his visitors, to whom he beckoned with an expressive come-hither wave of his hands immediately he spied our approach.

Gérard Duplessis is a great character with a knowing wicked smile just discernible beneath the grey bushy whiskers. Initially rather suspicious of his two wine writer visitors, he soon warmed to us and expounded on his family background and wines. He comes from four generations of *vignerons*, maybe more but he is not sure, and lives in an old farmhouse built in 1895 over much older cellars, surrounded by lovely old farm buildings which he admits are very decrepit. The approach is through an equally rustic garden fronting the river. Visitors are usually welcomed by the family's magnificent sloppy Basset Hound who more than likely will follow all into the *cuverie*.

The outward appearance of the estate does not reflect the quality of the winemaking. Gérard is immensely proud of his métier and takes pleasure in all his wines. The domaine is small and manageable with important holdings in fine crus, producing a total production of some 18,000 bottles in 1995 and 22,000 in 1996. Vinification is in stainless steel and ageing takes place *en futs* for 4 to 6 months with natural precipitation of the tartrates. The wine is bottled and kept about 16 months before release.

As for the wines, Gérard's soft spot for his Montée de Tonnerre soon became evident on our very first visit from the number of different vintages that he produced for us, proudly finishing with his 1989. We could not other than agree with him, his Montée de Tonnerre 1989 was delicious. Find it if you can! Next time around we soon discovered that his other Premier Crus are of equal quality and Grand Cru Les Clos is especially noteworthy. On this subsequent visit in February 1999, for some extraordinary reason we all forgot to taste the 1996 Montée de Tonnerre. A couple of days later whilst lunching in Bar Chablis, Gérard popped in for his daily packet of Gauloises. Catching sight of us in a corner devouring our Croques Messieurs, he immediately indicated that he would be home in an hour and we should drop by to taste the missing item. We did so, and afterwards we made a move to go. 'That's all?' he asked with feigned surprise, 'You don't want to taste this?' holding up a dusty bottle of some age. 'I opened this yesterday for my English importer Roy Richards, 'Certainly' we gulped. The mystery bottle was another Montée de Tonnerre, from 1952 – miraculous and an honour! Thank you, Roy! Apparently Gérard has a store of vintages going back to his birth year.

This is a two-star domaine, long may it prosper. The wines are marketed in France, with exports to the UK, and just a little to Canada, USA, Japan, Germany and Belgium.

Tasting notes

The following wines were tasted at the domaine in February 1999:

Montmains 97 – honeyed floral nose, lovely concentrated fruit, apricots, minerally and steely, balanced and very long. Very good. (2001–2005)

Montée de Tonnerre 97 – quite forward wine, lovely honeyed nose, voluptuous fruit, good depth and intensity, balance and length. Lovely wine. Fine. (2002–2006)

Vaillons 97 – en cuve – more minerals here, good fruit but perhaps not quite so concentrated. Good. (2001–2004)

Fourchaume 97 – en cuve – floral minerals, tremendous depth of fruit, flinty, very dry finish, lovely wine. Very good/fine. (2002–2006)

Montée de Tonnerre 96 – floral minerally nose, concentrated fruit, really long and lovely. Very good indeed. (2002–2006). We are glad we went back!

Les Clos 96 – closed nose, intense concentrated fruit, rich, complex, fabulous length, lovely acidity and balance, wonderful wine. Fine. (2003–2008)

The following wines were tasted at the domaine and BIVB in May 1998:

Chablis 96 – delicious wine, bursting with lovely fruit, well balanced and long. Very good.

Montée de Tonnerre 95 – lovely nose, good balance of fruit and acidity, delicate wine of elegance and finesse, long, good but not great. Drink now.

Montée de Tonnerre 93 – closed nose, low on acidity, lacks a bit of fruit, rather sour aftertaste. A typical 93. Fair. Drink up.

Montée de Tonnerre 92 – floral aromatic nose, lovely biscuity fruit, good acidity, not much length but a very good delicate wine. (Now to 2002)

Montée de Tonnerre 89 – deep colour, honeyed nose, alcoholic but gentle wine, very long, fine balance, very warm and generous. Lovely wine. Fine. Drink now.

Montmains 88 – fruit fading a bit, acidity still there, some length, still a good wine but drink up.

Montée de Tonnerre 52 – truffles, mushrooms and *sous-bois*, at the end of its life but what a life! Totally delicious. Farewell!

Wines available at the **CELLAR DOOR,** and from stockists in:

UK
Richards Walford, Stamford, Lincs. Tel: 01780 460451 Fax: 01780 460276

USA
Hand Picked Selections, 226 East Lee Street, Warrenton, Virginia 22186.

DOMAINE JEAN DURUP ★★

4 Grande Rue
Maligny   Tel: 03 86 47 44 49
89800 Chablis   Fax: 03 86 47 55 49

170 hectares

Production:

Chablis Premier Crus	Fourchaume	17.00 ha (inclusive of L'Homme Mort 13.00 ha)
	Montée de Tonnerre	2.00 ha
	Montmains	0.55 ha
	Vau de Vey	15.00 ha

Chablis Village (including 65 ha in one parcel at Maligny) and Petit Chablis

This is a no-oak domaine par excellence, established many years ago by Jean Durup president of La Fédération des Viticulteurs Chablisiens, the *syndicat* opposed to William Fèvre's attempts to restrict the limits of Chablis Appellation to the existing boundaries.

Chez Durup is a rather innocuous-looking block of buildings at the southern end of main street Maligny. Don't be fooled, behind those grey walls lurks an enormous operation, the nerve centre of over 170 hectares of productive Premier Crus and Chablis Village vineyards, and an immense *cuverie* and *chai*, stainless-steel, cement and fibreglass vats, not a scrap of oak anywhere, spotlessly clean and state of the art. Quality winemaking and *élevage* with the minimum of interference produce fine results, wines of *typicité*, fruity and flinty, a flowery aroma and wines which can age well, developing a delicious honeyed biscuity nose. Never wines of the greatest weight, but of fine character nevertheless.

Terroir is important to Durup, and this comes over well in the natural distinction between *climats*. We were fortunate to be able to see this distinction at first hand, when on one of our visits to the domaine, we were taken round much of the *vignoble* by son Jean-Paul in his Land Rover, indicating that this was a more practical way to traverse the vineyards than in Owen's BMW – how right he was and thankful we were to arrive back at domaine HQ in one piece visibly shaken but not stirred. But in between tracks, we mercifully stopped for explanations of the various *terroir* divisions. We even survived the steep rutted slopes of L'Homme Mort.

Although the estate has no Grand Cru vineyards, there is an impressive parcel of Premier Crus and individual *lieu-dits* of Village Chablis from part south-facing slopes. We particularly like the Vigne de la Reine and Carré de Caesar each with its own specific character. Jean-Paul claims the Vau-de-Vey as one of his personal favourites – this may not be one of the finest Premier Crus, but in the hands of Durup some lovely wine is made from his 15ha holding.

Jean Durup is a tax consultant in Paris, but spends about three days a week in Chablis. In his absence, Jean-Paul manages the estate and, in his dreams, Auxerre FC. A personable young man, Jean-Paul is immensely proud of his father's achievements and an immensely capable successor when the day comes to move fully into the driving seat. In the meantime the two Durups run an impressive empire with undoubted ability, charm, humour and results which are justly famed.

Jean-Paul holds the view that the standard of Chablis produced by the growers of the region has improved considerably over recent years, as sons and daughters of the domaines are now sent to wine schools in Dijon or Beaune rather than relying solely on guidance handed down over the generations. Durup Jnr is such a nice fellow that he wouldn't say anything bad about anybody!

The family now own the ruined Château de Maligny, a magnificent twelfth-century château, and restoration work is well under way, but it is a mammoth undertaking. This is a labour of love and Jean-Paul laughingly expresses the hope that he will live long enough to see its fulfilment! Work on the cellars has been completed, together with a fine tasting room where the lucky visitor is warmly welcomed with *gougères* and genuine hospitality. If you are very fortunate, you will be taken on a tour of the château and the neighbouring thirteenth-century nunnery, whose restoration is also nearing completion.

As one would expect, the Domaine Durup's markets are spread far and wide, exporting throughout Europe, the Antipodes, Brazil, Japan, Canada and the USA, This is one of the great Chablis estates. Buy with confidence.

The same wines also appear under the labels of Domaine de l'Eglantière, Château de Maligny, Domaine de la Paulière and Domaine des

Valéry – the importers choose the label.

Tasting notes
The following wines were tasted in London in August 1999:

Chablis 98 – bright sparkling colour, mineral and steely, good concentration of fruit, nice length and balance. Very good.

Vau-de-Vey 98 – mineral nose and palate, dry fruit, a little on the bitter side but citrus flavours, good length. Good wine but not special. (2001–2004)

Fourchaume 98 – lemony nose, steely Chablis, dry fruit, quite concentrated with good length. Very good. (2002–2005)

The following wines were tasted at the château in October 1998:

Petit Chablis 97 – what a super nutty biscuity nose, fruity and dry. A very good Petit Chablis.

Chablis Vieilles Vignes 97 – flowery nose and some depth here, old vine intensity, rich and long, good balance. Very good wine.

Chablis 97 – very flowery and perfumed, dry, intense austere fruit but a bit short, good though.

Vigne de la Reine 97 – gentle perfume, discreet elegance, a feminine wine, complex, balanced, long, delicious. Fine. (2000–2004)

Carré de Caesar 97 – typical Durup nuts, honey and biscuits on nose, lovely fruit, more earthy than Vigne de la Reine, long and really delicious, well balanced, long finish. Very good to fine. (2000–2004)

Fourchaume 97 – nose of *typicité* but closing up, good fruit and acidity, very dry, now needs time. Very good. (2002–2005)

L'Homme Mort 97 – more open typical mineral flinty nose, lovely fruit, intensity and length, concentration and depth, fine balance. Fine. (2002–2005)

Vau-de-Vey 97 – more aromatic nose than L'Homme Mort without quite the depth, but lovely fruit, concentrated and long. Very good. (2000–2004)

Montée de Tonnerre 97 – lovely open nose, this is a masculine wine, big on fruit and everything else, good *typicité*, wonderful balance and length. Almost as good as L'Homme Mort but not quite the depth. Very good. (2002–2005).

Montmains 97 – steely, minerally and flowery, complex, good fruit and balance, very dry. Very good. (2001–2005)

Fourchaume 90 – lovely golden colour, apricots, nuts and biscuits, voluptuous fruit, expansive and long, very long, fruit will last for years. Delicious. Very fine, incomparable, and lucky you if you have some! (2000–2005)

The following wines were tasted at the château in October 1997:

Petit Chablis 96 – light but fresh and delicious, some length. Fine for what it is, no pretensions.

Chablis 96 – deeper in colour and on palate, still fresh and delicious, well balanced. Good.

Chablis La Vigne de la Reine 96 – light greenish gold, slightly more flowery nose and depth, good length, soft and elegant. Very good. (2000 –2004)

Chablis Le Carré de César 96 – more mineral in character, and more typical, also delicious. Very good. (2000 –2004)

Chablis Vieilles Vignes 96 – more closed than the above, richness and depth, flinty Chablis character, good length. Very good.

Fourchaume 96 – wine of depth and concentrated fruit, soft and round, very long, delicious. Fine. (2001 –2005)

L'Homme Mort 96 – bigger mouthful of flavour, soft but depth and concentration, profound, needs 5 years at least. Fine. (2001 –2006)

Vau-de-Vey 96 – fuller on nose, wine of *typicité*, fine but L'Homme Mort is better and longer. Good. (2000 –2003)

Montmains 92 – good Chablis style, but seems a bit short, lovely nose, soft, nice wine, typical Montmains. Good. Drink soon.

Montée de Tonnerre 90 – very Chablis, flinty minerally fruit, long and expansive, lovely wine. Fine. Drink now.

Fourchaume 88 – wonderful fine old Chablis, honeyed, expansive, long, delicious. Fine but drink soon.

Montée de Tonnerre 86 – dark, almost golden, deep and honeyed, wonderful finish, very long, fabulous wine. Fine. Drink soon.

Chablis Vieilles Vignes 83 – from vines planted in 1895 and destroyed by frost in 1985. Nutty, rich tea biscuits and honey, tastes like a fine delicate Meursault, unforgettable and unrepeatable – no further comment.

The following wines were tasted on various occasions from late 1997:

Chablis 95 – mature nose of lemon biscuits, developing honeysuckle in glass, lovely and rich on palate, long, wonderful for a Village wine, fully mature, drinking beautifully. Tasted on several occasions and gets lovelier each time. Very good. (October 97/October 98)

Fourchaume 95 – gentle, flowery perfumed nose, honeyed, full of ripe fruit with fine acidity, good intensity and depth, long and delicious, will get even better. Very good. (2000–2005) (June 98)

Fourchaume 94 – the epitome of fine Chablis character on nose, steely and rich, good mouthful of flavour, depth and very good length, well balanced, fine for the vintage. (2000–2002) (October 97/February 99)

Petit Chablis 93 – lowest appellation, poor vintage, fine winemaker – just shows what can be done with the raw tools. Light colour, little on nose but character and *typicité* in glass, fruit and acidity in balance. Very good for the vintage and what it is! (January 98)

Chablis La Vigne de la Reine 92 – hard to believe this is only a Village wine, scintillating colour, light gold straw, spring flowers and a little honey on nose, mouthful of lovely fruit with just enough acidity, fully mature, good depth, perhaps just tails off a bit at the end but better than many a Premier Cru of the ilk. Drink soon. (January 98)

Fourchaume 89 – straw gold colour, nutty biscuity on nose and palate, vegetal in the nicest sense, fully mature, full, long and lovely. Very good. Drink soon. (January 98)

Wines available from the **CELLAR DOOR** and stockists in:

UK
Château de Maligny label:
Army & Navy Stores, London SW1. Tel: 020 7834 1234
Anthony Byrne Fine Wines, Cambs. Tel: 01487 814555
Thresher Group, branches nationwide including Bottoms Up and Wine Rack. Tel: 01707 328244 Fax: 01707 385000

Domaine de l'Eglantière label:
Ameys Wines, Suffolk. Tel: 01787 377144
John Arkell Vintners, Wilts. Tel: 01793 823026
Ben Ellis, Surrey. Tel: 01737 842160
H. Smith, Derby. Tel: 01335 342150
King & Barnes, W. Sussex. Tel: 01403 270470
Thorman Hunt, London SE11. Tel: 020 7735 6511
Thornham Wines, Thornham, Norfolk. Tel: 01485 512310
The Wine Bureau, N. Yorks. Tel: 01423 527772

Domaine de la Paulière label:
Mayfair Cellars Ltd, London SE1. Tel: 020 7329 8899 Fax: 020 7329 8880

Domaine des Valéry label:
Tanners, Shrewsbury, Salop. Tel: 01743 234500

Jean Durup label:
Domaine Direct, London WC1. Tel: 020 7837 1142
Eldridge Pope, Dorchester, Dorset. Tel: 01305 251251 Fax: 01305 258300
    e-mail: finewines@eldridge-pope.co.uk
Haynes Hanson & Clark, London SW1. Tel: 020 7259 0102
Peckham & Rye, Glasgow and Edinburgh. Tel: 0141 445 4555
Howard Ripley, London N21. Tel: 020 8360 8904 Fax: 020 8351 6564

Stones of Belgravia, London SW1. Tel: 020 7235 1612
Wine & Spirit International, London NW9. Tel: 020 8975 1023
   Fax: 020 8975 1025. e-mail: dale@wineandspirit.com
T. & W. Wines Ltd, Thetford, Norfolk. Tel: 01842 765646 Fax: 01842
   766407. e-mail: contact@tw-wines.co.uk
Noël Young Wines, Cambridge. Tel: 01223 844744 Fax: 01223 844736

USA
Parliament Wine Co., 3303 Atlantic Avenue, Atlantic City, New Jersey
08401.

DOMAINE d'ELISE

Frédéric Prain
Sur la Côte de Léchet
Milly   Tel: 03 86 42 40 82
89800 Chablis   Fax: 03 86 42 44 76

13 hectares

Production:
Chablis Village and Petit Chablis

This estate, created in 1970, is perched on the top of the hill above the Côte
de Léchet, and run since 1982 by Frédéric Prain, a public works engineer in
Paris, vintage Citroën car collector and wine buff. The vineyards unusually
are in one parcel, 13 hectares divided almost equally between Chablis and
Petit Chablis with a southern exposure. One hectare situated below the
road is virtually Côte de Léchet but cannot yet obtain Premier Cru status.
   Frédéric and his wife are an absolutely charming young couple, delightful, welcoming, busy, worrying, saying they can't spare more than five minutes as they are in the middle of late harvesting and then spending about a
half an hour with us before even the tour begins and a bottle opened.
Bushy-bearded Monsieur Prain speaks excellent English, and talks nineteen to the dozen enthusiastically about his wine and his vines. He hardly
needs the income from their wines to support his way of life, which is just
as well as he is still a businessman in Paris – a local government engineer –
but he loves life in the vineyards spending a third of the time in Chablis and
the rest of the year in the metropolis with the children. Out comes the
photo album, not of the family hols, but aerial views of his vineyards, and
there follows a detailed description of each *lieu-dit* and the vines, interestingly the Chablis and Petit Chablis appellations running into each other in
such a way that establishing a dividing line between them is well nigh impossible.
   M. Prain harvests as late as possible – which is always risky, and carries
out a very careful selection. As mentioned, our visit in October 1998 was

towards the end of the picking, and Frédéric needed just a few hours more of dry weather to finish his harvest. As we emerged from the house, Frédéric glanced southwards over the vineyards, and exclaimed in an excited voice 'My God, what's that?' 'The sun,' laughed Owen in reply. 'No, not that,' panicked Frédéric, 'behind it!' Indeed, looming up in the distance was a very dirty black cloud. Subsequent reports indicate that his 1998 vintage was very much rain affected, but this was not apparent in the wine tasted – see the tasting notes below. We took our leave of a delightful domaine and amusing man. We shall go again!

Yields are controlled and average 45-50 hl/ha on the older part of the vignoble, impressively low for the lower appellations. Traditional vinification in glass-lined concrete vats, temperature-controlled at 20°C, a long *élevage en cuve* on the fine lees, and a single filtration precede bottling of the Petit Chablis in May or June, and the Chablis in September.

It is interesting to note how Frédéric describes the two vintages 1995 and 1996:

1995 – distinguished by a fine balance of acidity and alcohol, already delicious, but can be kept for several years without problem. Freshness and crispness are perhaps second to aromas of mushrooms and *sous-bois*.

1996 – exceptional vintage in all respects, distinguished by three factors: pure, healthy fruit free from rot, optimum maturity – no need to chaptalise, beautiful acidity to support the making of *un grand vin de garde*.

The policy of the domaine is to give priority to everything which improves the quality of the wine and to maintain reasonable prices. Half the production is sold to the *négoce* (from the youngest vines) which enables the best to be kept for bottling – their words not ours.

The visitor to the domaine will be allowed to see the vintage car collection on request and to talk of many things, not just wine. But avoid harvest time!

Tasting notes
Tasted in London in August 1999:

Chablis 98 – dumb nose which needed encouragement, nice fruit with lots of crisp acidity and a delicious finish. No evidence of rain-affected fruit here. Good.

Tasted at the domaine in October 1998:

Chablis 97 – quiet flinty nose but lovely fruit, slight sulphur on the finish which will go. Good wine. Retasted March 99 – now no trace of sulphur, delicately perfumed nose, lovely concentrated fruit, *sous-bois*, mushrooms and overripe apples, good intensity and length but not exactly crisp and lacks a bit of zip. Still a lovely wine. Good/very good.

Chablis 96 – already some maturity on nose, lovely intense fruit and length, crisp delicious wine. This confirmed an earlier note in April 98 – mature lemon yellow colour with a lovely nose, very forward, full flavoured on palate, bursts with fruit and well balanced with attractive acidity, long delicious wine.

Wines available from the **CELLAR DOOR** and stockists in:

UK
Bentalls of Kingston, Surrey. Tel: 020 8546 1001
European Wine Growers, Nr. Lancaster. Tel: 01524 701723
Holland Park Wine, London W11. Tel: 020 7221 9614
McKinley Vintners, London SE1. Tel: 020 7928 7300
Wine Trading Co., Harrogate, N. Yorks. Tel: 01423 872425

DOMAINE JEAN-PIERRE ELLEVIN

7 Rue du Pont
Chichée
89800 Chablis   Tel. & Fax: 03 86 42 44 24

10 hectares

Production:

Premier Crus	Vaucoupin	1.40 ha
	Vosgros	0.80 ha

Chablis Village and Petit Chablis

Approach the pretty village of Chichée from Fleys, cross the bridge over the Serein and immediately on the right is Domaine Jean-Pierre Ellevin. The attractive stone-built house fronts the road but enjoys side views over the river, alongside which is found the *chai* and *cuverie* behind a very tidy newly laid courtyard.

Jean-Pierre Ellevin, a ruddy-faced youthful man, takes immense pride in his *vigneron* family's achievements, he is now the third generation to run this small but interesting estate. Although reluctant to respond to the many letters sent to him, on arriving unannounced we were greeted with open arms and a broad smile.

The grapes are vinified in temperature-controlled enamelled *cuves*, no wood is used here. The total annual production comprises some 20,000 bottles for *vente directe* and the restaurant trade plus bulk sales to the *négoce*.

At this stage Jean-Pierre does not export to the UK or USA but wines are available at the **CELLAR DOOR**. Beat your way to it, these are good wines: we particularly liked his Vaucoupin, a difficult Premier Cru in the best of hands.

Tasting notes
The following wines were tasted at the domaine in February 1999:

Chablis 97 – fruity wine with lovely floral overtones. Good basic Chablis.

Vosgros 97 – a light Premier Cru early maturing, lovely wine already. Good plus. (2000–2003)

Vaucoupin 97 – floral nose, very fruity wine with lovely length and aftertaste. Delicious. Very good. (2001–2004)

DOMAINE FELIX et FILS

17 Rue de Paris Tel: 03 86 53 33 87
89530 Saint-Bris-le-Vineux Fax: 03 86 53 61 64

Total 30 hectares – 2.3 hectares of Chablis

Production:
Chablis Village and Petit Chablis

In the main road of Saint-Bris on a prominent corner facing other local domaines, a large iron-gate leads through to the house and operation of Monsieur Felix, dominated by modern buildings, not unattractive in themselves, surrounding a gravel courtyard.

This family domaine boasts of its ancient origins, and the family records apparently show just that, the domaine having been handed down from generation to generation since its inception in 1690. Hervé Felix, who assumed control a few years ago from his father Jean Felix, surmises that the history may even stretch back further to Roman times, but we will be content with 1690. He is joined by his wife Marie-Claire on the commercial side, when she is not otherwise engaged in keeping the children at bay, the toys and paintings in Dad's office give heartening testament that this is a real family.

The estate produces a range of Yonne wines including Sauvignon de Saint-Bris, Bourgogne Aligoté, Côte d'Auxerre and Irancy as well as Chablis and Petit Chablis. The Petit Chablis comes from vineyards in Lignorelles, the Chablis vines are in Courgis. We preferred the Petit Chablis – so much for *terroir* here!

Vinification of the Chablis Appellations is in temperature-controlled stainless steel tanks installed in 1993 and some enamelled *cuves*. The wines receive traditional treatment including a *passage au froid* for the precipitation of tartrate crystals. Personal supervision by M. Felix for all stages of the winemaking process is essential to maintain control to his standards – he believes that the Chablis has ageing potential of up to 10 years in good vintages, 6 years for the Petit Chablis. Well, this maybe possible if everything gels!

The Sauvignon de Saint-Bris must be mentioned, as both the 97 and 98 vintages were found to be deliciously fresh, gooseberry-style fruit, crisp wines – fine summer drinking.

The methods may not be startling in themselves, but the Chablis produced is certainly not to be sneezed at – good honest wines and if you are passing through Saint-Bris or see them on a restaurant wine list give them a try! The total annual production of the estate amounts to about 8,000 bottles of Chablis and 10,000 of Petit Chablis. Some of these bottles find their way to Denmark, Holland, Belgium and Germany, but not as yet the UK or USA, except the Sauvignon de Saint-Bris.

Tasting notes

The following wines were tasted at the domaine in February 1999, except as stated:

Chablis 98 – Chablis nose of *typicité*, dry minerally fruit and concentration, crisp wine with some length. Good. (August 1999 London)

Petit Chablis 97 – bright colour, honeyed aroma, citrus fruits. Well-made wine. Delicious.

Chablis 97 – good nose but fruit rather lacking, slight bitter finish. Will it improve? We have doubts.

Chablis 96 – nose less obvious, rather sharp acidic wine but more fruit here than the 97. Should get better.

Chablis 95 – mature nose, honey and citrus flavours. Quite good Chablis, so perhaps these wines do age well.

Wines are available from the **CELLAR DOOR.**

DOMAINE WILLIAM FEVRE

14 Rue Jules Rathier   Tel: 03 86 42 12 51
89800 Chablis   Fax: 03 86 42 19 14

60 hectares

Production:

Chablis Grand Crus Bougros, Grenouilles, Les Clos, Preuses, Vaudésir and Valmur

Chablis Premier Crus Fourchaume, Montée de Tonnerre and Montmains.

Chablis Village and Petit Chablis

All is now changing at Domaine William Fèvre, as William – a staunch French *vigneron* with an English name – decided at the age of 67 in 1998 to sell his Chablis business to the Henriot family who control both Henriot Champagne and Bouchard Père et Fils.

William Fèvre comes from a noble line of *vignerons* from Fontenay-près-Chablis going back many generations: he was in the forefront of the battle against frost in the 1950s but made his name mainly for his presidency of Le Syndicat de Défence de l'Appellation de Chablis which he held until he handed over to Jean-Bernard Marchive of Domaine des Malandes in 1998. During this period he fought to maintain the reputation of Chablis by resisting any extension of the vineyards on to land without proper *terroir*, 'Le Kimmeridgien est sacré.'

The domaine has been the largest holder of Grand Cru vineyards in Chablis with parcels in each, the sole exception being Blanchots, but he also added grapes bought from other producers, effectively extending his wine production to some 100 hectares across the whole range of Chablis Appellations. Fèvre was also a strong advocate of new oak and the magnificent cellar constructed in 1979 is full of barrels imported from the Côte d'Or. Since 1990, however, he has vinified in oak and *cuve* switching from one to the other by stopping the fermentation as his 1,000 barrels were insufficient to cope with the production. Unfortunately, this led to rather irregular winemaking with quality variation. However, as we have said, this is history, and the vinification is now controlled from Bouchard HQ in Beaune by their chief winemaker Didier Seguier – and change is in the air!

Vinification and *élevage* is still taking place at the original *cuverie* in the centre of town situated alongside the Hostellerie des Clos. Expansion has already taken place with a new large *chai* having been built just outside the centre on the road to Tonnerre and the numbers of barrels increased by some 25 per cent to cope with the production.

The new owners have now introduced a much more controlled harvesting procedure with all grapes now manually picked and gathered into small baskets to protect from damage and maintain quality: a *table de trie* has been introduced in order to weed out unripe or rotten fruit and Bouchard believe it is the first in Chablis. Only 5 hectares are now picked by machine.

All Grand Crus are fermented and *élevé* in wood but only 20 per cent of the barrels are new each year, with the barrel age extended to 4 or 5 years. Vinification of the Premier Crus is now only 50 per cent in wood and only 30 per cent for the basic Chablis. Enamelled and stainless steel vats from the original Fèvre operation are still in use and traditional fermentation procedures are adopted using only natural yeasts. 1998 will be their first vintage.

New labels are being introduced keeping the separate names of William Fèvre and Domaine de la Maladière, other names used for the *négociant* wines Ancien Domaine Auffrey and Jeanne-Paule Filipi are expected to disappear. Champs Royaux – the prestige cuvée produced from selected Chablis Village vineyards – is being retained, and it is expected that whereas in the past this wine was totally overpowered with oak, it will now be much better balanced and more representative of a Cuvée Prestige.

We met Didier Seguier at the domaine where he explained these changes and we will note with interest how the William Fèvre wines develop for the future. First impressions are very favourable. At this time we feel it is inappropriate to give any rating or classification to this domaine in view of the new régime and the considerable changes taking place – at least two vintages 1998 and 1999 will be needed to form a better assessment.

Tasting notes
The following wines were tasted at the domaine on 1 March 1999:

Chablis 98 – fragrant, good fruit and acidity, good concentration from very low yield, balanced, good length.

Montmains 98 – this was *élevé* in *cuve*, no oak, rich ripe fruit with good maturity, appley, minerally, well balanced, soft finish. Should be very good. (2002–2006)

Vaillons 98 – 50 per cent in wood, well integrated. Mineral nose with good fruit and lovely balance, well structured, minerally and rich, elegant. Should be very good. (2002–2006)

Bougros 98 – malo not finished – fruit and acidity is there, rich and minerally. Should be a very good wine. Give it six years.

Les Preuses 98 – malo not finished – more delicate mineral nose, gorgeous rich fruit and balance, should be fine. Needs six years.

Les Clos 98 – malo not finished – very restrained nose, the fruit is hidden but very rich and concentrated, should be an elegant, long and lovely wine in seven years.

Champs Royaux 97 – much better than the 96, good fruit with dry mineral finish, well balanced. Good wine.

Vaillons 97 – too oaky on nose, mineral flavour but where is the fruit? Disappointing. (2000–2004)

Les Preuses 97 – little on nose, fruit a bit sour but not masked by oak. Fruit is expansive at back of throat suggesting probable improvement with age. Judgement reserved.

Fourchaume 96 – too oaky for us but a rich fruity wine. Oak should integrate with time. (2002–2005)

Les Preuses 96 – closed up here, concentrated fruit once again marked by oak, perhaps too much to integrate. Not exactly typical Chablis! May get better, only time will tell. A note from a bottle tasted in April 98 made the same comment. (2003–2008)

Montmains 94 – gentle perfumed nose, not a lot of concentration but fair balance with a dry mineral finish. Fairly good wine. Drink now.

Bougros 94 – delicate fruity nose but good fruit on the palate, Cox's apples, dry, minerally, balance and length. Very good for the vintage. (2000–2004)

The following wines were tasted at the domaine in May 1998 except as stated:

Chablis Champs Royaux 96 – fermented *en barrique* with 2 months' ageing. Tastes of oak and bitter.

Les Clos 96 – vinified in inox, racked to *barrique* and back again to inox. 2 months ageing in inox and 6 months in oak which masks the style of wine. Good intensity, but we shall see how it develops.

Grenouilles 96 – deeply coloured, nose smells of 'sulphured frogs', boiled sweet flavour, a no-no! (April 98)

Petit Chablis 95 – pale greenish tinged, very little nose but lovely gentle Chablis of good *typicité*, excellent with food. (January 98)

Montmains 95 – inox vinification and *élevage en barrique* 20 per cent new. Smells of new oak, nice fruit but tannin from oak masks and marks it.

Valmur 95 – same process as Les Clos. Still an oaky nose, more mineral, but again oak is masking the progress. This will *not* be like the wonderful 1990.

Monsieur and Madame Fèvre were present at the 1997 London Wine Fair, where a wide range of Chablis were available for tasting. Our tasting notes follow:

Chablis Champs Royaux 95 – oak aged, not for us. Although this is from selected grapes, it is still only a village wine and the oak flavour was too overpowering.

Fourchaume 94 – still closed, but beginning to show its quality. Lovely nose developing in glass with good fruit and a long lingering aftertaste. A good wine. (2000–2004)

Vaudésir 93 – a light year which tests a grower's expertise. This is becoming a lovely fragrant wine, delicious with fish. Very good for the vintage. Drink now.

Bougros 93 – a much fuller wine than the Vaudésir, opening up beautifully in the glass. This one please for poultry with sauces. Very good. (2000–2003)

Tasting notes from other occasions:

Chablis 93 – already showing good *typicité*, fruity and well balanced for the vintage. Fairly good. (September 94)

Les Clos 93 – Chablis nose of *typicité*, lovely fruit with good length, very good for the vintage, delicious. Drink now. (May 98)

Fourchaume 92 – very pleasant nose, nutty and biscuity, and on the palate the fruit was pineappley and quite exotic but with little depth, Chablis it isn't but a nice wine. Good. Drink now. (January 98)

Mont de Milieu 92 – streets ahead of the 91, lovely steely fruit and acidity, not a big wine, but some elegance. Good. Drink now. (September 94)

Vaudésir 92 – a very good Grand Cru, flowery, full and well balanced, lovely *typicité*. (2000–2002) (September 94)

Mont de Milieu 91 – some maturity, already drinking, little individual character, but this is the vintage. Fair. Drink up. (September 94)

Valmur 90 – stunning wine, wonderful vintage. Big, lovely fruit and balance, nuts and honey, very long, real quality. Fine. (2000–2005) (November 97)

Vaudésir 89 – this has 30 per cent new wood, but it is not obtrusive at all, wine of *typicité*, good weight and depth, full, long lovely fruit. Fine wine. Drink now. (November 97)

Bougros 87 – a very good Grand Cru for the vintage, already developed and drinking well. A good buy at the time. (October 90)

Wines are available at the **CELLAR DOOR** and through the named exclusive importers Heyman Barwell Jones in the UK and Seagram Château and Estate Wines in the USA. We also list below a fuller range of known outlets where at the time of writing these wines were available.

UK
Barwells of Norwich. Tel: 01603 723900
Berry Bros. & Rudd, London SW1. Tel: 020 7396 9669 Fax: 020 7396 9611 and at Basingstoke, Hants. Tel: 01256 323566 Fax: 01256 340106
Greene King, Bury St.Edmunds and branches. Tel: 01284 763222 Fax: 01284 706502

Heyman Barwell Jones, Suffolk and London SW1. Tel: 020 7730 0324 Fax:
020 7730 0575
Longford Wines, Sussex. Tel: 01273 480761 Fax: 01273 480861
or longwines@aol.com
Montrachet, London SE1. Tel: 020 7928 1990 Fax: 020 7928 3415
Thos. Peatling, Bury St.Edmunds and branches. Tel: 01284 755948 Fax:
01284 705795
Pomona Wines, Kent. Tel: 01634 235658
Freddy Price, London W5. Tel: 020 8997 7889 Fax: 020 8991 5178
e-mail: freddywine@aol.com
Reid Wines, Bristol. Tel: 01761 452645 Fax: 01761 453642
Charles Taylor Wines, London SE1. Tel: 020 7928 8151 Fax: 020 7928 3415
e-mail: charles.taylor.wines@dial.pipex.com
Waverley Vintners, Perth, Perthshire. Tel: 01738 629621 Fax: 01738 630338

USA

Garnet Wines & Liquors, New York, 10021. Tel: 212 772 3211
Fax: 212 517 4029
Seagram Château & Estate Wines Co., 375 Park Avenue, New York City,
NY 10152-0192. Tel: 212 572 7000 Fax: 212 572 1263
Sherry-Lehmann Inc., New York. Tel: 212 838 7500 Fax: 212 838 9285

DOMAINE DE CHATEAU DE FLEYS

André Philippon

Fleys	Tel: 03 86 42 13 73
89800 Chablis	Fax: 03 86 42 81 09

10 hectares

Production:

Premier Cru Mont de Milieu	4 ha
Chablis Clos de Château de Fleys	1 ha
Chablis Village	5 ha

As the name indicates, this domaine is centred on the old Château de Fleys
on the highest point of the village overlooking the *clos* to the Château and
the vineyards across the valley.

André Philippon, a wonderful character and an enthusiastic anglophile
(we can do no wrong), makes light of his not inconsiderable problems,
bound to a wheelchair having suffered polio as a child, and recently in
1998 his daughter being terribly injured in a motor accident. His ability
to keep so ebullient and smiling shows his strength of character. And for
the happy future, his son is at l'Ecole du Vin in Beaune and will soon follow
in the business.

We were received in the large lounge of the château, a lovely old building with a courtyard garden and patio leading down to the *clos*. The reception was warm and friendly, and if we did not have further appointments that day, we would probably still be there listening to this fascinating man and imbibing his lovely wines. Jean-Paul Durup tells us the story of the day that André was to attend a function at Le Petit Pontigny and as he was unable personally to manoevre his wheelchair down the stairs to the banqueting hall, he and chair were lifted shoulder high and carried below, André bellowing directions left and right, Roman-emperor style. The guests collapsed with laughter.

However, the wines are the thing, and André had a fine training in viticulture coming from a family of growers, but it was very largely due to his own perseverance that the estate was created in 1970. His father was a restauranteur in Auxerre and no doubt was one of the first customers to purchase the wine!

Yields are kept as low as possible, the average *rendement* for the Mont de Milieu being 45-50 hl/ha. Vinification is traditional, all in stainless steel. Although wood was used in the past, this practice has now ceased. The total annual production is about 600 hectolitres, 60 per cent of which is sold to the *négociant* firm Labouré Roi. The remainder is bottled and sold locally with some exports to Belgium, Germany and just a little to the UK.

We tasted the Mont de Milieu from four vintages. Lovely wines. This is definitely a domaine worthy of note.

Tasting notes

Wines tasted at the domaine in October 1998:

Mont de Milieu 97 — nose already opening out, lovely fruit with depth, balance and length. Fine wine. (2000–2003)

Mont de Milieu 96 — lovely nutty nose, intense concentrated fruit with a delicious dry finish. Fine wine. Needs time. (2001–2005)

Mont de Milieu 95 — perfumed nose, intense fruit, nuts, honey and apricots on palate, full but elegant, well balanced with a fine dry finish. Fine wine. (2000–2003)

Mont de Milieu 89 — lovely deep colour, honey and biscuit flavour, fine fruit, wine of depth now fully mature and perhaps past its best. Drink soon.

Wines tasted in London:

Chablis 96 — bit of a dumb nose, plenty of weight and fruit, but not quite enough acidity to balance. A good food wine though. (May 98)

Wines are available from the **CELLAR DOOR.**

DOMAINE FOURREY et FILS

9 Rue du Château
Milly
89800 Chablis

Tel: 03 86 42 44 04
Fax: 03 86 42 84 78

15 hectares

Production:
Premier Crus

	Beauroy	0.25 ha
	Fourchaume	0.25 ha
	Vaillons	2.20 ha
	Côte de Léchet	3.00 ha
	Mont de Milieu 1	.00 ha

Chablis Village and Petit Chablis

Domaine Fourrey comprises a range of rather old dilapidated buildings and the family house grouped around a yard which has visions of Steptoe & Son. However, a brand new building was erected in 1997 fronting the road immediately opposite the imposing Château de Milly so as to attract visitors to the domaine and this is very tastefully laid out with a shop, office and large comfortably furnished tasting room in the cellar below. The whole is designed with the passing trade in mind – wishful thinking perhaps!

We were greeted by Madame and Monsieur Fourrey (Mère et Père), father rather distrustful of his visitors and as usual Madame very charming and helpful. The son of the family was duly summoned, now clearly in charge of winemaking, a young man sharing his father's reluctance to smile and elaborate too much on his methods and quite what made him tick, if anything.

We did glean, however, that vinification of their not insignificant holdings was carried out in stainless steel, but some old barrels, 3 to 5 years old, are also in use. The production is 80 per cent sold *en vrac* to the *négoce* with some 20,000 bottles per annum available for the home market, plus exports to Holland and surprisingly to Australia. The UK and USA are not yet on the honoured list.

For a domaine with five separate Premier Crus, even though two are of a relatively small area, we found the wines rather disappointing. The ability to produce good wine is undoubted – e.g. the Côte de Léchet 97. The basis for a sound business is here with some recent investment in buildings; we can only hope that with time the yield will be evident in the quality of the wines.

Tasting notes
The following wines were tasted at the domaine in February 1999:

Chablis 97 – some nose, perfumed fruit comes through, but rather bland on palate. Disappointing.

Côte de Léchet 97 – closed on nose, good balance of fruit and acidity with a nice minerally aftertaste. We liked this wine. Good. (2001–2004)

Vaillons 97 – also closed on nose, rather sharp mineral flavours, apples and pears. Needs more depth and focus. The Côte de Léchet is better. Fair only. (2001–2004)

Fourchaume 97 – flowery nose, violets, fruit rather hidden with strange after-taste. Fair acidity but lacks a little concentration and personality. Fair. (2001–2004)

Wines are available from the **CELLAR DOOR.**

DOMAINE RAOUL GAUTHERIN et FILS

6 Boulevard Lamarque   Tel: 03 86 42 11 86
89800 Chablis   Fax: 03 86 42 42 87

16.5 hectares

Production:

Chablis Grand Crus	Vaudésir	0.81 ha
	Grenouilles	0.22 ha
	Les Clos	0.17 ha
Chablis Premier Crus	Vaillons	3.67 ha
	Montmains	0.68 ha
	Mont de Milieu	0.26 ha
Chablis Village and Petit Chablis		

This is a family domaine that has made wine for five generations and is now run by Alain Gautherin.

The entrance to the domaine is essentially rather low-key, concealed behind a wall with double gates, set at the far end of the large main town car park. Lifting the catch and venturing through, trying not to step on an assortment of children's toys and thus being involuntarily propelled feet first on the seat of your pants across the yard by an uncontrollable skate-board, one is struck by the similarity to a playground, obviously a meeting place for friends, customers and the younger members of the Gautherin household alike. Clearly it is no accident that the estate is surrounded by a wall! Within these walls are located the family home plus the *cuverie*, cellar and small tasting room on the opposite side of the yard.

We were welcomed by Alain, a young 30-ish friendly man and his charming wife, both with a lovely sense of humour but very sparing with the description of the domaine and winemaking.

The *vignoble* is quite extensive, totalling more than 16.5 hectares, of which 1.2 is Grand Cru and 4.6 Premier Cru. The largest holding is of Chablis Village – about 9.5 hectares with the remainder Petit Chablis. The wines are mostly vinified in the traditional way in enamel-lined vats, although there are also large old *foudres* of 6,300 litres for some of the Vaillons.

Alain regards his Grenouilles as the wine of the domaine, even though the area involved is very small. He prefers it for its richness when fully matured. Unfortunately, none was available for us to be able to verify his claim. To judge from the wines tasted, including wines from one of the greatest of Chablis vintages, the expertise is available here for the production of very good wines. So far the 98s do not please us, perhaps the fruit was affected by the late summer rains. We shall visit and taste again.

Apart from the French domestic market where they concentrate on the catering trade, they export to England, Germany and Holland, as well as Japan and Brazil. The total production is divided 60 per cent in bottle and 40 per cent to the *négoce*.

Tasting notes

Tasted in London August 1999:

Chablis 98 – quiet nose, dry bitter fruit, citrus flavours but rather bland. Fair.

Montmains 98 – gentle perfumed nose, appley fruit but not very substantial. Fair. (2001–2003)

Vaillons 98 – straw nose, somewhat lacking in fruit and low on acidity. Disappointing. (2001–2003)

Tasted at the domaine in May 1998:

Chablis 96 – closed nose, balanced fruit and acidity, drinkable basic Chablis.

Vaillons 96 – fruity nose, good ripe fruit, some intensity and length, fair wine, should improve (as it did – see below).

Vaudésir 96 – 35-year-old vines, obviously closed up but not enough fruit showing for the future. Not much to it. Disappointing.

Retasted in London April 99:

Vaillons 96 – minerally fruit on nose, a dry wine with plenty of fruit, good acidity and length, even intensity, wine of *typicité*. No great depth initially but returning to the bottle the following day (the litmus test = leave it till morning under seal) the wine had gained immensely, hazelnuts and biscuits on the palate, really delicious and with a lovely lingering aftertaste. Still needs a little time. Very good. (2000–2003)

Vaudésir 96 – intense tight nose showing underlying fruit, mineral characteristics, good concentration, fair length and balance, undeniably a very good wine but it doesn't quite stir the soul. Unlike the Vaillons, it did not pass the litmus test. (2002–2006)

Wines available from stockists in:

UK
Bordeaux Direct, Reading, Berks. Tel: 0118 948 1718
McKinley Vintners, London SE1. Tel: 020 7928 7300
Sunday Times Wine Club. Tel: 0118 903 0123 Fax: 0118 903 0401

USA
Dennis Sherman, Forum Worldwide Ltd, PO Box 339, Bridgeport,
  Pennsylvania 19405-9998.

DOMAINE ALAIN GAUTHERON

Fleys	Tel: 03 86 42 44 34
89800 Chablis	Fax: 03 86 42 44 50

18 hectares

Production:

Premier Crus		
	Vaucoupin	1.5 ha
	Mont de Milieu	1.0 ha
	Les Fourneaux	3.5 ha

Chablis Village and Petit Chablis

On the road from Chablis to Tonnerre, just into the village of Fleys, fork left down into the valley in the shadow of Mont de Milieu. Situated on the slopes below the village, Alain Gautheron's domaine clings to the steep sides, a Swissstyle house with a range of modern buildings incorporating the office, *cuverie* and warehouse overlooking the slopes of Premier Cru Fourneaux. All that is needed to complete the scene is 12 inches of snow and a ski-lift with an unending queue.

This domaine has been handed down from father to son over six generations. Alain is a verbose but amiable character with a take it or leave it attitude. His son is in his early twenties, rather overshadowed by father, but we are sure is in good hands to follow in the family tradition.

Vinification is mainly by traditional methods in stainless steel cuves, but a little oak does feature here in *barriques* of between one and five years of age, and used for the Fourneaux. The wines are fined *sur col* and given a kieselguhr filtration. There are normally 3 bottlings between July and September of the year following the vintage.

Alain likes the fruit of his Vaucoupin but as always preferences are varied by vintage. His English and Belgian customers lean toward the Fourneaux, so do we, whilst the Japanese like the very dry Mont de Milieu.

The wines have a wide market, exported to the UK, Holland, Belgium, Germany, Japan and a little to the USA. Yet again we have a domaine making variable wines where selection with care must be the byword. Perhaps earlier bottling would preserve freshness, and fewer of them to cut down the possibility of variation.

Tasting notes
The following wines were tasted at the domaine in October 1998, except as stated:

Fourneaux 98 – this needs time to develop. Mineral Fourneaux nose, the fruit is there with good concentration and depth, green apples, crisp clean finish. Very good. (2002–2006) (London, September 1999 by courtesy of Unwins)

Chablis 97 – quiet nose but lovely fruit, good balance and a good mouthful.

Vaucoupin 97 – little on nose for the vintage, appley flavour with good fruit, but rather sour.

Fourneaux 97 – a much better wine, lovely fruit with depth and concentration, crisp acidity, very elegant. Alain's Fourneaux is very good. (2000–2003)

Fourneaux Vieilles Vignes 97 – rather closed as would be expected, good concentrated fruit with length and intensity. Very good but perhaps the above has the edge on elegance. (2001–2004)

Mont de Milieu 97 – lovely nose, fruit, balance and depth, all there. Very dry wine. Good. (2000–2003)

Chablis 96 – lovely Chablis nose, good fruit with some depth, length and nice aftertaste. Good.

Vaucoupin 96 – pale colour, rather sour appley flavour, not for us! This is not Premier Cru quality.

Les Fourneaux 96 – pale lemon/straw, brilliantly clear, gentle but lovely flowery fruity nose, excellent *typicité*, bags of fine fruit, complex, good concentration and crisp acidity, well balanced, very long, drink from 2000 but delicious already. Very good. (April 98 in London)

Mont de Milieu 96 – lighter and less concentrated fruit here but nevertheless with some intensity. Rather sour aftertaste. This could improve with age. (2001–2003)

Chablis 95 – this was more like a generic Chardonnay from Oc, but those wines can be very interesting and extremely good value. This was just not interesting enough, rather bland. Fruit OK, some acidity but no length or depth. (April 98 in London)

Wines available from the **CELLAR DOOR** and stockists in:

UK
Anglo-International Wine Shippers, Esher, Surrey. Tel: 01372 469841
   Fax: 01372 469816
Unwins, branches nationwide. Tel: 01322 272711 Fax: 01322 220864

DOMAINE DES GENÈVES

Dominique Auffrère
Route de Collan
Fleys   Tel: 03 86 42 10 15
89800 Chablis   Fax: 03 86 42 47 34

13 hectares

Production:
Premier Crus   Mont de Milieu   1.50 ha
                        Les Fourneaux   1.22 ha
                        Vaucoupin   0.64 ha
Chablis Village and Petit Chablis

Many generations of Dominique Auffrère's vigneron family led to the creation of Domaine de Genèves in 1973. The domaine occupies an unmissable position at the entrance to the village of Fleys on the road from Chablis to Tonnerre, set behind an enormous car park and distribution yard, with the family cat and home to one side and the *cuverie* and *chai* facing the road. If an appointment is made for a visit, it is more than likely that Monsieur Auffrère will be waiting outside to welcome his visitors, and lead them directly into a very well equipped tasting room. Initially there was a problem with William Fèvre when Dominique started business, as Fèvre objected to the use of the name Domaine Auffrère on the grounds that it sounded too much like his own label Ancien Domaine Auffrey. Dominique, like the gentleman that he is, decided to bow to 'Big Brother' and change the name, but does not consider that he has lost anything in the process.

The domaine was fully equipped by 1985 and upgraded in 1992 with up-to-date vinification methods including temperature-controlled *cuves*.

This is an interesting domaine capable of producing very good wines. We particularly like the Chablis Vieilles Vignes cuvée and it is worth making a detour to get some from the cellar door. The total production is divided 60 per cent for the *négoce* and 40 per cent (approximately 50,000 bottles) for the home market and export mainly to Belgium, Germany and USA. At present we are not aware of any UK importer.

Tasting notes
The following wines were tasted at the domaine in October 1998, with the 98s tasted in London in August 1999:

Chablis Vieilles Vignes 98 – minerally nose, rather bitter from sulphur hiding the fruit, but this may dissipate. Judgement deferred.

Vaucoupin 98 – Mineral and fruity nose, lots of fruit on palate, fairly good concentration but no great length or depth. Fair. (2001–2004)

Mont de Milieu 98 – earthy minerals on nose and palate, sour apples but fruit comes out well on finish. May improve. Fair. (2001–2004)

Chablis Vieilles Vignes 97 – from 50-year-old vines. Lovely nose, great intensity and concentrated fruit, peaches and cream, lovely wine. Very good.

Les Fourneaux 97 – mineral *typicité* on nose, this is a good example, acacia and violets, lovely concentration, good balance, dry finish. Very good. (2000–2004)

Vaucoupin 97 – closed all round but the fruit is there, should develop well but is there enough concentration? Dry finish. Probably good. (2000–2003)

Mont de Milieu 97 – more on nose, more fruit although slightly astringent. This is a very good wine, nicely concentrated with a pleasant aftertaste. (2000–2004)

Petit Chablis 96 – good fruit and acidity, nicely balanced, crisp and clean finish. Good.

Chablis Vieilles Vignes 96 – from 50-year-old vines and it shows. Closed nose, old vine intensity, good concentration of fruit and well balanced. Needs time.

Mont de Milieu 96 – closed nose, the flinty mineral fruit is there but this is just a little rustic. Good wine with food. (2000–2003)

Vaucoupin 96 – from 30/40-year-old vines. Typical Chablis nose, appley fruit, fair concentration only and very dry. Good only. (2000–2003)

Wines are available from the **CELLAR DOOR** and stockists in:

UK

Anglo-International Wine Shippers, Esher, Surrey. Tel: 01372 469841
    Fax: 01372 469816
John Harvey of Bristol. Tel: 0117 927 5010

USA

Garnet Wines & Liquors, New York, 10021. Tel: 212 772 3211
    Fax: 212 517 4029

DOMAINE ALAIN GEOFFROY

4 Rue de l'Equerre
Beines   Tel: 03 86 42 43 76
89800 Chablis   Fax: 03 86 42 13 30

45 hectares

Production:
Chablis Grand Crus   Les Clos and Vaudésir (both *négociant* wines).
Chablis Premier Crus   Beauroy   7.0 ha
                        Fourchaume   1.5 ha
                        Vau Ligneau   3.0 ha
Chablis Village and Petit Chablis

This is a large commercially orientated domaine based in Beine, producing Chablis wines of good *typicité* for early drinking.

The house and domaine occupy a prominent corner position in the village receiving visitors in their large and busy front office. Alain Geoffroy very much in charge is an engaging and imposing man as befits his status as a past Mayor of Beine and patron of Auxerre Football Club where he can be regularly spied alongside his friend Jean-Marc Brocard.

At the domaine, Alain proudly leads the visitor through the *cuverie* and vast cellars closely accompanied by his black Labrador: this is clearly required as nobody else could find their way through this maze of interconnected buildings to his special tasting room. He is a supporter of the Durup case for the expansion of the Chablis vineyards and whilst we suspect the *rendements* are always up to the maximum permitted under AOC regulations, the wines are nevertheless well made and of a typical Chablis character.

Vinification is in stainless steel and the Village Chablis and Premier Crus are all bottled earlier than many other producers' wines. The Chablis Vieilles Vignes spends some six months ageing in oak barrels of between 2 and 5 years old. He sometimes adopts the same procedure for Grand Cru Les Clos, a *négociant* wine, depending upon the vintage. Alain regards his Beauroy as the most expressive wine in the stable.

These wines are easily found in UK wine shops on a regular basis. Ubiquitous they may be, but for once, do not let that put you off. This is a domaine to follow for easy drinking Chablis. What the wines may lack in individual personality and that last ounce of concentration are made up for by the steely and often refreshing crisp character, the perfect partner with white fish and seafood, especially oysters. This is definitely a domaine worthy of note.

Seventy-five per cent of the wines are for export to the UK, Germany, Benelux, Denmark, Switzerland, Japan and a little to the USA and Canada. The total production is 400,000-450,000 bottles a year. Labels may display either Domaine Alain Geoffroy or Domaine Le Verger but contain the same wine, although bottling dates may be different.

Tasting notes

The following 98s (cask samples) were tasted at BIVB/SOPEXA tasting in London (January 1999) and retasted at the London International Wine Trade Fair in May 1999:

Petit Chablis 98 – lovely fruit on the nose and on the palate, crisp acidity, even some depth. This is a very good Petit Chablis. By May 99 had developed lovely citrus flavours.

Chablis 98 – not quite so much here, fairly crisp wine but the Petit Chablis lingers on.

Chablis Vieilles Vignes 98 – more concentration and intensity here. Made entirely in 4-year-old wood. Lovely nose, mineral character and length. Oak doesn't mark too much. (London, May 99)

Vau Ligneau 98 – good typical nose, steely flinty fruit, some depth, good length. This is a good Vau Ligneau with potential. (2001–2004)

Beauroy 98 – closed on nose, dry fruit and plenty of it underneath but needs to come out. Not such a pleasant aftertaste. Judgement deferred. By May 99 this had not developed a great deal – showed good concentration of ripe sweet fruit with high acidity and fair length. Needs time. Good. (2002–2006)

Fourchaume 98 – this has a lovely floral fruity nose, concentrated fruit, long, comes out well on palate, plenty there for the future. Very good. (2001–2005)

The following wines were tasted at the domaine in May 1998:

Chablis 97 – fairly good Chablis of *typicité*, fruit and acidity balanced but just a bit bland.

Chablis Vieilles Vignes 97 – closed all round, a gentle but oaky wine, otherwise the same comments apply. Retasted at the London Wine Trade Fair where it had opened out a little and showed some citrus fruit flavours, no great concentration but a clean dry mineral finish. Good wine.

Vau Ligneau 97 – quiet nose, not much to report as not much wine here – we are still not convinced of the Premier Cru status of Vau-Ligneau! (Tasted at the London Wine Trade Fair 1998 – no change)

Beauroy 97 – absolutely nil on nose and just a little on palate, fruit hidden, mineral flavours, some length. Should develop well when it all comes together. Retasted in London at the Wine Trade Fair where it had come well forward, showing lovely minerally fruit with good concentration and a crisp finish, still developing well and should be very good. (2001–2003)

Fourchaume 97 – more fruit and length here, good balance but not the best Fourchaume. Fair. (2001–2004)

The following two wines were tasted in the old cellar off the bottling plant, the walls lined with an array of lovely old bottles including a 1927 Chablis and an 1870 Marc de Chablis:

Récolte Tardive 97 – bottled just 4 days. A real experience, gently sweet, obvious botrytis, but elegant fruit, wonderful aperitif wine.

Vin de Paille 97 – another rare experience, this is a new venture for Chablis and not generally available. Grapes dried on a bed of straw, which comes over deliciously on the nose, sweet and lovely.

Petit Chablis 96 – good fruity nose and palate, a fresh crisp Petit Chablis.

Chablis 96 – more restrained than the Petit Chablis, lovely fruit but not much depth. Domaine Le Verger later bottling.

Chablis 96 – earlier bottling. More character and more evolved on the palate than the above. Good wine. Is this the same wine as tasted at the London Wine Fair in 1997? See below.

Chablis Vieilles Vignes 96 – *barrique* on nose, a bit of character but oak too prominent. Is this for the US market?

Vau Ligneau 96 – closed nose, fruit hidden, nice concentration but a bit bland. The earlier bottling Chablis Village 96 was preferred. Fair. Drink now.

Beauroy 96 – closed nose once again as would be expected, lovely but reticent fruit, needs time to develop, and should be a good wine. (2000–2002)

Fourchaume 96 – not usually available in the UK, small production. Lovely floral nose, good fruit and acidity, well balanced but a bit sour on aftertaste. Good. (2000–2004)

Vaudésir 96 – what is there is totally closed, but how much fruit is there to evolve? (*Négociant* wine) Judgement reserved.

Les Clos 96 – vinification in *barrique*, same note as above, but perhaps the fruit shows better, needs a long time as oak overpowers the fruit. Should be good. (2002–2006) (*Négociant* wine)

Fourchaume 85 – wonderful nose of biscuits and toasted oak, fine fruit and length, well developed and balanced. Alain Geoffroy style and a fine wine just proving that these wines are capable of ageing beautifully when well made. Very good. Drink now.

Wines available from the **CELLAR DOOR** and stockists in:

UK
Anglo-International Wine Shippers, Esher, Surrey. Tel: 01372 469841 Fax: 01372 469816
Enotria Winecellars, London NW10 (trade only). Tel: 020 8961 4411 Fax: 020 8961 8773

Fullers, branches London and S.E England. Tel:.020 8996 2000 Fax: 020
    8996 2087
Oddbins, branches and fine wine shops nationwide. Tel: 020 8944 4400
    Fax: 020 8944 4411
Michael Peace, London W8. Tel: 020 7937 9345 Fax: 020 7937 7884
Thresher Group, branches nationwide including Bottoms Up and Wine
    Rack. Tel: 01707 328244 Fax: 01707 385000

USA

Atlanta Improvement, 1401 Dutch Valley Pl. NE, Atlanta, Georgia.
    Tel: 404 876 4500
Baron Francois Ltd. 236 W. 26th Street, Suite 304, New York City.
    Tel: 212 924 1414
The Williamsburg Winery, Williamsburg, Virginia. Tel: 757 229 0999.

DOMAINE GOISOT

Anne et Arnauld Goisot
8 Rue de Gouaix
4 bis Route de Champs   Tel: 03 86 53 32 15
89530 Saint-Bris-le-Vineux   Fax: 03 86 53 64 22

23 hectares − 3 hectares of Chablis

Production:
Chablis Village

This lovely domaine is run by the delightfully charming Anne Goisot and
her husband Arnauld from fine old buildings occupying a lovely setting.
The family house fronts the Rue de Gouaix with a picturesque terraced
garden at the rear also accessed from the Route de Champs. The cellars
and tasting room are set beneath the terrace where Anne Goisot met us
to discuss her wines and production.

Apart from the 3 hectares of Chablis Village, the Goisots also produce
Bourgogne Aligoté, Côte d'Auxerre red and white and, of course, Sauvignon de Saint-Bris. The total area of vines under cultivation is 23 hectares, so this is no small undertaking. The first vintage was in 1986 since
when the wines have received recognition every year from 1992. The family
involvement, however, goes back over three generations.

Vinification is totally in stainless steel *cuves* following traditional lines,
the grapes coming from six different parcels of Chablis Appellation in
Courgis.

These are well-made Chablis Village wines, and with a total production
of 22,000 bottles there is still some available for export, but we suspect this
is mainly sold in France and at the **CELLAR DOOR.**

Tasting notes

The following wines were tasted at the domaine in February 1999:

Chablis 98 – from *cuve* – good fruity Chablis, nice acidity and structure. Good.

Chablis 97 – rather bland but fair fruit, balanced, good crisp finish. Good.

Chablis 96 – floral honeyed nose, citrus fruits, some length, dry, delicious wine. Very good.

DOMAINE GRAND ROCHE

Erick Lavallée

16 Route de Champs   Tel: 03 86 53 84 07
89530Saint-Bris-le-Vineux   Fax: 03 86 53 88 36

6.45 hectares

Production:
Chablis Village

Domaine Grand Roche is run by the husband and wife team of Erick and Laurence Lavallée from their large house and farm situated up above the Route de Champs behind the local wine co-operative. However, the visitor having faithfully followed directions to the estate will inevitably be taken to the *cuverie* and *chai* which is housed in a new factory-type building on an industrial estate at the edge of town with all the aesthetic attraction of a shoe-box.

Erick Lavallée is an easy going friendly man who makes slight of his wine expertise but nevertheless tells us that from beginnings in 1987 he now produces 40,000 bottles of wine annually which includes his Bourgogne Blanc, Sauvignon de Saint-Bris, Côte d'Auxerre and Irancy as well as Chablis Village. Erick also owns a minuscule amount of Premier Cru but this is for very restricted sale and was not available for tasting – judging by the organisation here this was probably because he couldn't find any!

The vines are aged between 10 and 20 years and the vinification is traditional – the *cuverie* is very matter-of-fact with a row of stainless steel vats and a simple bottling line.

Tasting notes

The following Chablis were tasted at the domaine in February 1999, the 98 in London:

Chablis 98 – very pale, dumb nose, fruit is there but a little bitter. Fair only.

Chablis 97 – lovely nose, good depth of fruit, well balanced with light acidity. Good, basic Chablis.

Chablis 96 – mineral nose, fruit is there in abundance but perhaps a little short and lacked a bit of concentration. Nevertheless, quite good.

Wines are available at the **CELLAR DOOR** and **UK** stockists:
Hall Batson & Co., Norwich, Norfolk. Tel: 01603 415115
　Fax: 01603 484096

DOMAINE JEAN-PIERRE GROSSOT

Corinne Perchaud-Grossot and Jean-Pierre Grossot
4 Route de Mont de Milieu
Fleys   Tel: 03 86 42 44 64
89800 Chablis   Fax: 03 86 42 13 31

18 hectares

Production:

Chablis Premier Crus	Mont de Milieu	0.65 ha
	Vaucoupin	1.40 ha
	Fourneaux	1.60 ha
	Fourchaume	0.75 ha
	Côte de Troèmes	0.20 ha

Chablis Village and Petit Chablis

Driving eastwards out of Chablis on the Tonnerre road, entering the village of Fleys, the Grossot domaine is the first to be seen on the right-hand side, a complex of modern buildings set back from the road ranged round a courtyard and vineyard. You will probably be greeted by a large Doberman-cross, any encounter with undesirables likely to end in them being licked to death.

　The family estate was established in 1910, and there have been three generations of Grossots building to a respectable holding of 18 hectares including fine Premier Cru sites. Jean-Pierre Grossot and his wife Corinne are a young couple developing a reputation, Corinne herself coming from a *vigneron* family. Her name appears on some labels as Domaine Perchaud.

　Vinification here is traditional, stainless steel and enamelled *cuves*. There is some experimentation with oak but not all cuvées, e.g. the Chablis Grossot and part of the Mont de Milieu and Fourneaux is aged *en barrique*. The wines are fined with bentonite or isinglass, given *un passage de froid* for precipitation of the tartrates and finally kieselguhr-filtered before bottling which takes place between 9 and 15 months after the harvest.

　Very good wines emanate from this domaine, but we wonder whether there is too much interference during the *élevage*. And is the oak really necessary for a village cuvée? The style of the 96s seem to suit the Grossots very well. This is undoubtedly a domaine worthy of note.

　The markets for the wines are worldwide, including the UK, Europe, Japan and the USA.

Tasting notes

The following wines were tasted at the domaine in February 1999, the 98s at La Grande Marque in London in January 2000 by courtesy of Lay & Wheeler:

Chablis 98 – good fruit here but the wine doesn't sing. No great length. Good only.

Côte de Troèmes 98 – slightly earthy nose, a little dumb, good appley fruit on palate with fair length, no great depth but a good wine. (2001–2004)

Fourchaume 98 – nose reveals good fruit, Granny Smith apples, crisp acidity, good concentration and length, a wine of some depth. Very good. (2002–2006)

Chablis 97 – lovely green appley nose, minerally fruit, well balanced, crisp finish. Very good.

Chablis Part des Anges 97 – a little closed here, needs time for fruit to blossom, lovely balance. Very good.

Fourneaux 97 – steely mineral nose, needs time but this is very acidic, young vines so not a great deal of concentration, very dry wine. Good only. (2001–2003)

Fourchaume 97 – flowers and minerals, steely wine but still too much acidity for the fruit. Fair/good. (2001–2003)

Vaucoupin 97 – not a lot of concentration of minerally fruit, once again this is too acidic and short. Fair. (2000–2002)

Mont de Milieu 97 – brilliant greenish tinged colour, closed on nose but opens out a bit in glass, lovely Granny Smith apples with a hint of apricot, well balanced and long. This is very good. (2002–2005)

Chablis Grossot 96 – mildly oaky and perfumed, good fruit balance and length here. Good wine. This had improved since tasting in May 1998.

Vaucoupin 96 – lovely fruity nose which doesn't quite reflect on attack, not very elegant but well balanced and a nice dry finish. Good. (2001–2004)

Mont de Milieu 96 – very closed on nose but really lovely crisp juicy apple flavour if you work on it, clean dry finish. Very good. (2002–2005)

Tasted at the domaine May 1998:

Chablis Part des Anges 96 – more typical Chablis, good fruit but a bit short.

Fourchaume 96 – lovely floral and biscuity nose, masculine but elegant, good fruit, falls a bit dry on the finish, still very young and should open with time. Good. (2000–2004)

Chablis Grossot 95 – Chanel No. 5, fruit totally masked by oak, rather bland, not for us!

Fourneaux 95 – nice perfumed nose, lots of fruit, intensity and length, good acidity, good wine. Drink now.

Vaucoupin 95 – this is a good Vaucoupin, closed nose, minerally, lots of expansive fruit, very nice wine and no wood. Drink now.

Mont de Milieu 95 – part in wood, flowery perfumed nose, lots of fruit, a bit sharp and oak a bit too obvious, but could be a good wine given time. (2000–2003)

Wines currently available from stockists in:

UK

Enotria Winecellars, London NW10 (Trade only). Tel: 020 8961 4411
    Fax: 020 8961 8773
Ian G. Howe, Newark, Notts. Tel: 01636 704366 Fax: 01636 610502
Lay & Wheeler, Colchester, Essex. Tel: 01206 764446 Fax: 01206 560002
    http://www.layandwheeler.co.uk
O. W. Loeb & Co., London SE1. Tel: 020 7928 7750 Fax: 020 7928 1855
La Vigneronne, London SW7. Tel: 020 7589 6113

USA

Kysela Père et Fils, Chestnut Grove Road, Winchester, Virginia 22603.
    Tel: 540 722 9228
World Wine Source, Russell Herman, Berkeley Heights, NJ.

. . . .

DOMAINE GUITTON-MICHEL

2 Rue de Poinchy   Tel: 03 86 42 43 14
89800 Chablis   Fax: 03 86 42 17 64

6 hectares

Production:

Grand Cru	Les Clos	0.16 ha
Premier Crus	Montmains	0.80 ha
	Beauroy	0.10 ha

Chablis Village

On the road from Chablis to Poinchy at the right-hand fork, Rue de Poinchy, is found a small but attractive house clearly marked with the name of the domaine, a car park and access way leading to the office and well-equipped comfortable tasting room tagged on to the rear of the family home. This is a domaine run by Patrice Guitton and his wife Martine Michel, a cousin of Louis Michel of Chablis – wine verily flows through the family veins! The Guitton-Michels are now in their fourth generation of *vignerons*.

Domaine Guitton-Michel is a small estate with two tiny parcels of Premier Cru sites and one of Grand Cru Les Clos, the remainder made up of nearly 5 hectares of Chablis Village. The harvesting is done manually for the crus and the Chablis Vieilles Vignes with the rest carried out by machine.

Vinification is in enamelled *cuves* for the basic Chablis and *fût de chêne* with an average age of about four years for the Montmains, Beauroy and Les Clos. Before bottling in April, the wines are fined with bentonite and filtered.

A large part of the Chablis production is sold *en vrac* to the *négoce*, but some 30,000 bottles go for home consumption, with a little exported to Belgium and Germany.

Tasting notes
The following wines were tasted at the domaine in February 1999:

Chablis 97 – 40-year-old vines. Floral nose, slightly sour appley fruit, but good drinkable Chablis.

Beauroy 97 – floral fruit, a little closed but rather sharp. Fair. (2000–2002)

Montmains 97 – nose and palate of *typicité*, crisp fruit, fat and round, good length, lovely aftertaste. Very good. (2000–2003)

Chablis Vieilles Vignes 96 – 77-year-old vines. Good intense fruit, tight, some length here, good wine.

Beauroy 96 – closed nose, lots of fruit here but a touch sour, good concentration, depth and length, dry finish. Needs time to develop. Should be good. (2001–2003)

Montmains 96 – lovely fragrant flowers on nose, very minerally fruit, green appley, good length and aftertaste. Good/very good. (2002–2004)

Les Clos 96 – some minerals on nose, immense concentration of fruit but very tight now, lovely length and balance. Very good. (2003–2007)

Wines are available from the **CELLAR DOOR.**

DOMAINE THIERRY HAMELIN

1 Impasse de la Grappe
Lignorelles   Tel: 03 86 47 52 79
89800 Chablis   Fax: 03 86 47 53 41

37 hectares

Production:
Chablis Premier Crus   Vau Ligneau   3.50 ha
                       Beauroy   3.90 ha
Chablis Village and Petit Chablis

Domaine Hamelin, family owned for over six generations and centred on
the village of Lignorelles has grown slowly but surely from modest beginnings in 1840, when Gustave Hamelin cultivated a mere 2 hectares. By 1880
a further hectare had been added and because of Phylloxera the total
reached only 4 hectares by 1911. At this time polyculture was the norm
but hard times were to come with the advent of the First World War.

Georges Hamelin handed over to his son Pierre in 1936 and then began
the development of the estate. Mechanisation was introduced in the 1950s
and a gradual installation of enamelled metal *cuves* began. In 1970 Marc
Hamelin created his own estate adding it to his father's holdings. Today
the domaine has been regrouped, Thierry and his brother Bruno control-
ling an impressive 37 hectares from two separate estates around the communes of Lignorelles, Beines and Poinchy including two fine parcels of
Premier Cru sites, 3.5 hectares of Vau Ligneau in the Vallée de Vaux de
Long and 3.9 hectares of south-facing Beauroy. The Chablis and Petit Chablis vineyards are on Portlandian soil.

A corner shop on the main road approach is the outlet for cellar door
sales with the *chai* and family home situated round the corner occupying
old farm-type buildings. The large modern *cuverie* is located down the hill
on the other side of the main road.

The spotlessly clean *cuverie* houses a traditional operation, vinifying and
ageing the wines in stainless steel. A small amount of oak is available in the
chai but rarely if ever used. The whole operation is run with a quiet efficiency as befits the thorough and thoughtful approach of *les frères* Hamelin.

The wines can be very good as the notes below testify, generally minerally and dry, with crisp acidity and flowery fruit, the epitome of typical
Chablis, excellent with food.

Tasting notes
The following wines were tasted at the domaine both in May 1998 and
February 1999-and others as stated:

Petit Chablis 97 – fresh aromatic wine, good for early drinking. By February
99 this was not showing much length and was a bit slight.

Chablis 97 – good concentration of fruit with some depth, long clean finish. Good basic Chablis.

Chablis Vieilles Vignes 97 – 55-year-old vines. Intense wine, lovely citrus fruits, mineral *typicité*, good acidity and length. Needs a couple of years. Very good. (2001–2004)

Vau Ligneau 97 – this had improved from when first tasted, but still needs more time to show its fruit. Good fruit but lacks a little concentration and depth. Dry mineral finish. Fairly good (2001–2004)

Beauroy 97 – lovely fruity nose, floral perfumed, fruit a little tight but hints of hazelnuts and apricots, rich and concentrated, dry mineral finish. Very good. (2002–2007)

Petit Chablis 96 – little on nose, some fruit and plenty of acidity, as Petit Chablis goes it's OK, but not a lot to it. There are better. (April 98)

Chablis 96 – straw yellow colour, lovely fragrant flinty nose, big mouthful of green appley fruit with well-balanced mouth-puckering acidity, fresh and crisp, long, delicious Village wine. This would be an absolute marvel with a dozen oysters *aux naturelles*. (April 98)

Chablis Vieilles Vignes 96 – from 54-year-old vines. Floral nose, good fruit and concentration, good depth, good wine. (2001–2004)

Vau Ligneau 96 – closed nose, lacks a little fruit, too much acidity, a bit sour, perhaps it will blossom out but the Chablis Vieilles Vignes was preferred. Retasted in London: straw colour, nose opening out, lovely fruit of apricots with honey tones, good length. A much better wine than tasted at the domaine. Different bottlings? This is now a good wine. (May 98)

Beauroy 96 – straw coloured, gentle flowery nose with a flinty character, develops beautifully in glass, fine concentrated fruit and balancing acidity, depth and complexity, hazelnuts, green apples, apricots and honey, long, slightly austere at the moment but will blossom out, very good wine. (2000–2004) (April and May 98)

Wines available from the **CELLAR DOOR** and stockists in:

UK

Anglo-International Wine Shippers, Esher, Surrey. Tel: 01372 469841 Fax: 01372 469816
Avery's of Bristol, Nailsea. Tel: 01275 811 100 Fax: 01275 811101
Berkmann's Wine Cellars, London N7. Tel: 020 7609 4711
The Boxford Wine Co., Boxford, Suffolk. Tel: 01787 210187
Châteaux Vino, London N2. Tel: 020 8883 4365
House of Hallgarten, Luton, Beds. Tel: 01582 722538 Fax: 01582 723240
Le Nez Rouge, London N7. Tel: 020 7609 4711

USA

Calvert Woodley, Washington DC. Tel: 202 966 4400

Robert Kacher Selections, 28000 V. Street, NE Washington DC, 20018.
USA Wine Imports, 285 W.Broadway, New York, NY10013. Tel: 212 941
7133

DOMAINE LAROCHE ★

L'Obédiencerie
22 Rue Louis Bro
89800 Chablis

Tel: 03 86 42 89 09
Fax: 03 86 42 89 29
e-mail: lorraine.carrigan@domainelaroche.fr
http://www.vinternet.fr/DomaineLaroche

100 hectares

Production:

Chablis Grand Crus	Blanchots	4.50 ha
	Les Clos	1.12 ha
	Bougros.	0.31 ha
Chablis Premier Crus	Fourchaume VV	6.80 ha
	Vaillons VV	6.91 ha
	Montmains	1.42 ha
	Beauroy	2.80 ha
	Vau de Vey	10.20 ha
	Côte de Léchet	0.23 ha
	Montée de Tonnerre	0.04 ha

Chablis Village, Vieilles Vignes and Petit Chablis

Domaine Laroche has grown from small beginnings in 1850 when Jean Victor Laroche, a local vineyard worker, bought his first modest plot of vines, to more than 100 hectares today producing 4.5 million bottles a year.

For five generations the family has been dedicated to producing top quality Chablis, but expansion really took hold when in 1967 Michel Laroche, then a 21-year-old oenologist and his father Henri made substantial investments. At that time the local economy, although promising, was far from booming, and the opportunity was there and taken to buy land at reasonable prices.

Domaine Laroche is based at the Obédiencerie, the ninth-century monastery in the centre of Chablis, the home to the monks of Saint Martin who planted the first vines in the town. This lovely old building houses one of the oldest wooden presses ever used in Chablis, and is still occasionally brought into use to make a celebration *cuve*.

Michel Laroche constantly strives to achieve the perfect mix of techniques to obtain his ultimate goal, but the emphasis is strongly on the use of organic methods and less and less sulphur. Only natural fertilisers are used and chemical treatments of parasites are kept to a minimum. He also uses only traditional vinegrafts mainly taken from his own Vieilles Vignes which are more than 40 years old.

The *cuverie* and *chai* on the road to Milly are ultra-modern built in 1991 for the 1992 harvest. Even the method of transporting the fruit from the vineyards is impressively up to date, a trailer adapted to allow the free fall of juice away from contact with crushed grapes and into a tray underneath, thus preventing oxidation. Right up to the *débourbage* everything works by gravity. After pressing of the grapes, all the *vin de presse* is added back to the free-run wine. Fermentation temperature depends on the vintage and *cuvé*. Precipitation of the tartrates generally occurs in a controlled environment in inox, but one year recently an experiment was carried out encouraging the natural process by leaving the doors open during the winter months.

This is a domaine that believes in oak, and oak ageing for all the Grand Crus, the Fourchaumes and Vaillons using 228-litre Allier barrels at least four years old. Sometimes the provenance of the oak is mixed, to maintain complexity. Stainless steel vats are used to produce the other Premier Crus and the Village Chablis, emphasising their fresh mineral character. The wines are fined with casein for a later bottling, and bentonite or fish fining for an earlier *mis*. Filtration is used sparingly, but for the 96 Grand Crus not at all.

There are 6 hectares of Grand Crus and some 29 hectares of Premier Crus. Michel Laroche is particularly proud of his Réserve de L'Obédienc-erie made from only half a hectare of his best selected Grand Cru Les Blanchots. The estate also produces a Village Vieilles Vignes made from vines with an average age of 25 years which he regards of equal quality to many Premier Crus. Is this a veiled critique of the recent extension of Premier Crus in the outlying villages?

As can be seen from the tasting notes below, this is a very good and reliable source. 95 per cent of the total production is exported to the UK, Scandinavia, Asia and the USA. A star domaine.

Tasting notes
The following cask samples were tasted in London in August 1999:

Chablis Saint-Martin 98 — nose of real *typicité*, minerals and fruit, good concentration and length. Good Chablis.

Vaudevey 98, pale colour, dumb on nose but good apricot fruit and acidity with length. Good wine. (2001–2004)

Vaillons 98 — the fruit peeps out shyly here, but develops in glass to show minerally character, good concentration but we prefer the Vaudevey. (2001–2004)

Fourchaume 98 — a bit dumb on the nose but lovely fruit with concentration and depth, apples and pears, lovely balance, length and finish. Very good. (2002–2005)

Blanchots 98 — lots of earthy minerally fruit, hidden but revealed with encouragement, intense concentration, lovely balance and length. Should be a very good wine. Give it time. (2003–2008)

Les Clos 98 – oaky nutty nose, big wine but fruit smothered by the oak. Given time, should be a good wine. (2004–2009)

The following wines were tasted at the domaine in February 1999:

Chablis Saint Martin 97 – full of fruit and even drinking now, good balance of acidity, good length, clean and crisp. Good.

Vaudevey 97 – some perfume on nose but not a lot of depth or concentration here, still some steely fruit with acidity and dry finish. Good. (2001–2004)

Vaillons Vieilles Vignes 97 – gone into its shell and needs time. Good fruit here but is there enough acidity? Mineral flavours, oak well integrated. Good. (2002–2005)

Fourchaumes Vieilles Vignes 97 – vine age 30/35 years. Flowery fragrant nose with hazelnuts, lovely fruit and balanced acidity, nicely minerally, long. Very good. (2002–2005)

Blanchots 97 – delicate perfumed nose, nicely concentrated with intensity, depth and length, lovely wine. Lots there for the future. Very fine. (2003–2007)

Les Clos 97 – very closed, bags of elegant fruit, beautiful balance, this is a big wine for the future, but should have great finesse. Will be fine. (2004–2009)

Réserve de l'Obédience 97 – very closed, a bit woody on palate but good intense concentration of fruit, rich and stylish, needs time, should be fine. (2003–2007)

The following wines were tasted at the domaine in May 1998:

Chablis Saint Martin 96 – nose a little closed but lovely fruit and balance, very stylish. Another bottle tasted a few days later revealed no nose but a strong flavour – is it oak? Lacked fruit, short, not for us! Why was this so different from that tasted at the domaine and how spaced out were the bottlings? (May 98)

Vaudevey 96 – nose of *typicité*, wine of character, good fruit, balanced, gentle, long, oak does not obscure fruit, will open out into a very good wine. (2000–2004)

Vaillons Vieilles Vignes 96 – fine wine, fruity and balanced, good depth and concentration, very good length, but now closing up. (2000–2004)

Fourchaumes Vieilles Vignes 96 – concentrated wine of depth, excellent fruit and acidity, very long, but slight bitterness at back of throat (perhaps sulphur which will dissipate). Should be very good. (2002–2006)

Blanchots 96 – very closed, but very concentrated wine, great intensity, stylish. Fine wine. (2003–2008)

Les Clos 96 – oak apparent but should integrate, this wine has hidden depths, completely closed. Should be fine. (2004–2010)

Réserve de l'Obédiencerie 96 – from Blanchots. Wonderful intense nose, depth and concentration, wonderful fruit and balance, very long, very stylish. Fine wine. (2004–2010)

Further tasting in London and Chablis at varying times:

Chablis Saint Martin 95 – no nose here, dry flinty steely fruit, well balanced, clean finish. Good.

Chablis Vieilles Vignes 95 – quite a delicate wine, little on nose, good typical Chablis character, fine fruit but lacks a bit of zip. Perhaps it will develop. (December 97)

Blanchots 95 – perfumed nose, intense concentration, balanced, good acidity but slightly oxidised and faded in glass. Good only. Drink now.

Chablis Saint Martin 94 – lovely bright colour, gentle on nose and palate, good steely fruit, fair length, crisp, but could have a little more character even for a Village wine. (February 98)

Wines available from stockists in:

UK
Bottle & Basket, London N6. Tel: 020 8341 7018
Anthony Byrne Fine Wines, Cambs. Tel: 01487 814555
Percy Fox & Co., London and Essex. Tel: 020 7493 6174
Haverlock Wines, Bedford. Tel: 01234 272766
Majestic Wine Warehouses, branches nationwide. Tel: 01923 298200

USA
Garnet Wines & Liquors, New York, 10021. Tel: 212 772 3211
Fax: 212 517 4029

DOMAINE ROLAND LAVANTUREUX

4 Rue Saint Martin
Lignorelles
89800 Chablis

Tel: 03 86 47 53 75
Fax: 03 86 47 56 43

18 hectares

Production:
Chablis Village and Petit Chablis

Situated in the village of Lignorelles, this interesting domaine can be found behind the church, the house and buildings arranged around a small yard with a large *chai* at the rear.

Roland Lavantureux, a dapper friendly man, followed his father into the family business – his brother is located nearby in his own domaine, but not all the Lavantureux names throughout the village are related. His vineyards are all located in the area around the village, which makes for easier hands-on management both in the vineyards and the *cuverie*. The picking of the grapes is all done by machine and vinification is in stainless steel and en-amelled *cuves*. There are no startling practices here, just good honest and traditional winemaking.

Three quarters of the production is bottled producing some 70,000 bottles per annum. His wines, although limited to Petit Chablis and Chablis, are well made and this domaine is definitely worth a visit. The wines are exported to Germany, Belgium and Japan as well as the UK and USA.

Tasting notes.
The following wines were tasted at the domaine in February 1999:

Petit Chablis 97 – little on the nose but good fruit and crisp, a well made Petit Chablis.

Chablis 97 – little nose again but lovely ripe fruit and balance with distinct lemon flavour. Good clean finish.

Chablis 96 – light gold colour, more intense fruit, good acidity. Very good Chablis.

Wines are available from the **CELLAR DOOR** and stockists in:

UK

Adam Bancroft Associates, London SW8. Tel: 020 7793 1902 Fax: 020 7793 1897

USA

Kermit Lynch, Berkeley, California 94702. Tel: 510 524 1524 Fax: 510 528 7026

DOMAINE LONG-DEPAQUIT ★★

45 Rue Auxerroise	Tel: 03 86 42 11 13	
89800 Chablis	Fax: 03 86 42 81 89	

62 hectares

Production:

Chablis Grand Crus	Les Clos	1.60 ha
	Vaudésirs	2.60 ha
	Blanchots	1.10 ha
	Preuses	0.25 ha
	La Moutonne	
	Monopole	2.35 ha
Chablis Premier Crus	Beugnons	2.10 ha
	Les Lys	1.70 ha
	Vaucoupin	2.60 ha
	Vaillons	3.50 ha
Chablis Village		

The French Revolution hit Chablis at a time when a certain Jean Depaquy was the Abbot of Pontigny and his brother Simon Depaquy was public prosecutor. In 1790, both of them retired from public life 'for their health' – a wise decision. Simon retired to Chablis and on 31 March 1791 at the sale of national assets, confiscated by the new Revolutionary Assembly, bought the vines of the Abbey which included the famous 'Moutonne en Vaudésirs'.

In 1793 Simon married and had four children. He was Mayor of Chablis from 1795 to 1798, and one of his sons Benjamin became a wine broker on La Place de Bercy from 1824 to 1869. Benjamin had no children, but adopted a nephew François Auguste Long, thus the new family name of Long Depaquit. François had ten children from two marriages: it was his son Louis, a doctor of medicine, who managed the vineyards from 1910 to 1967 – this was quite amazing considering that he was blind as the result of a car accident at the age of 25. He devoted his life to his vineyards and his wines, and above all to the business, selling to Europe and the USA.

In 1927 Louis sold the property that Simon Depaquy had built, a fine house on the outskirts of Chablis, and acquired the eighteenth-century château situated on the Route d'Auxerre. This is today the Château Long-Depaquit with its 15,000 sq.m., its park and its cellars. Louis died without issue in 1967 at the age of 77. His legacy was a *vignoble* in excess of 10 hectares of the best crus in Chablis, and it was at this time that the Bichot family from Beaune, who had moved into Chablis, took an interest in the domaine. It was not until 1970 that the acquisition was completed, and two years later with the arrival of Gérard Vullien as *Régisseur*, Bichot decided that the estate should be run completely autonomously. Now there started a long period of development. Firstly, the planting in 1973 of 3 hectares in

Vaudésirs, Les Clos, Beugnons and Les Lys, then the acquisition and planting of 10 hectares of Chablis AOC in the commune of Viviers between
1974 and 1977. Six hectares of Vaucoupins followed and various other pur-
chases, and since 1987 the estate can boast a total area of about 62 hectares.
This development was rightly accompanied by improvements and new additions to the buildings including the restoration of the château in 1975 and
the construction of a new *chai* in 1991.

The domaine is very particular in its practices today. The grapes are
hand-picked in the Grand and Premier Crus, and part mechanically for
the Chablis village. Vinification and *élevage* are in stainless steel vats,
almost 100 per cent, with strict temperature control.

La Moutonne:
Included in the domaine is a small but revered Grand Cru Monopole
named La Moutonne with an area of 2.35 hectares, and situated at the
heart of the amphitheatre which forms the valley of Vaudésir, straddling
both the Grand Crus of Vaudésir and Les Preuses, its steep slope and Kimmeridgian outcrops protected from the cold north wind.

It is a name that applied already under the old régime to a vineyard of the
commune of Chablis situated in the Côte de Vaudésirs, one of the seven
Grand Crus. As has already been seen, La Moutonne was the property of
the monks of the Abbey of Pontigny and bought by Simon Depaquy in
1791.

In 1868, Doctor Guyot mentions La Moutonne amongst the best crus of
Chablis; Rousseau and Chappaz in 1904 name it before Vaudésirs, Les Clos
and Les Grenouilles. But La Moutonne acquired great notoriety during the
nineteenth century thanks to Benjamin Depaquit the Place de Bercy broker
who utilised 'Chablis Moutonne' as an appellation d'origine and also as a
brand-name. Moutonne is not the name of a brand but of a cru both by law
and custom, and to put an end to such abuse of the name, an agreement was
signed on 18 October 1950 between Monsieur Long-Depaquit and the
Syndicat Viticole de Chablis in the presence of the Service de la Répression
des Fraudes, ratified by INAO in July 1951.

In the not so distant past, Joseph Drouhin had an interest in the vineyard, and some bottles appeared with the Drouhin label. Today, La Moutonne has become the property of the Société Civile de la Moutonne, all
matters appertaining to the wine under the control of régisseur Gérard
Vullien. Like all the wines of the domaine, distribution is through
owners Maison Albert Bichot of Beaune.

The wine of La Moutonne tends to be soft and round, developing
honeyed tones after just a few years in bottle. Like all the wines of the
domaine, it has a personality, frequently very fine and seldom faceless,
very often charming. Gérard Vullien has stamped success all over this
estate.

All in all this is a wonderful domaine well deserved of two-star status.

Tasting notes

The following wines were tasted at the domaine in February 1999 and at the BIVB/SOPEXA tasting in London, January 1999:

Chablis 97 – good nose and fruit, and a good basic Chablis, but not as good as the 96. Dry mineral finish. Drinking already.

Les Lys 97 – fruit lacks a bit of concentration and a bit short, not very crisp. Rather disappointing. (2001–2003)

Beugnons 97 – very minerally fruit, some depth, well balanced. Good. (2001–2003)

Vaillons 97 – a lot to live up to with the last two vintages, and it just manages it! Lovely typical nose and fruity palate, good fruit, good concentration, good length, good acidity. Perhaps not the personality of the 95 and 96 but a good wine nevertheless. (2000–2003)

Vaucoupin 97 – this has more concentration and depth, lovely fruit. Needs time. Good wine. (2000–2004)

Vaudésir 97 – wine of intensity, violets on nose, lovely rich fruit of depth and concentration, well balanced and long. Very good. (2002–2007)

Moutonne 97 – this has all the elements expected of a fine Moutonne, obviously closed but bags of honeyed fruit waiting to burst out. Don't spoil it by drinking too soon. This will be fine. (2004–2009)

Les Clos 97 – 50 per cent in barrel. Closed as would be expected. Lots of lovely concentrated fruit here, gentle hint of oak, beautiful balance. Should be very good indeed. (2003–2008)

Chablis 96 – lovely nose, fruit and well balanced, drinking well now. Good.

Les Lys 96 – floral nose, violets, nice fruit with some depth. Delicious wine. Very good. (2002–2006)

Vaillons 96 – rather closed on nose but good fruit flavours. (May 98) Six months later this had developed into a lovely wine, still little on the nose, but a wine jam-packed with lovely concentrated almost sweet fruit, the honey and almonds are there just waiting to burst out, a big mouthful but elegant with it, fine acidity, beautifully balanced. Still needs time. Very good. Retasted many times since, a delicious wine. (2002–2006)

Vaucoupin 96 – minerally flinty wine of *typicité*, concentrated fruit with depth, balance and length. Fine. (2002–2006)

Blanchots 96 – very floral, lovely honeyed fruit, long and delicious, intense, well balanced, even lovely now, but a good keeper. Fine. (2003–2008)

La Moutonne 96 – reticent nose but gorgeous opulent fruit, fat, rich, delicate and elegant at the same time, concentration and depth, balanced and really long. Very fine. (2003–2008)

Les Clos 96 – 50 per cent in barrel. Intense fruit in abundance. Elegance and finesse. For the long term. The taste just goes on and on. Very Fine. Star wine! (2006–2010)

The following wines were tasted at the domaine in May 1998, and elsewhere as noted:

Vaucoupin 95 – nose still closed, stronger in flavour, bags of fruit with some acidity, not too long, not as good as the Vaillons. Good. (2000–2002)

Vaillons 95 – nutty and straw on nose, great fruit, good acidity for a 95, length and elegance. A really lovely wine. Delicious. Retasted several times in London – it gets better all the time! Very good. (2000–2004)

Les Clos 95 – 45 per cent oak of which 10 per cent new, remainder 2 to 8 years old. As would be expected, the oak is obvious but blends well, full flavoured, long and lovely. Perhaps not enough acidity for the very long term but that's the nature of the vintage. Very good. (2002–2006)

La Moutonne 95 – still quite closed but obvious *typicité*, wine of intensity, depth and concentration of fruit, very elegant, fine balance and aftertaste, long and delicious. Retasted at the Chartered Surveyors Wine Society July 1998 and just as delicious. Fine wine. (2002–2005)

La Moutonne 94 – more on nose here, honey and apricots, lovely deep concentrated wine, perhaps not as deep as the 95 but lovely open fruit flavours. This was tasted again at the BIVB tasting and once again at the domaine in February 99. What an utterly delicious wine! Fine. (2000–2004)

La Moutonne 93 – wonderful! Like walking through a field of spring flowers, a gentle perfume of violets, intense concentrated fruit, delicate, feminine, very elegant and very long. Truly lovely. Fabulous for the vintage. Fine. Drink now. (Bedford Fine Wine Club Tasting, March 1998)

La Moutonne 92 – a real treat. Tremendous bouquet of fruit, apricots and violets, absolutely delicious with *gougères*, very long, a delight! Fine. Drink now.

La Moutonne 90 – toasted oak, mushrooms and truffles, rich, full, fat, long and luxurious, absolutely delicious again. Fine. Drink now.

Wines available from the **CELLAR DOOR** and stockists in:

UK
Alliance Wines, Beith, Ayrshire. Tel: 01505 506060
Ballantynes, S. Glamorgan. Tel: 01446 774840 Fax: 01446 775253
Berry Bros. & Rudd, London SW1. Tel: 020 7396 9669 Fax: 020 7396 9611
    and at Basingstoke, Hants. Tel: 01256 323566 Fax: 01256 340106
Continental & Overseas Wines, Timperley, Cheshire. Tel: 0161 976 3696
F. & E. May, London WC1. Tel: 020 7405 6249

Unwins, branches nationwide. Tel: 01322 272711 Fax: 01322 220864
Waverley Vintners, Perthshire. Tel: 01738 629621

USA

Atherton Wine Imports, Georges Derbalian, PO Box 2305, Atherton, California, 94025.

Charmer Industries Inc., John Donnelly, 48-11 20th Avenue, Astoria, New York 11105.

Garnet Wines & Liquors, New York, 10021. Tel: 212 772 3211 Fax: 212 517 4029

Hi-Time Wine Cellars, Costa Mesa, California 92627. Tel: 949 650 8463 Fax: 949 631 6863

DOMAINE DES MALANDES ★★

| 63 Rue Auxerroise | Tel: 03 86 42 41 37 |
| 89800 Chablis | Fax: 03 86 42 41 97 |

25 hectares

Production:

Grand Crus	Vaudésir	0.90 ha
	Les Clos	0.53 ha
Premier Crus	Fourchaume	1.25 ha
	Montmains	1.18 ha
	Côte de Léchet	1.43 ha
	Vau de Vey	3.52 ha

Chablis Village and Petit Chablis

This family estate was started in 1986 by Lyne and Jean-Bernard Marchive from a sound base, for Lyne Marchive's family are the Tremblays of La Chapelle Vaupelteigne, an old established Chablis dynasty. The domaine is located just off the Route d'Auxerre, in a prominent attractive modern building housing the *cuverie*, *chai* and offices, the substantial family home set apart and back from the working part of the estate. The *cuverie* and *chai* were built in 1973 but the Marchives only moved into the house in 1996.

A charming smiling couple, the Marchives are welcoming hosts. Jean-Bernard, who took over the presidency of Le Syndicat de Défense de l'Appellation de Chablis from William Fèvre in 1998, strolls about the estate always followed closely by his faithful black Schnauser continually nudging guests for a pat or stroke. Every aspect of the viticulture and winemaking is clearly and lucidly expounded and explained.

Lyne and Jean-Bernard are enthusiastic about their vineyards, which include nearly a hectare of Vaudésir planted between 1967 and 1987, and half a hectare of Les Clos planted in 1962. The Premier Crus comprise 1.25ha of Fourchaume planted in 1952, plus impressive holdings in Montmains

1.18ha, Côte de Léchet 1.43ha and 3.5ha of Vau de Vey. There is just over a hectare of Petit Chablis, but the bulk of the domaine is the 14ha of Chablis Village.

Low yields are important here, with a strictly controlled harvest of only the ripest and healthiest fruit. The grapes are pneumatically pressed and vinification is in temperature-controlled stainless steel or enamel-lined vats, with the minimum of interference.

A tour of the domaine is followed by a fine tasting in the cellars below the *cuverie*, reached by a steep and precarious wooden staircase causing some anxiety when helping Jean-Bernard carry down an armful of precious bottles, after all you don't want to break any, never mind about broken legs. At the tasting, Lyne joins the party and warms with her Tremblay-smile an already happy occasion.

The Marchives also make the wine from about a third of a hectare of Vaudésir owned by Mark Reynier of La Réserve and Heath Street Wines in London, surely the only instance of British-owned vines in a Chablis Grand Cru (if there are any others, we shall be pleased to hear), but this wine is not vinified separately and is included in the main body of the Vaudésir cuvée. His reward is a few hundred bottles in a good year but little or none when hail causes a problem, as in 1998. Perhaps English growers should not put all their grapes in one basket.

The markets for the wines include the UK and mainland Europe, Japan, Hong Kong, Singapore, South Africa, Australia, Canada and the USA.

This is a fine two-star domaine, lovely people and lovely wines. Seek them out!

Tasting notes
The following wines were tasted in London in August 1999 by courtesy of Hall Batson:

Chablis 98 – pale colour, lovely nose, gentle and refined, minerally citrus fruit, fine balance and length. Very good.

Côte de Léchet 98 – well developed floral nose of acacia, lovely citrus fruit flavours bursting forth, lovely balance, sheer elegance in a glass, fine length and depth. Fine wine. (2003–2007)

Montmains 98 – pale colour, fragrant nose, bags of luscious fruit, minerally, dry, long, great depth. A very elegant Montmains. Fine. (2002–2006)

Vaudésir 98 – big nose of nuts and fruit but will close up, immense concentration of fruit, apricots and honey, great depth and richness, very long, complex and totally lovely. For the long term. Very fine. Star wine! (2004-2010)

The following wines were shown at the BIVB/SOPEXA tasting in London, January 1999:

Chablis 97 – lovely wine of *typicité*, good fruity perfumed nose, developing well, good length. Very good.

Vau de Véy 97 – typical nose of flint and minerals, good fruit balance and length. Good wine but not great.

Vaudésir 97 – closed right up on nose and palate as would be expected. Underlying rich concentrated fruit. Great potential for the future but going through a very dumb stage. Should be a very fine wine of elegance. (2003–2011)

Les Clos 97 – this will be a big wine, totally closed up but baskets of fruit just peeking through, intense concentration, finely balanced and the elegance shows. Great potential. Great wine. (2005–2013)

The following wines were tasted at the domaine in October 1998:

Chablis 97 – lovely limpid colour, discreet perfume, lovely mouthful of delicious fruit, long aftertaste. Very good indeed.

Vau de Véy 97 – selection clonal. Pale colour, more mineral nose, crisp expansive fruit, really quite lovely. Fine. (2000–2004)

Vau de Véy 97 – from cuve and awaiting bottling. Gentler than above, a bit of sulphur but a nice wine.

Côte de Léchet 97 – typical perfumed mineral nose, wine of elegance, lovely fruit, rich and good concentration, fine length, very stylish and complex. Fine. (2001–2005)

Montmains Vieilles Vignes 97 – selection massale. Very floral on nose but closed on palate. Fruit is there, very mineral, very dry finish. Should be fine. (2002–2007)

Vaudésir 97 – light floral nose but almost completely closed, intense concentrated fruit with a dry finish. Complex and long, elegant but rich. Needs time. Fine. (2002–2007)

Côte de Léchet 96 – lovely elegant wine, but now closing up, flinty mineral and steely fruit already approachable, fine balance and length, very complex structured wine. Delicious. Fine. (2000–2005)

Les Clos 96 – very closed but intense fruit all there for the future, very long. A complete wine, difficult to taste at this stage, but very fine. (2002–2008)

Vaudésir 95 – lovely golden colour, gives a little on nose, very fruity and minerally, citrus fruits, apricots and honey, lovely succulent fruit, very long. Very fine. (2001–2006)

Vaudésir 92 – coming out of its shell, lovely nose of biscuits, nuts and honey, fat, round, rich, complex, beautifully balanced and long. Lots of life yet.

The Hut at La Moutonne – on the slopes of Vaudésir

L'Homme Mort and Fourchaume in October

A really lovely fine wine. (Now to 2005)

Vaudésir 90 – lovely deep colour, wonderful nose, voluptuous steely fruit, deep and concentrated, very long, elegant, rich, complex, very lovely and still needs time. Very fine. (2000–2005)

Wines available from the **CELLAR DOOR** and stockists in:

UK

Berry Bros. & Rudd, Basingstoke, Hants. Tel: 01256 323566 Fax: 01256 340106

Bordeaux Direct, Reading, Berks. Tel: 0118 948 1718

CCM Wines, Underwood Bros., Kenilworth, Warwickshire. Tel: 01926 484386

Evingtons, Leicester. Tel: 0116 254 2702

Hall Batson & Co., Norwich, Norfolk. Tel: 01603 415115 Fax: 01603 484096

Charles Hawkins, Uppingham, Rutland. Tel: 01572 823030 Fax: 01572 823040

George Hill Ltd, Loughborough, Leicestershire. Tel: 01509 212717

Longford Wines, Sussex. Tel: 01273 480761

Montrachet, London SE1. Tel: 020 7928 1990 Fax: 020 7928 3415

New London Wine, London SW8. Tel: 020 7622 3000

Freddy Price, London W5. Tel: 020 8997 7889 Fax: 020 8991 5178
e-mail: freddywine@aol.com

Michael Ruddock Wines, Kingston-upon-Hull, Humberside. Tel: 01482 326487

Edward Sheldon, Shipston-on-Stour, Warwickshire. Tel: 01608 661639

T & W Wines Ltd, Thetford, Norfolk. Tel: 01842 765646 Fax: 01842 766407 e-mail: contact@tw-wines.co.uk

Charles Taylor Wines, London SE1. Tel: 020 7928 8151 Fax: 020 7928 3415
e-mail: charles.taylor.wines@dial.pipex.com

Wines of Interest, Ipswich, Suffolk. Tel: 01473 406611

The Wine Society, Herts. Tel: 01438 741177

Mark Reynier's Vaudésir label is sometimes available at:

Heath Street Wine Co., London NW3. Tel: 020 7435 6845 Fax: 020 7431 9301

Le Picoleur, London W2. Tel: 020 7402 6920 Fax: 020 7402 5066

La Reserve, London SW3. Tel: 020 7589 2020 Fax: 020 7581 0250

Le Sac à Vin, London SW6. Tel: 020 7381 6930 Fax: 020 7385 5513

USA

International Gourmet Corporation, 1754 Tullie Circle, Atlanta GA 30329

Monsieur Touton Selection Ltd, Suite 9b, 129 West 27th Street, New York NY 10001.

DOMAINE des MARRONNIERS

Bernard Legland
Rue de Chablis
Préhy   Tel: 03 86 41 42 70
89800 Chablis   Fax: 03 86 41 45 82

20 hectares

Production:
Chablis Premier Crus   Montmains   2.50 ha
                        Côte de Jouan   0.25 ha
Chablis Village and Petit Chablis

Situated on the high ground above the village of Préhy, the domaine is partly hidden by a high evergreen hedge no doubt to combat the oncoming south westerly wind. Bernard Legland's house, originally a farmhouse and a most impressive property, was built in 1850 over much older cellars, but his own small domaine was started in 1976, concentrating efforts mainly in Montmains and Chablis Village.

Bernard Legland himself is an extremely amiable man, very welcoming and extremely generous. Proud of his achievements in such a short time, he shows off his wares with an air of expectancy; the vineyards were completely replanted and therefore now have an average age of only 15 years. As the years progress, his expectancy will undoubtedly be rewarded, to judge by the winemaking skills employed.

Vinification is in stainless steel and enamelled *cuves*, and the wines are bottled after 6 to 8 months *élevage*.

At the moment, we regard this as a domaine worthy of note, but with their young vines gaining maturity and the undoubted expertise of Monsieur Legland we suspect this will soon be upgraded to star status.

The principal markets for the wines are France, the UK, Belgium, Holland, Germany, Brazil and just a little to the USA.

Tasting notes
The following wines were tasted at the domaine in May 1998 and February 1999, the 98s in London, August 1999:

Chablis 98 – lovely nose with a real mouthful of fruit, well balanced, lovely finish. Delicious.

Montmains 98 – quiet nose, green appley fruit, good acidity, little concentration or depth showing but could develop. Judgement reserved.

Petit Chablis 97 – good aromatic fruit and acidity, crisp, very good Petit Chablis.

Chablis 97 – lovely nose, good fruit with length and acidity, fine finish. Very good.

L'Obédiencerie – Exterior

L'Obédiencerie – Twelfth century press

Jean and Jean-Paul Durup – La Cave

Château de Maligny

Montmains 97 – 16-year-old vines. Quiet minerally nose, quite fruity and good acidity, steely, good concentration and length, dry finish. This had improved considerably since first tasted in May 98. Very good. (2002–2005)

Côte de Jouan 97 – 18-year-old vines. Quite forward, soft nose but nice appley fruit here, a feminine wine with finesse, well balanced and a dry finish. Good for the *climat*. (2000–2003)

Chablis 96 – flowery perfumed nose but a bit sour. Had just been bottled, maybe a bit of sulphur, did not show well. By January 99 the nose was showing some honey and the green appley fruit was very dry, austere and minerally. This is a good food wine.

Côte de Jouan 96 – less prominent nose than Village Chablis, some fruit and acidity, but not much length or depth. Vines too young again. Needs more time to show its paces. In January 99 this still had a backward nose only delicately flowery, but the fruit had developed well, crisp Granny Smith apples, steely acidity, good length. Good. (2001–2003)

Montmains 96 – two earlier notes were unimpressive. In May 98 the wine showed reluctance on the nose, fresh acidity, some length but lacked a bit of concentration. This showed better fruit by January 99, steely, dry and minerally with a nice finish, even some depth. Here is a wine that really does take its time to show. Now very good. (2002–2005)

Chablis 95 – lovely wine of *typicité*, good fruit, acidity and length, not a lot of concentration but good for the vintage. (now.

Montmains 95 – honeyed fruit, dry, but lots of it, lovely balance here with good length and dry finish. Very good. (2000–2004)

Côte de Jouan 95 – backward nose, lots of expansive fruit, mineral and citrus flavours, long and balanced, refined and delicious. Very good. (2000–2003)

Chablis 94 – minerally character, little depth or concentration, but a good wine for drinking now.

Montmains 93 – lovely floral nose, rather vegetal flavour but not unpleasant, some depth and concentration, even length. Good. Drink now.

Montmains 92 – greenish lemon colour, aged Chablis on nose, hazelnuts, but a bit disappointing on palate, lacks grace and charm, woolly, also lacks length. Disappointing. (November 97 at Mike Schuster's Chablis Tasting)

Montmains 91 – toast and biscuits, delicious fruit, still good balance but now fading a little and may not last too long. Very good. Drink up.

Chablis 90 – lovely rich-tea biscuits, promises well and delivers, good fruit and balance, fine length, delicious. Fine. Drink now if you can get it.

Montmains 88 – nose less prominent, don't forget then very young vines, but plenty in reserve, some concentration, caramelly but delicious, good length. Good. Drink now.

Montmains 85 – a lovely biscuity nose, honeyed, totally delicious, and the vine age then only 5 years, well there is an exception to every rule! Very good. Drink now.

Wines available from the **CELLAR DOOR** and stockists in:

UK

Bibendum, London NW1. Tel: 020 7916 7706 Fax: 020 7916 7705
    e-mail: sales@bibendum-wine.co.uk http://www.bibendum-wine.co.uk
Continental & Overseas Wines, Timperley, Cheshire. Tel: 0161 976 3696
Great Western Wine, Bath. Tel: 01225 446009
Peter Watts, Essex. Tel: 01376 561130

USA

Lionstone International, 55 Albrecht Drive, Lake Bluff, Illinois.
    Tel: 847 604 8733

DOMAINE de la MEULIÈRE

Chantal et Claude Laroche

Fleys	Tel: 03 86 42 13 56
89800 Chablis	Fax: 03 86 42 19 32

15 hectares

Production:

Chablis Premier Crus	Mont de Milieu	2.80 ha
	Vaucoupin	0.55 ha
	Fourneaux.	1.40 ha

Chablis Village and Petit Chablis

Located in the centre of the village of Fleys on the main road from Chablis to Tonnerre, the domaine arranged around an attractive courtyard includes the house, *cuverie* and *chai* with a delightful tasting room in the stone-built cellars.

Domaine de la Meulière, created in 1972, prides itself on manual harvesting, traditional vinification in stainless steel and no wood. Chantal and Claude Laroche come from a family of *vignerons*; they operate a very well run estate making lovely wines for early drinking, but with their largest parcel of Premier Cru Mont de Milieu producing wines for the longer term. This is their pride and joy. Interestingly, when comparing the 97 vintage with the 95 – as many *vignerons* do, the wines sharing a common softness and forward fruit – Claude exclaims that he feels that the 97s are more supple. We agree, a virtue we have found in many domaines.

The Laroches have a son in his twenties at L'Ecole du Vin in Beaune who will soon be joining the business, so the family continuance is assured.

Gérard Vullien – at Chemin de Vaudésir

Château Long-Depaquit

Vincent Dauvissat in his cellars

La Famille Moreau – Jean-Jacques, Louis and Anne

Production totals about 100,000 bottles per annum and apart from the home market, exports go to the UK, Belgium, Holland, Germany and Denmark. Come on US importers, get round there!

This is a domaine worthy of note. Seek out the wines where you can, especially the Mont de Milieu. We found a basic Chablis in a Copenhagen restaurant.

Tasting notes

The following wines were tasted at the domaine in October 1998, except as stated:

Chablis 98 – perfumed nose, bags of mineral fruit, apples and peaches, good depth and lovely length. Very good basic Chablis. (London, September 1999)*

Mont de Milieu 98 – flinty nose of *typicité*, very dry and steely on palate, good concentration of fruit with a lovely crisp finish. Very good. (2002–2006) (London, September 1999)

Fourneaux 98 – not the class or the personality of the Mont de Milieu. Good fruit and length, a slightly bitter finish which should dissipate. Good wine. (2002–2005) (London, September 1999)

Petit Chablis 97 – good fruit with some nuttiness, crisp acidity, a well-made early drinking Petit Chablis.

Chablis 97 – lovely perfumed nose, good supple fruit with some length and a lovely aftertaste, clean crisp finish. Good wine.

Vaucoupin 97 – light coloured, closed nose, rather austere flinty wine, but may develop more. Still a good wine. (2001–2004)

Fourneaux 97 – closed nose, lots of fruit and very dry mineral flavours with a somewhat strange aftertaste. Does not show well but the vines are young. Fair. (2001–2004)

Mont de Milieu 97 – perfumed nose, good concentrated fruit all there, good depth and length, impressive wine with nice aftertaste. Fine. (2001–2005)

Chablis 96 – good basic Chablis with nice fresh acidity. Good wine. (Chablis BIVB, May 98)

Mont de Milieu 96 – quiet nose just showing, good acidity and fruit, good length, well made wine. Good/very good. (2000–2004) (Chablis BIVB, May 98)

Chablis 95 half bottle – surprisingly restrained nose, fruity if light wine and drinking well. (Copenhagen, September 98)

Mont de Milieu 95 – quiet nose, more minerally flavour, not as interesting or as supple as the 97, but still a good wine. (2000–2002)

Mont de Milieu 93 – lovely perfumed nutty nose here, acacia flowers and honey, now reasonably mature for a difficult vintage. A long lovely wine but drink now.

Mont de Milieu 92 from magnum – quiet perfumed elegant nose, fruit well balanced and complex, long and lovely. Very fine. (Now–2002)

Wines are available from the **CELLAR DOOR**. To date, we have been unable to identify any UK or US stockists.

DOMAINE LOUIS MICHEL ET FILS ★★★

9-11 Boulevard de Ferrières	Tel: 03 86 42 88 55
89800 Chablis	Fax: 03 86 42 88 56

22 hectares.

Production:

Chablis Grand Crus	Grenouilles	0.54 ha
	Les Clos	0.50 ha
	Vaudésir	1.17 ha
Chablis Premier Crus	Montée de Tonnerre	4.00 ha
	Fourchaume	0.30 ha
	Montmain	6.50 ha
	Vaillons	2.00 ha
	Forêts	2.50 ha
Chablis Village and Petit Chablis		

A long-standing family business founded in 1850 and in its fifth generation. The domaine is now run by Jean-Loup Michel, also producing wine under another label Domaine de la Tour Vaubourg which, as can be seen from the photograph, reflects the ivy-covered tower which forms the lower end of the large family residence. The complex of imposing greystone buildings situated at the corner of Boulevard de Ferrières and Quai Voltaire in the centre of the village, facing the river, encompasses the extensive family home accessed from a courtyard by a double sided stairway to the raised ground floor, perfect for photographing the two Michels, the *cuverie*, *chai* and offices.

The expectant visitor is generally welcomed into the front room of the house by a smiling Madame Michel, and joined without any fuss by Louis in the old days, now by Jean-Loup, the spitting image of his famous father. A well-fitted tasting room is installed in the cellar, giving an unhurried and comfortable atmosphere.

This domaine, in our view one of the finest in Chablis, has produced superlative wines year-in, year-out, without an oak barrel in use, those in his cellar now being for decoration only. Interestingly, however, Alexis Lichine writes in *Wines of France* (1952): 'Michel will wave his hand at some

Jean-Loup Michel and the late Louis Michel

La Tour Vaubourg – Domaine Louis Michel

Bernard Raveneau – The old Cellar

Domaine Raveneau – Sign and cellardoor

barrels in the corner. "That is 49 Vaudésir over there, and this is 49 Les Clos."' Perhaps these barrels did have a use therefore in the 1950s?

Nowadays the grapes receive a slow gentle pressing, fermentation (temperature-controlled 18-20°C) and *élevage* on the fine lees takes place in stainless steel vats, allowing 8 months for the Village Chablis and 12 months for the Premier and Grand Crus. The wines are bottled after bentonite polishing and a light plate filtration.

Michel's Village and Premier Cru wines can be drunk young and are readily obtainable in the UK. They do, however, justify keeping for the longer term and the 90 and 92 Montée de Tonnerre, in particular, are now just coming out and showing their full flavours. The Grand Crus are for much longer keeping and Vaudésir 1988, the lightest of the three in the Michel stable, is only now just ready for drinking. The 1983 Vaudésir tasted blind in London in March 1999 was stunning, with still more time needed to fully develop.

Sales of the wines are worldwide, including the home market, the UK and the EEC countries, Japan, Singapore and the USA. 90 per cent of the production is exported.

Visits have been made to this domaine in 1990, 1994, 1997, 1998 and 1999 and listed below are tasting notes made on these occasions and other wines tasted in London. We shall continue to visit this superlative estate. This is a three-star quality domaine.

Sadly, Louis Père died in 1999. Although the domaine has been controlled by Jean-Loup for the past few years following his father's retirement, Louis will be sorely missed. His legacy is the superb domaine which continues to produce the wines of which he was so justly proud. A devoted family man and elder statesman among the Chablisiens, indeed the Burgundians, Louis Michel's memory will be cherished and revered as the man was in his lifetime. We are honoured to have known him.

Tasting notes
The following wines were tasted in London in August 1999:

Chablis 98 – lovely steely nose, delicious fruit, good concentration, balanced acidity and terrific length, all there and more. Very good.

Montmains 98 – quiet nose but flavour explodes in mouth, dry and minerally, good intensity but not quite the length of the Montée de Tonnerre below. Good to very good. (2002–2006)

Montée de Tonnerre 98 – reluctant nose but wine of hidden depths. Excellent fruit concentration, intensity and length. But has it the class of the 96 and 97? Time will tell. Very good. (2003–2008)

The following wines were tasted at the domaine in February 1999:

Petit Chablis 97 – this is a good crisp fruity Petit Chablis, gentle and well balanced.

Chablis 97 – little on the nose yet but lots of steely fruit, good acidity and length. Very good.

Vaillons 97 – delicate nose of violets, fruit and acidity in balance, a little tight right now but will open out, dry long finish. Very good. (2002–2006)

Montmains 97 – closed right up, quite dark for so young a wine, lots of fruit, very dry, very typical, mineral flinty and steely, good acidity, balance and length. Very good indeed. (2002–2006) A bottle consumed the following month confirmed this opinion, in fact the nose had opened out slightly and the dryness had moderated.

Montée de Tonnerre 97 – gentle on the nose, minerally, lovely apricots and green appley fruit, well balanced, good intensity and length. Very good indeed. (2002–2006) A bottle opened in April was just as lovely and passed the litmus test with flying colours. (litmus = leave it till morning under seal)

Vaudésir 97 – very closed, good concentration and depth, rich, Granny Smith apples, long, not as big as the 96 but still should be fine. (2004–2009)

Les Clos 97 – closed again, elegance here but this is a big concentrated wine, some minerals apparent, a wine of complexity and very stylish, very long and intense. Very fine. (2004–2009)

Grenouilles 97 – some fragrance on the nose, enormous depth of fruit and concentration, very classy, stylish and very lovely, very fine. (2004–2010)

The following wines were tasted at the domaine in May 1998 and others as stated:

Petit Chablis 96 – crisp fresh but a bit short, rather faceless, but it is only Petit Chablis. (November 97)

Chablis 96 – straw colour, perfumed nose, lovely basic Chablis, not too intense but fabulous for a Village wine. Very good. This confirmed many previous and subsequent tastings in 1997, 1998 and 1999.

Montmain 96 – intensity on nose, lovely fruit if a bit closed, minerally, fair length, very dry. Very good. (2000–2002)

Montée de Tonnerre 96 – once again good intensity of fruit on nose, more fruit and a more aggressive wine, really lovely, good length and fine balance. Fine wine! (2000–2006) This confirms an earlier tasting in April.

Vaudésir 96 – very low yield – only 20-22 hl/ha. Perfumed mineral nose, immense fruit, rich and fat, quite lovely, fine balance, wonderful length and aftertaste. Star wine! Very fine. (2004–2010)

Les Clos 96 – perfumed nose but more closed than above, big wine, difficult to taste as so closed, but all there in abundance, immense concentration and depth, brilliant balance. Should be a great wine. Very fine. (2004–2010)

Grand Cru vineyards

Grenouilles 96 – very perfumed and quite lovely, concentrated rich intense fruit, great length and wonderful aftertaste, elegance and finesse, absolutely fabulous. Star wine! Very fine. (2002–2008)

The following wines were tasted at the domaine in October 1997:

Montmain 95 – classic Chablis nose, good acidity and depth. Drinking well now but not necessarily one to keep. Good. Drink now.

Montée de Tonnerre 95 – usually the best of the grower's Premier Crus and this one is the best. Superb nose and depth of flavour but closing up. Very good. (2000–2004)

Vaudésir 95 – one of the lightest of the Grand Crus, but a delicate refined wine with terrific flavours that just jump out of the glass. If this is a better year than 1988 then this will be a really lovely wine by 2003–2006. Fine wine.

Montée de Tonnerre 94 – Tasted in London two years ago and again in Louis Michel's cellar as a comparison to the 95. Suffers a little by that comparison, but still a fine wine from an average/good year. Drink now.

Vaudésir 94 – now open, super balanced wine, creamy and dreamy. Advanced as are most this year, but don't let that put you off a lovely wine. Very good. Drink now.

Further wines tasted on previous visits and in London:

Montmain 92 – a lighter wine than the Montée de Tonnerre, less obvious nose, but opens out deliciously in the glass. Was drinking well throughout 1995. Very good. Drink up.

Montée de Tonnerre 92 – one of our favourite wines of the vintage, superb nose with opening fruit flavours of elegance and depth. 'The full Montée'! Fine. Drink now. (Many notes – last tasted May 98)

Vaillons 92 – somewhere between Montmain and Montée de Tonnerre in quality and taste, but this as always is personal preference. A lovely wine. Very good. Drink now. (October 94/September 95)

Montée de Tonnerre 90 – the Premier Cru wine of the decade so far. Quite superb in every way, weight, style, depth, flavour, fruit, acidity, balance, *typicité*, need we say more? Very fine. Drink now if you can find some!

Grenouilles 89 – tasted blind in London in October 97, when the Louis Michel character of mock oak flavour came through, it was mistaken by some to be a quality Puligny Montrachet. Tremendous depth of flavours giving a fragrant powerful wine, with a biscuity nose and long, very long. Yet another stunner from this domaine. Tasted again January 98 and just as beautiful, and yet again at Bedford Fine Wine Club Tasting in March 98 where it was the champion wine of the evening. Very fine. Drink now.

Vaudésir 88 – tasted separately to the Grenouilles in London when it was still only just ready. Still rather closed on the nose, but opened up in the glass after 15 minutes. A lovely buttery flavour with considerable length. Probably still not at its best. (March 95/May 96) – another bottle at the Chartered Surveyors Wine Society July 1998 revealed that this wine still has some while to mature. Fine wine. (2000 onwards)

Vaudésir 83 – no hint of age, gorgeous fruit, opulent, still with lovely acidity and length, wonderful aftertaste. Very fine. Will last 'for ever and ever'. Don't drink yet until you've invited us! (March 99)

Grenouilles 78 – a rich dark honeyed wine, amazingly supple and long. Delicious and probably unrepeatable. Fine. (May 97). But it wasn't unrepeatable! In February 1999 a superb bottle showed complex citrus fruit flavours, pineapple, mango and passion fruit, gloriously luscious and voluptuous with wonderful acidity and not a trace of old age. Star wine!

Wines available from the **CELLAR DOOR** and stockists in:

UK
Berry Bros. & Rudd, London SW1. Tel: 020 7396 9669 Fax: 020 7396 9611 and at Basingstoke, Hants. Tel: 01256 323566 Fax: 01256 340106
Corney & Barrow, London EC1. Tel: 020 7251 4051
Dreyfus Ashby, Tonbridge, Kent. Tel: 01732 361639
Enotria Winecellars, London NW10 (trade only). Tel: 020 8961 4411 Fax: 020 8961 8773
Findlater Mackie, London SW19. Tel: 020 8543 0966
Fortnum & Mason, London W1. Tel: 020 7734 8040
Haynes Hanson & Clark, London SW1. Tel: 020 7259 0102 Fax: 020 7259 0103 and at Stow-on-the-Wold, Glos. Tel: 01451 870808 Fax: 01451 870508
Ian G. Howe, Newark, Notts. Tel: 01636 704366
James Nicholson, Co. Down. Tel: 028 44830091
O. W. Loeb & Co., London SE1. Tel: 020 7928 7750 Fax: 020 7928 1855
Oddbins, branches and fine wine shops nationwide. Tel: 020 8944 4400 Fax: 020 8944 4411
Reid Wines, Bristol. Tel: 01761 452645
Thresher Group, branches nationwide including Bottoms Up and Wine Rack. Tel: 01707 328244 Fax: 01707 385000
The Wine Society, Herts. Tel: 01438 741177

USA
Burgundy Wine Co. Ltd, New York. Tel: 212 691 9092 Fax: 212 691 9244
Calvert Woodley, Washington DC. Tel: 202 966 4400 Fax: 202 537 5086
Garnet Wines & Liquors, New York, 10021. Tel: 212 772 3211 Fax: 212 517 4029

Robert Haas, Vineyard Brands – Birmingham, Alabama. Tel: 205 980 8802
or www.vineyardbrands.com

DOMAINE ALICE et OLIVIER DE MOOR

4 Rue Jacques Ferrand
Courgis
89800 Chablis   Tel: 03 86 41 47 94

6 hectares in total – 3 hectares of Chablis

Production:
Chablis Village – 'Rosette' and 'Bel Air'
Also produced – Bourgogne Aligoté, Chardonnay, and Sauvignon de
   Saint-Bris

How refreshing it is to find young newcomers to the demanding world of
growers and *vignerons* with so much enthusiasm and achieving widely ac-
claimed success virtually from the start.

This is a home grown estate: Alice and Olivier de Moor's parents were
not involved in the world of wine, the nearest connection being Alice's
grandfather who was a *viticulteur* in the Jura, and Olivier's uncle who owns
some land in Chablis which they have planted. As the de Moors say themselves, 'the domaine was created out of the passion and love of the work well
done'. Olivier himself is rather shy and unassuming, not the qualities usually associated with a fine winemaker, which he undoubtedly is. Alice is a
delightfully pert and charming *vigneronne*, very commercially minded. A
young, very young couple in harmonious partnership, and a pleasure to
meet.

The simple yet adequate premises are found in the heart of the village of
Courgis, along a narrow road of rough grey-stone buildings most of which
look as if they had seen better days, but nevertheless oozing rustic charm
and *chic*. The open polished wood doors to Chez de Moor is the first invit-
ing sign to what lies inside – a somewhat cramped but orderly array of
cellars on two levels, entrance to or from one to the other can lead to a
nasty 'burmp' on the head. Neat rows of barrels are a misleading give-
away to the winemaking, for here 3 to 4-year-old wood is used with respect
for the end product – the Bel Air *cuve*, and is well integrated into the wine
almost from the start. The other Chablis with the delightful name of Rosette is vinified and raised *en cuve* and is equally well made.

As qualified oenologists from Dijon, the de Moors planted up in 1988
and produced their first Chablis vintage in 1993. They have received cita-
tions in *Guide Hachette*, *La Revue des Vins de France* and Robert Parker's *Wine
Advocate* for every vintage since, not bad considering that their Chablis
holding is a little under 3 hectares, the remainder of the estate being
made up with generic Chardonnay, Aligoté and Sauvignon, the latter also

highly regarded.

Viticulture is fairly traditional with controlled yields and the harvest is picked manually. As stated above, vinification and *élevage* are *en cuve* for the Rosette and *en fût* for the Bel Air. Each operation, alcoholic and malolactic fermentation, fining, filtration, is thought through according to the vintage and necessity, nothing is done for the sake of it or because it was done last year or the year before.

The total annual production of Chablis is some 150 hectolitres part sold to the *négoce* to help pay the bills, thankfully leaving about 16,000 bottles earmarked for the home market and export to Europe, Japan and the USA.

Our visits here are truly memorable. On the first occasion, when we at last emerged on to Rue Jacques Ferrand, Alice ran across the road to the *boulangerie* van for her daily baguette, keeping a watchful eye on the mobile *boucherie* lest it sped away before she had the chance to bring in the supplies. It was raining, again. This was surprising, the sun was shining inside! Second time around, Olivier was less shy and talked non-stop about his wines, but always with extreme modesty. The future holds great things for the de Moors.

Undoubtedly, this is a domaine worthy of note and well on the way to future star status.

Tasting notes

The following wines were tasted in the cellars in October 1998 and February 1999, the 98s in London in August 1999:

Chablis Rosette 98 – very fragrant nose of violets, honey and peaches, fine concentration and depth taking the flowers through to the finish. Lovely. Very good. (2001–2004)

Chablis Bel Air 98 – lots of perfumed fruit on nose and palate, apricots and peaches, good concentration and balanced acidity, a little oak will dissipate very soon. Very good. (2001–2004)

Chablis Rosette 97 – lovely gentle nose of *typicité*, and a gentle wine on the palate, even some elegance. Delicious. A good wine. (2000–2003)

Chablis Bel Air 97 – lovely fruit here with the oak already well integrated, fine clean finish, delicious. Very good. (2000–2003)

Chablis Rosette 96 – deeper in colour than above but still very typical, gentle floral nose, fruit with a lovely lemony flavour, clean lingering finish. Very good. (2000–2004)

Chablis Bel Air 96 – fine deep colour, wine of generosity and character, beautifully balanced, apricots and honey, long, fine finish and oak well integrated. Is this really only a Village appellation? Very good indeed. (2000–2004)

Chablis Rosette 95 – lemon gold colour, hint of honey and apricots, delicious fruit and well balanced. Lovely wine. (2000–2002)

Chablis Bel Air 95 – this has developed well but plenty of life in it, nice concentrated supple fruit, balanced and long. Very good. (2001–2003)

Wines are available from the **CELLAR DOOR** and stockists in:

UK
Ian G. Howe, Newark, Notts. Tel: 01636 704366 Fax: 01636 610502
Villandry, London W1. Tel: 020 7631 3131

USA
North Berkeley Wine Imports, Richmond, California.

DOMAINE LOUIS MOREAU ★★

10 Grande Rue
Beine   Tel: 03 86 42 87 20
89800 Chablis   Fax: 03 86 42 45 59

120 hectares

Production:

Chablis Premier Crus	Vaulignot	10 ha
	Les Fourneaux	2 ha
Chablis Village and Petit Chablis		

Within the Moreau stable are the following:

Domaine de Biéville   Domaine du Cèdre Doré
2 Rue Jules Rathier   2 Grande Rue
89800 Chablis   Beines 89800 Chablis

Chablis Village −65 ha   Chablis Village 5 ha

Jean-Jacques Moreau's son Louis and his charming wife Anne run this significant estate from their winery in Beines, a small village and one of the twenty communes about 6 kilometres to the west of Chablis. In 1965, Jean-Jacques created the Domaine de Biéville, a single-parcel 65-hectare estate of Chablis Village appellation south-east of Chablis in the village of Viviers with south/south-western exposure. Development is a keyword in the Moreau philosophy, and further expansion occurred more recently with the creation of the Domaine du Cèdre Doré also in Viviers, following the purchase of an estate in Beines under the name Domaine Jean-Claude Dauvissat, now all brought under the mantle of Domaine Louis Moreau.

Louis spent eight years in California, where he majored in Oenology and Viticulture at Davis University followed by hands-on experience with Callaway Vineyard in Temecula California and Roederer Estate (Louis Roederer of Champagne fame) in Philo-Mendocino County. Louis and Anne now control the harvest production of some 120 hectares and the resultant winemaking.

The impressive Moreau mansion fronting Grande Rue is a two-storey nineteenth-century building housing the offices and comfortable tasting room leading into the *cuverie* and *chai*. The *cuverie* is ultra-modern, spotlessly clean and tidy, installed with numerous tall enamelled and stainless steel vats. Even in frantically busy periods after the harvest, all seems calm and well ordered. Vinification is traditional, no wood, *élevage* on fine lees during the winter months, precipitation of tartrates by refrigeration, and light filtration before bottling.

All the wine is sold in bottle, nothing for the *négoce*. This is a fine progressive estate which has no commercial relationship with the *négociant* house.

In a short while, Louis Moreau will be able to complete the range of wines with half of the Moreau vineyards belonging to his father Jean-Jacques which returns to them under an agreement:

Chablis Grand Cru Clos des Hospices – 1 ha monopole
Chablis Grand Cru Les Clos – 2.5ha
Chablis Grand Cru Valmur – 1 ha
Chablis Grand Cru Vaudésir – 50 ares
Chablis Grand Cru Blanchot – 10 ares
Chablis Premier Cru Vaillons – 4 ha

We wait with great anticipation. Fine estate, lovely people, and lovely wines. Hats off!

Tasting notes

The following wines were tasted at the domaine in February 1999:

Petit Chablis 98 – ripe fruit and crisp acidity, well balanced and delicious. Very good.

Chablis 98 – a little more restrained than the Petit Chablis but this is a well balanced fruity basic Chablis with no further pretensions.

Domaine de Biéville Chablis 98 – this is ready for bottling. Appley fruit, good acidity and some intensity. Should develop well. Good/very good.

Vaulignot 98 – nose closed, fruit and acidity well balanced, minerally and appley fruit with a nice dry finish. Very good. (2002–2007)

Les Fourneaux 98 – lovely minerally fruit, dry, steely, long, balanced and lovely. Very good. (2002–2008)

The following wines were tasted at the domaine in October 1998 and the BIVB/SOPEXA tasting in London, January 1999:

Petit Chablis 97 – a supple wine, lots of fruit and crisp, a very good Petit Chablis.

Chablis 97 – all from the plateau above the village. Lovely Chablis nose, good fruit with some concentration and depth. Not exactly crisp, but a good wine.

Domaine de Biéville Chablis 97 – what a lovely wine! All that could be expected from a basic Chablis and more. Good typical nose, fresh and minerally, really lovely fruit, long, luscious, concentrated. This has come out substantially since October 1998. Dry and flinty, good *typicité*. Very good indeed.

Domaine du Cèdre Doré Chablis 97 – fresh, crisp and green appley. Very good but the Biéville has greater depth and concentration

Vaulignot 97 – from 20-year-old vines. Obviously closed, immense fruit almost sweet, great intensity and depth, long long aftertaste. If this is how it's made, we're converted to Vaulignot! Bravo! Fine. (2002–2006)

Les Fourneaux 97 – closed since last tasted in October when it showed violets and apricots, but opens with encouragement, great fruit, long and flinty, this is an elegant wine and one to be savoured. Delicious. Still needs time. Fine. (2002–2007)

The following wines were tasted at the domaine in May 1998 – but beware! If you are given scrumptious *gougères* with the tasting, the family dog, a handsome Labrador, will place himself at your feet, and look with longing eyes – full marks if you resist!

Petit Chablis 96 – good nose, fruit and acidity in balance, lovely wine with food.

Chablis 96 – pleasant nose of *typicité*, good fruit and acidity, well-balanced, good basic Chablis. This had developed well by January 99 – why can't all others make basic Chablis like this? Lovely fruity wine, long, good balance, dry minerally finish, drinking beautifully.

Domaine du Cèdre Doré Chablis 96 – gentle perfumed nose, lovely fruit and balance, good length and aftertaste, lovely. Tasted again at London Wine Fair May 98 – not quite the intensity of the Biéville but still a lovely wine. Good.

Domaine de Biéville Chablis 96 – lovely floral nose, gentle wine of elegance, good concentration of fruit, good intensity and depth, nice length, beautiful wine. Tasted again at London Wine Fair May 98, what a wonderful wine for a basic Chablis! This is almost Premier Cru quality. Very good.

Vaulignot 96 – closed nose, good intensity, good fruit and quite concentrated, mineral flavour, tails off a bit, needs time. Tasted again at London Wine Fair May 98 where the wine had won a gold medal at the International Wine Challenge. By January 1999 it was still closed on the nose but the fruit and *typicité* were there, now long and expansive in the mouth with good intensity. Very good wine. (2001–2006)

Les Fournaux 96 – nose closed, intense fruit, minerally and steely, fine depth, great acidity and length, quite lovely. We do love this *climat*. Very good. (2002–2006)

Further wines tasted:

Domaine de Biéville Chablis 96 – if Wine Rack has any more of this, snap it up! Quite simply the best basic Chablis we have ever tasted. Simple note for a delicious wine. Should last well. (Tasted and drunk on many occasions over the past two years, see above)

Domaine de Biéville Chablis 95 – gentle fruity flowery nose, lovely green appley fruit and surprisingly good acidity for the vintage, well balanced, fresh, crisp, amazingly long – goes on and on, very good for a village wine. (London, May 98 and many times since)

Vaulignot 95 – very fruity wine, not a great deal of acidity but that's the vintage, a bit short but a nice wine. Good. (Now to 2002)

Mont de Milieu 92 – location of vines in section renamed Les Fournaux in 1994 – lemon gold colour, wonderful biscuity fragrant nose, delicious fruit and balance, voluptuous, finesse and elegance, very very long, a wine made with love, one of the best 92s we have ever tasted. Star wine! (Now to 2004) (Chablis, May 98)

Wines available from the **CELLAR DOOR** and stockists in:

UK
Earle Wines, N. Yorks. Tel: 01765 677296
Eurowines, London W4. Tel: 020 8994 7658 Fax: 020 8994 8054
Jascots, London W6. Tel: 020 8749 0022
Oxford Wine, Oxford. Lechlade Glos. and London. Tel: 01865 820789
    Fax: 01865 821375
Thresher Group, branches nationwide including Bottoms Up and Wine
    Rack. Tel: 01707 328244 Fax: 01707 385000
The Vineyard, London W14. Tel: 020 7371 6553 Fax: 020 7602 7742

USA
Maverick Brands, Ukiah, California. Tel: 707 462 3692

DOMAINE SYLVAIN MOSNIER ★

4 Rue Derrière les Murs
Beine   Tel: 03 86 42 43 96
89800 Chablis   Fax: 03 86 42 42 88

15 hectares

Production:
Chablis Premier Crus   Côte de Léchet   0.60 ha
                        Beauroy   1.00 ha
Chablis Vieilles Vignes, Village and Petit Chablis

Sylvain Mosnier is a jovial character oozing enthusiasm and confidence, not exactly modest, but not pretentious either as his accomplishments well testify. He runs an impressive domaine created in 1978 but *vigneron* links go back to 1890 and his father and grandfather before him.

The hub of the domaine is located in a fairly inconspicuous but not un-attractive building on the RN65 Route Nationale, the main road from Chablis to Auxerre, in the village of Beine alongside Domaine de Pisse-Loup, whose car park is most welcome in the pouring rain, and identified by his prominently displayed name. Entrance is straight into a fascinating tasting-room colourfully decorated with hundreds of empty wine bottles of widely varying provenance, the collection of Madame – there is even a bottle from a Sussex Vineyard, quite well spoken of by Monsieur Mosnier, and a bottle of Belgian wine – no doubt used to wash down a dish of *moules et frites*! The tasting room opens out into the *cave*, with the *cuverie* situated in the buildings at the rear and more easily accessed from Rue Derriere les Murs.

The Premier Cru vineyard holding is modest, but as they say, all good things come in small parcels, and this is certainly true of Sylvain Mosnier. He is particularly proud of his Chablis Vieilles Vignes which have a veritable age of more than 50 years. General *rendements* for the top wines average 45-50 hl/ha. Vinification and ageing is in enamelled *cuves* with the exception of one cuvée of Beauroy reared in old oak *pièces*.

This is a star estate with a fine reputation, but the wines are not the easiest to find. A search will be well rewarded. Monsieur Mosnier is moving towards a more practical approach to his sales; he told us that he is thinking of marketing the 97s before the 96s, sound reasoning which could be adopted by other producers in similar circumstances of relative vintage merits.

The markets for the wines are spread wide, including the UK, Switzerland, Sweden, Belgium, Germany, Japan and the USA.

Tasting notes
The following wines were tasted at the domaine in October 1998, the 98s in London, August 1999:

Chablis 98 – lovely fragrant Chablis nose, delicious exotic fruit flavours, pineapple and grapefruit, dry crisp and well balanced. Delicious. Very good.

Beauroy 98 – dumb nose but nice fresh ripe fruit on palate, appley dry, good length. Good. (2001–2004)

Côte de Léchet 98 – also a somewhat dumb nose, fruit is there but hidden, dry and minerally, good length as fruit flavours develop in mouth. Needs a bit of time to show its paces. Good to very good. (2001–2004)

Petit Chablis 97 – lovely perfumed wine, good fruit and crisp acidity. A good Petit Chablis.

Chablis 97 – marginally more characterful than the Petit Chablis, good typical nose, minerally and flinty, lovely fruit, a very good Village Chablis.

Chablis 97 Vieilles Vignes – totally closed, a more intense wine with excellent underlying fruit, good depth and balance. Fine. (2000–2003)

Côte de Léchet 97 – very minerally and very dry hidden fruit, good intensity with depth and some elegance. Will open out. Very good. (2001–2004)

Beauroy 97 – perfumed wine, lots of lovely concentrated fruit, good intensity, elegant. A very good wine. (2001–2005)

Beauroy 97 en pièces – oak already integrated, a little closed but lovely fruit there, very dry finish. Should be a good keeper. Very good. (2002–2005)

Petit Chablis 96 – lots of fruit here, and lovely at that, good clean crisp finish. Good wine.

Chablis 96 – lovely perfumed nose, just jumps out of the glass, bags of ripe fruit, fine finish, lovely intense wine. Very good.

Chablis 96 Vieilles Vignes – closed up, but all there for the future, good concentrated fruit, good balance, intensity and length. Very good. (2000–2003)

Côte de Léchet 96 – lovely perfumed nose of *typicité*, gorgeous fruit, this is a delicate, feminine and elegant wine of intensity, characterful mineral and flint, fine length, depth and complexity. Fine. (2000–2005)

Beauroy 96 – also perfumed fruit but a bit closed, rich ripe fruity and intense, lots of elegance here, very good but the Côte de Léchet was preferred. (2000–2004)

Beauroy 96 en pièces – oaky nose but will integrate, lots of lovely ripe fruit, fine depth, length and aftertaste. Fine. (2002–2006)

Petit Chablis 95 – this is good acceptable basic Petit Chablis, crisp and fruity for drinking now.

Chablis 95 – not so much character here, lacks a bit of bite but good basic Chablis of *typicité*. Drink now.

Chablis 95 Vieilles Vignes – better wine, good fruit and intensity, dry but good finish. Very good. This confirmed an earlier tasting in May 98. (2000–2003)

Beauroy 95 – lots of fruit here but rather a bitter finish. Doesn't quite hold together. Lacks a bit of acidity. Disappointing wine. (2000–2002)

Beauroy 95 en pièces – too much oak prominence here which overpowers the fruit, dry and bitter finish. Disappointing.

Côte de Léchet 95 – quiet gentle nose, nicely minerally but not as crisp as the 96. Lovely ripe fruit and elegant. Very good. (2000–2002)

Wines are available from the **CELLAR DOOR** and stockists in:

UK
Burgundy Shuttle, 12 Mandeville Courtyard, 142 Battersea Park Road, London SW11.

USA
Franklin Selections Inc. 12001 Guilford Road, Suite 109, Annapolis Junction, MD 20709.
Fruit of the Vine Inc. 161 W. 54th Street, Suite 203-204, New York, NY 10019.

DOMAINE DE LA MOTTE

Bernard Michaut
41 Rue de la Ruisseau
Beines   Tel: 03 86 42 49 61
89800 Chablis   Fax: 03 86 42 49 63

11 hectares

Production:
Premier Crus	Vaulignot	1.10 ha
	Beauroy	0.60 ha

Chablis Village, Chablis Vieilles Vignes and Petit Chablis

Within the village of Beines just behind the main road from Chablis to Auxerre, the D965, is located this interesting little domaine immaculately maintained in every way. To one side is a newly constructed two-storey function and tasting house, accommodating large parties on both floors in modern comfort – and a good time will be had by all! Central to this smart complex is a neatly laid out courtyard, containing an open air tasting garden with tables and chairs underneath a pagoda-type roof-cover, ensuring rainwater does not dilute the Chablis. Completing the complex on the opposite side is a newly refurbished and stylish family house with a delightful tasting-room furnished for the convenience and comfort of the customers.

All this, but are the wines up to scratch? The short answer is a resounding yes.

This is a small estate with two chunks of Premier Cru and Bernard Michaut, a very friendly smiling man, whose brother is a partner in Domaine Pisse-Loup, runs it with precision and pride, and more than a touch of individuality. Vinification for the Petit Chablis, Chablis and Vaulignot is in inox with *élevage en cuve*, whilst the Beauroy is vinified and raised in *fûts de chêne* of 1 to 4 years of age; 'Beauroy needs it and can take it', argues Monsieur Michaut. Perhaps he has a point, at least in his hands! Before bottling, the wines are fined with bentonite and given a kieselguhr filtration. To preserve freshness, bottling begins in January for the Petit Chablis and continues through the range until May or June.

The total production is some 80,000 bottles with none for the *négoce*, and export markets include Belgium, Germany, Denmark, Switzerland, Italy, Japan and the UK.

Seek out these wines, they are very good.

Tasting notes

The following wines were tasted at the domaine in February 1999:

Petit Chablis 98 – a fresh, young, fruity Petit Chablis, slightly too sharp.

Chablis Vieilles Vignes 98 – from vines 30+ years old. Once again a young, fresh, fruity Chablis, well balanced. Good.

Vaulignot 98 – no nose, good fruit with fair concentration and depth. Should be good.

Beauroy 98 – oak already integrated, fair fruit and balance, well-made wine but not a lot of backbone. Good.

Petit Chablis 97 – nice nose and fruit here, green appley, well balanced. Very good Petit Chablis.

Chablis 97 – toasty nuts, a mêlée of minerally citrus fruits, well-balanced acidity. Very good.

Chablis Vieilles Vignes 97 – closed nose and well-hidden fruit but comes out with encouragement, good length and balance. Needs a little more time. Very good.

Vaulignot 97 – perfumed mineral nose, steely flinty fruit of Granny Smith apples, long and delicious. Very good. (2001–2004)

Beauroy 97 – toasty nose, lovely fruit, concentration and depth, a little oak apparent but this is a delicious wine. Very good. (2002–2004)

Chablis 96 – nice mineral nose, crisp green apples, dry mineral finish a little bit short but this is only a Village wine. Good.

Wines are available at the **CELLAR DOOR.** We have not been able to identify a UK stockist.

DOMAINE ROBERT NICOLLE

55 Route de Tonnerre
Fleys   Tel: 03 86 42 19 30
89800 Chablis   Fax: 03 86 42 80 07

15 hectares

Production:
Premier Crus   Les Fourneaux   3.5 ha
                                   Mont de Milieu   1.8 ha
Chablis Village

Domaine Robert Nicolle is not easy to find as no signpost gives away its location, but on the road from Chablis to Tonnerre, pass through Fleys and note the last house on the left as you leave the village, a white house with a brown-tiled roof set back from the road and undoubtedly the prettiest private house in the village. Blink and you'll miss it! The rear of the house overlooks the slopes of Les Fourneaux, the mainstay of this estate.

The impressive *cuverie* and *chai* are situated in a large modern building at the back of the house, further down the slope and separately approached by a service road, understandably a better way of access during wet weather than scrambling down over rough unmade ground. The *chai* was enlarged in 1995 and there is clearly room for further expansion when required. The operation here is traditional – vinification and elevage in enamelled *cuves*, wood is not used. The wines are given a light plate filtration before bottling.

Monsieur and Madame Nicolle who come from a long line of *vignerons* run the domaine with a quiet efficiency but we feel here that the wines as good as they are, could do with a little more personality. At present, they do not quite hit the mark!

Tasting notes
The following wines were tasted at the domaine in October 1998, except as stated:

Chablis 97 – quiet Chablis nose, rather sour and a bit dull on the palate. Not exciting.

Les Fourneaux 97 – more typical nose but unfortunately this is also very ordinary and very unexciting. Fruit not there. (2000–2003)

Mont de Milieu 97 – good nose here and more *typicité*, good appley fruit, mineral flavours, very dry and crisp finish. This is a good Mont de Milieu. (2000–2004)

Chablis 96 – little on nose, sour apples and regrettably little elsewhere.

Les Fourneaux 96 – closed nose as would be expected, some concentration of fruit, reasonable balance with a lovely aftertaste, some sulphur present which should dissipate. Good wine. (2000–2004)

Les Fourneaux 95 – little on nose, wine of fair *typicité*, good acidity but a bit characterless at present, needs another two years. Good length, pleasant aftertaste. Unlikely to be a great wine, but good nevertheless. (2000–2003) (March 98 in London)

Wines available from the **CELLAR DOOR** and stockists in:

UK

Bordeaux Direct, Theale, Berks. Tel: 0118 903 0903 Fax: 0118 903 0130
  e-mail: orders@bordeaux-direct.co.uk
Hugh Johnson, London SW1. Tel: 020 7491 4912 Fax: 020 7493 0602
Verulam Vintners, Ashford, Middx. Tel: 01784 421822 Fax: 01784 421822-
  33

DOMAINE DE L'ORME

Société Civile Agricole
16 Rue de Chablis
Lignorelles   Tel: 03 86 47 41 60
89800 Chablis   Fax: 03 86 47 56 66

37 hectares

Production:
Chablis Premier Cru   Beauroy   3.00 ha
Chablis Village and Petit Chablis

Michel Boudin's Domaine de l'Orme is a family domaine with over a hundred years of history. Until the early 1960s, the estate ran with a modest 10 hectares, then development and modernisation over the next thirty years took the total to the present 37 hectares – 3 hectares of Premier Cru Beauroy, 24 of Chablis Village and 10 hectares of Petit Chablis in more than 20 parcels. M. Boudin, no relation of his namesake at Domaine de Chantemerle, is an enthusiastic and energetic man in his mid-years, with more energy than most; his *régisseur* Pascal Mercier and we had enormous difficulty in keeping pace as he darted here and there talking nineteen to the dozen, showing us every inch of the *chai* and *cuverie*, almost pushing us inside a vat, mercifully empty at the time, brandishing a hastily assembled light so we could inspect the accumulated sparkling tartrate crystals clinging to the rough concrete surface.

Viticulture is as near organic as possible, which involves cutting down on all toxic materials, the reintroduction of natural predators and the use of biological insecticides, hoeing rather than chemical weed-killers, severely limiting the use of fertilizers. The average age of the vines is 30 years.

Vinification is largely traditional and carried out with great care and devotion. The capacity of the pneumatic pressing of the grapes prevents any waiting period and thus oxidation of the must. Fermentation takes place in cement and enamelled *cuves*, temperature-controlled by a system of stainless steel heat exchangers. *Elevage* is entirely in *cuves* for a period of 6 to 15 months depending on the wine and circumstances of the vintage.

The style aimed for is a rich aromatic wine of finesse and character: unfortunately, we feel that this is not always achieved. The 97s were a success.

Tasting notes.

The following wines were tasted at the domaine in May 1998, the 97s from vat, and the 98s tasted in London in August 1999:

Chablis 98 – typical Chablis nose, sour green appley fruit with not a lot of concentration.

Beauroy 98 – pretty innocuous with little definition. What fruit is there is rather sour. A no-no.

Petit Chablis 97 – good fruit, fresh and crisp.

Chablis 97 – due for bottling, apples fizzed out of vat, difficult to taste and judge. Retasted in bottle March 99 – lovely perfumed ripe apples on nose, very forward, concentrated ripe sweet fruit on palate with good length and fair acidity. Not exactly crisp on finish but a delicious wine for early drinking. Very good

Beauroy 97 – good concentration of fruit but already closed. This should be a fair wine. (2000–2002)

Chablis 96 – lovely fruity nose, good concentration of fruit on the palate but is there enough acidity and depth? Only fair length. Fair.

Chablis 95 – little on nose, a bit flavourless, no depth or concentration. Below average wine.

Beauroy 95 – concentrated fruit, well-balanced acidity, good for the vintage. Drink now.

Beauroy 93 – more on nose, well mature, drink up.

Wines available from the **CELLAR DOOR** and stockists in:

UK

Direct Wines, Reading, Berks. Tel: 01189 481711

GILBERT PICQ & SES FILS

3 Route de Chablis
Chichée   Tel: 03 86 42 18 30
89800 Chablis   Fax: 03 86 42 17 70

13 hectares

Production:
Chablis Premier Crus   Vaucoupin   0.5 ha
                        Vosgros   1.5ha
Chablis Village and Vieilles Vignes

Since 1976, father and sons have been running this small domaine where all
the vines are situated in the commune of Chichée about 3 km south of
Chablis on the left bank of the Serein. The Picq family go back generations
as *vignerons* and are very proud of their tradition and their holdings, as can
be attested when we first met Picq Père in 1994, his chest swelling with
pride and a delightful grin spreading across his face as he talked about
the wines. Father is now retired and his sons run the show in a relaxed
and laid-back manner, Didier in charge of the cellars and Pascal the vineyards. Daughter Marilyn looks after the commercial side in the office – a
true family domaine.

The vineyards amount to 13 hectares in total – 2 hectares of Premier
Cru, Chablis Vieilles Vignes from 1 hectare of 45/50-year-old vines, and
10 hectares of basic Chablis Appellation. The Village Chablis is the first to
be harvested, but the Premier Crus and Vieilles Vignes are picked as late as
possible to take advantage of any extra ripening sunshine, 100 per cent
destemming for the Vosgros and Village, 50 per cent for the V.V. A slow
pneumatic pressing is followed by up to 24 hours static period for *débourbage*. The fermentation in inox is long and temperature controlled at 18 to
20°C to begin with, allowing it to rise to 24 to 25°C. After the malo has
finished, the wines are racked and *élevé* on their fine lees in stainless steel –
10 to 12 months for the two top wines, 8 to 10 months for the Vieilles Vignes
and up to a year for the Chablis. The wines are cooled for tartrate precipitation and filtered before bottling.

The total production averages 80/90,000 bottles per annum and are
widely exported.

These wines are typical Chablis, the best having all the flavours and
nuances that Chablis is capable of, and good for medium term ageing.
The Vosgros in a good vintage can age for 10-15 years – it is quite obvious
that both Picq *père* and Didier are particularly proud of this cuvée, and so
they should be. These wines should be keenly sought, a very good source.
This is definitely a domaine worthy of note, nudging star status.

Tasting notes

Most of the following wines were tasted at the domaine in February 1999, the 98s later in the year in London by courtesy of Morris & Verdin:

Chablis 98 – pale colour, very floral nose, lovely concentrated fruit and balanced acidity, succulent. Very good Chablis. Try it with Moules.

Chablis Vieilles Vignes 98 – more intensity on nose here, very honeyed concentrated fruit, well balanced, lovely long aftertaste with a hint of honey. Very good.

Vaucoupin 98 – more minerally on nose, fruit rather hidden but comes out in glass, not the greatest of length and a slight bitter finish. Needs time but should evolve well. Good. (2002–2005)

Vosgros 98 – tight nose, lovely fruit on palate, ripe and concentrated with depth. Good length and lovely aftertaste. Wine of character. Very good. (2002–2006)

Chablis 97 – restrained nose but good fruit. Lovely basic Chablis.

Chablis Vieilles Vignes 97 – fragrant nose, packed with ripe fruit and well-balanced acidity. Some old vine intensity here. Very good.

Vosgros 97 – aromatic nose, lovely fruit – Cox's apples, perhaps lacks a little acidity on the attack but it's there at the finish with good length. Very good. (2002–2005)

Vaucoupin 97 – from vines planted in 1990. Fruit comes through on the nose, as expected not a great amount of depth, but showing some restrained elegant fruit. Fair/Good. (2001–2004)

Chablis 96 – a very floral nose, violet creams, gorgeous fruit – citrus and apples, fresh fruit salad in the nicest sense, lovely crisp acidity, delicious wine. Very good.

Chablis Vieilles Vignes 96 – violets and apples on nose, great depth of fruit, intensity, crisp finish, needs more time. Very good.

Vosgros 96 – very lovely perfumed wine – like Diorissima, a mêlée of fruits, concentration, intensity and depth, crisp acidity, lovely finish. Very good. (2002–2005)

Vaucoupin 96 – flinty floral mineral nose, quite forward, more depth and concentration than the 97, citrus fruits, good acidity and a clean finish. Good. (2002–2004)

Vosgros 95 – nothing on the nose, but a mature wine on the palate. The fruit is there but not supported by enough acidity as is the character of the vintage. Delicious with Andouillette. Don't keep too long. Drink now. (May 98)

Vosgros 93 – brilliantly clear light lemon/gold, fresh fragrant nose of new-mown hay and green apples but didn't hold up in glass, more than a hint of maturity on palate, was a lovely wine with good length and depth, excellent for the vintage, but on its way out! (March 98)

Chablis 85 – mature biscuity nose, buttery fruit and honey, a touch of *sous-bois*, a lovely old Chablis proving that a well-made village wine can last, and still some life in it yet!

Wines available from the **CELLAR DOOR** and stockists in:

UK

Matthew Clark (Grants of St. James's), Bristol. Tel: 01275 891400
O.W. Loeb & Co., London SE1. Tel: 020 7928 7750 Fax: 020 7928 1855
Morris & Verdin, London SE1. Tel: 020 7357 8866 Fax: 020 7357 8877
Todd Vintners (Agent) – Tunbridge Wells. Tel: 01892 527335
Noël Young Wines, Cambridge. Tel: 01223 844744 Fax: 01223 844736

USA

Kent Beverage Co. 650 36th Street SE, Wyoming, Michigan 49548. Tel: 616 242 6900
New France Wine Co., PO Box 14205, Saint Paul, Minnesota 55114. Tel: 651 698 2533
Sante Wine Distributors, 112 S.Duke Street, 600 Durham, North Carolina, 27701. Tel: 919 688 6774
USA Wine Imports, 285 W. Broadway, New York, NY 10013. Tel: 212 941 7133

DOMAINE LOUIS PINSON ★

5 Quai Voltaire   Tel: 03 86 42 10 26
89800 Chablis   Fax: 03 86 42 49 94

11 hectares

Production:

Chablis Grand Cru	Les Clos	2.50 ha
Chablis Premier Crus	Mont de Milieu	4.75 ha
	Montmains	1.00 ha
	La Forêt	0.70 ha

Chablis Village
There is some Vaillons with 7-year-old vines, needing another three years of age before they come on-line.

This is a very old Chablisien family, and their small but significant estate, little changed over the years, is now run by Laurent and Christophe Pinson, handed down in the time-honoured tradition of father to son.

Legend has it that the Pinsons were established in Chablis even before Napoleon. Father Pinson, Louis, assumed control from his father in 1942 of a small parcel of three hectares, gradually adding to the vineyards, but remaining in control by limiting the expansion to a manageable size.

The family domaine is situated in the Quai Voltaire, facing the river. The entrance is through a courtyard overlooked by the residence on first floor level, with the *cuverie* and *chai* below. Very French and rustic, as Laurent Pinson leans over the balcony rail to greet his guests, one feels transported back to the days when D'Artagnon may have said farewell to his fretful mother as he set out on his adventures, or the inn at Amiens about to be invaded by the Lescaut entourage in Abbé Prévost's novel. All it needs is a handful of ducks, geese and chickens running around. History feels alive here, so does the winemaking.

Vinification is in enamelled *cuves*, but ageing of the top wines is in Allier oak, 6 months for the Grand Crus in 2 to 3-year-old wood, and 5 months for the Premier Crus where the oak is 4 to 6 years old. The wines are fined with bentonite and isinglass, and given a light plate filtration before bottling.

This is a fine estate producing fine wines, with the undoubted ability to ensure that the oak used complements and supports the wine without bruising it.

The markets here, not surprisingly, are worldwide, the UK and all Europe, Japan, Australia, Canada and the USA.

Tasting notes
The following wines were tasted at the domaine in May 1998, February 1999 (the 97s), and London:

La Forêt 97 – just a little oaky but should integrate well, good concentrated fruit and length, good acidity and balance. Should be very good. (2002–2005)

Montmains 97 – nicely mineral on nose, some flint and steel, fine floral fruit, quite a restrained wine, long and lovely with a clean finish. Very good. (2002–2005)

Mont de Milieu 97 – more closed on nose here, oak already integrated, lovely fruit extraction, fine balance, mineral dry finish, elegant wine. Fine. (2002–2005)

Les Clos 97 – completely closed on nose as would be expected but some oak apparent, immense and intense fruit concentration, great depth, lovely, long and beautiful. Fine. (2004–2009)

Montmains 96 – closed nose, lovely restrained fruit, good balance, intensity and length, oak is there but should integrate. Very good wine. (2000–2003)

La Forêt 96 – a bit of oak on nose but will integrate well, fine fruit, a bit low on acidity, surprisingly for a 96. Tasted again October 98 – no change! Fair. Drink now.

Mont de Milieu 96 – fairly closed nose, good wine of *typicité*, oak should integrate, good fruit, fine finish and length. Very good. (2000–2004)

Les Clos 96 – now totally closed up, this is a sleeping giant waiting to burst forth, packed tight with everything, try again in 15 years! (2005–2010)

Montmains 95 – flowery honeyed nose, delicious fruit but oak here is a little too dominant. Good concentration but it does tail off a bit at the end. Good. (2000–2002)

Les Clos 83 – yellow gold, lovely fragrant honeyed nose, big rich wine but with considerable elegance and depth, nuts and toasted oak, delicious and long, will last a few years more yet. Star wine! (April 98, London)

Wines are available from the **CELLAR DOOR** and stockists in:

UK

Bibendum, London NW1. Tel: 020 7916 7706 Fax: 020 7916 7705
e-mail: sales@bibendum-wine.co.uk http://www.bibendum-wine.co.uk
Majestic Wine Warehouses, branches nationwide. Tel: 01923 298200
Christopher Piper Wines, Devon. Tel: 01404 814139

USA

Petit Pois Corp., 50 Twosome Drive, Moorestown, New Jersey 08057. Tel: 609 608 9644
Michael Skurnik Wines Inc.,575 Undermill Boulevard, Syossett, New York 11791. Tel: 516 677 9300
Wine Warehouse, 6550 East Washington Boulevard, Commerce, California 90040-1800.

DOMAINE DE PISSE-LOUP

Jacques Hugot et Jean Michaut

30 Route Nationale	*cave*:	1 Rue de la Poterne
Beine 89800		Beine 89800
Tel: 03 86 42 85 11		Tel: 03 86 42 41 45

10 hectares

Production:
Chablis Village   8 ha
Petit Chablis   2 ha

Set back on the main road through Beine from Chablis to Auxerre is a large detached house facing an attractive garden and with a large parking area for visitors. The house, the domicile of the Hugot family, is also used for tastings and sales to the public, the *cuverie* and cellars being located in Rue de la Poterne at the rear of the village.

According to Jacques Hugot, the history of the family stretches back to

1697 when two family branches were tied together. Jacques's father was an active *vigneron* in Beine, but Jacques himself is both a vigneron and a Professor of Economics in Auxerre. The charming Madame Hugot teaches music three days a week as well as assisting her husband in running the domaine. Their 27-year-old son is now involved in the family business.

Jacques Hugot prides himself that they have no north-facing slopes, abundant in Chablis and Petit Chablis Appellations, and their best slope in fact faces due south on Kimmeridgian soil. All the vineyards were replanted by 1985 and the first harvest of Chablis was in 1987 followed by Petit Chablis in 1992. The general approach to viticulture is scientific, Jacques being a very exacting man with firmly held views on most aspects of viticulture and viticulteurs, not all of them repeatable here. Yields are controlled by propitious pruning and harvesting is partly manual, separate cuvées prepared for the hand- and machine-picked grapes. The picking is as early as possible to ensure the healthiest of fruit and not take chances with late summer rains.

Vinification is in enamelled and stainless steel *cuves*, and a small part is aged in old oak barrels before *assemblage*. Bottling is done as late as possible. Some 20,000 bottles are produced each year from 25 per cent of the total production, the remainder earmarked for the *négoce*.

Messieurs Hugot and Michaut suggest that in good years their Chablis can age up to ten years in the bottle. The wines serve as a fine accompaniment to Madame Hugot's scrumptious cuisine which accompanied the tasting below in October 1998, except the 98s which were tasted in London in August 1999. We like this domaine and especially Monsieur et Madame Hugot: a good address for basic Chablis – go for the manually harvested wines which have that additional degree of character, depth and complexity. This is definitely a domaine to watch.

Tasting notes

Chablis 98 – shy nose, lovely citrus fruit flavours, some concentration but little more. Some hours later, this had opened out with a lovely nutty nose, but still did not display any depth. Good though for easy quaffing.

Chablis 98 manual harvest – lovely steely fruity nose, terrific concentration of exotic fruit flavours, good length and depth. Lasted until the following day, really lovely. Very good.

Petit Chablis 97 – slightly bitter taste, not a lot there, but could open out.

Chablis 97 – more perfume on nose, but fruit rather bland. Fair wine.

Chablis 97 manual harvest – this is a different proposition altogether, a wine with extra dimension and with more depth. This is good.

Petit Chablis 96 – no chaptalisation, rather sharp on taste, not a lot there.

Chablis 96 – more perfumed nose, good fruit, even some depth, should keep well. This is a very good wine.

Chablis 96 manual harvest – lovely fruit here, more developed and with depth.

Great wine for a Village Chablis. Very good.

Petit Chablis 95 – good fruit and acidity. This has come together very well. Good wine.

Chablis 95 – good nose and balance of fruit and acidity, but a rather sour aftertaste. Fair.

Chablis 95 manual harvest – yet again the manually picked wine comes through much more developed and complex. Good fruit, intense and long. A bit atypical of the vintage but a good wine.

Wines are available from the **CELLAR DOOR** and so far as we are aware only exported to Belgium. UK and US importers take note.

DOMAINE DENIS POMMIER

31 Rue Poinchy	
Poinchy	Tel: 03 86 42 83 04
89800 Chablis	Fax: 03 86 42 17 80

8 hectares

Production:

Chablis Premier Crus	Fourchaume	0.25 ha
	Côte de Léchet	0.60 ha
	Beauroy	1.16 ha
Chablis Village and Petit Chablis		

The approach to the Pommier estate is directly off the main road from Poinchy to Chablis through a wide access to what looks like an old working farm. A surveyor would describe the family home and *chai* as a substantial period terraced property with original features: a wine writer would use the words 'very French and delightfully rustic'.

From this old-world setting, a young estate is being run by a delightful young couple Denis and Isabelle Pommier who built on 2.5 ha inherited from Denis's grandparents in 1990. This has now been increased to 8 hectares with some fine Premier Cru and Chablis Village vineyards. Denis gained his viticultural experience with other local growers and at the Ecole du Vin in Beaune, putting those skills to use in the rapid development of his own domaine.

Chaufferettes are used to protect all their Beauroy vines and part of the Village Chablis against frost. The remaining plots at present are unprotected, but no doubt this will follow in due course

Vinification is largely traditional in enamelled metal *cuves*, but 10 per cent wood is used for the *élevage* of the Beauroy which Denis says balances the mineral flavours and enables the full character to develop after several years in bottle. He is also particularly fond of his Côte de Léchet which is both powerful and fine, and a good keeper. His area of Fourchaume is very small and the vines are still too young having only been planted in 1990. Some further time is needed for these to develop.

On our return visit in February 1999, the Pommiers mentioned that from the 1998 vintage they will be producing an oaked cuvée of the Beauroy and Côte de Léchet at the request of one of their importers. We were not amused, and fear that such a practice has pitfalls, not least of which is damage to their not inconsiderable reputation. We beg them to reconsider, it is surely better to maintain the typicity of the wines than to embark on a road fraught with dangers. The thought of Côte de Léchet eventually ending up in new oak for six months — as is the plan — is mind-boggling. For the 97 vintage, 9 per cent of the Beauroy spent 6 months in 5-year-old wood, which is a world apart from the new proposals. Nevertheless, as it stands this is a domaine worthy of note, and to watch for the future. We shall visit here again in trepidation and anticipation, but judging by the stupendous 98s we don't appear to have too much to worry about, assuming that these wines were bottled for the European market.

The production is divided equally between the *négoce* and private clients, much of it exported to the UK, Belgium, Holland, Austria and Germany. Let us hope that as the domaine's reputation grows, the wine finding its way into bottle will be much the larger amount.

Tasting notes
The following wines were tasted at the domaine in May 1998 and February 1999, the 98s in London in August 1999:

Chablis 98 — lots of fruit here on nose and palate, wine of *typicité*, lovely length and balance. Very good.

Côte de Léchet 98 — lovely fragrant nose, elegant fruit, concentration and depth, well balanced and long. A text book example of a super *climat*. Very good. (2002–2005)

Beauroy 98 — perfumed nose, well-proportioned wine, quite forward, good concentration of delicious fruit, lovely balance of acidity, length and depth. A credit to the Pommiers and, of course, Beauroy, not the easiest of Crus to get right. Very good. (2001–2004)

Fourchaume 98 — perfumed nose again, lovely concentrated fruit, nuts and honey, lovely length and depth. Classic Fourchaume. What a pity this is such a small production. Very good. (2002–2006)

Petit Chablis 97 — fruity nose but a bit flat on the palate, lacks a bit of acidity. Fair.

Chablis 97 — little on nose but good fruit and length, fair acidity. Good.

Fourchaume 97 — lovely green tinged colour, mineral nose, good fruit but once again there is a question mark against the acidity. Good though. (2002–2005)

Côte de Léchet 97 – a bit closed, lovely fruit and gentle acidity, good concentration and balance. Very good. (2002–2005) This is their best Premier Cru, no wood please!

Beauroy 97 – nice minerally nose, good depth and concentration of fruit, a little woody but will integrate. Good. (2002–2005)

Petit Chablis 96 – little on nose, a bit astringent on palate, but some good appley fruit, good with food.

Chablis 96 – lovely colour, quite deep, open nose of good fruit and on palate, perhaps a little short on acidity but good basic Chablis.

Côte de Léchet 96 – gentle bouquet, lovely fruit, length and aftertaste, a delightful young wine. Very good. (2001–2004)

Beauroy 96 – closed nose, good concentrated fruit, mineral flavours develop in the mouth, tails off a bit but leaves a pleasant aftertaste. Good. (2001–2004)

Fourchaume 96 – only 2,000 bottles from 0.25 ha young vines 9 years old. Quiet nose, but hasn't the concentration, nice fruit but little complexity. Needs a few more years of vine age. Good. (2001–2003)

Wines are available from the **CELLAR DOOR** and from stockists in:

UK
Ian G. Howe, Newark, Notts. Tel: 01636 704366 Fax: 01636 610502

USA
Robert Kacher Selections, 28000 V. Street, NE Washington DC, 20018.

DOMAINE LAURENCE et DENIS RACE

5a Rue de Chichée		Tel: 03 86 42 45 87
89800 Chablis		Fax: 03 86 42 81 23

15 hectares

Production:

Grand Cru	Blanchot	0.30 ha
Premier Crus	Côte de Cuissy	0.40 ha
	Mont de Milieu	0.55 ha
	Vaillons	0.90 ha
	Montmains	5.50 ha

Chablis Village and Petit Chablis

Domaine Laurence et Denis Race is a conveniently situated domaine one-minute's walk from the town centre in old village buildings steeped in Chablis tradition. Everything is housed within a cramped complex of buildings yet the individual parts are far from cramped. An impressive *cuv-*

erie and *stockage* are located alongside the visitor's reception and tasting room.

The thirtysomething Denis Race was initially very wary of his writer visitors, almost reluctant to talk openly about his wines or even open a bottle or two, but after a testing few minutes' trial he soon relaxed, darting to and fro to produce bottle after bottle with equal enthusiasm. Unfortunately, as good as our French isn't, his French is spoken as if his listeners were on the point of departure and three sentences have to be delivered in the time and space normally devoted to one, and with a strong regional accent. Never mind, we coped! On our next visit, hurriedly disposing of a family group of Parisian tourists, he greeted us like long lost friends, talking nineteen to the dozen, and it was as much as we could do to extricate ourselves without causing offence and not be too late for our next appointment. Denis Race really is a very nice fellow, and he also makes good wines as can be seen below.

Vinification is traditional in temperature-controlled stainless steel *cuves* and no wood is allowed within sniffing distance of the domaine – 'Je le contre' ('I'm agin it') growls Denis who produces some 80,000 bottles per annum, allowing just a little to the *négoce*. The remainder is for the home market and export to the UK, Belgium, Holland and Germany.

This is definitely a domaine worthy of note.

Tasting notes
The following wines were tasted at the domaine in October 1998 and February 1999, the 98s in London in August 1999 by courtesy of Morris & Verdin:

Chablis 98 – restrained nose, steely appley fruit on palate, not too much concentration but a good Chablis.

Montmains 98 – quite closed on nose but fruit peeps out underneath, concentration with some hidden depth, bitter aftertaste. Needs a retaste.

Montmains Vieilles Vignes 98 – very closed on nose, more concentrated fruit here, apples and pears, good length, shows much better than the above. Good wine. (2002–2006)

Chablis 97 – good fruit and balance here with a little sulphur on the finish – this should disappear. Quite good.

Côte de Cuissy 97 – from 35-year-old vines. Strange nose in spite of good fruit and acidity. Not exactly typical Chablis. We are still not convinced by this Premier Cru.

Montmains 97 – floral nose, minerally, better fruit, good balance but a bit short. Nevertheless a good wine. (2000–2003)

Montmains Vieilles Vignes 97 – from 65-year-old vines. More mineral, concentrated fruit, good intensity and depth, well balanced, very dry, needs time. Should be a very good wine. (2001–2005)

Mont de Milieu 97 – typical Chablis nose, mineral flinty flavour, steely, very dry, needs time for fruit to show. Should be very good. (2001–2004)

Vaillons 97 – gentle perfume on nose, mineral fruit with length and some elegance. Better than the Mont de Milieu. Very good wine. (2000–2004)

Blanchots 97 – totally closed but intense concentrated fruit, very lovely, good balance, quite complex, very long, needs time. Should be a very good wine. (2002–2007)

Chablis 96 – floral nose, good fruit and acidity. Good basic Chablis.

Montmains 96 – floral flinty fruit with a hint of honey, good balance and length, slightly bitter aftertaste but a good wine. (2001–2004)

Montmains Vieilles Vignes 96 – very closed, good concentrated fruit and intensity but perhaps not the depth of the 97. Quite good nevertheless. (2002–2006)

Vaillons 96 – lovely delicate nose, flinty fruit, well balanced, very dry clean finish. Very good. (2001–2004)

Blanchots 96 – nose a bit tight, bags of lovely fruit and well-balanced acidity, good length. Very good wine. (2003–2006)

Wines are available from the **CELLAR DOOR** and stockists in:

UK
Beaconsfield Wine Cellar, Beaconsfield, Bucks. Tel: 01494 715376
Bentalls, Kingston. Tel: 020 8546 1001
Fields, London N5. Tel: 020 7704 1247
Hicks & Don, Dorset. Tel: 01258 456040
Ian G. Howe, Newark, Notts. Tel: 01636 704366 Fax: 01636 610502
Morris & Verdin, London SE1. Tel: 020 7357 8866 Fax: 020 7357 8877
Verulam Vintners, Ashford, Middx. Tel: 01784 421822 Fax: 01784 421822-33
Uncorked, London EC2. Tel: 020 7638 5998

DOMAINE RAVENEAU ★★★

9 Rue de Chichée   Tel: 03 86 42 17 46
89800 Chablis   Fax: 03 86 42 45 55

7 hectares

Production:

Grand Crus	Les Clos	0.54 ha
	Blanchot	0.60 ha
	Valmur	0.75 ha
Premier Crus	Montée de Tonnerre	2.90 ha
	Montmains	0.36 ha
	Forest	0.40 ha

Chapelot	0.20 ha
Butteaux	1.50 ha
Vaillons	0.39 ha

François Raveneau's domaine, now in effect run by his sons Jean-Marie and Bernard, enjoys the justifiable reputation as the greatest domaine in Chablis. It is to Chablis what Bonneau du Martray is to the Corton. Anyone who is fortunate enough to be allowed an annual allocation of the minuscule production can look forward to the finest of Chablis drinking when the wines come of age, and that can be a long time.

The traditional *chai* is located in town, marked by an elegant hanging wrought-iron father-time sign outside the front door *à la* Getreidegasse Salzburg, and this is most appropriate, as the wines are sheer Mozart, like the magic of *Die Zauberflöte*. The cellars underneath the family home are accessed direct from the main road down a flight of concrete and stone steps, forcing the visitor to bend double to avoid a nasty blow on the forehead. Once inside, you are faced with four long rows of oak *feuillettes* packing the old vaulted cellars.

Jean-Marie taps the barrels lightly to indicate which one is to be raided. How he tells which is which is a total mystery. The wines are aged in these oak *feuillettes* for twelve months, the barrels having an average age of seven or eight years. Fermentation in *cuve* is followed by the *élevage en fût,* fining if necessary with bentonite and a very light kieselguhr filtration. But despite the traditional adherence to oak, the wines are the epitome of Chablis and quality: steely flinty fruit, long and lingering, depth and concentration with elegance and finesse. And to cap it all, Raveneau still uses wax capsules on the bottles. This is an oak producer *par excellence.*

On our visit in May 1998, we cheekily asked Bernard, now happily returned from his sojourn in Vezelay, what was the Raveneau secret. 'Secret? What secret?' An all-knowing smile spread across his jovial face. 'To making the finest wines in Chablis, and almost every year.' The smile turned to laughter, a shrug of the shoulders and two upturned hands! With a twinkle in the eye he replied 'It's a full time task, you know, hard work and many hours in the vineyards and cellars.' We still don't know the answer! Or do we? Bernard obviously didn't object to the question as he welcomed us back a few months later. But he still did not answer it!

As for ageing in bottle, the Premier Crus should not be touched for at least 5 years, and Les Clos, Blanchots and Valmur need 10 years to avoid the charge of infanticide. A great estate, fabulous wines. Three stars plus.

Tasting notes

The following wines were tasted at the domaine in February 1999:

1998s – Forest, Montée de Tonnerre, Valmur and Blanchot from enamelled *cuves*. Detailed tasting notes were not taken, owing to the unfinished state of the wines which still had to be *élevé* in barrel, but we can generally report lovely fruit and acidity indicating good wines in what Bernard described as a difficult vintage.

The 97s were tasted again from barrel:

Forest 97 – rich concentrated fruit, long, delicious. Fine. (2004–2010)

Montmains 97 – minerally, fruity, very concentrated. Fine. (2004–2010)

Butteaux 97 – lovely pale straw colour, citrus fruit flavours, great depth and concentration of fruit but only fair length. Still a lovely wine. Very good. This is a great improvement on our previous tasting in May 98 – just shows the danger of pre-judging an incomplete wine. (2003–2007)

Chapelot 97 – closing up already, good depth of fruit, elegant wine with more structure than the Butteaux. Fine. (2004–2010)

Montée de Tonnerre 97 – minerally nose, very lovely concentrated fruit, but perhaps a trifle short on acidity. Not as initially lovely as when tasted last May. Still it is a very good wine. (2002–2006)

Vaillons 97 – good flinty fruit with lovely length and a dry finish. Great concentration and depth. This is a fine wine. (2004–2010)

Blanchot 97 – closed nose, lovely acacia flavours, very elegant and concentrated, immense wine, a bit austere and dry on finish, but brilliant. Very fine. (2005–2012)

Valmur 97 – perfumed and elegant, great depth of fruit and opulent, good length, a lovely wine. Fine. (2005–2012)

Les Clos 97 – honeyed perfume, more open than expected, wonderful wine, elegance and finesse in a glass, rich fruit, acidity, balance, length, finish, in other words, the lot; had gained since last tasted, it must be a Star wine! Very fine. (2005–2012)

The following wines were tasted at the domaine in October 1997, all from barrel:

Montmains 96 – a deeply concentrated wine of style and character. Very good. (2004–2010)

Vaillons 96 – fabulous wine, more profound and even more fruit than the Montmains. Fine. (2004–2010)

Butteaux 96 – another profound wine, perfect balance of fruit and acidity. Retasted at MW 96 Burgundy Tasting in March 1999: quiet nose but blossoms out on the palate, delicious buttery fruit, lovely balance with a long, wonderful aftertaste. Fine. (2002–2008)

Montée de Tonnerre 96 – not showing well on the day, needs a retaste. Retasted at MW 96 Burgundy Tasting in March 1999: quite restrained nose, but bags of fruit there, good grip, nice crisp acidity, minerally and steely, perhaps a slight bitter finish but still very good. (2002–2008)

Blanchots 96 – very fine wine, but totally closed. Underneath it was immense. (2006–2014)

Valmur 96 – brilliantly concentrated wine, deep, but obviously dumb. Fine. (2006–2014)

Les Clos 96 – Big Daddy! Showing little, but what is there, is there in abundance. Fabulous wine. Very fine. (2006–2016)

Further wines tasted at the domaine and in London and Chablis:

Chapelot 95 – guilty of infanticide, this case was opened in Hampshire in October 97. Although not too long in bottle, the wine had already developed a lovely nose, luscious fruit and depth of flavour. Now expected to close up for a few years. Do not touch until 2002 at least. Very fine. (2002–2010)

Forest 95 – closed as expected, fruit so intense that it hurts to hold the mouthful, immense concentration, fine balance, but despite all this some doubt over its future. Only time will tell. (2002–2010) (Nitry, October 98)

Butteaux 93 – lovely biscuity nose but somehow does not deliver on the palate. The fruit is there and some acidity, no great length or depth. Good but not great, therefore disappointing. Drink soon. (London, December 99)

Vaillons 93 – fully mature on nose and palate, fair depth of buttery tropical fruit, apricots and honey, pineapple and mango, with length and intensity. Good but drink soon. (January 2000)

Chapelot 92 – closed up but underlying depth and concentration of delicious fruit, very long, very lovely, very fine. (2002–2008) (October 94)

Les Clos 92 – obviously closed but encouragement reveals a wonderful Big Daddy of a wine, all that is wanted in a bottle, luscious elegant fruit, firm, great acidity, and long, very long, very fine. (2002–2010) (October 94)

Valmur 91 – tasted after a Ramonet Chassagne Morgeots 90 and blew it away. Fabulous wine, rich, elegant and very long. Just proves how a great winemaker can produce a quality wine in an indifferent year! (Drink now until 2006) (London, August 98)

Vaillons 85 – lovely nose, tremendous fruit, superb length, honey nuts and butter-biscuits, delicious mind-blowing Chablis. Star wine! (Drink now until 2003) (London, May 98 and December 99)

Blanchot 82 – lovely restrained nose, but rather disappointing on palate. Fruit and acidity still there but a bit musty and bitter on finish. (April 98)

Wines are not available from the cellar door, but may be obtained from stockists in:

UK

John Armit Wines, London W11. Tel: 020 7727 6846 Fax: 020 7727 7133
e-mail: info@armit.co.uk http://www.armit.co.uk

Haynes Hanson & Clark, London SW1. Tel: 020 7259 0102 Fax: 020 7259
0103 and at Stow-on-the-Wold, Glos. Tel: 01451 870808 Fax: 01451
870508

USA

Burgundy Wine Co. Ltd., New York. Tel: 212 691 9092 Fax: 212 691 9244

Hi-Time Wine Cellars, Costa Mesa, California 92627. Tel: 949 650 8463 Fax:
949 631 6863

Kermit Lynch, Berkeley, California 94702. Tel: 510 524 1524 Fax: 510 528
7026

DOMAINE GUY ROBIN

13 Rue Berthelot	Tel: 03 86 42 12 63
89800 Chablis	Fax: 03 86 42 49 57

20 hectares

Production:

Grand Crus	Blanchot	0.20 ha
	Valmur	2.60 ha
	Les Clos	0.20 ha
	Bougros	0.50 ha
	Vaudésir	0.25 ha
Premier Crus	Vaillons	1.10 ha
	Montmains	2.00 ha
	Mont de Milieu	1.00 ha
	Montée de Tonnerre	3.80 ha
Chablis Village		

Located in the back streets of old Chablis town, simple but substantial
buildings mark the home and domaine of the Robin family, an old-established Chablis family steeped in tradition. The whole has a rather austere
appearance backing onto multi-storey blocks of flats, London's East End or
New York tenement style. The estate and complex of farm-type buildings is
protected by iron railings, behind which a quadruple canine reception
committee seems totally bored with the absence of activity on either side
of the fence.

Within the courtyard is an assortment of agricultural implements, an old
wooden press on a floral decorated cart and various motor vehicles of
doubtful vintage. A muddy approach leads to an attractive domicile
facing a pretty garden. To the rear of the yard is a barn, storing tractors
and other equipment, together with the wine press, presumably the one
in use and, believe it or not, various enamelled *cuves*. Disorganisation

seems to be the order of the day.

Regrettably, the large concrete cellars are not much better, arrayed with rows of barrels aged from 2 to 15 years old, with a rather musty smell.

The domaine itself has been run for three generations. The vineyards were established 40 years ago and include some fine Grand and Premier Cru holdings. Harvesting is still by hand, with fermenting in old oak *pièces* except the Village Chablis which is *en cuve*.

This is a domaine which reminds one of the nursery rhyme about the little girl with the curl in the middle of her forehead. The results are varied. Madame Robin, who took us around the domaine and conducted the tasting, was helpful and friendly. Monsieur Robin was we believe recovering from the efforts of bringing in the 98 harvest and was not available.

Tasting notes

The following wines were tasted at the domaine in October 1998. The 97s were just three weeks in bottle, and obviously recovering from bottling shock. We will taste again.

Chablis 97 – fair wine, sourish apples, sulphur on nose, needs time to dissipate.

Vaillons 97 – pleasant nose, lots of fruit, but odd aftertaste. Fair only. (2000–2002)

Montmains 97 – closed as expected, fruit rather hidden but slightly sour again. Needs time. Fair. (2002–2004)

Mont de Milieu 97 – better fruit, best of the bunch so far. Fairly good. (2000–2002)

Chablis 96 – fruit still hidden but sulphury when tasted. Should get better. Needs time.

Montmains 96 – good Chablis nose, good fruit and fairly pleasant aftertaste but still a bit bitter. This might get better. Fair. (2000–2002)

Vaudésir 96 – totally closed but not much there anyway. Once again bitter and some sulphur which will probably dissipate. Not Grand Cru quality.

Tasted in London:

Chablis 95 – this is odd, plenty of fruit on the palate and with supporting acidity, but a lingering whiff of sulphur like the Montmains and not the most pleasant of aftertastes. (March 98)

Montmains 95 – slightly stale nose, flowery scented taste, maybe over-sulphured and thus not to our liking, short unpleasant aftertaste (March 98). A bottle the following month showed some variation, for it had lovely fruit and some length, but rather low acidity. Not a great Montmains but very drinkable now. The sulphur is obviously dissipating. (2000–2002) (April 98)

Montée de Tonnerre 95 — this is better, very much better. Pale straw colour, lovely fruity nose, citrus overtones in the nicest sense, concentrated fruit bursts out of the glass, good length, well balanced, not exactly a wine of *typicité* but very good indeed. Needs another year. If they can do it like this, why not all the time? (2000–2003) (March 98).

Wines are available from the **CELLAR DOOR**, the retail shop in town and stockists in:

UK
Playford Ros Ltd, Thirsk, Yorks. Tel: 01845 526777 Fax: 01845 526888

USA
Calvert Woodley, Washington DC. Tel: 202 966 4400 Fax: 202 537 5086
Garnet Wines & Liquors, New York, 10021. Tel: 212 772 3211 Fax: 212 517 4029
Hi-Time Wine Cellars, Costa Mesa, California 92627. Tel: 949 650 8463 Fax: 949 631 6863
North Berkeley Wine Imports, Richmond, California.

DOMAINE DES RONCIÈRES

Régis et Yves Ségault
10 Rue de Picardie
Maligny   Tel: 03 86 47 55 69
89800 Chablis   Fax: 03 86 42 84 14

11 hectares

Production:
Chablis Village and Petit Chablis

Just outside the village of Maligny on the way to Chablis, make a left and first right towards Fontenay-près-Chablis, up and up a narrow country road through fields, meadows and vines. After three kilometres or so, at the top of the hill and slap bang in the middle of nowhere the working farm buildings of Domaine des Roncières appear on the right. Drive in and be greeted by Farmer Giles – alias Régis Ségault, a congenial friendly young man in his late thirties. The domaine literally comprises cramped rustic farm buildings well adapted for vinous use.

This small family estate is run by the two brothers Régis and Yves Ségault who, after making wine for family consumption, concentrated on commercial production turning out their first vintage in 1987. Their ancestors had always cultivated the vine at the same time as other agricultural activities, but Régis and Yves made a mean Chablis and realising their ability took the opportunity to expand on their activities. However, polyculture has not been abandoned as Yves still looks after his sheep and cows plus 170 hectares of cereals, leaving Régis very largely in charge of the vines.

Vinification is traditional in stainless steel – temperature-controlled, with *élevage en cuve*. No wood is used here. These are quite good wines, nothing startling, but good honest Chablis for early and easy drinking, produced with love and affection. It is a fun place to call for the casual visitor, and the odd bottle or so. Taste first if you can! Most of the production is destined for the Burgundy *négoce* but about 10 per cent (5-6,000 bottles per annum) finds its way to the home market and **CELLAR DOOR**.

Tasting notes
The following wines were tasted at the farm in February 1999, the 98 in London in September 1999:

Chablis 98, lovely mineral and fruit nose, not exactly concentrated or crisp, some Granny Smith character, slight bitter finish but good and drinkable.

Chablis 97, little on nose, some fruit here but lacks a bit of crispness. Not a lot of personality but good.

Chablis 96, this is delicious, lovely fruity nose, steely appley fruit and well-balanced acidity with length. Very good.

Chablis 95, light gold in colour, nutty honeyed nose but a bit medicinal in character. Quite good though.

DOMAINE VINCENT SAUVESTRE

Rue de Monthèlie   and at: Rue de Poinchy
21190 Meursault   La Chapelle Vaupelteigne
Tel: 03 80 21 22 45   89800 Chablis
Fax: 03 80 21 28 05

26 hectares

Production:
Premier Crus   Beauroy
                        Montmains
Chablis Village

Originally known as Maison Pierre Bitouzet, this business, which includes a large *négociant* arm in Meursault for Côte d'Or wines, has been renamed Domaine Vincent Sauvestre following the succession by Pierre Bitouzet's son-in-law in 1988.

The domaine now has 26 hectares under vine in Chablis including parcels of Premier Cru Beauroy and Montmains. The wines are vinified at their *cuverie* in La Chapelle Vaupelteigne just a few kilometres north of Chablis located by the bridge over the River Serein which at the time of our visit in February 1999 was almost entirely surrounded by flood waters.

At present, the vinified wine is transported to Sauvestre's large *cuverie* in Meursault for *élevage* in enamelled *cuves*. In due course the *cuverie* in Chablis is to be enlarged so that the local operation becomes self-sufficient.

Pierre Bitouzet continues to oversee the vineyards, and vinification is under the control of winemaker Pierre Jean and Vincent Sauvestre himself. Vincent, at only 37 years old, is clearly an ambitious man but also has a shrewd business head on his shoulders

This domaine makes good wines and we shall continue to note its progress with great interest.

Tasting notes

The following wines were tasted at the *cuverie* in Meursault and Chablis in February 1999; the 98s were from *cuve*:

Chablis 98 La Valée – a fresh and fruity village wine from the *lieu-dit* of this name at La Chapelle, perhaps a little short on length but good nevertheless.

Chablis 98 Chapiteau – a different cuvée with a lovely nose, good fruit with more concentration and length. Good Chablis.

Beauroy 98 – very mineral, fat and lovely, good structure, should be a good wine. (2002–2005)

Montmains 98 – more aromatic, pear drops, lovely length, should be very good. (2003–2006)

Chablis 97 – 3 months in bottle, quite austere, fruit not so obvious, but a good Chablis with a dry mineral finish.

Beauroy 97 – a little more closed on nose, fat wine, almost opulent, good length and delicious. Very good. (2001–2004)

Montmains 97 – 2 months in bottle-typical nose, steely mineral wine, good length, supple, dry finish. Good. (2001–2004)

Beauroy 96 – good nose and fruit, more rich and concentration than the Montmains below. Good/very good. (2001–2004)

Montmains 96 – minerally nose, fruit there but rather short. We prefer the 97. Fair only. (2001–2003)

The domaine produces a low-priced basic Chablis under the *sous-marque* Margherite Carillon, available at Majestic Wine Warehouses; this is a quick, quaffable thirst quencher but has no further pretensions.

The wines are not sold direct but are available from the following stockists:

UK

Alliance Wine Co., Beith, Scotland. Tel: 01505 506060

Everton Wines, Droitwich, Birmingham. Tel: 01905 775536

DOMAINE FRANCINE ET OLIVIER SAVARY

4 Chemin des Mates
Maligny
89800 Chablis

Tel: 03 86 47 42 09
Fax: 03 86 47 55 80

13 hectares plus a further 3.5 to be added in 1999

Production:
Premier Cru   Fourchaume 0.75 ha
Chablis Village and Petit Chablis

Based on the outskirts of Maligny to the north-east of Chablis, this domaine has a rather austere location with an aspect of electricity pylons, uncultivated land and a distant view of vineyards. The buildings themselves
are very modern, grouped around a small courtyard, the *cuverie* and *chai*
having the capacity to increase production by 50 per cent when needed,
the total already standing at some 100,000 bottles per annum.

Francine handles the business side in a friendly and helpful manner,
which is fortunate, as Olivier, a graduate in wine technology at Dijon,
was clearly preoccupied with other matters at the time of our expected visit.

The set-up is what one would expect from a young couple with modern
ideas. The loading of the presses is by gravity, *débourbage en cuve* and temperature-controlled vinification in stainless steel and enamelled vats. There are
eight *barriques* aged between one and four years old for *élevage* of some of the
Chablis production. Why? The parcel of Fourchaume is small but hopes
remain that this can be increased.

The Savary's first vintage was in 1984 so these are still early days, but on
present form a learning curve is required if these wines are to reach star
status. Right now, they are good but generally unexciting.

Apart from the home market, the wines are exported to the UK, Holland, Belgium, Japan and the USA.

Tasting notes
The following wines were tasted at the domaine in October 1998, except as
stated, with the 98s tasted in London in August 1999 by courtesy of Adam
Bancroft Associates:

Chablis 98 – nose of *typicité*, good concentration of fruit, lovely balance of
acidity. Good Chablis.

Chablis Vieilles Vignes 98 – quiet nose, concentration of fruit but a bit bitter
with a sour finish. Not much to it.

Chablis 97 – a basic Chablis without pretensions, sulphur rather too prominent and will hopefully dissipate with time.

Fourchaume 97 – yellow/green colour with some nose, more depth of peachy
fruit, good clean finish. Good to very good. (2001–2004)

Chablis 96 – flinty and mineral open nose, good fruit with a long lingering aftertaste. Good wine.

Chablis Vieilles Vignes 96 – more fragrant wine with fruit partly vinified in oak already integrated. Good concentration. Good wine.

Fourchaume 96 – closed nose as would be expected, fruit hidden but should come through, good clean finish. Good wine. (2002–2006)

Chablis Vieilles Vignes 95 – nutty toasty nose, mineral dry fruit, Granny Smith apples, with length and good balanced acidity, mouth-puckering finish. Lacked a little depth initially and some old vine intensity but evolved quite well in the glass. Needs a year or so. Passed the 'litmus' test (*leave it till morning under seal*). Very good. (April 99)

Fourchaume 95 – pale lemon gold, gentle mineral fragrant and fruity nose, nice fruit and good balance with fair length and a dry finish. But not very profound and unlike the Vieilles Vignes it did not pass the 'litmus' test. Good only. (2000–2002) (April 99)

Wines available from the **CELLAR DOOR** and stockists in:

UK

Adam Bancroft Associates, London SW8. Tel: 020 7793 1902 Fax: 020 7793 1897

Ian G. Howe, Newark, Notts. Tel: 01636 704366 Fax: 01636 610502

USA

Kermit Lynch, Berkeley, California 94702. Tel: 510 524 1524 Fax: 510 528 7026

DOMAINE ROGER SÉGUINOT

4 Rue de Méré
Maligny   Tel: 03 86 47 44 42
89800 Chablis   Fax: 03 86 47 54 94

23 hectares

Production:
Chablis Premier Cru   Fourchaume
Chablis Village and Petit Chablis

Roger Séguinot, 75 years young and with more energy than a person half his age, runs this estate with his family. His son exploits 12 hectares of his own and Roger's daughter, not directly involved in the business, has two children, the elder son Jean-Frañois having been to l'Ecole de Viticulture de Beaune, so a long family tradition is assured of continuity.

The domaine is based in Maligny where the family house and garden is found in a side street off the main Chablis road through an archway leading on to the *cuverie* and *chai*. An attractive mural on the outside wall identifies the property.

The work in the vineyards follows standard Chablis practice, as far as it is standard, Guyot pruning, with weedkiller and anti-mildew, oidium and parasite treatments according to the norm and to the need. The harvest is done mechanically and has been for the last 10 years: M. Séguinot remarks that at the time of the change-over from manual picking, extensive tasting was carried out to ascertain any differences with that part of the harvest which was still done by hand – at the time of the tastings, no difference was noticed, and this is still the case in retrospect.

The vinification and *élevage* in resin-epoxy *cuves* is traditional and the resultant wine is Chablis of *typicité*. The production is part bottled 8-10 months after collage and filtration, and about 30 per cent sold to the *négoce*. The wines are good, and can be very good, but we feel that a steadier hand should control the sulphur bag.

As an example of the active nature of this charming man, M. Séguinot still participates in the Fêtes du Vin, has been President of the Commission of Chablis within BIVB, President of the Yonne Section of Viticulture, Secretary of the Federation of Chablisien Vignerons and a prominent re-spected member of other viticultural associations.

The markets for the wines include France, Belgium, the UK and USA.

Tasting notes
The following wines were tasted at the domaine in May 1998:

Chablis 96 – quiet nose, good fruit and acidity in balance, *le vrai Chablis!*

Fourchaume 96 – nose of *typicité*, good fruit and acidity, long, a touch of sulphur at the back of the throat which should go. Good wine, but may not develop further. (2000–2004)

Chablis 95 – wine of *typicité*, but good fruit and acidity for the vintage, a bit yeasty, good though.

Fourchaume 95 – gentle nose, good fruit, some length, but still a little sulphur present. Fair to good. (2000–2003)

Wines available from the **CELLAR DOOR** and **UK** shippers:

Anglo-International Wine Shippers, Esher, Surrey. Tel: 01372 469841 Fax: 01372 469816

DOMAINE SERVIN ★

20 Rue d'Oberwesel   Tel: 03 86 18 90 00
89800 Chablis   Fax: 03 86 18 90 01

32 hectares
Production:

Grand Crus	Les Clos	0.88 ha
	Bougros	0.46 ha
	Blanchots	0.90 ha
	Preuses	0.90 ha
Premier Crus	Vaillons	3.50 ha
	Montée de Tonnerre	2.50 ha
	Forêts	0.50 ha
Chablis Village		

This is one of the larger estates of Chablis, farming about 32 hectares under vine with prime sites in four Grand Crus and three Premier Crus. Although they boast a family tradition going back to 1654, it is with Francis Servin's grandfather Marcel that the modern story begins, a one-time *tonnelier* with Simonnet across the road, but owning some vines of his own.

The domaine which fronts the main road on the entrance to the town from Tonnerre comprises a complex of old buildings, rather haphazard in shape enclosing its own access road and yard. Plenty of land is available for expansion on which new buildings are already planned. Francis Servin with his *régisseur* Mark Cameron, imported from the Antipodes to deal with English-speaking customers and wearisome wine writers, now run the domaine with a quiet efficiency and high reputation for making fine wines.

The grapes at Domaine Servin are harvested mechanically, except for the Grand Crus which are partly manually picked as conditions permit, some of the slopes being very steep. In fact, Servin was one of the first to experiment with a mechanical harvester back in 1982. The domaine reports low yields where in 1996 for example, Chablis Village Appellation was only 37 hectolitres per hectare as against 46 hl/ha for the Montée de Tonnerre. In 1994 the Vaillons reached 58 hl/ha, surprising for this vintage, in spite of frost damage. The 1998 vintage affected by hail on 14 May that year has resulted in the crop of Blanchot, Preuses, Vaillons and Montée de Tonnerre being only 50 per cent of the usual amount – devastation indeed. The Forêts was unaffected, but as this was replanted between 1992 and 1993, the vines will have only recently come on line.

The average age of the vines is around 25 years, but specifically 40 years for Preuses and Bougros and 15 years for Les Clos. Francis Servin particularly likes his Bougros which he recommends with Gibier and Crustaces.

A new vinification plant was installed in the early 1980s with temperature-controlled stainless steel vats for fermentation and *élevage*. However, the Vaillons is put into oak barrels from 3 to 9 years old in the proportion of 80 per cent to 20 per cent inox. Les Clos sees 100 per cent oak, Preuses and Bougros get about 30 per cent depending on the vintage. After the malo and ageing, the wines are fined *sur col*, filtered and usually bottled in June or July following the vintage.

The total production in an average year is 120,000 bottles with exports to the UK and USA as well as mainland Europe.

This is a very well run domaine producing quality wines with thoughtful customer control – wines found badly stored in a warehouse in England were withdrawn when it was clear that this did not meet the high quality expected. This is a star domaine, but we would like to see more controlled use of oak.

Tasting notes
The following wines were tasted at the domaine in October 1998, except as stated, with the 98s tasted in London in August 1999:

Chablis 98 – pleasant nose of *typicité* with fruit in the background, good concentration and length, lovely exotic fruit flavours. Very good.

Vaillons 98 – lovely perfumed nose, a little oak still to integrate, bags of peach and apricot fruit, lovely acidity, lovely wine. Very good. (2002–2005)

Montée de Tonnerre 98 – another lovely wine from Francis Servin, elegance and finesse, intensity, concentration and length, perhaps not the character of the Vaillons but still very good. (2002–2005)

Bougros 98 – tight nose, intense fruit comes through on palate, lovely concentration, length and depth. Very good. (2003–2008)

Chablis 97 – good fruit and acidity, lemon flavours, lovely crisp clean finish. Very good.

Montée de Tonnerre 97 – nose rather closed as expected, a masculine wine with good fruit and great intensity, quite dry, very long. Fine. (2000–2004)

Vaillons 97 – flinty Chablis, lots of ripe fruit, peaches, good length and depth, lovely wine. Very fine. (2002–2005)

Blanchots 97 – closed right up, great concentration of fruit here, lovely intensity, for the future. Fine. (2003–2007)

Preuses 97 – vinified and *élevé* in oak which, although still apparent, is well integrated already. Still needs a lot of time but should be very good. (2003–2007)

Bougros 97 – oak very obvious but a fat wine with good fruit and acidity. Should be a very good wine in time if the oak integrates. (2003–2007)

Les Clos 97 – generous nose with voluptuous concentrated fruit if slightly bitter, apricots and vanilla, fine balance and some intensity. However, the oak is rather too prominent and judgement is reserved. Perhaps the vines are too young to cope with 100 per cent oak in this vintage. Should be a great wine – we shall see!

Chablis 96 – lovely floral nose, apricots and honey, ripe fruit, long and luscious, crisp clean finish. This note confirms an earlier tasting in London in December 97 which already showed a lovely nose and soft round fruit. Very good.

Montée de Tonnerre 96 – closed nose but depth and concentration of fruit is obvious, apricots and honey again, delicious long finish. Fine. (2002–2006)

Vaillons 96 – totally closed, but once again lovely concentration of apricot and honeyed fruit, good acidity. Oak, what oak? Beautifully integrated, this is the way it should be done, at the service of the wine, not in conflict. A very fine wine. Drink (2003–2007)

Chablis 95 – nose lost, fruit going, acidity dull, disappointing. In January 98, a bottle was just as disappointing.

Preuses 95 – dumb nose, fruit still hidden by vanilla flavours but toasty, wine just emerging from its shell, lacks a little crispness and a bit short. Perhaps too much oak for the vintage. Good only. (2000–2003)

Montée de Tonnerre 93 – light gold straw coloured, fruit on nose and palate with some depth, not over long, a very good wine with food. Drink now. (January 98 in London)

Bougros 93 – dark yellow colour, lemon vanilla flavours, good length and intensity. Oak now reasonably well integrated but still a bit much for the vintage. Not likely to get any better. Good wine though. (2000–2003)

Wines available from stockists in:

UK
Anglo-International Wine Shippers, Esher, Surrey. Tel: 01372 469841 Fax: 01372 469816
Avery's of Bristol, Nailsea. Tel: 01275 811100 Fax: 01275 811101
Bordeaux Direct, Theale, Berks. Tel: 0118 903 0903 Fax: 0118 903 0130 e-mail: orders@bordeaux-direct.co.uk
Corney & Barrow, London EC1. Tel: 020 7251 4051 Fax: 020 7608 1373
Majestic Wine Warehouses, branches nationwide. Tel: 01923 298200
Peckham & Rye, Glasgow and Edinburgh. Tel: 0141 445 4555
Robersons, London W14. Tel: 020 7371 2121

USA
Julienne Wines, Chicago, Illinois
Purveyor of Fine Wines, New Orleans, Louisiana. Tel: 504 523 5230

DOMAINE PHILIPPE TESTUT

38 Rue des Moulins   Tel: 03 86 42 17 50
89800 Chablis   Fax: 03 86 42 14 75

12 hectares

Production:

Grand Cru	Grenouilles	0.55 ha
Premier Crus	Montée de Tonnerre	1.00 ha
	Beugnons	0.50 ha
	Vaucoupin	0.50 ha
	Forêts / Montmains	0.17 ha

Chablis Village and Petit Chablis

Close by a beautiful stretch of the river is located this domaine, approached through a door in the stone wall into an attractive garden. A covered walkway leads to the vaulted cellars on two levels, partly below ground, full of old barrels and immaculately tidy but still with a fine ambiance.

Philippe Testut, smiling and congenial, leads his visitors to the tasting table where they are made to feel welcome and comfortable. If you are very lucky, you will be entertained with a plate of home-made *lapin terrine* to accompany the tasting, and joined by the charming Madame Testut, a very knowledgeable lady with a wicked sense of humour.

Philippe Testut's family was well known in France as manufacturers of weighing machines, but in 1966 added winemaking to their other skills with the purchase of some vineyards adding Château Grenouille to the estate in the 1970s. Philippe was by no means a novice in the field, having gained his experience with Long Depaquit in the early 1960s. In fact Dr Long Depaquit's own chair is located in the *chai* for the comfort of the fortunate taster. After the disposal of Grenouille to La Chablisienne, Philippe left in 1974 and in 1980 started his own domaine. The wines produced carried the name of Testut Frères on the labels up to 1994, and from then on just his own name.

The wines are all important to the family. Fine *climats* are included in the domaine, some *en fermage*. Vinification is in enamelled *cuve* or stainless steel for the Chablis and Premier Crus, but a little wood is used for the Grenouilles which receives up to two years *élevage*. In general, the Chablis Village and Petit Chablis are given 6 months *élevage* but the Premier Crus 1 year. The wines are given a light plate filtration but from the 1997 vintage the system will change to a new method called *tangentielle*, in which the filter plates are placed tangentially to the norm, thus reducing pressure on the wine. The Premier Crus are bottled September to November the year after the vintage for release the following spring.

Ten per cent of the total production is exported mainly to the UK, Belgium and Germany, the remainder being for the home market.

The future of this estate is in good hands – son Cyrille Testut is a graduate of the Viticultural School in Beaune and is now involved in the family business. This is a domaine worthy of note.

Tasting notes

The following wines were tasted at the domaine in May 1998:

Petit Chablis 97– little on nose, but a full delicious wine.

Chablis 97 – nose a bit closed but lovely fruit and acidity in balance, good length. Lovely wine.

Montée de Tonnerre 97 – very floral, almost intensely perfumed, fine depth of fruit with good length and balance. Very good. (2002–2005)

Chablis 96 – gentle nose, good fruit and acidity, long and delicious, a wine of true *typicité*. (Tasted with M. Testut's home-made rabbit terrine)

Montée de Tonnerre 96 – wine of *typicité* on nose but still fairly closed, just a touch of sulphur which will disappear, lovely fruit and balance, good length, big wine, expansive, a five-year wine (the terrine lasted to this point). Very good. (2002–2006)

Montée de Tonnerre 95 – rather dumb nose, slightly bitter taste, good balance of fruit and acidity but did not show well. Fair/good. (2000–2003)

Marc de Château Grenouille 25-30 years old – distilled at 60 per cent but loses with time, now at 43 per cent volume, a production which is still continuing. This nearly takes your head off. A strong biscuity flavour, expansive, wonderful experience.

Wines available from the **CELLAR DOOR** (if it is open – Madame Testut's quip) and stockists in:

UK

M. & W. Gilbey Ltd, Pheasants Ridge Vineyards, Hambleden, Henley-on-Thames, Oxon.

House of Townend, Red Duster House, York Street, Wincolmlee, Hull HU2 0QX.

DOMAINE GERARD TREMBLAY ★

Domaine des Iles

12 Rue de Poinchy
Poinchy
89800 Chablis

Tel: 03 86 42 40 98
Fax: 03 86 42 40 41

33 hectares

Production:

| Grand Crus | Valmur | 0.50 ha |
| | Vaudésir | 0.60 ha |

Premier Crus	Fourchaume	6.00 ha
	Côte de Léchet	3.00 ha
	Montmains	1.50 ha
	Beauroy	0.50 ha

Chablis Village and Petit Chablis

This well-established and respected domaine is now in the reliable hands of Gérard Tremblay and his wife Hélène with their well-travelled daughter now involved in the family business. The Tremblay family is one of the best-known in Chablis, with the name connected with many other domaines – Pascal Bouchard-Tremblay and Lyne Marchive-Tremblay of Domaine des Malandes to name just two of the most famous.

Gérard's portfolio is impressive: substantial holdings in Chablis Village land, a large parcel of Premier Cru Fourchaume from 4 different *climats*, three other important Premier Cru sites and a small area of Grand Cru Valmur produce some 200/250,000 bottles per annum and from the 1997 vintage Gérard has added over half a hectare of Vaudésir.

This up-to-date domaine, situated two minutes from Chablis just off the main road to Auxerre, is approached over a beautifully laid garden with an ornamental pond. The impressive 8-year-old *cuverie*, chalet-style, with its pitched pine-clad close-boarded roof, is most attractive and very tasteful.

The harvesting of the grapes is carried out by machine, with the exception of the steep-sloped Grand Crus. Vinification proceeds in temperature-controlled stainless steel vats for both alcoholic and malolactic fermentations. The bulk of the wine remains in inox for *élevage*, but a small part of the Grand and Premier Crus, perhaps 15 to 20 per cent, is aged in 1 to 4-year-old wood for five to six months before *assemblage* with the inox cuvée, and just a light bentonite or kieselguhr fining prior to bottling.

The wines are marketed worldwide, including the UK and all Europe, Japan and the USA.

We like the guy, we like his wines! A star estate.

Tasting notes
The following wines were tasted at the domaine in February 1999, the 98s at the London International Wine Trade Fair in May 1999:

Petit Chablis 98 – lots of lovely fresh fruit with good balancing acidity. This is a good Petit Chablis.

Chablis 98 – more typical on nose, good fruit and acidity, dry and steely. Good.

Fourchaume 98 – only two weeks in bottle and suffering shock. Perfumed nose, fair concentration of fruit, acidity is there, dry but a bit short. Should improve. Fairly good. (2002–2005)

Petit Chablis 97 – pleasant nose but fruit is a little thin, very dry. Fair.

Chablis 97 – good fruit here, quite forward, some length and a dry mineral finish. Good.

Beauroy 97 – nose quite forward, floral fruit well balanced, crisp, good length. Very good. (2002–2005)

Côte de Léchet 97 – a little closed but opens up with encouragement, lovely minerally fruit, balance and length, very elegant, lovely wine. Very good. (2002–2005)

Montmains 97 – nicely mineral and steely, lovely ripe fruit, crisp acidity, good length and aftertaste. Very good. (2002–2005)

Fourchaume 97 – lightly floral, violets, acacia and hazelnuts, very rich elegant fruit beautifully balanced, delicious acidity. Fine. (2002–2006)

Vaudésir 97 – first vintage from 20-year-old vines. Very closed nose but lots of intense rich fruit there, fine concentration and depth, even complexity, long dry finish, lovely wine. Very good indeed. (2003–2008)

The following wines were tasted at the domaine in May 1998 except as stated:

Petit Chablis 96 – minerally nose, fresh Petit Chablis, clean and crisp.

Chablis 96 – flinty mineral nose, fruit OK but a bit sour on the finish.

Beauroy 96 – from 40-year-old vines, lovely lemon/straw colour with a greenish tinge, 15 per cent old oak beautifully integrated, bursts with lovely sweet fruit, fine balance, clean finish, good length, lovely wine. Very good. (2002–2006)

Côte de Léchet 96 – greenish tinged, brilliantly clear, nose developing, oak is a little too noticeable, but nice fruit. Not sure that C. de Léchet needs oak but this should integrate as this is a well made wine. Good. (2000–2004)

Montmains 96 – fine floral and minerally nose, good fruit and balance, a little dry on finish, but nice wine. Very good. (2000–2004)

Fourchaume 96 – lovely lemon/green tinged colour, closed nose, lovely fruit, comes out in glass, good acidity, crisp and clean finish. Lovely wine. Very good. (2000–2006)

Valmur 96 – pale greenish tinged, nose just jumps out of the glass – 30 per cent wood – oak and honey perfumed, quite delicious but for home market only. Very good/Fine. (2003–2008)

Chablis 95 – rather acidic for the vintage, some fruit, a little unbalanced but pleasant enough, not a lot of character. (March 98 in London).

Montmains 95 – yellow/straw, maturity on nose, some fruit but a bit short, falls away in glass. The wine showed better when returning to the bottle two hours later, but still too short. Fair. Drink now. (April 98 in London)

Montmains 93 – quiet nose, some fruit but a little sharp, rather sour. Drink up. (May 98 in London)

Fourchaume 89 – darker yellow but youthful colour, petit-beurre biscuits, honey and flowers, lots of lovely succulent fruit, well balanced and with good length, absolutely delicious, fine wine. Drink now.

Wines available from the **CELLAR DOOR** and stockists in:

UK

Anglo-International Wine Shippers, Esher, Surrey. Tel: 01372 469841 Fax: 01372 469816

Bottleneck Wine, Bucks. Tel: 01908 560904

Le Bon Vin, Sheffield. Tel: 0114 256 0090

Enotria Winecellars, London NW10 (trade only). Tel: 020 8961 4411 Fax: 020 8961 8773

Eurovines, Isle of Wight. Tel: 01983 811743

Hall Batson & Co., Norwich, Norfolk. Tel: 01603 415115 Fax: 01603 484096

Daniel Lambert, Cardiff. Tel: 029 2066 6128

William Morrisons Supermarkets, N. England. Tel: 01274 494166 Fax: 01274 498395

Noble Rot Wine Warehouse, Worcs. Tel : 01527 575606

Option Wines UK, Maidstone, Kent. Tel: 01622 744139

Christopher Piper Wines, Devon. Tel: 01404 814139

USA

Classic Wine Imports, Brighton, Boston MA 02134. Tel: 617 731 6644

Garnet Wines & Liquors, New York, 10021. Tel: 212 772 3211 Fax: 212 517 4029

Gateway Wine & Spirit, Pittsburgh PA 15214. Tel: 412 682 1099

Ginday Imports, Washington DC 20037. Tel: 202 333 3680

DOMAINE LAURENT TRIBUT ★

15 Rue de Poinchy
Poinchy   Tel: 03 86 42 46 22
89800 Chablis   Fax: 03 86 42 48 23

5.2 hectares

Production:

Premier Crus	Beauroy	1.00 ha
	Côte de Léchet	0.55 ha
	Montmains	0.20 ha
Chablis Village		

A very small but significant estate run by Monsieur and Madame Laurent Tribut, Monsieur Tribut being the brother-in-law of Vincent Dauvissat whose name often appears on the labels as Tribut-Dauvissat.

A modest and delightful couple, the Tributs live in a lovely old house in the village of Poinchy, just a stone's throw from Chablis. Their daughter is at the viticultural school in Beaune and will eventually join the family firm; and what a fine firm to join!

The Premier Crus between them account for only 1.8 hectares, a mere 780 cases, and only 1,400 cases of Village Chablis from 3.4 hectares. This is a tiny production, but quality is paramount, hence the emphasis on low yields e.g. 37-40 hectolitres per hectare for the 1996 vintage.

Alcoholic and malolactic fermentations are in temperature-controlled enamelled *cuves*, and *élevage* follows in *fût de chêne* – oak *pièces*. There is no fining but a kieselguhr filtration. When we asked what they did for precipitation of tartrates, the reply was a smile and a waved hand towards the *cuverie* door. Like some other domaines in Chablis, if wood is used correctly, an open door in the winter months causes natural precipitation, and no doubt a few colds. The provenance of the oak is mixed, to encourage complexity (Allier, Vosges, Nevers and Chatillons) and is on average 7 to 8 years old. Surely this is one of the secrets of fine Chablis production when using oak? There are two bottlings, in September and April. Lovely wines. The Premier Crus need four or five years in bottle for optimum pleasure.

This is a star domaine.

The wines are marketed throughout Europe, Japan, New Zealand and the USA.

Tasting notes
The following wines were tasted at the domaine in May 1998 and February 1999, except where stated:

Chablis 97 – good nose and fruit, fresh and crisp wine. (February 99)

Côte de Léchet 97 – quiet nose, oak had integrated since tasting in barrel, great fruit and acidity, elegant, fine length and clean finish. Still needs time. What a lovely *climat*! Very good. (2001–2004) (February 99)

Beauroy 97 – once again well integrated oak, gentle floral nose, bags of fruit – apricots and Cox's apples, and well-balanced acidity, concentrated, good intensity, long and lovely. Very good/fine. (2001–2004) (February 99)

Montmains 97 – 40-year-old vines from René Dauvissat. Very closed but good mineral *typicité*, good length with a dry appley finish, lovely aftertaste. Fine. (2002–2005) (February 99)

Chablis 96 – packed with lots of fine fruit, nutty, well balanced, long. A very good village wine. (January 98/May 98/September 98 in London)

Côte de Léchet 96 – this is an oaky wine, lots of ripe fruit, lovely balance, but the wood is integrating well. Good clean mineral finish, very long. Very good. (2001–2004) (May 98)

Beauroy 96 – closed on nose as would be expected, bags of fine fruit and nicely concentrated, well balanced, very good length, delicious. Fine. (2001–2004) (January/May 98)

Montmains 96 – quite closed on nose and palate, needed a lot of encouragement, but then showed good concentrated fruit and acidity, good length. This is a good wine. (2001–2004) (May 98)

Wines available from stockists in:

UK

Domaine Direct, London WC1. Tel: 020 7837 1142

The French Wine People, Matlock, Derbyshire. Tel: 01629 57166

Ian G. Howe, Newark, Notts. Tel: 01636 704366 Fax: 01636 610502

Justerini & Brooks, London SW1. Tel: 020 7493 8721 Fax: 020 7499 4653 and Edinburgh. Tel: 0131 226 4202 Fax: 0131 225 2351

Lea & Sandeman, London branches. Tel: 020 7376 4767

USA

Calvert Woodley, Washington DC. Tel: 202 966 4400 Fax: 202 537 5086

Garnet Wines & Liquors, New York, 10021. Tel: 212 772 3211 Fax: 212 517 4029

Robert Haas, Vineyard Brands, Birmingham, Alabama. Tel: 205 980 8802 or http://www.vineyardbrands.com

DOMAINE DE LA VALLÉE AUX SAGES

Vincent Gallois
3 Route de Bleigny-Le-Carreau
Lignorelles   Tel: 03 86 47 51 16
89800 Chablis   Fax: 03 86 47 57 01

14 hectares

Production:
Chablis Village and Petit Chablis

Monsieur Gallois, whose parents were associated with La Chablisienne, is Beaune-qualified and exploits about 8 hectares of Chablis Appellation and 6 hectares of Petit Chablis. He built his *cave* in 1985, a building which gives the appearance of a large garage/motor works set well back from the road, unannounced, surrounded by vines and therefore difficult to find. Gradually, little by little, within a few years this modest domaine was fitted out to sell the wine in the bottle. An energetic and enthusiastic *vigneron*, Vincent personally controls all aspects of production, modern traditional vinification, filtration, bottling, not hesitating to roll up his sleeves and get mud on his hands in the vineyard, admitting that this leaves little time to devote to clients and the business of selling, but the wine comes first. He also has little time for wine writers and reviewers who do not take the trouble to visit the growers, hence we turned up in anticipation.

This is a small progressive estate with a refreshing attitude. That Monsieur Gallois can make good wine is undoubted, see the note on the 96 Chablis Village. But just think what could be done with a little Premier Cru or a site on Kimmeridgian soil, as most of the *vignoble* is at present located on Portlandian soil. A stricter régime of yield control and less adherence to over-sulphuring would also benefit the results.

In the meantime, one third of the production is sold on the domestic market, and the remaining two thirds finds its way to the UK and Japan.

Tasting notes

The following wines were tasted at the domaine in May 1998:

Petit Chablis 96 – fair nose and fruit, not particularly characterful, but good food wine.

Chablis 96 – nose of *typicité*, lots of fruit with good acidity and nice length. This is a good wine.

Petit Chablis 94– some maturity on nose, fruit to the fore, a bit blousy, not a very pleasant aftertaste.

Chablis 94 – no nose at all, fruit there but no length. Not a good wine.

Wines available from stockists in:

UK

J. T. Davies (Mayor Sworder), Croydon, Surrey. Tel: 020 8686 1155

DOMAINE DE VAUROUX ★

Claude et Olivier Tricon

Route d'Avallon   Tel: 03 86 42 10 37
89800 Chablis   Fax: 03 86 42 49 13

28.7 hectares

Production:

Grand Cru	Bougros	0.69 ha
Premier Crus	Montmains	1.65 ha
	Montée de Tonnerre	1.11 ha
Chablis Village		

After an impressive drive along the Route d'Avallon about 4 km out of Chablis, forging through hills and countryside, Domaine de Vauroux can be spied perched on the top of *une petite colline*. The domaine is approached over a long, very well maintained private road giving a very favourable early impression that this may be a well-run estate, and on further acquaintance those impressions are confirmed.

The small detached house and garden with converted old farm buildings have been dramatically enlarged over the last few years. The very large new *cuverie* has only recently been extended again above the extensive concrete cellars.

As we approach, Claude Tricon – a dead ringer for Sir Georg Solti and highly flattered by the comparison, pointing out that his direction of the estate is not with a *baton* – greets his visitors with a warm welcome. His family purchased the domaine in 1954 on their return from a sojourn in South Africa, and following the retirement of father Olivier the lead fell to Claude. Four sons are waiting in the wings to continue the family tradition, but in the meantime in March 1999 Claude handed the reins to his nephew Olivier and took a well-earned rest.

Apart from holdings of Grand and Premier Crus, the domaine owns 14 hectares of Chablis Appellation entirely with a southern exposure and facing the property across the valley, with gentle slopes and possible Premier Cru potential in the future. Most of the vines here were planted over 20 years ago. The work in the vineyard is all important: to aid complexity, 12 hectares of the estate were replanted *selection massale,* 3 hectares planted each year for four years, the remainder of replanting was *clonal* mostly between 1972 and 1980.

The Bougros and Montée de Tonnerre are harvested manually, the remainder by machine. Vinification is in enamelled and stainless steel *cuves*, no oak here. *Passage au froid*, bentonite fining and kieselguhr filtration precede bottling and all wines are kept in bottles for 7 or 8 months before being released.

Claude Tricon has left a well-organised and rapidly expanding operation making wines of very good quality. This is a star domaine. It remains to be seen whether the vinification methods are changed in any way and to what extent the wines differ in the future, if at all. The most recent tasting of the 1998 vintage indicates that the wines are getting even better and this may warrant further upgrading in the future.

Olivier, as well as taking over control of Domaine de Vauroux, operates his own domaine from the same address with separate vineyards and vinification, the wines labelled as Domaine Olivier Tricon. The estate comprises about 6 hectares, including 1 ha of Petit Chablis, 4 ha of Chablis Village and 1 ha of Montmains. In addition Olivier runs a substantial *négociant* business producing Montée de Tonnerre, Les Preuses and Les Clos plus a range of other wines from the Yonne and Oc. A new venture moves into Champagne – Guy Michel et Fils – and further Chablis production under the name Domaine Baillard. This *négociant* arm is known as Maison Olivier Tricon.

Tasting notes

Domaine de Vauroux

The following wines were tasted at the domaine in October 1998 and February 1999. The 98s, a masterly flight of wines, were tasted at La Grande Marque in London in January 2000 by courtesy of Lay and Wheeler:

Chablis 98 – lovely typical steely nose, flinty mineral fruit, great length, crisp acidity, fresh and truly delicious. This is an outstanding Village Chablis.

Montmains 98 – slightly retroussé nose of complexity but lovely minerally fruit on palate with great concentration and depth. Very long and delicious, very good. (2002–2005)

Montée de Tonnerre 98 – gentle elegant nose, lovely concentrated fruit, beautifully balanced, hints of apricots, peaches and Cox's apples, great depth, rich, very lovely, delicious, the taste just goes on and on. Fine. (2002–2006)

Chablis 97 – aromatic nose, good fruit and balance, drinking well now but perhaps without the depth of the 96. Still a good wine.

Montmains 97 – lovely colour, florally, nice flinty character with good depth of fruit and length, crisp finish. This wine was tasted on both occasions and had advanced well by February 99. Very good. (2002–2005)

Montée de Tonnerre 97 – bags of lovely flinty fruit, good concentration and length, touch of sulphur which should disappear. Good wine. (2001–2004)

Bougros 97 – lemon gold colour with a green tinge, closed nose as would be expected, great depth and concentration of fruit, good balance and length. Fine wine. (2003–2008)

Chablis 96 – nose rather closed, but a good depth of fruit underneath, terrific length for a Village Chablis and a wonderful aftertaste. Confirmed by a bottle opened later in London. Very good wine.

Montée de Tonnerre 96 – closed nose as expected, but fruit clearly there in abundance, great depth, finely balanced. Will be a fine elegant wine but needs time to develop. (2001–2006)

Chablis 95 – wine of *typicité* on nose and palate, good balance of fruit and acidity, not exactly spectacular but a very good Village wine. Tasted March 98 and later at the domaine.

Domaine Olivier Tricon

The following wines were tasted at the London International Wine Trade Fair 1999:

Petit Chablis 98 – light fruity nose, not exactly crisp acidity but good flavour.

Chablis 98 – minerally and a little sulphur, lots of fruit here and good acidity but sulphur at present dominates. Suffering from bottling shock but should get better.

Montmains 97 – *élevé* in tank on fine lees. Mineral nose, good concentration and intensity with some length. Will be a very good wine. (2000–2004)

Wines are available from stockists in:

UK

Alexander Wines, Glasgow. Tel: 0141 882 0039 Fax: 0141 882 0041

Connolly's Wine Merchants, Birmingham. Tel: 0121 236 9269 Fax: 0121 233 2339

Enotria Winecellars, London NW10 (trade only). Tel: 020 8961 4411 Fax: 020 8961 8773

Fullers, branches London and S.E England. Tel:.020 8996 2000 Fax: 020 8996 2087

Lay & Wheeler, Colchester, Essex. Tel: 01206 764446 Fax: 01206 560002 http://www.layandwheeler.co.uk

James Nicholson, County Down. Tel: 028 44830091

Peckham & Rye, Glasgow and Edinburgh. Tel: 0141 445 4555

USA

Julienne Importing, Chicago, Illinois.
Wines of France Inc., New Jersey.

. . . .

DOMAINE VERRET

7 Route de Champs   Tel: 03 86 53 31 81
89530 Saint-Bris-le-Vineux   Fax: 03 86 53 89 61

8.7 hectares of Chablis Appellations

Production:
Premier Cru   Beauroy   6.30 ha
Chablis Village   2.40 ha

Domaine Verret is a commercial concern producing some 350,000 bottles of wine including a Chablis Village and Premier Cru Beauroy as well as a large range of Bourgogne Blanc and Rouge and Sauvignon de Saint-Bris. Chablis accounts only for about 17.5 per cent of their total vineyard area. The domaine is located on the fringe of the town of Saint-Bris-le-Vineux at two levels, the site sloping towards farm land at the rear.

This is a family-run domaine now in its fourth generation run by Bruno Verret. The Chablis Beauroy vineyards were purchased in 1979, the Village Chablis more recently. The whole operation is very up to date with vinification in stainless steel *cuves*. Wood is used for their special cuvée Beauroy L'Ame de Domaine.

As the tasting notes indicate, the Chablis wines lack the usual *typicité*. More needs to be done if the domaine is to compete successfully in the quality Chablis market. We cannot report on the major part of the domaine's production, i.e. the Bourgogne wines and Sauvignon de Saint-Bris for which they have a reputation. Wines are available at the **CELLAR DOOR** only. No exports as yet to the UK or USA.

Tasting notes
The following wines were tasted at the domaine in February 1999:

Beauroy 98 – this is a very recent bottling and was found to be too stressed to taste. Retasted six months later in London when it displayed a pleasant nose of perfumed fruit, some concentration and length with crisp acidity but a trifle sour. Good though. (2001–2004)

Chablis 97 – lacking any aroma, but fruit is there and fairly well balanced.

Beauroy 97 – closed up, mineral flavours indicate Chablis character, but fruit is lacking a degree of concentration. Fair. (2001–2003)

Chablis 96 – little on nose, fruit there but rather astringent. But it may settle.

Beauroy 95 – L'Ame du Domaine. This is their special cuvée *élevé* in wood. The fruit lacks a bit of concentration and the oak is too prominent. We do not have great hopes for this wine's future.

DOMAINE DU CHATEAU DE VIVIERS

Viviers	Tel: 03 80 61 25 02	
89700 Chablis	Fax: 03 80 24 37 38	

17 hectares

Production:

Grand Cru	Blanchots	0.50 ha
Premier Crus	Vaillons	0.50 ha
	Vaucoupin	1.70 ha
Chablis Village		

This domaine is part of the Albert Bichot empire and is under the control of Gérard Vullien of Domaine Long-Depaquit.

The lovely château in the centre of the village is fourteenth century. The courtyard at the rear is surrounded by converted old stables now used for the *cuverie*.

The emphasis here is on a large holding – some 14 hectares – of Chablis Village. The wines are vinified in Viviers but transported to Beaune for bottling. The vinification is in temperature-controlled stainless steel *cuves* followed by the *élevage en cuve*.

Good basic wines perhaps, without quite the intensity and elegance of Long-Depaquit. Distribution is by Bichot's *sous-marque* Lupé Cholet based in Nuits Saint Georges in the Côte d'Or.

Tasting notes
The following wines were tasted at Domaine Long Depaquit in February 1999:

Chablis 97 – this has good fruit and balance. May not set the world on fire, but it's not intended to.

Vaillons 97 – this has house style, steely mineral fruit, good depth and length. Very good. (2001–2004)

Vaucoupin 97 – good typical nose, very aromatic, mineral and flinty, good depth and intensity, similar house style, lovely wine. Vine age 25+ years and shows. Very good. (2001–2004)

Blanchots 97 – very pale colour, intense fruit but closes up on finish, a bit short. Fair. (2002–2005)

Chablis 96 – a very good basic Chablis, lovely fruit, length balance and intensity. Very good.

Vaillons 96 – wine of *typicité*, showing good mineral steely fruit, dry finish, perhaps a bit short. Fair. (2001–2003)

Vaucoupin 96 – quiet floral nose, plenty of fruit here with a dry mineral finish, acidity not quite crisp enough. Good. (2001–2004)

Blanchots 96 – closed nose, lovely depth of fruit of some concentration. Forward for what it is. Very good. (2000–2006)

Chablis 95 – good typical nose, fruit and good acidity for the vintage, gentle character. Pleasant drinking with food. Good wine. (March 98)

Wines available from stockists in:

UK
World Wines Direct – Lancs. Tel: 0800 864000

DOMAINE VOCORET ★

| 40 Route d'Auxerre | Tel: 03 86 42 12 53 |
| 89800 Chablis | Fax: 03 86 42 10 39 |

40 hectares

Production:

Grand Crus	Blanchot	1.77 ha
	Valmur	0.28 ha
	Vaudésir	0.11 ha
	Les Clos	1.61 ha

Premier Crus	Vaillons	5.00 ha
	La Forêt	6.00 ha
	Montmains	1.00 ha
	Montée de Tonnerre	1.50 ha
	Mont de Milieu	0.18 ha
	Côte de Léchet	1.40 ha

Chablis Village and Petit Chablis

Domaine Vocoret (pronounced with a hard c), adjoining the Hotel Ibis on Route d'Auxerre, is a family business of 40 hectares including around 14 hectares of Grand Cru and 15 hectares of Premier Cru vineyards. Three generations have run the same estate vineyards founded by Robert Vocoret in the 1930s. Robert himself is now contentedly retired in the knowledge that his domaine is in capable family hands. He was succeeded at the helm by his sons Claude, Michel and Patrice: Claude and Michel are also now *en retraite* and the domaine is ably run by Michel's son Jérôme in charge of the cellars and vinification whilst Patrice is responsible for the vineyards – yet he is frequently to be found in the *chai* or office, seemingly to possess the ability to be in two places at the same moment – pinning him down to one location is a true accomplishment.

The *vignoble* with an average age of 25 years is run in traditional style, with the harvest gathered 80 per cent mechanically. Modern ideas and equipment are employed in the *chai* – fermentation in stainless steel vats is fully temperature controlled, but *élevage* is in large oak *foudres* for the Grand and Premier Crus generally for about 10 months.

This is a popular and successful estate selling their fine wines worldwide, the principal markets being the EEC, Japan, USA, Switzerland and the Scandinavian countries.

We like this star domaine and are happy to recommend it. Hopefully it will become better known in the UK.

Tasting notes

The following wines were tasted at the domaine in May 1998 – the 97s *en cuve,* and, where noted, later in February 1999 in bottle. The 98s were tasted *en cuve* – other wines as noted:

Chablis 98 – still in an unstable state, but plenty of fruit and acidity. This had not greatly improved when tasted in bottle 6 months later – vegetal nose and a little sour. Disappointing.

Chablis Vieilles Vignes 98 – citrus fruity nose, good basic Chablis but falls a bit short. (August 1999, London)

La Forêt 98 – intense concentration of fruit finely balanced, should be very good. (2003–2007)

Montmains 98 – a little marked by the wood, lovely fruit and balance. Should be very good. (2003–2007)

La Forêt Vieilles Vignes 98 – marked by the oak as yet, intense fruit with good acidity, also should be very good. (2003–2007)

Vaillons Vieilles Vignes 98 – good fruit and acidity, minerally finish. Another good wine. (2003–2007)

Vaillons 98 – this wine was in an eight-year-old *foudre*. Nice up-front fruit, concentrated and balanced. Good/very good. (2002–2005)

Montée de Tonnerre 98 – nicely minerally, lovely steely flinty fruit, dry finish. Should be very good indeed. (2003–2006)

Blanchots 98 – intense fruit, good concentration and acidity. Should be very good. (2003–2008)

Les Clos 98 – great perfumed nose, good attack, intense concentrated fruit and acidity. Should be very good indeed. (2003–2009)

Chablis 97 – floral nose, lots of fruit, good length. By February 99 this had crept slightly into its shell but lots of lovely fruit there, good acidity and length. Still needs a year. Delicious basic Chablis. Drunk many times recently with equal pleasure.

Côte de Léchet 97 – quiet nose, appley and grapefruit flavours, lovely elegant fruity wine. Very good. (2001–2004)

Montmains 97 – quite nutty, lots of fruit, good length but closing. Good. (2000–2003)

Mont de Milieu 97 – nice fruity nose but a bit restrained, intense fruit with good balance, long finish, not too dry, lovely wine. Very good. (February 99) (2001–2004)

Vaillons 97 – oak on nose and palate, marks the fruit at back of throat, but a big wine. Very good. (2002–2005)

Vaillons Vieilles Vignes 97 – this has closed already, a bit of oak, tremendous fruit, a more complex wine with good length. Very good. (2002–2005)

La Forêt Vieilles Vignes 97 – more floral, delicate wine, good intensity and concentration, long, fine wine. (2002–2005)

Montée de Tonnerre 97 – bags of fruit on nose and palate, almost painful intensity in the mouth, oak should integrate well, will be a great wine. (2002–2006)

Blanchots 97 – closing up already, lots of sweet lovely fruit, good length, very individual wine. This was still tightly closed in February 99, but the intense fruit was there, concentrated, sour appley in the nicest sense, a lot there for the future. Should be very good. (2003–2007)

Les Clos 97 – lovely fruit, nose still open, will be a big, but fine elegant wine. (2003–2007)

Valmur 97 – already closing up, but soft and perfumed, fine wine. (2003–2007)

Chablis 96 – nicely forward nose, minerally with apricots and nuts, lovely fruit, perhaps the acidity is not as crisp as the 97 but this is a good basic Chablis, nice length and aftertaste. (June 98)

Montmains 96 – fruity mineral nose, concentration and depth, fat, steely, lovely acidity, very long. A bottle tasted in January 98 was utterly delicious, showed acacia and honey on nose and typicity *par excellence*. Very good/fine. (2002–2005)

Côte de Léchet 96 – mineral floral fruity nose, lovely elegant fruit and balance, delicious acidity and finish. Fine. (2002–2005)

Wines are available from the **CELLAR DOOR** and stockists in:

UK

H & H Fine Wines, Godmanchester, Cambs. Tel: 01480 411599

Ian G. Howe, Newark, Notts. Tel: 01636 704366

Majestic Wine Warehouses, branches nationwide. Tel: 01923 298200

Noël Young Wines, Cambridge. Tel: 01223 844744 Fax: 01223 844736

USA

Garnet Wines & Liquors, New York, 10021. Tel: 212 772 3211 Fax: 212 517 4029

Seagram Château & Estate Wines Co., 375 Park Avenue, New York City, NY 10152-0192. Tel: 212 572 7000 Fax: 212 572 1263

Sherry-Lehmann Inc., New York. Tel: 212 838 7500 Fax: 212 838 9285

DOMAINE YVON VOCORET

9 Chemin de Beaune

Maligny   Tel: 03 86 47 51 60

89800 Chablis   Fax: 03 86 47 57 47

16 hectares

Production:

Chablis Premier Cru   Fourchaume

Chablis Village and Petit Chablis

This domaine has produced Chablis for four generations of the Vocoret family of Maligny, not to be confused with Domaine Vocoret in Chablis itself. In the days of great-grandfather Vocoret the production was only 8 to 15 *feuillettes* – the old traditional Chablis barrel of 132 litres – from a mere 3.25 hectares. One part of the harvest was reserved for family consumption, while the other part was sold to the highest bidding merchant. This situation lasted until the end of the Second World War, when grandfather Henri decided to put away some bottles and in 1947 the first vintage filled the racks of the old vaulted cellars. Yvon's father Maurice recalled that this great vintage was responsible for much inebriation among the unwary, falling like flies after 4 or 5 glasses – an 'unbalanced' vintage? Thus the decision was taken to bottle every year.

It is thanks to the will and foresight of Maurice Vocoret that the family can boast a collection of Fourchaume going back 35 years, the earlier vintages being decimated by the ravages of a thirsty family. This collection is *not* for sale, but sometimes a sample of 20 or 25 years of age will miraculously appear on the dining table.

The family believe that the work in the vineyard is as important as the work in the cellar. Traditional vinification is the order of the day here in order to preserve *la typicité*. A new *cuverie* was completed in 1994. Yvon Vocoret himself professes that his wines are produced and *élevé* with the heart of a *vigneron* who loves his 'métier'. Some good wines here.

The wines are marketed mainly in France and Belgium.

Tasting notes
The following wines were tasted at the domaine in May 1998:

Chablis 96 – nice nose, good fruit and balance, good clean finish and fine length.

Chablis Vieilles Vignes 96 – from vines planted in 1939: strange nose but good fruit and length, a bit of sulphur on the aftertaste – should disappear. Good.

Fourchaume 96 – from L'Homme Mort: some sulphur on nose but will disperse, flinty, good fruit, acidity and length, good wine. (2001–2003)

Chablis 95 – quite fruity nose, but more fruit on palate, good acidity, fresh, quite crisp, but a bit bland overall.

Fourchaume 95 – quiet nose, good concentration and depth, plenty of fruit there for the future, very long, very good wine for the vintage. (2000–2003)

Wines available from the **CELLAR DOOR.**

DOMAINE VRIGNAUD

10 Rue de Beauvoir
Fontenay-près-Chablis
89800 Chablis

Tel: 03 86 42 15 69
Fax: 03 86 42 40 06

12 hectares

Production:

| Chablis Premier Cru | Fourchaume | 7 ha |
| Chablis Village | | |

This is a domaine identified from a London hotel wine list, run by Michel Vrignaud and his wife. Although most of his production is sold to La Chablisienne, since the 93 vintage he has thankfully bottled 2 hectares of wine for direct sales himself and hopefully this will increase.

The domaine comprises some very rustic old farm buildings in the centre of Fontenay, some in need of a little repair. Vrignaud owns some 7 hectares of Fourchaume, the remainder being basic Chablis. Vinification is traditional with no surprises, just hard work and dedication. Monsieur Vrignaud's 20-year-old son is at present working in a vineyard in South Africa and will join the family business in due course.

The private markets for the wines are mainly the UK and Belgium. This is a domaine to keep to oneself – come to think of it, don't read this profile!

A delightful tasting was given by the Vrignauds of the 95 and 96 vintages, and we returned with expectation for the 97 vintage – we were not disappointed – the tasting notes below tell the story.

This is a domaine worthy of note.

Tasting notes
Tasted at the domaine in May 1998 and February 1999, the 98s in London in August 1999:

Chablis 98 – pale colour, dry minerally nose and palate, good fruit, apples and pears, reasonable length. Good wine.

Fourchaume 98 – dumb nose, nice fruit, crisp apples, fair length. Returning to the bottle a few hours later, the wine had broadened considerably displaying a typical Chablis nose, expansive fruit and lovely length. Very good. (2001–2004)

Chablis 97 – lovely ripe luscious fruit, good balance of acidity, nice finish with a little kick at the end. Lovely wine.

Fourchaume 97 – a little closed on the nose, but lots of ripe fruit here, minerally green apples, crisp, well balanced and long. Very good. (2001–2004)

Chablis 96 – quiet nose but plenty of fruit, good acidity, better than most village wines, good length and good wine.

Fourchaume 96 – flowery nose, very good appley fruit, steely and minerally, good acidity and length, delicious, lovely wine. Retasted in London many times – delicious. (2001–2005)

Fourchaume 95 – quiet nose but opens out in glass, quite forward, very nice fruit, good acidity for the vintage, well balanced, lovely now. Retasted at Lifeboat Inn, Thornham, Norfolk and many times in London during 98/99 and just as lovely. (2000–2003)

Wines available from the **CELLAR DOOR** and stockists in:

UK
Matthew Clark (Grants of St. James's), Bristol. Tel: 01275 891400

Come on importers, get round there and persuade Monsieur Vrignaud to cut down on his allocation to the Co-op if he can, and get some more of these lovely bottles into UK and US stockists.

Section B

The Co-operative

and Chablis-based *Négociants*

LA CHABLISIENNE

8 Boulevard Pasteur   Tel: 03 86 42 89 89
89800 Chablis   Fax: 03 86 42 89 90

No mention of the wines of Chablis would be complete without reference to the co-operative, one of the largest co-operatives in France founded as long ago as 1923, having reputedly some 300 members and producing one third of the total production of the Chablis appellations. Hervé Tucki who now runs the co-operative is vague about the actual number of participants since family members often register in their separate names although the grapes may well be coming from the same vineyard. Never mind, that all helps with the mystique. What is certain is that once a grower has joined, it is very difficult and a very expensive exercise to un-join!

The wines produced include a full range of Village and Premier Crus, and some impressive Grand Crus from Les Clos and Grenouilles, Château de Grenouilles comprising some 7.2 hectares totally owned and controlled by La Chablisienne (see separate note that follows). La Chablisienne vinifies and markets two separate cuvées here, Grenouilles as separate and distinct from Château de Grenouilles.

The total production of the co-operative is 3–4 million bottles per annum, vinification being in large stainless steel vats but with 600 oak *pièces* in operation of which 100 are renewed each year, oak forming an important part of the process here. Monsieur Tucki seemed a little guarded as we started to talk about the use of wood, even defensive, stressing that using oak or not as a process is not the point, but that all that matters is that the wine should express the *terroir* of its origins, and that oak should be used to that end. Admirable sentiments – why then is 100 per cent used for the Mont de Milieu?

However, this is a very modern and well-run operation having considerable clout in marketing worldwide, with Marks and Spencer as one of its best-known customers. And here we take issue, for Monsieur Tucki admits that M & S, according to its marketing and sales policy, can influence the winemaking and thus the end result, a practice not unknown in other French and New World wine regions by other influential market concerns. So be warned, the wine you get in a bottle of M & S La Chablisienne may not be the same as that purchased elsewhere.

For the most part, Chablis *typicité* may not always be obvious in some of the wines of La Chablisienne where in our view oak is sometimes too prominent. The co-operative also lacks the care and close scrutiny of an individual grower picking and vinifying his own grapes to give an individual identity. Nevertheless, on the standard of quality, these can be good and often very good wines although sometimes a little pricey in comparison with their peers.

Tasting notes

The following wines were tasted in London, August 1999:

Petit Chablis 98 – little on nose and regrettably little on palate. Where was the fruit? Disappointing.

Chablis 98 – dry mineral nose, dry on palate, fruit and acidity are there but falls a bit short. Fair only.

Côte de Léchet 98 – shy nose with just a hint of oak, good fruit but not very deep or concentrated. Does not display the elegance of this Cru. Disappointing.

Beauroy 98 – dry minerals on nose, palate not revealing a great amount of fruit concentration at present and little depth, but some length and aftertaste indicates that in time this could improve. Judgement deferred.

Fourchaume 98 – That's better! Perfumed nose with a hint of oak, good concentration of fruit, apples and apricots, good depth and length. Very good. (2002–2005)

The following wines were tasted at La Chablisienne in October 1998 in a selected tasting kindly offered by Monsieur Tucki:

Petit Chablis 97 – quiet nose, but a fresh crisp dry and lovely basic Petit Chablis.

Chablis 97 – good acidity, appley flavour, good balance and length, a more intense aromatic wine.

Montée de Tonnerre 97 – 50 per cent oak. Floral nose, nutty intense flavours, oak well integrated here. A very good wine. (2002–2007)

Grenouilles 97 – 50 per cent oak. From the lower slopes near the river. The oak here is far too overpowering. Would be better vinified in stainless steel alone. Disappointing.

Chablis-La Chablisienne Cuvée 96 – typical Chablis nose here, mineral flinty fruit with good balancing acidity. Good wine.

Chablis Vieilles Vignes 96 – 45/50-year-old vines, 5 per cent oak. Closed nose, more intense fruit, oak a little obvious but will develop well with time. Good. (2000–2003)

Côte de Léchet 96 – 50 per cent oak. Elegant nose and lovely peachy fruit, good length. No problem with oak here. Drinking beautifully already but will keep. Very fine. (2000–2006)

Bougros 96 – 100 per cent oak. Closed up except for obtrusive oak, doubtful whether it will integrate. Simple wine. Judgement deferred.

Petit Chablis 95 Special Cuvée – lovely nose and very nice fruit, well balanced, lovely wine. Very good and highly recommended.

Chablis Vieilles Vignes 95 – 5 per cent oak. Open nose, very forward wine. Oak more obvious than the 96. Good intensity. Good wine.

Mont de Milieu 95 – 100 per cent oak. Deep yellow, chewy wine, fruit totally hidden by oak flavours. Usual Mont de Milieu dry mineral flavour not there. Doubtful whether the fruit can come through even with time. This vintage needed very different vinification.

Château Grenouille 95 – 100 per cent oak. Higher slopes than basic Grenouilles. Much better fruit extract, but still totally masked by the oak. May integrate in time. Good. (2002–2006)

Other wines tasted in London and Chablis:

Fourchaume 97 – gentle floral fruity nose, and gentle on the palate. Slightly bitter fruit, not a great deal of length. Fair. (2001–2004) (BIVB/SOPEXA Tasting London January 99)

Côte de Léchet 97 – this a wine of character, little on nose yet, but lovely expansive fruit on palate, good length, intensity, good concentration and depth. Very good wine. (2001–2004) (BIVB/SOPEXA Tasting London January 99)

Chablis 96 – good flinty nose, opens out in glass, good fruit and acidity, some concentration but little depth, good length but sharp dry mineral aftertaste. (June 98)

Montmain 96 – nose of Chablis *typicité*, very minerally, fruit is there, mouth puckering acidity, moderate intensity, reasonable length, good Montmain but not great. (2001–2003)(May 98)

Chablis 95 – lovely nutty nose, minerally, good fruit, fair acidity but a dry finish, some length and even depth, good *typicité*. Good for the vintage and for drinking soon. Don't leave too long. (July 98)

Vaillons 95 – little on nose, reasonable fruit but no concentration, not Premier Cru quality, well made but no more. Drink now. (October 97)

Grenouilles 95 – low on acidity, not fat enough, a bit flat and characterless. (BIVB/SOPEXA Tasting London January 99)

Château de Grenouilles 95 – certainly much more here, better balance, reasonable fruit with good acidity, oak not too obtrusive, length and concentration. Not exactly Grand Cru quality but nevertheless a good wine. (2000–2005) (BIVB/SOPEXA Tasting London January 99)

Chablis Vieilles Vignes 88 – oak totally dominates, no fruit, short, a disgrace to call it Chablis at all. (May 98 at La Chablisienne)

Wines available from the **CELLAR DOOR** and stockists in:

UK
Centurian Vintners, Gloucester. Tel: 01453 763223
London Wine Emporium, London SE11. Tel: 020 7587 1302
Marks and Spencer, nationwide. Tel: 020 7935 4422
Majestic Wine Warehouses, branches nationwide. Tel: 01923 298200

Howard Ripley, London N21. Tel: 020 8360 8904 Fax: 020 8351 6564
Stevens Garnier, Oxford. Tel: 01865 263303 Fax: 01865 791594
Thresher Group, branches nationwide including Bottoms Up and Wine
   Rack. Tel: 01707 328244 Fax: 01707 385000

CHÂTEAU DE GRENOUILLES

89800 Chablis

7.2 hectares

Taking its name from the Grand Cru, the 'château' is a large but very modest farm building accessed from the Maligny road, and stuck incongruously in the middle of the vineyard. It is in fact the only building among the Grand Crus. The prefix 'Château' was intended as a joke, but has stuck.

The estate and 'castle' were acquired by the Testut family during the 1970s, adding to their own holding bought in 1966. But family disputes led to the disposal of the estate to a private company of growers set up for the purpose, with the appropriate financial backing.

The wine is now vinified and marketed exclusively by La Chablisienne, and similar comments apply.

Wines available from stockists in:

UK
Berkmann's Wine Cellars, London N7. Tel: 020 7609 4711
Walter Hicks, Cornwall. Tel: 01726 74444
Marks & Spencer, nationwide. Tel: 020 7935 4422
Nadder Wines, Wiltshire. Tel: 01722 325418
Le Nez Rouge, London N7. Tel: 020 7609 4711
Stevens Garnier, Oxford. Tel: 01865 263303 Fax: 01865 791594

USA
Sazerac Co. Inc., dba Mr Henri Wines, 803 Jefferson Highway, New Orleans, Louisiana 70121.

MAISON LAMBLIN ET FILS

Maligny
89800 Chablis

Tel: 03 86 47 40 85
Fax: 03 86 47 50 12

7 hectares

Production:
Vineyards include Chablis Grand Crus Les Clos, Vaudésir and Valmur.
Chablis Premier Crus Fourchaume, Mont de Milieu and Beauroy.
Chablis Village and Petit Chablis.

This domaine is located at the northern extremity of Maligny within a modern high-tech looking building which dominates the Maligny/Chablis road. Originally and still a family firm, their connection with Chablis goes back to 1690 when Edme Lamblin worked the vine, and every succeeding generation has followed him. The first steps towards commercialisation were taken by Louis Lamblin in the 1890s, when to his work as a *vigneron* he added a brokerage business. His son Henri established the firm of Lamblin et Fils as *négociants* in 1920: he was a man who exercised great influence on the Chablis Vignoble and Burgundy in general, contributing to the writing of many legal texts concerning the Chablis Appellations. Henri's son Jacques carried on the work of the company by abandoning the magnificent old but non-functional *caves* in the centre of the village and constructing in 1973 an ultra-modern state-of-the-art building in Maligny, a building which is regularly enlarged and upgraded. He was the first Chablisien to equip his cellars with a refrigeration plant for precipitating the tartrates before bottling, a technique used today by most producers.

Since 1987, Didier and Michel Lamblin have successfully carried the torch for the family, continuing the traditions and standards for which they are known, particularly as a large *négociant* firm.

The wine production is by temperature-controlled stainless steel monsters and every type of machinery imaginable. A light filtration precedes bottling. Lamblin have their own bottling plant fully equipped with two production lines, one with a capacity of 6,000 bottles per hour, the other with 4,000 – this slower line is hand operated and used for the AOC wines. No surprise, then, that the cellars have a capacity for ageing an incredible 450,000 bottles.

The total production from this enormous operation is about 4.5 million bottles per annum covering all the Appellations, and includes Bourgogne Rouge et Blanc, Bourgogne Aligoté, Sauvignon de Saint-Bris and commercial Vin de Table. 30 per cent of this total stays in France, the remainder is exported principally to the UK, Germany, Holland, Belgium, Japan and Canada.

Wines are also sold under the following *sous-marques*: Paul Favey, Jacques Arnoul, Bernard Mille, Charles Montserat, Jacques de la Ferté, Paul Jarry, Paul Ferrand.

Didier Lamblin informed us that all the grapes, his own as well as those bought in, are vinified together, and there are no solely domaine-produced wines sold separately; tasting notes are nevertheless included below as an indication of quality levels to be expected. The past few years have not yielded wine of universal praise, no doubt due mainly to the requirements of mass production, but the 97s and 98s, creditable wines indeed, perhaps show that the quality corner has been turned. We shall watch this space with interest.

Tasting notes

The following wines were tasted at Maison Lamblin in May 1998, with the 97s and 98s tasted in London in August 1999 by courtesy of F. & E. May:

Chablis 98 – restrained Chablis nose but good citrus fruit and balanced acidity, even length, lovely aftertaste. Very good.

Fourchaume 98 – dumb nose but some lovely ripe fruit of concentration and depth, well balanced, good length. Very good. (2002–2006)

Chablis 97 – quiet nose with some Chablis *typicité*, good fruit and acidity with fairly good length. A very pleasant wine. Good.

Fourchaume 97 – shy nose, fair concentration of fruit but not up to 98 standards, appley flavours, fair length. Fairly good. (2001–2004)

Chablis 96 – reasonable nose, some fruit but ordinary and rather bland.

Beauroy 96 – better fruit here but very acidic – almost sour. Doubtful.

Vaillons 96 – lovely typical nose, better balance than above wines. Fair to good. (2000–2002)

Montée de Tonnerre 95 – a poor sample, did not show well – replacement not available.

Fourchaume 94 – sulphur still present, spangley fruit with a rather sour finish. Fair only.

Fourchaume 90 – good nose here, with good fruit and some length and depth. Why can't they all be like this! Good wine. Drink soon.

Tasted in London:

Vaudésir 90 – two bottles drunk and on both occasions little nose was apparent and the fruit lacked depth and concentration. This was not Grand Cru quality! (1998)

Wines are available from the **CELLAR DOOR** and stockists in:

UK
F. & E. May, London WC1. Tel: 020 7405 6249

MAISON S.A. J. MOREAU et FILS

Route d'Auxerre
89800 Chablis

FAMILLE MOREAU

No history of Chablis and the wine would be complete without the Moreau family. There is still some confusion over the differences between the old-established *négociant* house J. Moreau et Fils and the growers Domaine Louis Moreau, both descendants of the same family concern. We will attempt to clarify this situation.

The Moreau family have been inextricably linked to Chablis for six generations since its creation in 1814 by Jean-Joseph Moreau. Marrying into a *vigneron* family, as did his son and grandson, a sound basis was established on which to build. The family house was purchased in 1830 plus the beginnings of their Grand Cru holdings, in Les Clos and Vaudésir. The family own the estate of Les Clos des Hospices within the Grand Cru itself, that part of the cru reserved for the Hospital at Chablis, pre-revolution.

The casual visitor to the area, one not knowing very much or indeed anything about wine production, will call at the tourist office and be directed to organised tours of the major houses of Chablis, usually La Chablisienne, William Fèvre, Simonnet-Febvre, Lamblin or J. Moreau. This is such a pity, for it is in the smaller domaines that the real essence of Chablis is to be found, and the visitor would be better rewarded with a closer insight into the growing of the grape and its vinification into wine by individual hands-on non-delegating *vignerons*. Admittedly the larger concerns have more time and capacity to cope with PR, and that is one responsibility never shirked by J. Moreau.

Their prominent building, often sarcastically referred to in Franglais as 'Le Factoire' (or *L'Usine* en Français) dominates the Route d'Auxerre. Perhaps it is somewhat reminiscent of a modern transport depot with five loading bays, but there are worse. This is the nerve centre of a massive white wine production, very commercially successful. In 1974, the Moreau family sold 50 per cent of the *négociant* business to Hiram Walker and thus through inter-company transfers to the Allied Lyons Group, but in 1986 Jean-Jacques Moreau decided to retire and sold the remaining 50 per cent to the Allied Domecq Group as they had become known, retaining the vineyards in family ownership. And this is the crux of the matter – Domaine Moreau and their Grand Cru vineyards are the property of Jean-Jacques and Christian Moreau and never belonged to the *négociant* house of S.A. J. Moreau et Fils. Finally, the Jean-Claude Boisset Group of Beaune purchased J. Moreau et Fils from Allied Domecq in 1997, continuing the operation as before.

The house at present makes the wine from the vineyards in the private ownership of the family. The arrangement is under a lease which terminates shortly, half of the land transferring to Jean-Jacques's son Louis (see Domaine Louis Moreau). In the meantime, and historically speaking, the wines produced include:

Grand Cru Clos des Hospices – Monopole
Grand Cru Les Clos
Grand Cru Valmur
Grand Cru Vaudésir
Grand Cru Blanchot
Premier Cru Vaillons

These wines are considered 'own' labels appropriately distinguished from and not lumped together with the *négociant* grapes and wine. Indeed the

Clos des Hospices Monopole, that section of Grand Cru Les Clos owned pre-revolution by the l'Hopital de Chablis with a history going back almost to the origins of Chablis itself, has always been a very individual wine with a reputation and price to match.

Vinification of all wines is a thoroughly modern affair, stainless steel with not a whiff of wood to be found anywhere. Le Factoire is well equipped for this massive operation, a major part of which is the production of a whole range of *négociant* wines and an innocuous little white *vin de table* known as Moreau Blanc, which has not helped its reputation in quality wine production of this historic house amongst more demanding consumers, but commercially very successful worldwide – hence the physical emphasis on a massive distribution area.

During the winemaking process, the malolactic fermentation is sometimes blocked to maintain acidity levels, but this is a rare practice. In most years the wines are left on their lees until just before bottling so as to preserve freshness, but not in years such as 1996. Bentonite fining and a light plate filtration precede bottling.

S.A. J. Moreau et Fils, now controlled by the Boisset Group, is continuing in the path set for it, and therein lies the problem – a commercially successful company and deservedly so, but not exactly turning out the Chablis made famous by a great family, but this is the style and price of wine demanded today by an undemanding public. The writers well remember the early 1980s when bottle after bottle of Moreau Chablis was first blind tasted, then consumed at their wine-tasting society, the infamous Wednesday Wine Club. We gradually observed over just a few years the diminished depth and concentration of the wines and the less apparent vineyard typicity. Strange that the change-over from a family-run business was in 1986! We have not yet noticed any apparent return to former glories, but we live in hope! The organisation is in place.

Tasting notes

The following wines were shown at the BIVB/SOPEXA tasting in London in January 1999, and at La Maison in Chablis, February 1999, with the 98s in London in September 1999:

Chablis 98 – dry minerally nose, not much depth and rather bitter, little concentration and length.

Vaillons 98 – dry on nose, also rather bitter and seems to be lacking in fruit. Disappointing. (2000–2002)

Fourchaume 98 – no nose, earthy flavours but again where is the fruit? This example was not a good Fourchaume. (2000–2003)

Petit Chablis 97 – little on nose, some fruit, a light but good Petit Chablis.

Chablis 97 – typical minerally nose, good fruit, no great depth on the palate but a drinkable basic Chablis, some length, crisp acidity, good clean finish.

Vau de Véy 97 – good typicity on nose and palate, good fruit and length even some depth, steely and flinty. Not to be sneezed at! A surprisingly good wine. (2000–2003)

Vaillons 97 – fair nose and mineral typicity, fair fruit but little length, and the fruit is a bit shallow, clean finish, crisp but not sharp. Fair/good. (2000–2003)

Valmur 97 – acacia blossom and honey, concentrated fruit with some depth, but is there enough to last the distance? Good balance though. Should be very good. (2002–2006)

Vaucoupin 96 – single vineyard. Good nose of violets and fruit salad flavours, promises well on the attack but fails to deliver. Could be more concentrated but still good. (2000–2002)

Vaillons 96 – once again a fairly good typical nose, minerally fruit, but on returning to the previous wines there appears to be little individuality. Fairly good fruit on the palate and this time some length and depth. Not deeply concentrated but nevertheless a good wine. (2000–2003)

Montmain 96 – honeyed perfume, very forward wine, fruit is a little bland and there appears to be a lack of acidity. Some length but little depth. Fair. (2001–2003)

Les Clos 96 – gentle but quite closed on the nose, concentrated fruit with earthy flavours, well-balanced acidity, good potential for the future, a gentle wine, even elegant and with lovely length. Should be very good. (2003–2008)

Clos des Hospices 94 – a Cinderella year! Lovely complex nose of Madeleine biscuits, buttered toast, nuts and honey, great depth of delicious fruit and balanced acidity, long and lovely. Fine. (2000–2004)

Valmur 90 – refined floral nose, honey-coated nuts, this is a big wine with bags of concentrated fruit, fine acidity, long finish and balance. Fine wine. Drink soon but no hurry.

Les Clos 83 – another wonderful old Chablis, lovely depth of fruit, biscuity honeyed nose, still some acidity to lift the wine out of the glass, but it will not last too long. Delicious. (February 99 at Hostellerie des Clos)

Wines are available from the following stockists in:

UK
John Harvey of Bristol. Tel: 0117 927 5010

Thresher Group, branches nationwide including Bottoms Up and Wine Rack. Tel: 01707 328244 Fax: 01707 385000

USA:
Frederick Wildman & Sons Ltd. – 307 East 53rd Street, New York, NY
10022-4996. Tel: 212 355 0700 Fax: 212 355 4719

MAISON RÉGNARD

28 Boulevard Tacussel	Tel: 03 86 42 10 45
89800 Chablis	Fax: 03 86 42 48 67

10 hectares

Production:
Chablis Grand Crus Les Clos, Bougros, Blanchots, Grenouilles, Preuses,
Valmur and Vaudésir
Chablis Premier Crus Fourchaume, Montmains, Vaillons, Montée de
Tonnerre and Mont de Milieu
Chablis Village and Petit Chablis

Maison Régnard was established in 1860 by Zéphir Régnard and is one of
the last houses of Chablis to have all of its *caves* in the historic centre of the
town, testifying to its long and inseparable association. In 1957, Régnard
absorbed the family firm of Albert Pic, an old Chablis name dating back
to 1755, and marketed these wines until well after the death of the last family
member in the 1930's. We both remember the superb Albert Pic 83s, sublime wines and we suspect long gone.

The name of Régnard is the maiden name of the wife of Michel Rémon
who sold the firm in 1984 to le Baron Patrick de Ladoucette of Pouilly
Fumé and Sancerre fame, and who has continued the style and *typicité* of
the Chablis wines. Philippe Rossignol is the wine maker in Chablis but the
Baron is apparently very much involved.

Leading off the Place de le République, the elegant frontage of Boulevard Tacussel well conceals the houses and domaines behind and indeed
the depth and space revealed is quite amazing. The offices and commercial
hub of this Empire are approached from the Boulevard leading through to
the vast *cuverie* and historic cellars. The big surprise, however, is situated
round the corner in Avenue de la République where clients and customers
are received and often housed in an elegant eighteenth-century mansion –
except it is not eighteenth century, not even nineteenth and very nearly not
even twentieth century, for this *bâtiment* was entirely rebuilt in 1989 in
period style – and very beautifully and tastefully realised. Now, that is
planning for you! The smart tasting-room is off the courtyard and most
welcoming.

The house owns about 10 hectares of Chablis, Premier and Grand Crus,
and buys in the grapes for the rest of its production from some 50 growers.
The entire harvest is from about 125 hectares: the company claims the resultant diversity aids the complexity of the wines. Usually, the *négociants'*

grapes are included with the estate's own, but the Grenouilles is a separate production from half a hectare owned by the house.

Vinification is traditional. After a gentle pressing, the first run juice is allowed to rest in small *cuves* for the *débourbage*. Fermentation with selected yeasts in stainless steel vats is temperature controlled at 20°C. After the malolactic fermentation the wines are left *sur collage* for clarification with isinglass, the Premier and Grand Crus being *élevés* on their fine lees for between 8 and 12 months. Finally, the wines are given a light plate filtration before bottling under inert gas.

Total annual Chablis production is about 500,000 bottles.

Each Régnard wine should be produced according to the stated principles of the house:

1. A true Chablis is self evident, it does not need the taste of oak or barrel to attain better quality.
2. Finesse and freshness are the two qualities essential to a great white wine, due particularly to a perfectly controlled vinification.
3. A long ageing in bottle necessary for the Premier and Grand Crus reveal and elevate the wines to their finest expression.

The tasting notes below show whether these aims are always achieved or not.

Tasting notes
The following wines were tasted at La Maison in February 1999:

Petit Chablis 97 – gentle nose, good fruit, light acidity, a bit short but a nice Petit Chablis.

Fourchaume 97 – flowery fragrant nose, fine fruit extraction with gentle acidity, good balance and length. Quite forward. This is for early drinking. Very good. (2001–2005)

Chablis 96 – lovely fruity nose, fruit and acidity well balanced, good length. Very good.

Mont de Milieu 96 – a bit closed on nose but some perfume works its way through, good minerally fruit and dry finish, well balanced. Very good. (2002–2006)

Montée de Tonnerre 96 – closed up on nose and palate, but encouragement reveals lots of steely flinty fruit, concentration and depth. Dry finish again. Wine of *typicité*. Very good. (2002–2006)

Montmains 93 – No nose to speak of, and little fruit. Why show this wine?

Vaudésir 91 – lovely elegant fragrance on nose but disappoints in the mouth. Fruit is dry and a bit flat with no length and little acidity. Can't get excited here! (2001–2003)

Bougros 90 – honey and flowers on nose, lovely fruit, well balanced but lets down a bit with a slightly bitter aftertaste. Good only. Drink now.

Valmur 90 – slightly smokey nose, more fruit and intensity than the Bougros but fades a fraction at the end. Still a lovely wine. Good/very good. (2000–2005)

Bougros 1989 – gentle nose, good fruit and acidity, but lacks zip and personality. Comes out a little at the end, but such hard work! We'll give it the benefit of the doubt – maybe it's still not ready. Good. (2000–2005)

Les Clos 83 Albert Pic – well, here's a surprise, one left thanks to Michael Schuster. Still shows as a fine wine, honeyed and buttery nose but tired fruit on palate, a big wine, slightly bitter finish, drink up. (April 98 in London)

Wines available from stockists in:

UK
La Vigneronne, London SW7. Tel: 020 7589 6113

USA
Maison Marque et Domaine, Oakland, California.

DOMAINE SIMONNET

SARL Simonnet-Fèbvre et Fils

Route de Tonnerre
89800 Chablis
e-mail: simonnet@chablis.net
http://www.chablis.net/simonnet

Tel: 03 86 98 99 00
Fax: 03 86 98 99 01

5 hectares

Production:
Own wines:
Chablis Grand Cru Les Preuses
Chablis Premier Cru Mont de Milieu
Chablis Village
(*Négociant* wines include a wide range of Premier and Grand Crus, especially Montée de Tonnerre, Mont de Milieu, Fourchaume, Vaillons and Les Clos.)

This domaine was founded in 1840 by Jean Fèbvre, a *tonnelier*, who used to work as winemaker for a M. Tisserand, producing sparkling wine sold as Möet et Chandon. Branching out on his own account, his daughter then married a M. Simonnet, and the rest, as they say, is history.

The *négociant* side of the business buys in must from some forty growers over a wide range of crus, and this remains the bulk of the overall production. Other wines produced include Sauvignon de Saint-Bris, Aligoté, Irancy, and Coulanges-la-Vineuse. The house remains the only producer of sparkling wine – Crémant de Bourgogne within the commune of Chablis. This really is the bulk of their business. The domaine owns only a small amount of vineyard, about 5 hectares in Grand Cru Les Preuses, Premier Cru Mont de Milieu and Chablis Village.

This is not an oak domaine, but the visitor is likely to be surprised at the array of old oak casks in the cold dank *chai*, *in situ* for historic effect. Vinification is mainly carried out in temperature-controlled concrete enamelled vats with ageing in concrete epoxy-resin *cuves*. The wines are fined with bentonite and given a kieselguhr filtration. They are bottled young, and require some ageing.

Jean-Pierre Simonnet – *le père* – receives visitors to his historic and prominently located *chai* in the centre of Chablis with a broad smile and warm welcome. We made our first visit with CSWS in 1990. On a subsequent visit, turning up unexpectedly, he was still accommodating despite preparing for an invasion by a coach party of Women's Institute members from Dorset. And he enjoys the *dégustation* himself just as much as his guests, proudly proclaiming over a tasting sample of Mont de Milieu that he was a supplier to the QE2, Claridges and the Savoy Hotel as well as some of the most famous airlines, but on this subject he shrugs his shoulders in disbelief that anyone could enjoy a fine wine at 30,000 feet when changes in air pressure undoubtedly affect the evaporation and aromatic qualities of a wine. (We have been let in to the secret that his *négoce* wines are used for airlines, his limited own Mont de Milieu being kept with their feet on the ground – the tasting notes tell the story well.)

The domaine is now in the capable hands of Jean-Pierre's son Laurent, who appears to have inherited not just a little of his father's charm and wit.

Simonnet-Fèbvre wines have received mixed criticism by some wine writers and unfortunately mud sticks, which is rather unfair when one considers the efforts to improve quality over the past 10 years or so. However, the wines are successfully marketed worldwide and are still to be found on international airlines and hotel wine lists. We must confess that we do find the wines from Monsieur Simonnet's own 5-hectare domaine, known as Domaine Simonnet and so labelled on the bottle, significantly superior to the *négociant* wines.

Tasting notes

The following domaine wines were tasted in London in September 1999:

Chablis 98 – good fruity nose, lots of fruit on the palate without any great individuality, not exactly crisp but a good clean drinkable basic Chablis.

Mont de Milieu 98 – tight nose, needs to be worked on palate but good steely mineral fruit there, fair acidity, clean finish. Perhaps not quite the class of the 97 below, but a good wine. Needs time. (2002–2005)

Preuses 98 – totally closed up, lots of concentration lurking within and needs time to show its paces. The acidity is soft leaving a question mark over the balance. Like the 97 below only time will tell if all the elements will knit together. Should be good. (2002–2007)

The following wines were tasted at Simonnet-Fèbvre in February 1999:

Petit Chablis 97 – very fruity young wine on the nose but fails to deliver on palate. A little bitter and a bit short.

Chablis 97 – quieter nose but not a lot of difference here.

Montée de Tonnerre 97 – gentle fruity minerally nose, good fruit and balance, just a little short but this is a fairly good wine. (2001–2004)

Vaillons 97 – very minerally wine, almost obscures fruit, dry and a bit short. Not for us.

Mont de Milieu 97 – some nose, quite good fruit with fair concentration but a short dry finish. Fair only. (2000–2003)

Mont de Milieu 97 – Domaine Simonnet. What a difference! Perfumed, gentle on attack, lovely concentrated fruit and balance, nice finish and aftertaste. Very good. (2002–2005)

Fourchaume 97 – from l'Homme Mort. Perfumed minerals but fruit not over concentrated. Fairly good only. (2002–2005)

Valmur 97 – closed right up, but not a lot of concentration here to be concerned about. Might improve with time. Judgement reserved. *Négoce* wine. (2002–2007)

Preuses 97 – domaine wine. Totally closed as expected, there is some concentration and depth for the future, but will it hold? This should be good. (2002–2007)

Preuses 96 – domaine wine. 3 months in 1- to 3-year-old wood. Oaky on nose, lovely concentrated fruit underneath but will oak integrate? Judgement reserved.

The following domaine wines were tasted in Chablis in May 1998:

Chablis 96 – bottled end of March: a bit of sulphur left but a nose of *typicité*, sweet fruit, good balance but rather insipid, tails off on aftertaste.

Mont de Milieu 96 – Chablis nose of *typicité*, fullish wine but fruit could be more concentrated, a bit short, not a lot of depth. Fair/good. (2001–2003)

Les Preuses 95 – gentle floral nose just coming out, somewhat austere fruit, some depth, some length, may develop. Should be very good. (2002–2005)

Les Preuses 88 – biscuity nose, minerally and flinty, this has depth and concentration to a degree and some length, very intense but a slight sour aftertaste. Good/very good. Drink now.

Further wines tasted on earlier visits to the domaine:

Chablis Montée de Tonnerre 92 – approachable already, crisp wine of character and style, but the Mont de Milieu was preferred. (October 94) (*Négoce* wine) Bottles opened in November 97 and March 98 showed that this wine had developed well, nutty and honeyed, mature, but won't get any better. Good/very good. Drink now.

Chablis Mont de Milieu 92 – rich, steely Chablis, plenty of depth, lovely fruit and acidity, should develop well. (October 94) By December 97 and May 98 this had indeed developed, pale gold in colour, it revealed a gentle nutty nose almost Meursault in character, a mature wine, fair length, nice aftertaste but lacked a bit of intensity. Still very good. Drink now.

Chablis Les Clos 92 – a big wine, totally closed, but underlying depth and concentration, needs 8 years. (October 94) (*Négoce* wine) A bottle drunk in November 98 showed good development, mature nose and good fruit. Not exactly the depth expected of this Grand Cru, but a nice wine nevertheless. Good/very good. Drink now.

Chablis Mont de Milieu 88 – tasted in Chablis, this wine has similar characteristics to the 92, lovely wine, rich and steely, well balanced. (October 90) Very good. Drink now.

Wines available from **CELLAR DOOR** and stockists in:

UK
Château Wines, Tockington, Bristol. Tel: 01454 613959
Craven's Wine Merchants, London W2. Tel: 020 7723 0252
J. T. Davies (Mayor Sworder), Croydon, Surrey. Tel: 020 8686 1155
Davy & Co., London SE10. Tel: 020 8853 0585

USA
Bercut Vandervoort & Cie., Pier 19, The Embarcadero, San Francisco, California 94111. Tel: 415 391 0560
Premiere Wine, 1350 Avenue of the Americas, 7th Floor, New York, NY 10019. Tel: 212 399 4200
World Wine Classics Ltd, 35 Portman Road, New Rochelle, NY 10801. Tel: 914 235 2500

Section C

Beaune-based *Négociants*

MAISON CHANSON PÈRE et FILS

10 Rue du Collège   Tel: 03 80 22 33 00
Beaune   Fax: 03 80 24 17 42

Founded in 1750, Chanson is one of the oldest houses in the Côte d'Or and their cellar-book records that at the time Voltaire died in 1778 his wine was being stored for him in their cellars – was this perhaps the best of all possible wine in the best of all possible cellars? – with apologies to Candide!

The Chanson domaine includes some of the finest growths of Beaune, Savigny and Pernand Vergelesses. Their *négociant* business which includes Chablis has three Premier Crus, Montmains, Côte de Léchet and Mont de Milieu and Grand Cru Blanchots.

Head office with the lovely garden by the old town wall is rather reminiscent of a well-respected firm of provincial solicitors – lawyers to our American cousins – and the delightfully charming Philippe Marion-Chanson is the epitome of the venerable senior partner. He succeeded his father Maurice who died in 1970 as this is still very much a family-owned business. Within the town wall there is a fortress known as the Bastion de l'Oratoire, a fascinating fifteenth-century structure with Cyclopean walls built by King Louis XI to strengthen the fortifications of the town: this building on four floors is the firm's principal storage cellar.

A new press house with its own cellars has been built outside Beaune on the Savigny road and it is here that the Chablis wines are vinified in temperature-controlled stainless steel and enamelled vats, the Blanchots alone being partly *élevée* in oak *barriques*. Wines are bought in from individual growers and also from La Chablisienne.

As an overall comment we would say that the Chanson wines are very good, and some very good indeed. So the *négociants* can do it, and do it well. We wish that was always the case!

Tasting notes
The following wines were tasted in the magnificent period tasting room at Rue du Collège in February 1999:

Chablis 97 – golden colour, round fat wine with good fruit and balance, crisp. Very good basic Chablis

Montmains 97 – soft minerally nose, apricots and honey, mineral and flinty fruit, fat, dry, long, crisp and lovely. A textbook Montmains. Very good. (2002–2005)

Montmains 96 – closed on nose, apricots and honey again, dry minerally fruit, beautiful balanced mouth-puckering acidity, long, stylish and lovely aftertaste. Another textbook example. Very good. (2002–2006)

Blanchots 97 – closed on nose, flinty and aromatic wine with good concentration, opens out at back of throat, big wine, very long and lovely. Very good. (2002–2007)

Blanchots 96 – bright yellow colour, nuts and honey, bags of fruit, well balanced, deep and long, needs a long time to come out. Very good. (2002–2007)

Blanchots 93 – similar nose to the 96 but surprisingly reticent, fruit hidden on the attack but the whole thing opens out in glass, dry, lovely fruit, concentrated and balanced. Lovely wine for the vintage. Very good. (2000–2003)

Wines are available from the following importers:

UK
Hall & Bramley, Liverpool. Tel: 0151 524 2749

USA
Baron Francois, 236 West 26th Street, New York. Tel: 212 924 1414

MAISON LOUIS JADOT

21 Rue Eugène Spuller   Tel: 03 80 22 10 57
Beaune   Fax: 03 80 22 56 03

The old-established House of Louis Jadot is one of the most respected in Beaune famous for its range of red and white Côte d'Or wines generally of the highest quality, the pick of the bunch being the Chevalier Montrachet Les Demoiselles. Its reputation is due in no small measure to its winemaker *extraordinaire* Jacques Lardière.

Jacques Lardière, a very swarthy, gentle, upright and articulate man and one of great sensitivity, has been at Jadot for some 30 years and is now supported by his oenologist Christine Bodton whom he meets at the modern *cuverie* on the fringe of town on the Route de Dijon most mornings to assess his wines' progress, before proceeding to his office in Rue Spuller in the old part of Beaune.

The *cuverie* on three levels (allowing maximum gravity feed) is circular in shape with an attractive domed glass roof lighting up an array of stainless steel vats and a cellar full of Burgundian wooden casks. Built as recently as 1996, its very modernity and pristine condition goes hand in glove with a forward-looking and progressive organisation, one which puts quality as its prime consideration.

In addition to their Côte d'Or activities, Jadot produce around 100,000 bottles of Chablis specialising in a fine range of Premier and Grand Crus. Here all the wines are transported from vineyards in Chablis for fermentation and *élevage* in Beaune, the lighter wines in stainless steel and the more structured crus in 228-litre barrels. Jacques tells us that he firmly believes in blocking the malolactic fermentation of *all* his wines, Montrachet as much as Chablis, to maximise acidity and to ensure longevity. We are not here to comment on the Montrachet or other Côte d'Or wines, but we can report that the 1971 and 1967 Fourchaume proved just how beautifully these Chablis wines can keep and age.

Jacques Lardière believes in indigenous yeasts and as little interference with the developing wines as possible. Skimmed milk is used for fining, followed by a light plate filtration.

These are very well made Chablis wines which do great credit both to Chablis itself and to Maison Louis Jadot.

Tasting notes
The following wines were tasted in Beaune in February 1999:

Three Village Chablis were tasted, the 1997, 1996 and 1995 – these were wines of lovely citrus fruits with good concentration and acidity. We particularly liked the 1995 vintage but all were delicious. Our tasting notes of the Premier and Grand Crus are as follows:

Montmains 97 – steely flinty typical nose with good citrus fruits, fat, quite full yet delicate, lovely acidity, balance and length. Very good. (2001–2004)

Côte de Léchet 97 – lovely perfumed nose, intense mineral appley fruit, good concentration, supple. A beautiful Côte de Léchet. Very good. (2001–2004)

Montmains 96 – floral mineral nose, citrus flavours, terrific concentration, crisp acidity, great length and lovely aftertaste. Very good. (2002–2006)

Fourchaume 96 – good nose, quince and citrus fruits, good intensity, but perhaps slightly over acidic, green appley, clean finish. Should still be very good. (2002–2006)

Fourchaume 95 – less obvious nose, apricots and lemons, again rather too acidic but very good. (2002–2006) We preferred the 96.

Grenouilles 96 – oak more obvious on nose, nuts and biscuits, the fruit is there in abundance, very full. Should be fine but needs time. (2003–2008)

Preuses 97 – a bit too oaky at this stage smothering honeysuckle and acacia aromas. Good structure and should come through with time. Good. (2002–2007)

Valmur 89 – toasted oak, nuts and honey, apples and apricots, great structure, long, intense lovely wine. Fine. (2000–2004)

Fourchaume 71 – light gold colour, biscuity, very refined apricot and peach flavours, honeyed, still very youthful, lovely. Very fine. Drink now.

Fourchaume 67 – bright gold, amazing depth of fruit, complex citrus and soft fruit flavours, still some lovely acidity, fabulous, voluptuous. Star wine! Drink now if you get the chance!

All wines are sold through their main distributors:

UK

Hatch Mansfield, Old Bank House, Thames Street, Windsor, Berks. Tel: 01753 621126

USA

Kobrand Corporation, 134 East 40th Street, New York NY 10016. Tel: 212 490 9300 Fax: 212 983 0774

LABOURÉ ROI

Rue Lavoisier	Tel: 03 80 62 64 00
21700 Nuits Saint Georges	Fax: 03 80 62 64 10

Chablis is in first place in Labouré Roi's Burgundy sales and they regard this as a very important appellation. It was through Michael Morgan Ltd that they first launched and developed their sales of Chablis in the UK. They won a contract with British Airways to supply their Premier Cru 1994 when this was selected at a blind tasting. Apart from the 'world's favourite airline' they have contracts to supply Grand Cru 95/96 to rivals American Airlines and Chablis 95/96 to Japan Airlines. Labouré Roi sales are really taking off.

Their range of wines includes both Petit Chablis and Chablis, Premier Crus Fourchaumes, Montmains, Mont de Milieu, Beauregard, Montée de Tonnerre, Vaillons and Côte de Léchet. They also produce four Grand Crus Vaudésir, Valmur, Bougros and Les Clos. The production totals some 127,000 cases of Chablis of which 10,000 are Premier Crus with the Grand Crus accounting for 1,700 cases.

Labouré Roi buy their grapes from a number of well known domaines including Roger Séguinot, de L'Orme and André Philippon's Château de Fleys. All their wines are vinified at their large production unit based on the outskirts of Nuits Saint Georges under the name Cottin Frères, Chairman Louis Cottin being very much in charge, the most recent extension of their *cuverie* being completed at a cost of 25 million francs. The actual vinification process takes place in stainless steel vats, with the Premier Crus 30 per cent – 40 per cent in large barrels and the Grand Crus totally in wood.

A house style of wine is aimed at, but because of their substantial airline contracts, this may be varied to give the customer a special cuvée. Apart from the separate Premier and Grand Cru wines, an *assemblage* of each is made from unspecified crus under the labels Chablis Premier Cru and Chablis Grand Cru. We gather that you have to travel first class to get the latter! These wines are well made under strict laboratory control and the whole operation is spotlessly clean. As our tasting notes will testify, the wines do vary in style and in our opinion the general Premier and Grand Cru wines do not compare favourably with the individual crus. Perhaps this is to be expected, we are sure they are priced accordingly. Well, who's to know at 30,000 feet anyway!

Tasting notes
The following wines were tasted in Nuits Saint Georges in February 1999:

Chablis 97 – sweet nose with oaky overtones, but oak not used, intensely concentrated wine, good basic Chablis. (January and February 99)

Chablis Premier Cru 97 – lovely nose, lots of citrus fruit flavours, very mineral and round, but where is the identity – too general but good.

Fourchaume 97 – floral nose, well integrated oak, delicious minerally fruit with good length. Very good. (2001–2004)

Chablis Grand Cru 97 – closed on nose, fruit is there, good intensity, some length but no personality or zip! Good though.

Vaudésir 97 – elegant wine, floral, citrus fruit flavours, concentrated, good balance and length, lovely aftertaste. Very good. (2002–2007)

Wines are available from the importers:

USA
Lauber Somerville, New Jersey.

MAISON LOUIS LATOUR

18 Rue des Tonneliers	Tel: 03 80 24 81 00
Beaune	Fax: 03 80 22 36 21

Founded in 1797 Maison Louis Latour is one of the most famous and respected Houses in the Côte d'Or. Apart from owning 50 hectares of vineyards themselves, including prestigious sites in Corton Charlemagne, Chambertin, Chevalier Montrachet and Romanée-Saint-Vivant, they also act as *négociants* for a wide range of other wines.

A family-owned business, succeeding generations of Latour have directed the company, the last six of them each being named Louis. The current Louis Latour now heads the company with the help of his son Louis-Fabrice who joined him in 1989. They oversee all aspects of the winemaking and it is this hands-on approach that ensures their high reputation. Every cuvée of wine that is produced is personally tasted by Louis before it is passed fit for marketing.

Their delightful old *cuverie* in Corton, reputedly one of the oldest working *cuveries* in Burgundy, is used for vinifying their Côte d'Or wines. The Chablis and other white wines, however, are vinified at their modern winery in Savigny.

The Chablis portfolio includes basic Village, Premier Crus Fourchaume and Montmains and Grand Cru Vaudésir. In all, about 25,000 cases are produced. They insist on retaining the mineral flavours of their Chablis wines and all vinification is in stainless steel vats, with just a little wood –

10 per cent to 20 per cent – used in *élevage* for the Grand Cru.
Good wines here, but they won't cause a revolution!

Tasting notes

The following wines were tasted at Corton in February 1999:

Chablis 98 – from *cuve* – good mineral citrus flavours, well balanced acidity. Should be good.

Fourchaume 98 – *from cuve* – good fruity nose, bags of ripe fruit with good acidity. Should be good.

Chablis 97 – good basic Chablis with lovely length, lots of fruit, crisp apples. Good.

Montmains 97 – lovely nose of *typicité*, well balanced minerally fruit, good length, lovely wine. This had improved greatly from when tasted a year earlier. Very good. (2002–2006)

Fourchaume 97 – only just bottled. Rather four-square, good fruit and balance but probably stressed from recent bottling. Not a patch on the Montmains. Fair/good. (2002–2006)

Chablis 96 – minerally nose, good fruit, citrus flavours, well-balanced acidity, long. Good/very good.

Vaudésir 96 – lovely perfumed nose, rather tight but good fruit and length, dry mineral finish. Good/very good. (2002–2007)

Vaudésir 95 – brilliantly clear, nose of violets, fleshy mêlée of fruits, lovely length, very good. (2001–2005)

Wines can be obtained through:

UK

Louis Latour Ltd, 7/8 Grafton Street, London W1. Tel: 020 7409 7276
Fax: 020 7409 7092

USA

Louis Latour Inc., San Francisco. Tel: 415 479 4616 Fax: 415 479 4604

MAISON OLIVIER LEFLAIVE FRÈRES

Olivier Leflaive

Place du Monument	Tel: 03 80 21 37 65
21190 Puligny-Montrachet	Fax: 03 80 21 33 94

Domaine Leflaive is synonymous with the village of Puligny-Montrachet and famous for its holdings in its finest Premier and Grand Crus.

Olivier Leflaive, the nephew of Vincent Leflaive, for so long the doyen of the domaine, ran the business with his uncle until Vincent died, when his daughter Anne-Claude also became involved. Pierre Morey then joined the domaine as winemaker working alongside Anne-Claude. In 1984 Olivier, with Uncle Vincent's approval, had started up a *négociant* business in order to expand the family interests.

The family shareholdings are apparently equally shared for both the domaine and *négociant* sides but the business of Olivier Leflaive Frères is under the sole direction of Olivier where Frank Grux from Domaine Guy Roulot in Meursault joined as winemaker. Likewise Olivier has no direct control over the domaine where he acts more in the capacity of consultant.

Olivier has now built up the business from some 10,000 case sales in 1984 to 60,000 cases in 1998 almost entirely Côte d'Or wines and in the process has established a high reputation worthy of the Leflaive name. When we met him in February 1999 he explained that further expansion in the Côte d'Or was becoming increasingly difficult owing to the high prices now being sought for those wines, and as a result a sortie had been made to Chablis with a view to setting up a business in that area.

Chablis was therefore added to the portfolio with the 1997 vintage, the grapes coming from the slopes behind Milly from a reputable grower close to the Premier Cru vineyards of Les Lys and Vaillons, not a million miles from the Côte de Léchet.

Vinification is entirely in stainless steel, no wood at all, in order to retain the unique Chablis flavour as distinct from the Côte d'Or. Interestingly, the alcoholic fermentation takes place without temperature control, making a lie of the mistaken belief that this is automatic if inox is used. We know of another grower from Milly who has the same philosophy with considerable success as readers of this book will already have discovered.

Both young and old vines are used in the final *assemblage* as Olivier is anxious to retain all the fruit and mineral flavours to give Chablis *typicité* and to aid complexity. The vinification at present takes place at the grower's own *cuverie* and the wine is bottled and labelled with the name Chablis Selectionée pour Olivier Leflaive Frères.

Only 1,000 cases were produced in 1997 and 1998 of which some 250 were sold to the UK and a similar amount to the USA, the remainder being reserved for the French market. 50 cases of Premier Cru Côte de Léchet were added in 1998 and it will be interesting to see how these evolve. Olivier's ultimate aim is to increase Chablis sales to 5,000 cases and to have total control over its production by becoming directly involved.

The 1997 vintage, tasted in Puligny in February 1999, indicates that this is serious business. The 1998 wines, tasted in London in August 1999, continued this success with a knock-out Côte de Léchet. We wish him well in his Chablis expansion.

Tasting notes

Chablis 98 – lovely Chablis nose, succulent concentrated fruit with well balanced acidity, good length and lovely aftertaste. Very good.

Côte de Léchet 98 – restrained nose, delicious fruit, *goût de terroir* minerals, intense and concentrated, elegant, long and lovely. Very good. (2002–2005)

Chablis 97 – fragrant lemon tinged nose, aromatic, round opulent fruit, mineral flavours, elegant and long. This is very good Chablis and with *typicité*.

Wines are available from the following importers:

UK

Corney & Barrow, London EC1. Tel: 020 7251 4051 Fax: 020 7608 1373

USA

Frederick Wildman & Sons, 307 East 53rd Street, New York, NY 10022. Tel: 212 355 0700 Fax: 212 355 4719

MAISON VERGET

Jean-Marie Guffens
71960 Sologny

Tel: 03 85 51 66 02
Fax: 03 85 51 66 09

Négociant Chablis

Production:
Grand Crus Bougros, Valmur and Vaudésir
Premier Crus Vaillons, Montée de Tonnerre and Fourchaume
Chablis Village

No book on the wines of Chablis would be complete without a profile on Verget, the Macon-based company owned by the eccentric Jean-Marie Guffens.

Unfortunately our visit to the Côte d'Or coincided with a visit M. Guffens was making to the USA and a tasting was duly arranged at the smart City of London tasting-room of Lay & Wheeler on our return.

M. Guffens has a reputation of being rather arrogant and immodesty does not seem to be his middle name. He is often referred to as 'Motormouth' and legend has it that in visits to Chablis he wears a bullet-proof vest. No marksman has been contracted on a shoot-to-kill basis by the Chablisiens and we are happy to report that he is alive and well. As expected, Jean-Marie gave a very guarded response to our telephone enquiries, but we found that he soon relaxed on finding that his wine-writer caller was not bound by any pre-conceived ideas of his wines or reputation.

A Belgian married to a Belgian, M. Guffens, a proud family man, ended up in Burgundy by chance. He started with a tiny domaine in the Maconnais of only 4 hectares – at that time in the 1970s land was relatively inexpensive. He soon proved that his idiosyncratic ideas could produce his special style of wine in the region.

Verget was formed as recently as 1992 with a fellow Belgian as a partner. This has now developed into a large commercial concern based in Sologny, a little village high in the hills about 10 kilometres to the west of Macon. Here he produces a large range of wines from the Maconnais for which he has gained great acclaim, as well as Côte d'Or appellations.

It was perhaps through Robert Parker that he leapt to fame, with his Chablis wines receiving rave revues in the USA. Is this fame justified? We examined his strategy, as well as tasting his wines and the conclusion to this profile gives our answer, but we stress that this is our opinion, and there are many others.

Guffens buys grapes from selected growers in Chablis who are prepared to allow him to control their viticulture from pruning to vendage. He pays top prices but expects low yields and fruit of top quality. Once when asked whether he was the best winemaker in Chablis, he replied 'I am not the best winemaker but all the others are worse.' He has also stated that the Chablisiens have forgotten how to pick grapes, so he employs his own team of pickers. His popularity in Chablis is not too high.

Now to answer the question of whether these wines are good. The range of wines tasted by courtesy of Lay & Wheeler came from four vintages and included both Premier and Grand Crus plus a Vieilles Vignes. The tasting notes record our findings that these are all very well made wines and some are exceptionally good. The 1997 vintages were less exciting than the 1996s, but still very good. The striking point was the difference between the Fourchaume and the other major crus. The Fourchaume Vieilles Vignes in particular was a brilliant wine but it is not Chablis: surely at any blind tasting it would be said to be a Puligny-Montrachet or even a Meursault. The oak used was clearly very new and this is the dominating factor, as it is in the Vaillons 1998.

The Valmur 95, given such an accolade by Parker, is drinking well and is a delicious elegant wine. The Valmur 96 is, however, absolutely brilliant, an outstanding wine, and it tastes like Chablis. No more need be said!

Tasting notes
The following wines were tasted at La Grande Marque in London in March 1999 and January 2000 by courtesy of Lay and Wheeler:

Chablis 98 – little nose, elegant hidden refined fruit and balanced acidity, but not over-long. Good basic Chablis.

Vaillons 98 – noticeably oaky nose which follows through to the palate and somewhat hides the appley character of the fruit. There is some length here but it needs time to develop. Judgement reserved. (2003–2006)

Chablis 97 – well developed nose, lovely fruit with a hint of apricots, not really crisp but good definition and depth for a Village Chablis.

Vaillons 97 – more discreet perfumed nose, minerally fruit, not much length but good. (2001–2003)

Fourchaume 97 – very minerally nose but otherwise closed, earthy fruit with lovely depth and length, a slight kick at the end. This is very good. (2002–2005)

Fourchaume 96 – warm fruit salad and oak very obvious on nose, peachy fruit but again oak on palate which may not totally integrate. Good length and finish. Very good. (2003–2006)

Fourchaume Vieilles Vignes 96 – surely new oak barrels here but the wine can take it. Rich steely fruit flavours that just go on and on. Tremendous concentration, length and finish. Puligny style. Fine. (2004—2008)

Montée de Tonnerre 96 – barley sugar nose, earthy mineral flavours, good balance of acidity, crisp finish. Very good. (2003–2007)

Valmur 96 – green/yellow tinge, closed on nose as expected, lovely balanced Granny Smith fruit with a hint of oak, great intensity, tremendous concentration and finish again. Very fine indeed. (2003–2009)

Valmur 95 – nose rather dumb but opens out a little with encouragement, good grapefruity fruit with lovely balance and depth, very elegant. Perhaps not too long but good crisp finish. Very good. (2002–2006)

Wines are available from the following stockists:

UK
Lay & Wheeler, Colchester, Essex. Tel: 01206 764446 Fax: 01206 560002 http://www.layandwheeler.co.uk.
Lea & Sandeman, London branches. Tel: 020 7376 4767.
James Nicholson, County Down. Tel: 028 44830091.
Robersons, London W14. Tel: 020 7371 2121.

USA
Barrique Wine Co., Illinois.
Estate Wines Ltd, San Rafael CA.
Fongrenier Wine, Texas.
Fruit of the Vine Inc., 161 W. 54th Street, Suite 203-204, New York, NY 10019.
Ideal Wine and Spirits Co. Inc., Massachusetts.
Willett Distributing, Alexandria, Kentucky.
The Wine Company, Minnesota.

APPENDIX A

Production areas in hectares (ha) and yields in hectolitres (hl)

Year	G.Cru ha	G.Cru hl	P.Cru ha	P.Cru hl	Chab. ha	Chab. hl	PChab. ha	PChab.hl
1945	37	53	200	241	116	65	139	122
1946	37	621	200	4477	116	2067	139	3783
1947	34	847	225	6332	122	3379	143	4801
1948	34	565	225	4718	122	2300	143	3253
1949	34	600	225	4202	122	2071	143	2732
1950	34	1040	225	8747	122	4321	143	6966
1951	34	32	225	3903	122	2705	143	3812
1952	29	687	225	5749	140	3291	150	3709
1953	29	104	225	1974	140	1430	150	1973
1954	29	677	225	7108	140	4229	150	5171
1955	29	671	225	7824	140	4772	150	6255
1956	29	386	225	3301	140	2238	150	2808
1957		1.3		735		355		600
1958		655		5470		2650		2304
1959		760		6838		6590		3193
1960		681		6689		7426		2991
1961		673		5359		5052		2372
1962		1111		9868		9393		4202
1963		1389		11625		11956		5044
1964		1340		9723		9240		3727
1965		1240		8437		9295		3522
1966	41	1896	273	12000	304	13000	115	5209
1967		1420		8770		9200		3934
1968		1485		7894		15752		4050
1969	51	1720	276	7520	342	8145	120	2458
1970	59	2670	257	14035	313	17770	128	6415
1971		356		8984		11778		3753
1972		2295		11233		16245		5283
1973		3492		14850		21859		8000
1974	71	2685	260	10956	534	28282	163	9300
1975	83	3907	306	15591	544	29443	174	9543
1976	87	4444	333	16721	589	31934	184	8387
1977	85	1856	410	16958	733	26251	105	4147
1978	89	3850	437	17731	805	25179	104	2332
1979	83	6124	439	33988	856	66126	112	7989
1980	90	5113	463	25491	895	46601	106	5359
1981	91	2864	474	15686	924	22749	113	1723
1982	92	6075	477	33775	989	69682	110	7375

Year	G.Cru ha	G.Cru hl	P.Cru ha	P.Cru hl	Chab. ha	Chab. hl	PChab. ha	PChab.hl
1983		6772		41359		83260		8724
1984		5617		35603		68129		5161
1985		2693		25650		65294		6218
1986		4676		32339		65602		5811
1987	94	5060	593	34849	1432	82228	160	9673
1988	91	4920	615	36815	1543	91827	183	10693
1989	93	4915	650	35929	1730	94252	215	10782
1990	97	5223	669	42138	1958	114609	259	14709
1991	98	5072	692	39870	2104	102670	305	11325
1992	93	4994	717	42539	2321	138300	360	21224
1993	101	5806	664	43291	2122	141508	342	23864
1994	100	4330	711	36702	2415	128943	396	19819
1995	106	5731	747	44891	2680	160523	475	28096
1996	106	5198	747	42040	2678	154418	475	26451

These figures are a compilation from a number of sources, including Rosemary George M.W., Jean-Paul Durup, BIVB and INAO, unfortunately not available for every year, but they do indicate trends. Our thanks are due to Rosemary George for providing the figures for the earlier years.

APPENDIX B

Sauvignon de Saint-Bris

VDQS, and AOC from 1995

year	quantities in hl	production area in ha
1989	3,680	59
1990	3,652	61
1991	1,607	69
1992	5,909	68
1993	5,845	
1994	4,838	
1995	6,725	

Yonne AOC Blancs excluding Chablis and Sauvignon

1989	25,453	455
1990	22,212	472
1991	13,255	518
1992	38,897	561
1993	44,255	
1994	30,651	541
1995	43,999	

Yonne AOC Rouges

1989	22,062	438
1990	22,794	456
1991	13,831	470
1992	31,782	504
1993	29,007	
1994	24,146	481
1995	32,382	

Yonne AOC Grand Totals including Chablis and Sauvignon

1989	197,073	3,638
1990	223,337	3,972
1991	187,630	4,292
1992	283,645	4,643
1993	293,546	
1994	249,429	4,645
1995	322,347	

Once again, note throughout the region how production was affected by frost damage in 1991 and 1994. The figures also show an undramatic but steady increase in production levels since 1989, and hence maintenance of the popularity of the wines. The total AOC figures include Bourgogne Blanc et Rouge, Bourgogne Aligoté, Bourgogne Grand Ordinaire Blanc et Rouge, Passetoutgrains, Bourgogne Irancy, Bourgogne Rosé, Crémant de Bourgogne Blanc et Rosé.

Figures have been supplied by M. Durup, June 1995, through the offices of BIVB.

GLOSSARY

Assemblage: The blending together of the various vats to form a single cuvée for bottling.

Ban de vendange: The official date for commencement of the vintage as declared by the local office of INAO.

Batonnage: The agitation or stirring of the contents of a barrel so as to evenly distribute the lees throughout the wine. Only appropriate for white wines.

Cépage: The grape variety/varieties used in the make-up of the wine.

Chaptalisation: see Chapter 10.

Climat: Vineyard site, also sometimes referred to as *lieu-dit*.

Cold maceration: A short period of undisturbed and unheated settling of the must prior to the start of fermentation, generally a few hours up to a day.

Cordon de Royat: A system of vine training by which several vertical fruit-bearing shoots are taken off a single horizontal cane trained along a wire.

Coulure: The failure of vines to flower properly, thus causing reduced yield.

Courson: The short fruiting cane which will provide the vine's fruit the following year.

Court-noué: A viral disease of the vine which affects the leaves and reduces photosynthesis.

Cuve: The fermentation vessel, be it oak, stainless steel, glass-lined concrete, enamelled, etc.

Cuvée: A vat of a particular wine, or the vats making up a particular wine, e.g. a single vat of Chablis Village, or equally the Chablis Village vats for bottling.

Débourbage: The process of settling the gross lees to the bottom of the containing vessel before proceeding to fermentation.

Elevage: The period of ageing after fermentation to the time of bottling, and includes racking, refrigeration, fining and filtration.

Fermage: A landlord–tenant relationship, whereby the tenant works the land and keeps the fruits of his labour in return for an annual rental payment to the landowner based on current market prices of the wine produced. The rent is payable whether or not there is a harvest. See *Métayage* below.

Feuillette: The traditional Chablis barrel of 132 litres capacity.

Fining: The process of adding an agent to a wine prior to bottling for the purpose of aiding clarification. This process can take weeks or months, and is usually effected by the addition of egg whites, bentonite, isinglass or other material which collects the impurities and clouding particles on its way down to the bottom of the containing vessel. Carried out in addition to or instead of filtration or often not at all.

Foudre: A large oak fermentation vessel.

Guyot: The double-Guyot system of training vines adopted in Chablis, is described in Chapter 9.

Kieselguhr: A chemically inert earth sometimes used in the filtration process.

Lees: Gross lees – particles of fruit and the bunches, impurities and other matter within the must prior to fermentation. Fine lees – the dead yeast cells after fermentation.

Lieu-dit: An interchangeable term with **Climat** – denoting a vineyard site whether named or unnamed. Not generally used for Premier or Grand Cru vineyards, but not incorrect to do so.

Malolactic fermentation: The second fermentation process caused naturally by bacterial action, converting apple-tasting malic acid to lactic acid, thus reducing harsh acidity. Chablis, however, is sometimes complemented by a slight green-appley taste which is not necessarily indicative of an incomplete malo.

Métayage: A landlord and tenant relationship, whereby rent is paid by the tenant to the landowner in the form of a proportion of the grapes or wine produced. The tenant or métayer is usually responsible for the upkeep of the vineyard with the exception of replanting, and the cost of posts and wires.

Millerandage: The formation of embryo bunches of grapes which fail to develop further, thus reducing the yield of the plant. But quality can sometimes be achieved as these small unripe berries contain highly concentrated juice.

Monopole: A vineyard in single ownership, e.g. La Moutonne.

Must: The crushed grapes and juice before it is transformed into wine.

Oidium: A fungal disease known as Powdery Mildew, originating from America, which attacks the leaves and shoots of the vine, splitting the skins of the grapes and causing rot. The disease caused widespread havoc in the French *vignoble* in the middle of the last century. The effective method of control is by sulphur spraying.

Phylloxera: see Chapter 2.

Pièce: The Burgundy barrel of 228 litres.

PLC or **Plafond Limite de Classement:** The ceiling limit for yields, expressed in hectolitres per hectare, generally 20 per cent above the *Rendement de Base* – see below, and Chapter 4.

Pourriture: General name for 'rot'. *Pourriture noble* is encouraged in the production of sweet wines, all other types are unwelcome.

Racking: The process of drawing off the wine from its fine lees by syphonage or gravity, and from one vessel to another.

Rendement: Yield, usually in hectolitres per hectare.

Rendement de base: Maximum yield in hectolitres per hectare as set by Appellation law and issued by INAO. See Chapter 4.

Répiquage: Replacing individual plants in the vineyard when necessary, as opposed to grubbing up a whole section, thus keeping the average age of the vines as high as possible.

Sélection massale: The practice of replanting vines from cuttings taken from the best and healthiest plants in the vineyard, as opposed to clonal selection.

Sulphur: Used in various forms as a disinfectant in the wine-making process, and for the control of oidium.

Sur-col: A wine in the course of fining.

Terroir: see Chapter 11.

Triage or **Trie:** The manual sorting of the crop in the *cuverie* or in the vineyard to eliminate unripe, substandard or rotten fruit.

Typicité: Literally 'typicity', applied to any wine which does or should have the true recognisable Chablis characteristics.

Vendange verte: Green pruning, or the elimination of excess foliage and bunches in the summer in order to increase the circulation of air around the grapes on the vine, thus limiting the conditions for rot, increasing the level of sunshine reaching the fruit and concentrating the vines' activity on the remaining bunches. Not all viticulteurs agree with the practice.

Notes on measurements

Area
1 hectare = 10,000 sq. metres = 2.471 acres = 100 ares = 24 ouvrées

Volume
1 hectolitre = 100 litres = 133 bottles = 11 cases
1 bottle = 0.75 litres
1 magnum = 2 bottles
1 tonneau = 1 pièce = 228 litres = the Burgundy cask
1 feuillette = 0.5 tonneau

N.B. Just to confuse the issue, the traditional Chablis *feuillette* is 132 litres.

At 60 hectolitres per hectare, one vine produces about three-quarters of a bottle of wine.

Bibliography and Further Reading

CHARLES ALBERT D'ARNOUX – *Dissertation sur la Situation de Bourgogne*, London 1728.

CHARLES WALTER BERRY – *A Miscellany of Wine*, Constable & Co. Ltd, London, 1932.

CHARLES WALTER BERRY – *In Search of Wine, A Tour of the Vineyards of France*, Constable & Co. Ltd, London, 1935

MICHAEL BROADBENT – *The Great Vintage Wine Book II*, Mitchell Beazley, London, 1991.

CLIVE COATES – *Côte d'Or*, Weidenfeld & Nicolson, London 1997.

ROGER DION – *Histoire de la Vigne et du Vin en France des Origines au XIX Siècle*, Flammarion, Paris 1959.

ROSEMARY GEORGE – *The Wines of Chablis and the Yonne*, Philip Wilson Publishers Ltd, for Sotheby Publications, 1984.

BERNARD GINESTET – *Chablis*, in the series Bernard Ginestet's *Guide to the Vineyards of France*, English Edition 1990, Jacques Legrand, distributed in the UK by Longman.

STEPHEN GWYNN – *Burgundy*, Constable & Co. Ltd, 1934.

DR. JULES GUYOT – *Études des Vignobles de France*, Paris, 1868.

ANTHONY HANSON – *Burgundy*, 2nd edition, Faber and Faber, 1995.

A. L. HENDERSON – *The History of Ancient and Modern Wines*, Baldwin Cradock & Joy, London, 1824.

HUGH JOHNSON – *Wine Companion*, 3rd edition, Mitchell Beazley, 1992.

ANDRÉ JULLIEN – *Topographie de Tous les Vignobles Connus*, Paris, 1822, 1832 and 1866.

ALEXIS LICHINE – *Wines of France*, 2nd edition, Cassell & Co. Ltd, 1955.

JASPER MORRIS – *The White Wines of Burgundy*, Octopus Books Ltd, 1988.

P. MORTON SHAND – *A Book of French Wines*, Alfred A. Knopf, London, 1928.

ROBERT PARKER – *Burgundy*, Simon and Schuster, New York, 1990.

CYRUS REDDING – *A History and Description of Modern Wines*, Whittaker Treacher & Arnot, London, 1833.

JANCIS ROBINSON – *Vines, Grapes and Wines*, Mitchell Beazley, 1986.

FRANK SCHOONMAKER and TOM MARVEL – *The Complete Wine Book*, Simon & Schuster, New York, 1934.

SERENA SUTCLIFFE – *The Wines of Burgundy*, 2nd edition, Mitchell Beazley, 1992.

CHARLES TOVEY – *Wine and Wine Countries*, London, 1877.

WINES of CHABLIS

INDEX OF DOMAINES, GROWERS AND NEGOCIANTS

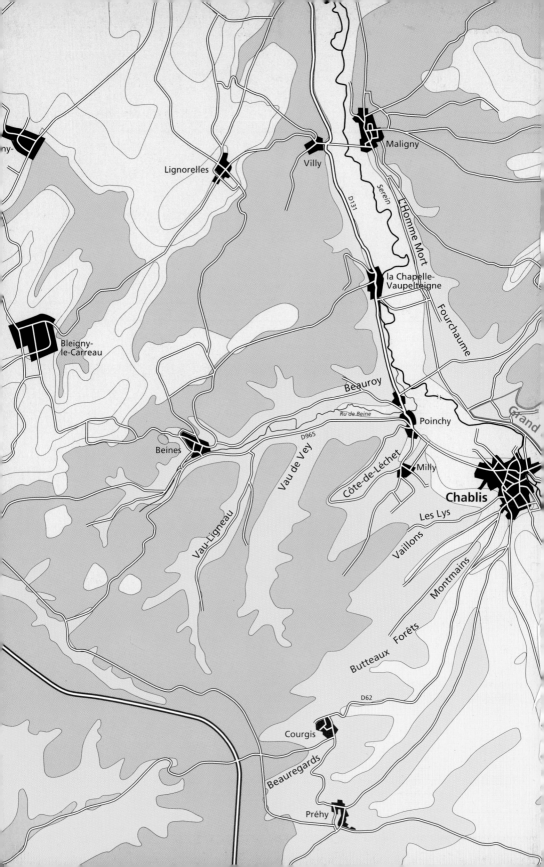